THE U.S. CRIMINAL JUSTICE SYSTEM IN THE PANDEMIC ERA AND BEYOND

T0146168

Taking Stock of Efforts to Maintain Safety and Justice Through the COVID-19 Pandemic and Prepare for Future Challenges

Brian A. **Jackson**   Michael J. D. **Vermeer**   Dulani **Woods**   Duren **Banks**
Sean E. **Goodison**   Joe **Russo**   Jeremy D. **Barnum**   Camille **Gourdet**
Lynn **Langton**   Michael G. **Planty**   Shoshana R. **Shelton**
Siara I. **Sitar**   Amanda R. **Witwer**

Sponsored by the National Institute of Justice

PRIORITY
Criminal Justice
NEEDS INITIATIVE

A project of the **RAND Corporation**,
the **Police Executive Research Forum**,
RTI International, and the **University of Denver**

RAND SOCIAL AND ECONOMIC WELL-BEING

For more information on this publication, visit www.rand.org/t/RRA108-8

Library of Congress Cataloging-in-Publication Data is available for this publication.
ISBN: 978-1-9774-0685-9

Published by the RAND Corporation, Santa Monica, Calif.
© Copyright 2021 RAND Corporation
RAND® is a registered trademark.

Cover Images: AdobeStock/Ulf; Honcharuk
Design by Peter Soriano

Support RAND
Make a tax-deductible charitable contribution at
www.rand.org/giving/contribute

www.rand.org

Preface

Starting in spring 2020, coronavirus disease 2019 (COVID-19) swept through the United States, infecting millions of people and resulting in hundreds of thousands of Americans killed. The pandemic caused a major disruption to all facets of life, along with significant economic damage and dislocation. This report focuses on one part of the effects of the pandemic: how the U.S. criminal justice system adapted to respond to the threat posed by the COVID-19 pandemic. The research effort is an "in-progress stock-taking" based on information gathered at the end of September 2020. We examine the changes that had been made across the justice system up to that point, the effects of those changes on communities, and whether the lessons learned suggest ways in which the justice system could be improved and strengthened going forward.

During the pandemic, a national protest movement—triggered by the killing of George Floyd by police officers in Minneapolis, Minnesota—occurred that focused on the equity and fairness of the justice system. Significant protests in many areas and cities once again raised the issue of criminal justice reform. The responses by the justice system to the pandemic are difficult to fully separate from the changes made during and after the protests. It is also difficult to consider the continuation and expansion of the lessons learned from the COVID-19 pandemic absent that national context. In some ways, that reality is fortuitous. Some of the changes made to respond to the threat of the pandemic—including changes that reduced incarceration and expanded access to justice—also could contribute to the response to the concerns of those seeking justice reform. Furthermore, considering some of the potentially promising innovations made in response to the pandemic through the lens of equity and fairness that was put front and center by the protests could contribute to better decisions about what should be preserved going forward.

In this report, we describe the results of a set of workshops carried out by the Priority Criminal Justice Needs Initiative (PCJNI), a joint effort managed by the RAND Corporation in partnership with the Police Executive Research Forum (PERF), RTI International, and the University of Denver on behalf of the U.S. Department of Justice's National Institute of Justice (NIJ). The goals of the Initiative are to identify needs for innovation in technology, policy, and practice across the criminal justice sector to inform NIJ and other justice system stakeholders.

Our COVID-19 workshops included separate events that were focused on law enforcement, court systems, institutional corrections, community corrections, victim services, and community concerns in the criminal justice response to the pandemic. A variety of common challenges and innovations were identified in those discussions that not only assisted in the continued operation of the system through the pandemic but also might support broader reforms and justice system innovation going forward. In presenting the results of the workshops, we include anonymized direct quotes from participants in an effort to relate the lessons from the pandemic as directly as possible in the words of those who were involved in responding to it.

The results of this effort should be of interest to readers in criminal justice and service-providing organizations, policymakers, and members of the public who are interested in public safety, public health, and the response to the COVID-19 pandemic in the United States. The report is organized such that readers with interests in a specific part of the justice system have the option of reading only the chapters of interest, while the entirety of the report is relevant to more–broadly focused readers who are interested in public safety, criminal legal system reform, and the justice system's ability to adapt to large-scale disruptions in the social and physical environments.

Other recent products of the PCJNI that might be of interest are

- Brian A. Jackson, Michael J. D. Vermeer, Kristin J. Leuschner, Dulani Woods, John S. Hollywood, Duren Banks, Sean E. Goodison, Joe Russo, and Shoshana R. Shelton, *Fostering Innovation Across the U.S. Criminal Justice System: Identifying Opportunities to Improve Effectiveness, Efficiency, and Fairness*, Santa Monica, Calif.: RAND Corporation, RR-4242-NIJ, 2020
- Joe Russo, Michael J. D. Vermeer, Dulani Woods, and Brian A. Jackson, *Risk and Needs Assessments in Prisons: Identifying High-Priority Needs for Using Evidence-Based Practices*, Santa Monica, Calif.: RAND Corporation, RR-A108-5, 2020
- Camille Gourdet, Amanda R. Witwer, Lynn Langton, Duren Banks, Michael G. Planty, Dulani Woods, and Brian A. Jackson, *Court Appearances in Criminal Proceedings Through Telepresence: Identifying Research and Practice Needs to Preserve Fairness While Leveraging New Technology*, Santa Monica, Calif.: RAND Corporation, RR-3222-NIJ, 2020
- Sean E. Goodison, Jeremy D. Barnum, Michael J. D. Vermeer, Dulani Woods, Siara I. Sitar, and Brian A. Jackson, *The Law Enforcement Response to Homelessness: Identifying High-Priority Needs to Improve Law Enforcement Strategies for Addressing Homelessness*, Santa Monica, Calif.: RAND Corporation, RR-A108-6, 2020
- Joe Russo, Michael J. D. Vermeer, Dulani Woods, and Brian A. Jackson, *Data-Informed Jails: Challenges and Opportunities*, Santa Monica, Calif.: RAND Corporation, RR-A108-1, 2020
- Joe Russo, Dulani Woods, George B. Drake, and Brian A. Jackson, *Leveraging Technology to Enhance Community Supervision: Identifying Needs to Address Current and Emerging Concerns*, Santa Monica, Calif.: RAND Corporation, RR-3213-NIJ, 2019.

Mentions of products or companies do not represent endorsement by NIJ, the RAND Corporation, PERF, RTI International, or the University of Denver.

Justice Policy Program

RAND Social and Economic Well-Being is a division of the RAND Corporation that seeks to actively improve the health and social and economic well-being of populations and communities throughout the world. This research was conducted in the Justice Policy Program within RAND Social and Economic Well-Being. The program focuses on such topics as access to justice, policing, corrections, drug policy, and court system reform, as well as other policy concerns pertaining to public safety and criminal and civil justice. For more information, email justicepolicy@rand.org.

Contents

Figures

Tables

Summary

By the end of November 2020, the coronavirus disease 2019 (COVID-19) was estimated to have resulted in the deaths of between 268,000 and 360,000 Americans.[1] The spread of the disease stressed the U.S. health care system, with the number of people needing care overwhelming available resources in some parts of the country. Both the disease and the actions taken to respond to it stressed the country as a whole and had broad impacts on the economic system and government agencies at all levels.

Although the COVID-19 pandemic affected the United States as a whole, it was not the same everywhere at all times. From its local points of introduction, the virus spread through neighborhoods and towns at different rates. This reality meant that how and when COVID-19 affected specific states and locales varied considerably, and the circumstances to which government, the private sector, and the public had to respond varied. Washington State and New York City were the epicenters of the initial phase of the pandemic. They endured early spring spikes of the disease and had to wrestle with the effects on their governmental, health, local economic, and criminal justice systems. Spikes in infection and disease burden occurred later in states in the South and Midwest, putting the majority of the summer burden of the pandemic in those regions. In fall 2020, still other areas were driving national numbers, with states in the Northern Midwest experiencing rapidly increasing infection rates. By late fall and early winter 2020, COVID-19 had spread explosively and near uniformly across the country.

Local responses to the pandemic also varied considerably. Because there was not a unified public health response that was driven from the national level, different states, cities, and localities made different decisions about what steps should be taken, and these different jurisdictions did so at markedly different speeds. The palette of options available to decisionmakers was the same—closures of schools, restrictions of gatherings or events, stay-at-home orders, mandates to wear face masks, and so on—but what measures those decisionmakers chose to use in a particular state or city ended up being quite different.

The Pandemic Posed Major Challenges to the U.S. Criminal Justice System

The outlines of how the justice system functions in the United States are understood relatively broadly. Law enforcement agencies investigate crime and arrest the suspected perpetrators of crimes; they also conduct other crime-prevention initiatives. Suspects are transferred

---

[1] See Johns Hopkins University School of Medicine, "COVID-19 United States Cases by County," data set, updated December 6, 2020, and Centers for Disease Control and Prevention, National Center for Health Statistics, "Excess Deaths Associated with COVID-19," webpage, updated December 2, 2020, respectively.

to the courts, where they are charged, their cases are resolved (most frequently through plea bargaining but sometimes through trial), and they are sentenced for their crimes. Depending on their sentence, they are transferred to the corrections system either for incarceration in a jail or prison or for supervision in the community corrections system on probation (or—after completion of a sentence in custody—on parole). The steps and connections among these three main components—law enforcement, the courts, and corrections—are shown in Figure S.1. The figure shows the path of justice-involved individuals through the system and the many entities involved in that process, with the involvement of members of the public and victims of crime supported by and involving other organizations and agencies. The functioning of the system creates what researchers and practitioners often describe as a flow of people through the system; an individual accused of a crime passes through the different steps with the relevant actions taken and decisions made in sequence.

Although it is frequently thought of as a purely governmental function, effective and efficient criminal justice depends on and involves a variety of actors and organizations beyond police, courts, and corrections agencies. The public plays a role as a participant in community policing and in reporting crime to law enforcement. Individuals or entities affected by crime have multiple roles in—and, in some states, a constitutional right to participate in—the justice process for the individuals accused. Some organizations associated with government and some nongovernmental organizations (NGOs) exist to assist, compensate, and counsel victims of crime in an effort to meet their needs. Other service-providing agencies are key players for justice-involved individuals, providing them with substance abuse treatment, counseling, education, and other services during their time in custody, under community supervision, or in reentry to reduce the chance that they will offend in the future.

Although the justice system often is viewed as a single river of people flowing from arrest to the corrections system, it is much more complex in reality. There are people whose charges were dropped or were acquitted at trial, and there are even more options: Depending on the context and the programs that are available, other paths might be available to divert people from that central flow. For example, there is prearrest diversion to treatment for substance abuse or mental health issues, diversion to specialty courts that serve specific populations or deal with specific types of offenses, or diversion to alternatives to incarceration later in the process. In some cases, intervention outside the criminal justice system might be better suited to address specific problems, and options have been developed to reduce the rate of growth of the significant portion of the U.S. population under some form of correctional custody or supervision.

Although this outline generally reflects the operation of criminal justice in the United States, the U.S. justice system is not a single system. Rather, it is hundreds of individual systems built locally and operating *similarly*, although by no means *identically*. There are more than 18,000 law enforcement organizations in the United States, some of which have thousands of officers and some of which have only a few officers. Some serve urban areas that might be geographically compact but population-dense, while others serve rural areas where many fewer people live in much larger jurisdictions. Court systems in different states have different administrative and management structures, which means that legal options that might be available in one state could be off the table in another. Corrections systems in different areas might have very different constraints on how they can manage their populations in custody and under supervision. How these agencies—and the service providers on which they depend—are funded also varies significantly. Some agencies are funded from line items in state or local bud-

Figure S.1
The Criminal Justice System

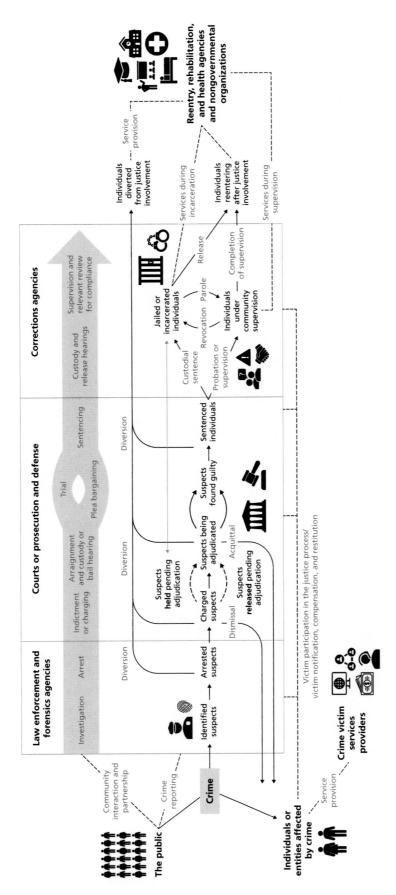

gets, some are supported by specific tax revenues, and others rely on fees paid by people filing cases in courts, paying fines, or paying the costs of their own correctional involvement.

Each individual justice system also exists in its own context. Some types of crime that are a major concern in one area might not be an issue in another area. The relationship between justice agencies and the communities they serve might be very strong in one city but strained to the breaking point elsewhere. Although correctional populations are significant nationwide, some areas had focused on reforming corrections and reducing the number of individuals in custody or under supervision before the COVID-19 pandemic. These local contexts, along with the differences in local policy, legal, and funding frameworks, had different effects nationally—enabling or constraining police, court decisionmaking, and what corrections agencies could do in response to unprecedented circumstances.

Because this diversity shapes how systems *could* respond, it also shapes the broader relevance of lessons learned from how agencies in different areas *did* respond. As a result, recognizing the diversity of the system must be the starting point for taking stock of the responses to the pandemic, planning for the future, and identifying lessons that are useful broadly and those whose value depended much more on the specific circumstances of the agencies or areas where they were used.

The COVID-19 Pandemic Created Multilayered Stresses on the Criminal Justice System

The high-contact nature of many criminal justice processes meant that the pandemic created the following major challenges to the standard ways of operating in the justice system:

- **Organizations were affected immediately by staff becoming infected or exposed to COVID-19.** Since the beginning of the pandemic, organizations in the justice system have been hit hard by staff and officers contracting COVID-19. According to a national tabulation of publicly reported deaths, as of November 2020, more than 156 police officers had lost their lives to COVID-19,[2] which is approaching the average number of officers who were killed in the line of duty from all causes from 2009 to 2019.[3] It is estimated that, as of November 2020, between 98 and 191 corrections staff members had died from COVID-19, and more than 46,000 staff had been infected.[4] In addition to losing key justice personnel to the disease, agencies across the system—including police departments, service agencies, and NGO reentry providers—have had their operations disrupted from staff exposure to COVID-19 because staff are forced to isolate themselves to reduce the chances of spreading the disease.
- **Justice organizations were forced to adapt to reduce the risk that they would be a driver for the spread of the virus.** From the face-to-face interactions of a police officer with a citizen on the street to a group education session supporting the reentry of a justice-involved person to the community, many justice processes had the potential to hasten the spread of the virus. Court processes bring together many people from different areas and

---

[2]   National Law Enforcement Officers Memorial Fund, "COVID-19 Related Law Enforcement Fatalities," webpage, undated.

[3]   National Law Enforcement Officers Memorial Fund, "Officer Deaths by Year: Year-by-Year Breakdown of Law Enforcement Deaths Throughout U.S. History," webpage, September 29, 2020.

[4]   The Marshall Project, "A State-by-State Look at Coronavirus in Prisons," webpage, updated December 2020b; American Correctional Association, "The Wall of Honor," webpage, undated.

put them in a single room, and many of the participants have no choice about being there. Crowded prisons house residents in close proximity, creating the potential for the rapid spread of the virus from person to person. If it did not make substantial changes, the justice system had the potential to make the pandemic worse, harming public health as it sought to protect public safety.

- **The pandemic significantly changed the types of problems and needs that justice agencies had to address.** Although trends appeared to differ across the country, there were substantial shifts in crime and victimization during the pandemic. Trends also differed with time, with analyses performed early in the pandemic reaching different conclusions than those conducted later. However, it appeared that some areas saw substantial increases in domestic and family violence, which were shaped by the different responses in different areas, and there was added difficulty in identifying and responding to such incidents. Some areas saw increases in violence whose intensity and scope rivaled that seen during earlier spikes in urban violence, such as in the 1990s. Other areas saw reductions in overall crime but spikes in specific types of property crime. There also were significant increases in calls to police about individuals in mental health distress, which were ascribed both to the stresses of the pandemic and the challenges created for other organizations that respond to people with mental health needs.

- **There were secondary effects on justice system organizations from the economic consequences of the pandemic, with reductions in both government agency and service provider budgets.** The pandemic reduced economic activity, which reduced local tax revenues. Funding streams that usually supported justice agencies, such as fines and fees, dried up because of fewer cases and court filings and as a result of the inability of many to pay what they owed because of job losses. Moratoria on the collection of fines and fees was part of pandemic responses in some areas. Service organizations that depend on philanthropy and donations from businesses and individuals saw those funding streams dry up. Agencies including government agencies and NGOs had to reduce staff and cut services because of budget cuts, which strained their operations as needs caused by the pandemic increased.

The differences in the path of the pandemic and the nature of government responses to it meant that the circumstances faced by justice agencies and related organizations differed from place to place. However, whether they felt the impact of COVID-19 early or late, and whether their area chose to use such measures as lockdowns, justice agencies were presented with challenges, and most had to make significant changes in how they operated to continue to play their public safety roles while protecting public health and the health of their staff.

> The courts are likely the largest convener of people . . . in [our state]. . . . On a typical day in our courthouses, we require or bring in . . . 1 percent of our [state's] population, and a large percentage of those people do not have a choice about whether to attend, because we've ordered them to appear. . . . We have an obligation not only to those people, but to the rest of the country to get it right, because if we don't get it right, we can set the whole community, state, country back.
>
> – Court system panelist

Tensions Between Justice System Roles and the Groups the Justice System Serves Complicated Adaptation and Change

Changing how the justice system operates in response to the pandemic—and innovating or reforming it for other reasons—is more challenging because of the complexity of roles the system has evolved to play and the different populations it serves. The first population considered is often justice-involved individuals and, by extension, their families and communities. People in the justice system are there because they have committed a crime, and part of their involvement is to be sanctioned for their behavior. But the reality that police, courts, and corrections agencies have become the front line for responding to many individuals with mental health challenges and substance abuse problems means that their involvement in the system is not *solely* about punishment. The justice system often seeks to serve this population in important ways by delivering treatment, counseling, and other services in a composite process that—in theory—sanctions them for their criminal behavior and attempts to address its causes to reduce the chances that they will reoffend in the future.

How the justice system chooses to do its business is responsive to the organizations and individuals who make up the system itself. It is also responsive to the communities to which justice organizations drive jobs and economic activity. The general public, including individuals or entities who are affected directly by the crimes that justice-involved individuals are accused or convicted of committing, is also a key population served by the system. Public safety is maintained for the benefit of the public, and victims of crime have rights and roles in the justice process, some of which are guaranteed by law.

When we consider making changes to how the justice system functions in crisis response or more broadly, the perspectives and needs of these three different groups—organizations in the system, justice-involved individuals and their communities, and the general public—can be in tension. Changes that make the system itself more efficient might go against the needs of crime victims or make it more difficult to deliver counseling and rehabilitative services to incarcerated populations. Changes that make the system more rehabilitative (e.g., to achieve broader societal goals more efficiently or to reduce recidivism by delivering more-extensive services to incarcerated populations) might be viewed as reducing the legitimacy of the system in the eyes of victims of crime. Although there is broad agreement that all three populations are important, different people weigh their importance differently, meaning that when change in the justice system must be made—whether because of immediate need to respond to the threat of a global pandemic or because of a desire for longer-term reform—these tensions can make such changes much more difficult to navigate.

The National Climate Challenged the Justice System and Its Responses to the Pandemic

The effect of the COVID-19 pandemic on the criminal justice system was complicated by other factors and circumstances. From the outset of the pandemic, both the disease and the response to it became intensely politicized, and there was substantial controversy regarding public health interventions. This meant that there also was controversy about the role that different parts of the general public wanted justice agencies to take in enforcing compliance with public health directives, such as wearing masks, closing businesses with indoor or significant in-person contact, or prohibiting such events as concerts, parties, or gatherings of large numbers of people. In some parts of the country, law enforcement actively enforced mask-wearing and shut down events where transmission could occur across large numbers of people. In other parts of the country, intervention was much more limited. In some broadly publicized cases, it was justice agencies themselves that resisted taking on—or outright refused to take on—a role of enforcing compliance with public health measures indented to reduce the spread of the virus.

As the country was beginning to deal with the effects of the COVID-19 pandemic, the killing of George Floyd by police officers in Minneapolis, Minnesota, triggered large-scale protests and unrest. Echoing the response to the killing of Michael Brown in Ferguson, Missouri, in 2014, the Black Lives Matter protests that started in May 2020 were more widespread and focused intensely critical attention on law enforcement and on the justice system more generally. The focus of the protests was on the first of the three groups described earlier—justice-involved populations and their communities—but they had consequences for the other two, including broader public participation in the protests and the consequences of the protests for justice agency officers and staff. The resulting push to cut funding from law enforcement agencies and reallocate it to non–criminal justice approaches for dealing with violence and other societal problems gained significant momentum in some areas, and other areas adopted changes to policing practices and implemented civilian oversight of justice agencies.[5] Both the law enforcement actions and policy actions taken in response to the protests differed significantly across the country. However, national-level reactions to extremely local-level actions—sometimes the actions of individual officers—taken during the protests intensified scrutiny of law enforcement agencies, further complicating the challenge of policing during the pandemic.

Past efforts to explore the potential role of criminal justice agencies in response to a pandemic, and the role of law enforcement agencies in particular, emphasized that close relationships and trust between members of the public and the justice system are needed for that involvement to be most effective.[6] The combination of the national environment and the protests therefore strained that trust (in some areas, apparently to the breaking point), reducing the opportunity for public safety agencies to contribute to protecting public health during this period. Although the limited involvement of justice agencies had some benefits because it reduced concerns about the criminalization of noncompliance with public health regulations, the reality meant that a possibly important player in reducing the impact of the COVID-19 pandemic on the country faced practical constraints in its ability to do so.

---

[5]   See Andrew Welsh-Huggins, "In Cities Across U.S., Voters Support More Police Oversight," Associated Press, November 21, 2020.

[6]   Edward P. Richards, Katherine C. Rathbun, Corina Solé Brito, and Andrea Luna, *The Role of Law Enforcement in Public Health Emergencies: Special Considerations for an All-Hazards Approach*, Washington, D.C.: U.S. Department of Justice, Bureau of Justice Assistance and Police Executive Research Forum, September 2006, p. 17.

The Priority Criminal Justice Needs Initiative Held a Virtual Summit to Better Understand the Challenges and Responses of the Justice System to the COVID-19 Pandemic

It is difficult to separate how the criminal justice system had to adjust to the realities of operating under pandemic conditions from the national political environment and backlash triggered by George Floyd's death. The fact that both occurred at the same time—multiplying the challenge to appropriately address either in isolation—is simply historical reality. Responses to the pandemic, including significant decarceration, also aligned with some of the demands made during the protests. Similarly, while some of the organizations involved in protests were calling to defund the police as part of reform efforts, the economic consequences of the pandemic for state and municipal budgets were resulting in the defunding of criminal justice agencies in very real ways. As a result, the reality of this period makes it difficult (perhaps even impossible) to fully separate the effects of the pandemic on the justice system from the broader national environment created by calls for justice reform.

Acknowledging this fundamental difficulty from the outset, the Priority Criminal Justice Needs Initiative (PCJNI)—a joint effort managed by the RAND Corporation in partnership with the Police Executive Research Forum (PERF), RTI International, and the University of Denver on behalf of the U.S. Department of Justice's National Institute of Justice (NIJ)—held a virtual summit made up of separate online workshops that explored the justice system's response to the COVID-19 pandemic. The workshops were held in the second half of September 2020, as the summer lull in viral spread was beginning to come to an end and the fall increase in case rates was starting. The goal of the workshops was a combination of an "in-progress stock-taking" on the way the justice system had responded to the pandemic up to that time and a look toward what those responses could teach us about the future. The workshop was designed to be cognizant of both the enormity of what has happened in the country and the responsibility (1) to seek out lessons we can use to prepare for similar future incidents and (2) to gain insight that could be valuable for addressing broader challenges and concerns.

The seven four-hour virtual workshops focused on

- **law enforcement services and operations,** including the shifts in crime during the pandemic and changes that had to be made in performing police tasks
- **law enforcement management,** including issues of staff safety and the workforce (e.g., recruiting and training), overall policing policy and strategy, and interactions with other justice agencies
- **court system operations and services,** including staff safety and workforce issues, case prioritization and backlogs, virtual court operations, and the effects of changes in the courts on other elements of the justice system
- **institutional corrections operations and services,** including staff safety and workforce issues, inmate safety and contagion prevention, technology issues, and effects of changes made in corrections on other justice system sectors
- **community corrections operations and services,** including safety issues, changes in policies and strategies, use of technology, measures taken when in-person interactions were needed, and the effects on other facets of the justice system of the issues facing community corrections

- **victim services delivery,** including the safety of staff in service-delivery organizations, issues contacting clients, changes that had to be made in how services were delivered, and the use of technology to do so
- **the public and the provision of justice during the COVID-19 pandemic;** specifically, the bigger picture of how changes made in policing, courts, and corrections affected communities; equity issues in how public health guidelines were enforced; and changes in service provision during the pandemic.

For the sectoral workshops, we designed each group to reflect representatives from state and local criminal justice agencies and organizations that had been significantly affected by the pandemic, individuals with public health expertise who had worked with the sector, representatives of national organizations, and participants with knowledge of how changes in the sector had affected communities and justice-involved individuals. In the workshop that focused on victim services, we sought out representatives from organizations that served a variety of needs, used different approaches (e.g., hotlines and direct service-delivery organizations), and were organized in different ways (e.g., stand-alone entities versus services delivered by staff from criminal justice agencies). For the public and the provision of justice panel, we sought representatives from a variety of communities, faith-based organizations, service providers with knowledge of how the COVID-19 pandemic and the changes made to the system had affected communities, and individuals with other relevant expertise.

Although the discussion in the panels was designed to focus on the responses to the pandemic rather than to the community protests, it quickly became clear that it was impossible to fully separate the two. Multiple panelists emphasized the importance of learning from the pandemic for the short term, but many were looking further out in search of more-fundamental lessons about ways the justice system could be improved going forward. As a result, the difficulty in separating the response to the pandemic and the response to the protests began to appear to be an opportunity more than a challenge, with some successful adaptations to the COVID-19 pandemic suggesting ways in which the system could adapt to address broader concerns as well.

PCJNI researchers synthesized the discussions from the workshop and drew on available published data and broader reporting about the pandemic and the justice system's response to it to provide context for drawing conclusions from the panelists' remarks. As part of this synthesis, PCJNI researchers compiled research, evaluation, and data-collection questions suggested by the discussions to begin to build a national research agenda for understanding the justice system's response to the COVID-19 pandemic and evaluating potential promising practices within that response for the future. Although we sought to bring practitioners and experts from departments across the country and with a variety of experience to the panels, it is important not to lose sight of the fact that—as is the case for all such efforts—the discussion likely would have been somewhat different with other groups of participants or in workshops held at different points during the pandemic. The authors did not fact check or seek to verify the statements made by participants beyond looking for contextual information or other sources to expand on the discussion of points that seemed particularly salient. As a result, although we generalize from the often very powerful discussions that occurred during the events, we seek to do so cautiously, and we recommend the reader do so as well. Indeed, many of the generalizations drawn are useful for further examination of key problems and promising solutions.

The Response to the COVID-19 Pandemic Involved Major Changes in Technology, Policy, and Practice by Organizations Throughout the Justice System

When the virus began to spread, the criminal justice system initially halted some of its activities to reduce infection risk. In some areas, police scaled back their activities; for example, deprioritizing traffic enforcement to minimize person-to-person contact. Some courts shut down. Some corrections institutions stopped visitation and many other activities that involved close contact, and in-person community supervision was minimized or stopped. Many actions were taken to try to reduce the flow of individuals into the justice system, including deferring arrests or charging, delaying trials, and limiting reincarceration for, e.g., nonviolent infractions of supervision conditions during probation and parole. Like many other organizations, justice agencies sought to reduce the chances that infected people would come into their buildings through screening and other measures, sought out protective equipment, and changed policies to try to protect their employees. However, many other adaptations were made to allow justice system functioning to continue in some capacity and to respond to the specific issues created by the pandemic. In Table S.1, we summarize the key top-level findings from our sector-by-sector examination, and in the next section, we pull together common responses to the pandemic from across the justice system.

> We went . . . looking for more discretionary ways to deal with crimes. A lot of citations were handed out. A lot of warnings were handed out rather than arrest[s]. Only those arrests that were of a violent nature, serious misdemeanor nature were actually physically taken into custody.
>
> – Law enforcement operations panelist
>
> We stopped all visitation, which was a dramatic change for us. We stopped—I hate using this term *nonessential staff*—but we basically only kept the security staff and other staff in the facilities that were necessary for the immediate safe operation of the facility. So all our vocational instructors, all of our teachers, etc., all of our program, recreation leaders, they had to stay home. And we had to basically run a bare-bones operation.
>
> – Institutional corrections panelist

Common Responses to the Pandemic Were Built on Past Innovation and Reform Efforts

The pressures placed on the justice system by the pandemic affected different parts of the system in different ways, but, in many cases, the responses to those challenges had common causes and required similar responses. As a result, in our panels' deep dives into each component of the justice system, the following common themes emerged with respect to successes in dealing with the pandemic and lessons that could be valuable to maintain in the long term:

- **Shifts in crime and need that occurred during the pandemic had implications throughout the system.** The pandemic resulted in reductions in some types of crimes but increases in others; these shifts were shaped by the effects on behavior and the responses taken to control infection. Increases in such offenses as domestic and family violence simultaneously created needs (e.g., the requirement for courts to maintain access

Table S.1
Key Findings from Each Sector Discussion

	Law Enforcement	Court System	Institutional Corrections	Community Corrections	Victim Services
Reducing the number of people in the justice system	• Many police departments adjusted their strategies for crime prevention and enforcement to limit officer contact with the public and reduce the flow of people into the justice system. • In some cases, there were changes to non-arrest approaches, including greater use of citations as an alternative to arrest. In others, departments merely deferred arrest until after the public health crisis improved, building a backlog of "to-be-arrested" individuals who will have to go through the system in the future.	• Courts were central in reducing populations in other parts of the justice system, including by reducing pretrial detention, limiting issuance of warrants, and facilitating release of individuals from custody where appropriate.	• Corrections facilities are limited by the space they have, and facilities that were overcrowded before the pandemic had great difficulty controlling the spread of the virus. In concert with other parts of the system, institutional corrections agencies sought to reduce jail and prison populations to open up space and enable disease control.		

xxiv   The U.S. Criminal Justice System in the Pandemic Era and Beyond

Table S.1—Continued

	Law Enforcement	Court System	Institutional Corrections	Community Corrections	Victim Services
Reducing transmission in facilities by using virtual and other models where possible	• Some police agencies closed stations to public entry to limit the potential for people to bring the virus into the station. • Some departments made significant shifts to virtual service delivery. Although some departments had already taken such steps, the pandemic pushed the changes and increased public receptiveness to online and virtual police response.	• Because of significant concern about virus transmission at courts, which are major conveners of people drawn from across wide jurisdictions, many court processes were initially stopped to reduce the risk of transmission. • To restart operations, some courts made significant shifts to virtual models for many types of proceedings and services. That has worked very well and has been viewed as providing benefits to both justice agencies and individuals who must appear. As a result, it is a potential practice to continue after COVID-19 has receded. • Although some areas have resumed jury trials, e.g., in alternative locations where physical distancing is possible or in alternative courtroom arrangements, capacity is still limited.	• Some facilities closed their doors to visitors and many types of nonsecurity staff, which reduced the chance of the virus entering facilities but hobbled many types of programming. Although such approaches were fine for short periods, as the pandemic wore on, they became more difficult to maintain. • Shortages in testing and the difficulty of managing large-scale testing programs made it difficult to keep the virus out of facilities and manage outbreaks when they occurred. Facilities had to develop management strategies for isolation and quarantine of multiple populations to limit risk. • Masks and hygiene practices were central components of many facilities' responses.	• Distanced and virtual supervision was viewed as beneficial by both staff and supervisees, increasing efficiency, allowing greater contact with supervisees, and reducing the burden of meeting justice obligations. It was viewed as a practice to continue, although outcome evaluation is needed. • The pandemic resulted in a major reduction in the dosage of supervision for many people in the community corrections system, with reduced drug testing and less direct contact. So far, results appear positive, suggesting potential routes to further reform and improve the supervision system. • Meeting the needs of individuals receiving treatment for substance use or mental health concerns was more difficult, requiring significant changes in models for treatment delivery.	• Victim services providers went to virtual and remote models to continue to operate and reach crime victims during the pandemic, but providers had reservations about cybersecurity, the ability to deliver services securely, and the effectiveness of some counseling and intervention delivered by phone or videoconferencing. New approaches to delivering some services appear promising to continue after the pandemic recedes. • Some critical services, including shelter and food, require in-person interaction, and delivering them in a safe way was more difficult and costly for providers.

Table S.1—Continued

	Law Enforcement	Court System	Institutional Corrections	Community Corrections	Victim Services
Reducing transmission in facilities by using virtual and other models where possible (continued)		• Because virtual hearings are viewed as inappropriate by many for serious felonies and other cases requiring a jury trial, large backlogs of unresolved cases have formed in many court systems, raising concerns about the rights of the accused. This has led to efforts to develop safe approaches to resume in-person proceedings.			• Bandwidth limitations and the digital divide can hamper serving all those who need assistance.
Digital divides limited how broadly virtual models could replace traditional approaches	• Public communication and community policing was very difficult during the pandemic, but departments had success using virtual modes, such as video platforms Facebook Live or Zoom. Reaching some groups required alternative methods, such as direct mail. • Some forensic labs were able to transition rapidly to significantly distributed work models, although agencies that had not invested in technology (e.g., those that were still dependent on paper files) had more difficulty.	• Limitations in bandwidth, connectivity, and available technology make it difficult for some individuals or organizations to participate in virtual court processes. To address concerns about these digital divides, systems had to develop such approaches as loaning technology or providing other ways to join virtual proceedings.	• Corrections institutions that already had invested in digital infrastructure (notably, inmate access to tablets for connectivity and communication) had options available to them other institutions did not.	• Transitions to virtual models for both supervision and service delivery were made more difficult by major digital divides, with technical limitations for both supervisees and providing organizations. In some cases, technology had to be provided rapidly to staff and supervisees to allow activity to continue.	

Table S.1—Continued

	Law Enforcement	Court System	Institutional Corrections	Community Corrections	Victim Services
Public communication and justice system transparency posed major challenges	• Community crime prevention and violence interruption efforts were much more difficult because limiting face-to-face contact and restricted entry to hospitals hurt their efforts to connect with crime victims. • The national environment and conditions created by the criminal justice reform protests made law enforcement involvement in public health initiatives very problematic. Although police can have a role in such situations, doing so effectively requires trust between police and the public.	• Virtual proceedings raised concerns about public access to courts and transparency. Some courts responded by streaming proceedings widely on the internet. However, that approach raised different concerns about the effect on participants in proceedings.	• Many institutions had difficulty managing public messaging regarding the situations within facilities and the steps they were taking in response. Agencies that had provided their residents with tablets or other ways to communicate with family cited transparency benefits because inmates could give their families, counsel, and other audiences updates.		• Pandemic conditions, including stay-at-home orders and visitor restrictions at such sites as hospitals, made it more difficult to reach victims. New approaches had to be developed to do so that might be valuable to maintain after the pandemic.

Table S.1—Continued

	Law Enforcement	Court System	Institutional Corrections	Community Corrections	Victim Services
The COVID-19 pandemic caused major staff health and stress concerns	• Protecting officer health and safety and, by extension, agency operational capacity required changes in staffing models (e.g., using staff cohorts, or an exclusive group of staff that works the same shift or in the same area), changes in procedures, and the use of protective equipment. In some cases, departments had difficulty with staff compliance with the use of protective equipment, reducing its effective risk reduction. • Operating in pandemic conditions and concerns about bringing exposure home to their families were significant stressors and mental health challenges for law enforcement staff. In response, some agencies implemented new mental health support and intervention resources, including remote counseling options.	• Court systems had major concerns about the safety of staff in older, sometimes crowded court facilities. Protecting court staff with high risk of COVID-19 complications was a driver for closing courthouses and seeking alternative ways to operate.	• Correctional and service provider staff faced major stress and health concerns, both from the broader pandemic and the specifics of their occupational exposure. Strategies to protect staff included procedural measures and providing protective equipment, although agencies sometimes had issues with staff use of personal protective equipment.	• Community corrections organizations used virtual and work-from-home models that reduced infection risk and provided more flexibility to staff. However, balancing work and home life was a stressor for staff. Where in-person work was required, agencies used various cohorting models to reduce the exposure risk to large factions of their workforce.	• Providers faced significant challenges protecting their staff because of being at a lower priority for access to protective equipment. Providers working from home faced the additional challenges of stress and managing the collision of their work and home lives. • Victim service providers had difficulty with staffing levels, and recruiting during the pandemic was a challenge.

Table S.1—Continued

	Law Enforcement	Court System	Institutional Corrections	Community Corrections	Victim Services
Justice system interconnections affected response	• Decisions made by other parts of the justice system and social services agencies significantly affected law enforcement, including increasing demands to respond to individuals in mental health crises, which were exacerbated by the pandemic.	• Court systems likely will have major backlogs of cases to address even after the COVID-19 pandemic recedes, requiring additional innovation to more rapidly resolve cases.	• Delivering health care in hard-hit facilities was difficult, particularly for agencies that relied on outside hospitals to provide advanced care to residents. COVID-19 control procedures made meeting residents' other care needs (e.g., for substance use disorders or mental health challenges) more difficult. Doing so was facilitated by virtual technologies for telecare.	• Efforts to decarcerate to reduce the risk of contracting COVID-19 in corrections institutions created a significant burden for supervision and service-provider organizations. For NGO service providers in particular, the demand for services was intense in some areas. Because of backlogs in other upstream parts of the justice system, community supervision participants expect another wave of cases in the future as those backlogs are resolved.	• Changes made by police and the courts in how they responded to some crimes—including nonarrest or rapid release of some individuals—made it tougher to meet the needs of crime victims.
Budget and fiscal concerns from the COVID-19 pandemic are acute	• As a result of the economic consequences of the COVID-19 pandemic, police agencies are facing reductions in budgets. Such cuts—although seemingly in agreement with the calls during protests to defund the police—will create additional issues for the remainder of the pandemic and during the recovery period.	• Because of pressure on the funding streams on which some courts depend to operate, including filing fees or specific tax revenues, these systems face resource constraints and have had to reduce staff. These constraints could make resolving court backlogs even more challenging.	• Institutional corrections agencies face funding pressures as a result of the effects of the pandemic on municipal and state budgets. There are concerns that those budget constraints will limit the ability of agencies to maintain the reduced density that has enabled infection-control strategies but that also could enable the system to improve performance and implement reforms going forward.	• There are major funding challenges facing both the government and NGO components of the community corrections system. These challenges will require more than considering how funding will affect individual entities in isolation. Instead, jurisdictions must address how the different pressures on their individual funding streams will affect the viability of the system as a whole.	• Many provider organizations face acute funding shortages from changes made by government, reduced revenues from fines paid by justice-involved individuals, reduced philanthropy, and financially strapped businesses that are unable to provide pro bono services or in-kind contributions. The pandemic has put the continued viability of many service providers at significant risk.

to protective orders, the need for law enforcement to change how they responded to some calls), made some strategies for responding more difficult (e.g., the decision in some areas to generally not arrest individuals accused of misdemeanors), and magnified demands on service providers to meet victims' needs. Some of those changes might enable better response to such concerns as domestic violence going forward. The nature of the pandemic also created needs within the justice system, causing stresses among incarcerated individuals and practitioners across justice organizations that built on similar concerns that preceded the pandemic.

> Looking across the domestic violence field nationwide, generally demand for services, including shelter, was up. Over 160 cities, counties, or states . . . reported at least double-digit increases in hotline calls, police calls, visits to helplines, or even homicides.
>
> – Victim services panelist
>
> Effectively, what happened here was every single social service agency on top of the courts being just turned off, every social service [agency]also kind of turned off. . . . We've seen . . . mental health [calls significantly] up, but overall we've seen crime go down. . . . That's kind of a weird juxtaposition because I think you would think these things would move together, but they're moving apart in this situation.
>
> – Law enforcement operations panelist

- **Physical infrastructure can put unforgiving constraints on responses to infectious disease.** Responding to the pandemic required space to physically distance, and the high density of many facilities in the criminal justice system made that exceedingly difficult—and required such strategies as decarceration to create the needed space. Across our panels, participants described difficulties in using physical distance to manage the disease—in small police stations, in court buildings where the design goal had been to fit as many courtrooms in as possible, in overcrowded jails and prisons, and in congregate shelters for reentry and to serve victims of crime. As a result, reducing the risk of broad spread of the virus within the justice system required such strategies as significant decarceration from jails and some prisons, holding court in alternative sites, and having many justice practitioners operate in the field.

  From one perspective, those challenges raise questions about what the true capacity of existing justice system infrastructure should be and whether it should be much lower than the pre-pandemic approaches of high-density facilities (unless investments are made to make that infrastructure less vulnerable to future pandemics). However, the experience also led some of the panelists to argue for the value of "de-infrastructuring" future justice activities—i.e., with more people working in the field, working from home, and using other distributed approaches to reduce the need for physical buildings and offices.

> If you're at a hundred percent capacity or above, you have an outbreak, there is *nothing* you can do. You can't quarantine people. You're stuck. If you have a little bit of breathing room, there's a lot of things you can do to help manage an outbreak and keep people safe, both inmates and staff.
>
> — Institutional corrections panelist

- **A massive shift to virtual access to justice and services could be valuable to both justice agencies and society, but it could leave areas and individuals behind.** For some time, analysts and practitioners have argued that there could be substantial benefit from adding telepresence and other virtual technologies to the justice system. Those benefits were dramatically realized during the pandemic. However, the pandemic led agencies to apply virtual models for tasks and functions that had not been the focus before. The expansion of online police services saved officers time. Virtual connections between courts and correctional facilities were valuable to both systems, allowing some tasks to be done with less transportation cost and security risk than physically moving people from place to place. The ability for members of the public to connect virtually—to go to court, to speak with incarcerated family members, to report during community supervision, and to receive services—saved them money and time, and made their participation in justice processes much less burdensome.

  However, our panelists raised questions about efficacy and appropriateness as well: While some panels were nearly unanimous on the value of virtual modes, others cautioned that—particularly for counseling and service delivery—the effectiveness of virtual modes might not be sufficient. And although there are clearly some types of virtual interactions and processes that are entirely unproblematic (e.g., providing individuals virtual ways to file paperwork or perform other transactions), important questions remain about the effect of virtual modes on the outcomes of trials and other hearings. Therefore, additional evaluation is needed to assess whether justice truly is deliverable virtually.

  Furthermore, although the potential value of virtual connections was clear to many, the issue of the digital divide came up across essentially all of our panels. Not every justice agency or supporting organization has invested in technology that will allow it to rapidly "go virtual."[7] Not everyone in every area of the country has ready access to technology and connectivity. To the extent that the justice system maintains virtual models, the needs of those populations without access to technology must be addressed so that the increase in access to justice for some is not offset by a decrease in access for others. However, potentially limited access to virtual justice is only one result of the shortfalls in digital infrastructure that exist in many areas of the country. Both before and during the pandemic, shortcomings in the availability, speed, and capacity of internet infrastructure in poorer or more-rural areas has affected economic activity, the education system, and

---

[7]   As we were completing this report, the National Commission on COVID-19 and Criminal Justice, an effort of the Council on Criminal Justice, published its final recommendations. Where their findings parallel those of our panels, we note the agreement. The National Commission also recommended upgrading the digital infrastructure of the criminal justice system—i.e., focusing on the *internal* system shortfalls in capability and digital divides (National Commission on COVID-19 and Criminal Justice, *Experience to Action: Reshaping Criminal Justice After COVID-19*, Washington, D.C.: Council on Criminal Justice, December 2020b, p. 16).

other societal functions. Efforts to address the digital divide to facilitate virtual justice system models would pay dividends in many other areas as well.

> This time, this year has really propelled the courts into the technology age, and the courts have never historically embraced technology in a big way. But my imagination stops at the point where a person might be losing [their liberty] over Zoom. . . . [T]here's something about being in the courtroom that makes the gravity of the situation real.
>
> — Court system panelist
>
> We really hope that the things that have served us well [during] COVID are here to stay. You think about people who are impoverished and . . . they have to make court appearances. If these people have jobs, they could lose their job for having to make that court appearance. Whereas now, they can show up to court remotely for a traffic ticket or for a misdemeanor charge. I think that's a net positive for society.
>
> — Law enforcement operations panelist

- **A justice *system* can respond more effectively in a crisis than a group of justice organizations acting independently.** In our panels, multiple participants flagged the importance of organizations collaborating to effectively respond to crises of this magnitude. The importance of collaborating with public health agencies came up multiple times, and the information and guidance health experts could provide to justice agencies was noted as important.[8] Other collaborations were highlighted as well, such as sharing protective equipment, bringing together information, coordinating different elements of response, and cooperating to try to meet the needs of both justice-involved individuals and crime victims. Our panels provided a multitude of examples where the decisions in one part of the system affected others and, although those choices might have been unavoidable in the face of the crisis, more coordination and information-sharing might have cushioned the effects of those choices throughout the system.[9]

> People [were] sitting in jail for [an extended period] before they were able to have their day in court. And that's just not fundamentally what the role that police officers should be put into is—to take someone's freedom away . . . without any type of judicial review, other than a paper review of the probable cause statement or something very minimal like that. So I think it erodes the public trust in the whole system.
>
> — Law enforcement operations panelist

---

[8]   The National Commission recommended institutionalizing such connections to sources of medical knowledge, including public health agencies (National Commission on COVID-19 and Criminal Justice, 2020b, p. 33).

[9]   One of the recommendations of the National Commission was maintaining "standing coordinating panels for [the] public health emergency preparedness" of criminal justice agencies (National Commission on COVID-19 and Criminal Justice, 2020b, p. 13).

> We also heard about instances where survivors would have no idea that their abuser has been released until they run into them on the street.
>
> – Victim services panelist

- **Serious challenges remain for successfully protecting the health and safety of emergency responders and critical personnel during large-scale disasters.** Large-scale events, whether natural or manmade, have always created serious challenges with regard to protecting the health and safety of emergency responders and critical personnel. Echoing the experiences of the September 11, 2001, terrorist attacks (9/11), panelists questioned whether today's responders would have long-term consequences from COVID-19 that would create long-term costs for them and for the United States. The potential for long-term physical effects is still uncertain, although it appears to be a significant concern for some. It *is* certain, however, that mental health consequences from the stresses of the pandemic already are occurring. As was the case for 9/11, there likely will be a need to remain attentive to how the consequences of this disaster evolve and how both the availability and use of protective options by practitioners and key personnel shape those consequences.

> We also don't know the long-term health consequences of COVID. For instance, there seems to be some lasting consequences on heart health, which we already know is a big concern in the law enforcement community. So we don't know whether survivor benefit claims will be lasting [for] decades.
>
> – Law enforcement operations panelist

Across our panels, the ability of organizations to adapt was supported by previous reform efforts or earlier initiatives to use new technologies. Areas that already had taken steps to reduce jail or prison populations had fewer constraints on how they could implement infection control measures in their less crowded facilities. Organizations that had made investments in information technology and converted paper case files into electronic files could shift to remote and distributed work models much more easily than those that had not. Past experiments with virtual court processes or telemedicine made it more straightforward to virtualize different parts of the justice process. And past relationships with other justice agencies—or with community organizations and the public more broadly—meant that social capital was already in place and could be drawn on when needed. In some cases, agencies that did not have such pieces in place before the pandemic put them in place quickly, with a speed of innovation and technology adoption that was nearly unprecedented for the justice system, but they had a more difficult time adapting than those that already had the needed elements in place.

> Really, it's the pace of change. [It's] unprecedented in my experience in over 32 years of court administration.
>
> – Court system panelist

Some Responses to the Pandemic Have Delayed Rather Than Resolved Challenges

Although reducing justice populations by halting or deferring processes did reduce infection risk, those strategies have created significant backlogs in the system that will have to be addressed later. Panelists described growing numbers of individuals who have been arrested but not charged, or whose court cases are accumulating in deep backlogs of unresolved cases and delayed trials. Across our panels, the metaphor most often used was that the flow of people through the system was blocked and the backlogs were growing like water behind a dam, with the pressures on the justice system increasing as the numbers of cases increase. The pressures are compounded by budget cuts, which are affecting both government and NGOs that are critical to the functioning of the system, essentially shrinking the size of the pipes available to drain the backlogs once the pandemic recedes. We summarize these constraints in Figure S.2 and flag backlogs and constrictions that were identified across our panels, which affect nearly every part of the justice system.

Although strategies of deferral might have been sufficient to manage a short-term event—which is consistent with the early narrative that the pandemic would pass through the country quickly—they were not enough for a longer-term crisis. Over the course of the pandemic, strategies of deferral managed the current crisis at the price of a future one, and dealing with that future crisis might require additional cycles of change and adaptation to relieve the pressure.

Figure S.2
Pressures Building at Different Points in the Justice System from Backlogs and Capacity Constraints

> We work as a system, and our courts have been doing everything just about virtually . . . but a real downside, and we're looking at this statewide, is the dockets aren't moving . . . and the backlog is huge. I've seen it [before], the court shut down, obviously [after the hurricane we experienced]. I saw the impact of that. But the courts are going to have to be able to function at over a hundred percent to be able to actually even make a dent into the docket. So, I don't know if that's going on in other places or not, but there's a backlog and it's a big deal.
>
> – Community corrections panelist
>
> Community engagement has been a challenge. . . . Over the last three or four years, we've really made strides in community engagement and we're missing that. We're missing that component from our agency. And I'm concerned about the long-term effects of that.
>
> – Law enforcement operations panelist

Research and Evaluation Are Needed to Assess Responses to the Pandemic and Inform Future Innovation and Reform Efforts

Across the different parts of the system, the adaptations made to confront the COVID-19 pandemic suggest a slate of research and evaluation needs to measure (1) the effectiveness of such adaptations in responding to the current crisis, (2) their potential value for strengthening preparedness for future infectious disease outbreaks, and (3) the value of maintaining them over the longer term, even when the risks of the pandemic are no longer dominating decisionmaking.

Some of the steps that were taken, such as the use of teleconferencing for many processes, were relatively well defined and previously explored changes that were made on a very broad scale. Before the pandemic, research and evaluation efforts had suggested the potential value of using telepresence in the justice system. However. multiple panelists suggested that it had not been broadly adopted because of the justice system's organizational and technological risk aversion. The COVID-19 pandemic changed that, with the pressure to continue operations breaking such barriers and, in the assessment of some of our panelists, causing the system to make years of progress in weeks. Therefore, these changes represent a major expansion in the scope and depth of an available technology across the justice system.

> The pandemic was not the disruption that we wanted in the court system, but maybe [it was] the disruption we needed to really make change happen. . . . [W]e're a big old-fashioned institution that doesn't change very easily. And this pandemic has really pushed the pace of change.
>
> – Court system panelist

Some of the other initiatives pursued during the pandemic—notably, major efforts to reduce arrests to limit flows of people into the justice system and rapid increases in releases from jails and some prisons—represented much more-substantial changes. Although some efforts to reduce incarceration in correctional institutions already were underway, the significant population reductions that occurred in some areas represented a massive, near–national-level experiment in a very different approach to managing criminal justice. Such changes were in line with some of the changes that were being sought in national protests, but they were implemented for infection-control rather than justice-reform purposes.

> I think there is a lot of support in the general public for the concept of scaling back on mass incarceration. And I think that is one of the very few things that consistently—in the last five or ten years—has been a bipartisan issue that pretty much everybody can agree that we want to cut back incarceration.
>
> – Institutional corrections panelist

Our panelists were generally positive about the results of many of these experiments of necessity, but some were cautionary about outcomes. Panelists viewed virtual models as extremely valuable and as having many possible benefits, but some were concerned about the effect of digital divides and whether virtual processes would be as effective as in-person ones. Several panelists were optimistic about the changes in arrest and incarceration policies because such policies did not appear to have resulted in major increases in crime. In Table S.2, we summarize the most promising practices that came out of the discussion in each of our panels.

However, for nearly all of these promising practices, our panelists emphasized the need for longer-term, empirical evaluations of outcomes to see whether their initial optimism held up to analysis and to assess whether the outcomes were driven by the circumstances of the pandemic. As a result, a variety of research and evaluation questions came out of the discussions in each panel, which showed commonalities and differences across the system. In Table S.3, we summarize those research questions, which represent an initial contribution to a research agenda for weighing the system's response to COVID-19 and determining what lessons can be learned for the future.[10]

> I think there's a real opportunity to fundamentally shift the reach of the criminal justice system in the lives of the poorest people in the community. But there's also tremendous resistance. . . . I think it's going to be up to researchers to be able to really evaluate the impact of COVID and bail reform and these arguments around police legitimacy and the link between that and crime to really help us better understand the impact.
>
> – Community organization panelist

---

[10] The National Commission argued for the development of minimum standards across a wide variety of these topic and practice areas to strengthen preparedness for the next pandemic. It also called for a "national research agenda concerning COVID-19 and criminal justice" for which the questions in this report could provide a jumping-off point; furthermore, the results of such questions could support standards development (National Commission on COVID-19 and Criminal Justice, 2020b, p. 31).

Table S.2
Promising Practices Identified in Each Sector Panel Discussion

Category	Law Enforcement	Court System	Institutional Corrections	Community Corrections	Victim Services
Virtual components of justice processes	• **Maintain virtual access to the courts.** Participants saw major advantages in making court appearances virtual for criminal justice practitioners (including forensic examiners and police officers) and citizens. The option was viewed as cost-saving when resource constraints likely will affect both government organizations and individuals. • **Continue using virtual calls for service and alternative ways to efficiently meet the public's needs.** The use of web-based reporting and nontraditional responses to some crimes have been explored by some agencies as a cost-saving measure for some time. The pandemic pushed the adoption of these modes, but their value to the public and likely significant resource constraints are arguments for maintaining them.	• **Maintain virtual access to the courts.** The ability of individuals to attend court remotely not only improves efficiency but also appears to have improved access to justice by making it easier and less costly for individuals to participate. Although digital divide concerns—which might increase because of the economic effects of the pandemic—must be resolved, the value of virtual options appears to be considerable. • **Maintain routine virtual connectivity between courts and corrections agencies.** In both the courts and corrections panels, participants noted the high value of bringing individuals to court virtually because it increased safety for all and cut costs involved with prisoner transportation and security at court. • **Maintain virtual elements of in-person processes.** Although a return to traditional in-person jury trials is a priority, maintaining virtual components wherever possible—in jury selection and voir dire—would increase efficiency and make jury service less burdensome.	• **Maintain routine virtual connectivity between courts and corrections agencies.** Corrections agencies flagged virtual court appearances as a major opportunity to save money and reduce safety risk. In an era of likely constrained resources, reducing costs for inmate transportation will be attractive.	• **Maintain virtual supervision and service-delivery models.** Virtual approaches to supervision and service delivery during the pandemic appeared to be beneficial to both supervisees and staff. Initial experience suggested that virtual approaches might have other advantages over standard methods, for example, by allowing customization of supervision. Although the effectiveness of these approaches should be evaluated formally, these approaches appear to be very promising, particularly for lower-risk supervisees.	• **Explore maintaining virtual service-delivery options.** Although victim services providers were less convinced than others that virtual models were as effective as traditional modes of counseling and service delivery, they could provide alternative modes when in-person delivery is not available. More-rigorous assessments of their effectiveness and the identification of specific services where virtual delivery is advantageous are needed.

Table S.2—Continued

Category	Law Enforcement	Court System	Institutional Corrections	Community Corrections	Victim Services
Work models	• **Maintain remote work options and schedule flexibility.** Although remote work options and schedule flexibility were driven by the necessity of minimizing the risk of transmitting the virus, panelists viewed such options as valuable for improving staff morale and retention in the long term. As a result, like in many private-sector firms, flexible schedules and remote work options were viewed as something to maintain in the longer term.	• **Maintain remote and paperless work processes for courts.** Even before the pandemic, courts were pursuing paperless processes and other improvements in information technology. Although models that allowed easy work from home were valuable in the pandemic, they also would improve efficiency after the pandemic.	• **Explore maintaining flexible work models as part of corrections.** Although many parts of corrections practice must be done in person and in facilities, providing some roles with more flexibility to the extent possible could make corrections careers more attractive.	• **Maintain teleworking models in community supervision and service-provider agencies.** Because they allow more flexibility for corrections practitioners, telework and flexible work models could help reduce infrastructure costs and make corrections careers more attractive to potential employees.	
Communication and connectivity	• **Use virtual connectivity and new information technology platforms to support leadership and community situational awareness.** In panel discussions, participants noted the value of law enforcement leaders being able to connect remotely and get information about what was going on. They thought it was useful in responding to questions from political leaders or the public. In addition, providing more data resources on department websites was noted as a strategy to strengthen communication when staff were not connecting with people in person. Both appear valuable to maintain.		• **Maintain expansions of virtual and video visitation systems.** Facilities that had strong virtual connectivity between inmates and others, including family, legal counsel, program providers, and electronic content sources, made disease-control measures that limited in-person contact easier to implement.		• **Maintain alternative contact approaches to reach victims in need.** Alternative ways that organizations developed to reach out to and communicate with victims under stay-at-home and restricted contact conditions of the pandemic, including text lines and modified practices with law enforcement agencies, could make it possible to better identify and serve victims in need after the pandemic recedes.

Table S.2—Continued

Category	Law Enforcement	Court System	Institutional Corrections	Community Corrections	Victim Services
Sector-specific issues			• **Better integrate corrections agencies into public health planning.** Because of their confined and dense populations, corrections institutions have always been a potential flash-point for infectious disease outbreaks. Because community spread into and out of facilities was a contributor, the COVID-19 pandemic demonstrated that facilities should have a seat at the table not only for emergency planning in their areas during crises but also on a long-term basis. • **Preserve reductions in inmate density to reduce disease risk.** Although infrastructure changes (e.g., ventilation) could reduce the chances of facilities becoming hotspots of disease, facilities that had lower population density had many more options available to reduce the risk of viral spread and respond when outbreaks occurred.		• **Strengthen partnerships and collaborations to enable service delivery during crisis periods.** Relationships and linkages between service providers, which are important even under normal circumstances, were viewed as particularly important in responding to the extremely complex and demanding circumstances of the pandemic.

Table S.3
Key Research and Evaluation Questions Identified from Panel Discussions

Category	Law Enforcement	Court System	Institutional Corrections	Community Corrections	Victim Services
Understanding COVID-19's effects on criminal justice	• What explains the differences from place to place in how crime and victimization changed during the pandemic? • What is the extent of the long-term physical and mental health consequences of COVID-19 for law enforcement officers? How has the pandemic affected officer suicide, which was a significant concern before the pandemic?	• Can the effects of the pandemic on plea bargaining behavior and outcomes be identified and measured? Can concerns about the potential coerciveness of COVID-19 in correctional facilities (i.e., increasing bargaining power of prosecution) be distinguished from ways that the push to reduce jail and prison populations might lead to a greater desire to reach agreement rapidly?	• Given concerns about the pandemic's effect on different racial and ethnic groups and disparities in incarceration, data need to be collected to better understand the burden of disease across demographic groups within facilities. • What have been the mental health effects of the pandemic on both incarcerated populations and correctional staff, and how long do such effects last?	• Given the importance of employment as a component of reentry and a driver of success, can the effect of the pandemic's economic dislocation on justice-involved individuals be directly measured to better understand supervision success rates going forward?	• Changes in reporting behavior by victims during the pandemic risks future analyses of crime and justice responses reaching distorted conclusions. For example, if many victims delay reporting because of fear of COVID-19 or other reasons, crime at different stages of the pandemic may appear lower than it actually was. How can this be addressed in research and evaluation studies? • Given differences in data on needs reflected in calls to helplines versus calls to police, how can the totality of the changes in victim service demand caused by the pandemic be better characterized?

Table S.3—Continued

Category	Law Enforcement	Court System	Institutional Corrections	Community Corrections	Victim Services
Improved disease management	• How has the level of community trust and the public perception of the legitimacy of police departments affected their ability to contribute to managing COVID-19? Have more-trusted departments been more effective or more trusted with access to sensitive data or other resources to enable pandemic response? Are there other roles that law enforcement could productively play in public health response? • How can areas better plan for future pandemics to limit the conflicts and imprecision in public health orders (e.g., what businesses were classified as essential, what level of enforcement by police is appropriate or useful) that made law enforcement participation in managing the crisis more difficult and controversial? Can a consensus be reached around definitions and categories to make it possible to respond more quickly, collaboratively, and effectively to future outbreaks?	• Can resources be developed to educate court system stake-holders about Health Insurance Portability and Accountability Act (HIPAA) requirements regarding the sharing of COVID-19 case information to enable protection of both staff and the community?	• What can be learned from the significant differences in COVID-19 spread in separate correctional systems and even across facilities within the same system? Was the variation mostly attributable to the nature and time of introduction of the virus, or were there key differences in initial conditions (e.g., more- versus less-crowded conditions) or in the practices, policies, or infection-control actions taken that explain the different experiences? • What disease-testing strategies are effective in minimizing infectious disease in correctional institutions, taking into account the limits of tests, their costs, and the information (and the uncertainty of that information) provided by a positive or negative result?		• Given resource constraints and victims in need of sheltering, can better strategies be identified to reduce infection risk in group shelters while keeping barriers to utilization low for clients?

Table S.3—Continued

Category	Law Enforcement	Court System	Institutional Corrections	Community Corrections	Victim Services
Improved disease management (continued)	• Are there more-effective ways to address the increase in mental health calls that has been observed during the pandemic, and how might alternative models inform consideration of police reform efforts? • How can law enforcement officers be better protected from infection risks during large-scale outbreaks, including increasing their compliance with the use of available protective equipment?		• Given concerns about individual isolation for disease prevention and controversy around the levels of transparency of correctional systems during the pandemic, can consensus models for such activities be developed that meet the needs of both corrections systems and advocates? • How can corrections officers and staff be better protected from infection risks during large-scale outbreaks, including increasing their compliance with the use of available protective equipment? • Given the lessons learned from the pandemic and the significant infectious disease risks to both incarcerated populations and the public from high-density, mass incarceration, what should the capacity of existing correctional institutions be?		

Table S.3—Continued

Category	Law Enforcement	Court System	Institutional Corrections	Community Corrections	Victim Services
Improved disease management (continued)			• Are there architectural or other retrofitting options that would make correctional institutions more resilient to future infectious disease threats? • What are the implications of the pandemic's lessons on the capacity of carceral facilities' medical care–delivery systems?		
Assessing the outcomes of reductions in arrest, incarceration, and supervision	• What have been the effects of nonarrest policies and actions taken in response to lower-level crimes during the pandemic? Do initially positive perceptions hold up over the longer term?	• Has the significant reduction in pretrial detention and money bail had an effect on appearance rates?	• How has the reduction in detention, reduction in jail use, and expedited release from prison incarceration affected crime and recidivism rates? • How can the effects of the changes made as a result of the pandemic be distinguished from the effects of other initiatives (e.g., bail reform) that were already underway in some areas?	• How has the substitution of supervision for incarceration and the reduction in the dosage (i.e., intensity) of supervision for many individuals affected crime and recidivism rates? • How have the major changes to the use of revocations—and, therefore, a significant reduction in a flow of individuals back into institutional corrections—affected outcomes? • How has the reduction of the use of such techniques as drug testing or electronic supervision affected outcomes? Do the changes made provide a template for reducing costs and intrusion into supervisees' lives going forward?	

Table S.3—Continued

Category	Law Enforcement	Court System	Institutional Corrections	Community Corrections	Victim Services
Assessing the outcomes of reductions in arrest, incarceration, and supervision (continued)				• How can the effects of the changes made as a result of the pandemic be distinguished from the effects of other initiatives (e.g., bail reform) that were already underway in some areas?	• What are the differences in outcomes for individuals served in alternative housing supports or hotel or motel models versus standard sheltering?
Assessing distanced criminal justice models	• What have been the effects of alternative work schedules and models on staff and law enforcement agencies, and how should those effects shape the decision to continue them over the longer term? • What should be measured to better assess the effects of pandemic restrictions on alternative approaches, such as violence-reduction interventions, and assess the effectiveness of efforts to create virtual options for generally relationship-intensive face-to-face interventions?	• Is there a measurable effect on case outcomes of trial participants being socially distanced or wearing face coverings? • How can courts proactively identify alternative facilities where jury trials could be held in the community? • Can tools be developed to solicit community input on case prioritization to ensure that community views are reflected in which cases are allocated scarce court resources and acted on for backlog reduction?	• Can the effectiveness of virtual visitation and other virtual options be measured to support investments in their expansion?		

Table S.3—Continued

Category	Law Enforcement	Court System	Institutional Corrections	Community Corrections	Victim Services
Assessing virtual delivery of justice services	• How satisfied has the public been with the provision of virtual police services during the pandemic, and how much have those alternative models saved departmental resources? • How effective have efforts to train staff and new officers virtually been? Over time, how do the skills and capabilities of officers who went to the Academy in cyberspace differ from those of officers who were trained in person? • What technologies are needed to support more law enforcement practitioners in flexible work models (e.g., systems to better enable dispatchers to work remotely)? • Did digital divides among different groups in the public affect the effectiveness of communication and other strategies? Were alternatives used by departments that encountered such problems effective?	• Have remote-appearance options reduced failure-to-appear rates? • Do victims of crime have a different perception of whether justice is served in remote hearings and proceedings? • How do jurors perceive the experience of serving on a virtual jury? • In virtual proceedings, do outcomes differ from those of in-person court processes on measurable factors, such as bail, sentences, or other outcomes? • Could online dispute-resolution processes be applied in the criminal area to help reduce the backlog while maintaining procedural justice? • Does the potential for integrating virtual technology into future court operations suggest a need to revisit court design and security standards? • If virtual juries are used, are there issues maintaining the representativeness of the jury pool? • How has the shift to virtual proceedings affected self-represented litigants?		• Are virtual models as effective as in-person supervision, counseling, and treatment? How have key outcomes—both from the individual and societal perspective—been affected by the shift? • What are the full net savings for corrections agencies from virtual models? Estimates should include variable costs (e.g., staffing, transportation time) and potential savings from infrastructure costs. What are the net savings to the individuals under supervision? • How have digital divides across different parts of the community corrections system—including government agencies, NGO service providers, and entities serving urban and rural communities—affected the ability to continue operations through the pandemic?	• How effective are virtual models for delivering services to victims, and how satisfied are those victims with the outcomes (including virtual court participation)? • How can organizations that might not have as strong a technology infrastructure as government criminal justice agencies more-effectively address the information security and other concerns with delivering services remotely? Similar to questions raised in the past regarding law enforcement, are there challenges (e.g., with legal discoverability) with providers using personally owned devices in performing their roles? • Given concerns about the digital divide significantly affecting the ability of victims from locations with low broadband or little communications infrastructure to access services and participate in the justice process, can levels of true access be better mapped to inform assessment of the impact of virtual models?

Table S.3—Continued

Category	Law Enforcement	Court System	Institutional Corrections	Community Corrections	Victim Services
Assessing virtual delivery of justice services (continued)		• Can the positive effects of virtual proceedings on litigants—in easier access, lower costs, and other factors—be quantified? If costs are lower, is access to justice increased? • Can the effects of streaming or broadcasting court proceedings online be measured to allow for the weighing of broader access versus greater exposure for victims, defendants, and other parties?			
Improving justice funding models	• Given likely funding constraints on departments going forward, what are the implications of the types of programs and initiatives that will be cut? How do such cuts interact with reform efforts arguing for the reallocation of resources from police budgets?	• How have the mechanisms through which court systems are funded affected their ability to respond to and operate through the pandemic?	• How can institutional corrections systems respond to budgetary pressures that could push toward a return to high-density facilities, therefore increasing vulnerability to infectious diseases?	• How can both supervision agencies and the service providers on which they depend be sustainably funded, given what we have learned during the pandemic?	• Given the importance of services to victims of crime and the importance of supporting their involvement in the justice process, how can sustainable support for organizations delivering those services be put in place given the vulnerability revealed by the pandemic and its economic consequences?

There Are Long-Term Challenges to Face, but There Is Also Opportunity to Substantially Improve Justice System Performance for All

At the time of this writing, there is optimistic news about vaccines for the virus becoming available that could mean that the end of the pandemic is approaching. But that good news is also coming at a point when case numbers are spiking to unprecedented levels in states across the country and average daily deaths once again number in the thousands. Furthermore, our panelists emphasized that, like people who have recovered from COVID-19 but are still experiencing symptoms, the effects of the pandemic on the criminal justice system are not going to go away rapidly. Because of the consequences of how agencies responded to deal with the immediate pressure of the pandemic, enduring pressures—backlogs of cases, demands, and needs—were created that might take months or even years to work through, even after pre-pandemic capacity is restored. And that recovery will be made more complicated by the scars that the pandemic will almost certainly leave on municipal budgets, on the philanthropic funding streams on which many service providers rely, and on the economy as a whole. The fiscal and economic fallout means not only that justice agencies likely will have fewer resources to address the backlogs that have built up but also that that need in particular will continue to expand as some stresses experienced by individuals and families during the pandemic persist beyond it. Although national protests called for defunding the police as part of demands for change, it might be the economic consequences of the pandemic that result in justice agencies having fewer resources to work with and constrained options going forward.

> I think it's also helpful just to think about [the fact that] it's going to be years before real recovery happens. I mean . . . you've got a really high rate of unemployment just across the board. And so when you talk about helping a population who doesn't have credit, who doesn't have job experience, who doesn't have a resume, trying to provide some of those supports just for employment, which is essential for any sort of long-term independence and self-sufficiency.
>
> – Victim services panelist

However, in spite of concerns about very serious challenges, there was optimism among our panelists as well. Long before the pandemic, there were concerns about the consequences of the number of people channeled into the justice system in the United States. The focus of calls for reform regarding mass incarceration have generally focused on the consequences for justice-involved individuals and their communities and how the intermingling of responses to mental health issues, substance abuse, and crime has affected the system's overall effectiveness.[11] Beyond such concerns, the pandemic made it undeniable that the public safety goals of criminal justice and public health are inexorably intertwined, and that past efforts to prepare the system for pandemic threats had only limited success. The pandemic itself represented a massive forcing function to decarcerate, giving the United States the opportunity to consider how a justice system that relies less on arrest and incarceration might look and what public

---

[11] The final report of National Commission argued for the expansion of diversion and alternative interventions to reduce the flow of such individuals into the justice system (National Commission on COVID-19 and Criminal Justice, 2020b, pp. 21–24).

safety outcomes it might produce. The pursuit of that outcome aligns with the calls for reform that were prominent in the protests through summer 2020, but it predates both those calls and the pandemic. The pandemic disproved—on a nationwide scale—the argument for slow progress in past reform and innovation in the justice system, potentially opening up new options and possibilities for the future. Although there are good reasons for a level of risk aversion in justice agencies, adapting to the pandemic involved rapid change on a very broad scale. Having demonstrated that inertia can be overcome, there is the potential for change that might have looked unrealistic before.

> So that's where we're standing at this moment in time, it's a big moment and we're not going to waste it. We're gonna go big and we're gonna do the investments in the community that we've talked about for a long time, but have never done.
>
> – Court system panelist
>
> I don't think instinctively that as a system we're inclined to be introspective. . . . I think if there is a silver lining, [it's that] we are being forced to be introspective. Ironically, some of the things that we were considering well before the pandemic where "old school resistance prevailed," now we're really considering it.
>
> – Community corrections panelist

Given the terrible loss caused by COVID-19, which has claimed the lives of many members of criminal justice and service organizations, of medical professionals fighting the disease (including those treating justice-involved individuals who became infected), and of hundreds of thousands across the United States, realizing the potential for improvement seems to be a critical goal. Drawing on lessons they learned in responding to this crisis, our panelists saw a chance for innovation that could make the criminal justice system both more effective in managing public safety and fairer to those who become involved in the justice system. In our discussions, panelists talked about the inherent tension that exists between the desire to craft justice interventions that are effective at the individual level and responding uniformly across large categories of people, offenses, or problems. Responses to the pandemic to reduce populations in jails or prisons, allowing the system to focus on fewer people at a time, make it easier to customize interventions for greater effectiveness. Technologies that the pandemic forced on the usually risk-averse justice system—most notably, virtual modes of interaction and supervision—further enable the development of one-size-fits-one models that can conserve resources, improve fairness, reduce the intrusiveness of the justice system in the lives of individuals and their communities, and be more effective. Although the likely enduring fiscal pressure on the justice system might make this sort of innovation practically important, learning to build a stronger justice legacy could be, to paraphrase one of our panelists, a way to find at least a thin silver lining in what has been a very darkly clouded time for the United States.

Acknowledgments

The research team gratefully acknowledges the contributions of all of the panel members and interviewees who participated in our virtual summit, even as they and their agencies were continuing to respond to the pandemic. The names and affiliations of our panelists are listed in the appendix to this report. We could not have assembled the information and insights needed for this effort without their contributions.

The PCJNI team also acknowledges the contributions of a broad group of NIJ staff who were involved in the planning and execution of these events. We are very grateful that NIJ director David Muhlhausen was able to join each of the workshops during our virtual summit. Steven Schuetz, Angela Moore, Mallory O'Brien, and Lucas Zarwell were the core planning team from NIJ for this effort.

In addition, the authors would like to specifically acknowledge the multiple research groups and organizations that have assembled data sets tracking the effects of COVID-19 on the country and the health and justice policies that have been implemented in different areas and regions. Throughout this project, we have drawn on a large number of such data sets as we discuss the differences in the effects of the disease on parts of the justice system and how the actions that were taken and not taken have shaped those effects. Although any research effort always relies on the foundations built by others, in this case, the extensive work by others across the country and around the world was so valuable to seem to merit thanks beyond the usual footnotes that flag where we drew on their data.

The authors also would like to acknowledge the contributions of the peer reviewers of the report, Meagan Cahill of the RAND Corporation and Greg Ridgeway of the University of Pennsylvania, and the anonymous NIJ reviewers of the final report. We are also grateful for the contributions of Babitha Balan, Kristen Meadows, Sandra Petitjean, Blair Smith, and Chandra Garber from RAND's Publications and Research Communications Departments for their work on this report and the companion research briefs.

Abbreviations

9/11	September 11, 2001, terrorist attacks
APA	American Psychiatric Association
APPA	American Probation and Parole Association
CDC	Centers for Disease Control and Prevention
COVID-19	coronavirus disease 2019
DUI	driving under the influence
EMS	emergency medical services
ExiT	Executives Transforming Probation and Parole
FBI	Federal Bureau of Investigation
FTC	Federal Trade Commission
GMU	George Mason University
IACP	International Association of Chiefs of Police
IT	information technology
NGO	nongovernmental organization
NIJ	National Institute of Justice
NLEOMF	National Law Enforcement Officers Memorial Fund
PCJNI	Priority Criminal Justice Needs Initiative
PERF	Police Executive Research Forum
PPE	personal protective equipment
PSAP	public safety answering point
UCLA	University of California, Los Angeles

VPN   virtual private network

VSP   victim services providers

CHAPTER ONE

Introduction

As of November 2020, the coronavirus disease 2019 (COVID-19) pandemic had resulted in the deaths of between 268,000 and 360,000 Americans.[1] The spread of the disease stressed the U.S. health care system, with the number of people needing care overwhelming available resources in some parts of the country. Both the disease and the actions taken to respond to it stressed the country as a whole, including the economic system and government agencies at all levels. Prominent among these systems is the criminal justice system—police departments, court systems, corrections agencies, victim services providers, and organizations that provide services as part of treatment and reentry support—whose activities traditionally involve face-to-face contact that could put both practitioners and the public at risk.

The high-contact nature of many criminal justice processes meant that infection-control approaches to promote socially distanced and virtual interactions challenged standard ways of operating. Furthermore, such approaches were difficult or even impossible to implement in custodial settings, where large populations of people held in correctional institutions resulted in rapid spread of the disease in some state and local prison systems.[2] According to public tabulations of reported deaths, as of November 2020, between 156 and 282 police officers had lost their lives to COVID-19,[3] which is approaching the average number of officers who were killed in the line of duty from all causes from 2009 to 2019.[4] It is estimated that, as of November 2020, between 98 and 191 corrections staff members had died from COVID-19, and more than 46,000 staff have been infected.[5] COVID-19 fatalities alone exceed the number of corrections workers killed in 2018 by between six and 12 times.[6]

---

[1]   See Johns Hopkins University School of Medicine, "COVID-19 United States Cases by County," data set, updated December 6, 2020, and Centers for Disease Control and Prevention, National Center for Health Statistics, "Excess Deaths Associated with COVID-19," webpage, updated December 2, 2020, respectively.

[2]   Megan Wallace, Liesl Hagan, Kathryn G. Curran, Samantha P. Williams, Senad Handanagic, Adam Bjork, Sherri L. Davidson, Robert T. Lawrence, Joseph McLaughlin, Marilee Butterfield, et al., "COVID-19 in Correctional and Detention Facilities—United States, February–April 2020," *Morbidity and Mortality Weekly Report*, Vol. 69, No. 19, May 6, 2020, updated May 15, 2020.

[3]   National Law Enforcement Officers Memorial Fund, "COVID-19 Related Law Enforcement Fatalities," webpage, undated; Fraternal Order of Police, "COVID-19 Line-of-Duty Deaths," webpage, updated December 7, 2020.

[4]   National Law Enforcement Officers Memorial Fund, "Officer Deaths by Year: Year-by-Year Breakdown of Law Enforcement Deaths Throughout U.S. History," webpage, September 29, 2020.

[5]   The Marshall Project, "A State-by-State Look at Coronavirus in Prisons," webpage, updated December 2020b; American Correctional Association, "The Wall of Honor," webpage, undated.

[6]   The number of corrections workers killed in 2018 was 16 (U.S. Bureau of Labor Statistics, "Injuries, Illnesses, and Fatalities: Census of Fatal Occupational Injuries [CFOI]—Current," webpage, updated December 17, 2019). The 2018 number

To maintain the justice system's ability to perform its functions for the country, agencies were forced to adapt to the reality of the new risk environment. Many made changes in an effort to limit face-to-face interaction to reduce the chances of viral spread and of staff becoming infected. Courthouses across the country ceased many—if not all—in-person proceedings. Agencies bought personal protective equipment (PPE) for their staff as a component of worker safety and public health efforts. Some agencies stopped delivering certain services or sought alternative—and largely virtual—ways to interact with the public, deliver counseling, or supervise justice-involved individuals in community supervision. Other agencies in the system simply stopped enforcing certain laws (e.g., traffic enforcement was significantly curtailed in some areas to limit contact between police and the public, and some community supervision agencies stopped sending individuals back to jail for technical violations of their conditions of probation and parole). Some institutional corrections systems released significant numbers of people in an effort to reduce population density to enable social distancing for infection control. To respond to the spread of the disease, agencies had to make major changes quickly, adjusting what they were doing to balance the risks of the pandemic with risks to communities from curtailing policing, court, corrections, and other justice system activities.

The National Climate Made Responding to the Pandemic More Difficult

The effects of the pandemic on the criminal justice system were complicated by several other circumstances. From the outset of the pandemic, both the disease and the response to it became intensely politicized, and there was substantial controversy regarding public health interventions. Despite mounting fatalities from the disease, the need for a public health response at all was controversial, and conflicting narratives about COVID-19 made coordinated efforts to contain it near impossible. This meant that there was also controversy about the role that different parts of the community wanted justice agencies to play in enforcing compliance with public health directives, such as wearing masks, closing businesses with indoor or significant in-person contact, or prohibiting such events as concerts, parties, or large gatherings. In some parts of the country, law enforcement actively enforced mask-wearing and shut down events where transmission of the virus could occur across large numbers of people. In other parts of the country, intervention was much more limited. In some areas, it was justice agencies themselves that resisted taking on—or outright refused to take on—the role of enforcing compliance with public health measures intended to reduce the spread of the virus.[7]

As the country was beginning to deal with the effects of the COVID-19 pandemic, the killing of George Floyd by police officers in Minneapolis, Minnesota, triggered large-scale protests and unrest. These protests also demanded action in response to the 2020 deaths of Breonna Taylor and Ahmaud Arbery. Echoing the response to the killing of Michael Brown in Ferguson, Missouri, in 2014, the Black Lives Matter protests that started in May 2020 were more widespread and focused intensely critical attention on law enforcement and on the justice system more generally. The resulting push to cut funding from law enforcement agencies and

---

also was higher than the average of 11 per year (Srinivas Konda, Hope Tiesman, Audrey Reichard, and Dan Hartley, "U.S. Correctional Officers Killed or Injured on the Job," *Corrections Today*, Vol. 75, No. 5, November/December 2013).

[7]   For example, see Scott Neuman, "Florida Sheriff Orders Deputies and Staff Not to Wear Face Masks," NPR, August 12, 2020.

reallocate it to non–criminal justice approaches for dealing with violence and other societal problems gained significant momentum in some areas. Other areas adopted changes to policing practices and implemented civilian oversight of justice agencies.[8] Both the law enforcement actions and policy actions taken in response to the protests differed significantly across the country. However, national-level reactions to extremely local-level actions—sometimes the actions of individual officers—taken during the protests intensified scrutiny of law enforcement agencies, further complicating the challenge of policing during the pandemic.

> Let's not forget that 2020—a pivotal year—is also the greatest civil rights reckoning of our lifetime. And there's tremendous pressure in my community. And I assume in yours too, to scrutinize what we're doing in the criminal justice system.
>
> – Court system panelist
>
> All of this has become too politicized. Information and data have become weaponized and that's unfortunate. I think that that relates to this kind of larger systemic or structural problem . . . that affects who we trust, what we trust, what we read, what we believe, how we do these analysis and so forth. I don't think government in general or the criminal justice system has done enough to be transparent. I realize that politics . . . are involved with everything. But right now, I think one of the major concerns that you have is that no one really trusts anyone. And . . . in that environment, it's really hard to have the kinds of coordination, collaboration, communications, and collective actions that we want across law enforcement, courts, prisons, and beyond.
>
> – Community organization panelist

We Held a Series of Workshops to Collect Lessons from the Justice System's Response to the Pandemic

It is difficult to separate how the criminal justice system had to adjust to the realities of operating under pandemic conditions from the national political environment and backlash triggered by George Floyd's death. Responses to the pandemic, including significant decarceration, aligned with some of the demands made during the protests. Similarly, while some of the organizations involved in protests were calling to defund the police as part of reform efforts, the economic consequences of the pandemic for state and municipal budgets were resulting in the defunding of criminal justice agencies in very real ways. As a result, the reality of this period makes it difficult (and perhaps even impossible) to fully separate the effects of the pandemic on the justice system from the broader national environment created by calls for justice reform.

Acknowledging this fundamental difficulty from the outset, the Priority Criminal Justice Needs Initiative (PCJNI)—a joint effort managed by the RAND Corporation in partnership with the Police Executive Research Forum (PERF), RTI International, and the University of Denver on behalf of the U.S. Department of Justice's National Institute of Justice (NIJ)—held a virtual summit made up of separate online workshops that explored the justice system's response to the COVID-19 pandemic. The goal of our efforts was to focus on the pandemic,

---

[8]   See Andrew Welsh-Huggins, "In Cities Across U.S., Voters Support More Police Oversight," Associated Press, November 21, 2020.

to seek out insights into how justice agencies had responded to the unprecedented set of circumstances the pandemic produced, and to learn lessons that might be valuable to maintain for the future. That focus was not to suggest that the pandemic was more important than the broader—and ongoing, even predating the most-recent protests—conversation around civil rights and criminal justice reform. Rather, we believed that an attempt to take on both at one time would risk doing justice to neither set of concerns. As will become clear in the discussion of the results of the workshops, it was indeed impossible to fully separate the two. However, the reality that many of the actions taken to adapt to the COVID-19 pandemic were consistent with policy changes called for in these protests and previous reform efforts made it seem to be more an opportunity than a challenge.

> I don't think we can look at COVID-19 entirely separate from the protests that have occurred. And it's really important that we realize that some people were willing to risk their health and the health of people they love in order to make their voices known in the protest that went all across the country. And so this whole idea of "we're all in this together," it's a nice concept, and yes, we all are in some ways, but our experiences are very different of the pandemic.
>
> – Community organization panelist

Our approach to gathering insight into the justice system's responses and adaptations was to go to those who had been directly affected by those challenges—practitioners in justice agencies and service-providing organizations from areas that had faced varied challenges from the pandemic. Because covering the entirety of the justice system was too broad for a single discussion, we held seven four-hour virtual workshops organized around different topics. The workshops focused on

- **law enforcement services and operations** (which we abbreviate to the *law enforcement operations workshop* throughout this report*)*, including the shifts in crime during the pandemic and changes that had to be made in performing police tasks
- **law enforcement management,** including issues of staff safety and workforce (e.g., recruiting and training), overall policing policy and strategy, and interactions with other justice agencies
- **court system operations and services** (which we abbreviate to the *court system workshop*), including staff safety and workforce issues, case prioritization and backlogs, virtual court operations, and the effects of changes in the courts on other elements of the justice system
- **institutional corrections operations and services** (which we abbreviate to the *institutional corrections workshop*), including staff safety and workforce issues, inmate safety and contagion prevention, technology issues, and effects of changes made in corrections on other justice system sectors
- **community corrections operations and services** (which we abbreviate to the *community corrections workshop*), including safety issues, changes in policies and strategies, use of technology, measures taken when in-person interactions were needed, and the effects on other facets of the justice system of the issues facing community corrections

- **victim services delivery** (which we abbreviate to the *victim services workshop*), including the safety of staff in service-delivery organizations, issues contacting clients, changes that had to be made in how services were delivered, and the use of technology to do so
- **the public and the provision of justice during the COVID-19 pandemic** (which we abbreviate to the *community organizations panel*); specifically, the bigger picture of how changes made in policing, courts, and corrections affected communities; equity issues in how public health guidelines were enforced; and changes in service provision during the pandemic.

The number of panelists in each workshop ranged from 11 to 18 people, with an average of approximately 15 individuals. The panels were designed to be large enough to have a variety of participants but small enough that a robust discussion was still possible in a virtual setting. For each sectoral workshop, we designed each group to reflect representatives from state and local criminal justice agencies and organizations that had been significantly affected by the pandemic, individuals with public health expertise who had worked with the sector, representatives of national organizations, relevant researchers, and participants with knowledge of how changes in the sector had affected communities and justice-involved individuals. For the victim services panel, we sought out representatives from organizations that served a variety of needs, used different approaches (e.g., hotlines and direct service-delivery organizations), and were organized in different ways (e.g., stand-alone entities versus services delivered by staff from criminal justice agencies). For the community organizations panel, we sought representatives from multiple communities, faith-based organizations, service providers with knowledge of how COVID-19 and the changes made to the system had affected communities, and individuals with other relevant expertise.

Panelists were identified by members of the research team via existing networks, focused searches for organizations and individuals with relevant experience, searches for participants who had studied specific topics, and through referrals. During the invitation process, when invitees were unable to participate, substitutes were identified by the research team or alternates were suggested to the team by our initial invitees. Where the discussion in the workshops suggested the need to consult with individuals with expertise or experience that the attendees lacked, additional one-on-one interviews were conducted to address that shortfall. The full list of attendees, interviewees, and their affiliations is provided in Appendix A.

All workshops were held during a two-week period between September 22, 2020, and October 1, 2020. The discussions were held on a not-for-attribution basis, but were transcribed for analysis. The input provided by the participants was examined and qualitatively grouped by topic to support the writing of this report. Quotations in this report are from cleaned transcripts of the discussion and are anonymized to maintain nonattribution, as promised to the participants.

PCJNI researchers synthesized the discussions from the workshop and drew on available published data and broader reporting about the pandemic and the justice system's response to it to provide context for drawing conclusions from the panelists' remarks. As part of this synthesis, PCJNI researchers compiled research, evaluation, and data-collection questions suggested by the discussions to begin to build a national research agenda for understanding the justice system's response to the COVID-19 pandemic and evaluating potential promising practices within that response for the future.

Although we sought to bring practitioners and experts from departments across the country and with a variety of experience to the panels, it is important not to lose sight of the fact that—as is the case for all such efforts—the discussion likely would have been somewhat different with other groups of participants or in workshops held at different points during the pandemic. We did not fact check or seek to verify the statements made by participants beyond looking for contextual information or other sources to expand on the discussion of points that seemed particularly salient. As a result, although we generalize from the often very powerful discussions that occurred during the events, we seek to do so cautiously, and we recommend the reader do so as well. Indeed, many of the generalizations drawn are useful for further examination of key problems and promising solutions.

Tensions in the Justice System's Response to the COVID-19 Pandemic Reflect Broader Concerns About Reform and Change Going Forward

Given the national environment at the time these workshops were held and how that environment increased the complexity of responding to the pandemic, we sought to gather information not just on the justice system itself—on police officers, court employees, correctional staff, and others—but also on the broader populations with an interest in the justice system. As a result, this virtual summit, which is made up of our seven separate workshops, included organizations serving victims of crime and community and civil-society organizations. Panel members emphasized the importance of including those perspectives because the needs of distinct populations differ and the effects of responses to the COVID-19 pandemic had varied impacts across those populations. A participant in our community workshop framed the challenge in terms of three different perspectives—of justice system agencies, of justice-involved individuals (who are simultaneously punished and served by justice intervention) and the communities they come from (which experience broader collateral effects of justice intervention), and of the broader public the system is charged to protect. Among the broader public, victims of crime are most prominent, because the actions of the justice system respond to individuals and the events that affected them directly. Those three perspectives are important not only in considering whether the way systems responded to the pandemic worked well but also in the assessment of which of those lessons or innovations might be worthwhile to carry into the future.

I think one of the biggest struggles with the justice system . . . [is that] there is a continuing incompatibility between the different audiences that we're trying to speak to in these moments.

If we're going to talk about the justice system from the perspective of impacted communities and what the system needs to do in order to kind of create some opportunities for healing and redemption, then that's one conversation.

If we're going to have a conversation about how the system is deployed to respond to incidences of harm and violence for victims or for harmed communities, that's another conversation.

But if we're going to have a conversation about how the justice system can just be made more efficient while also maintaining its status as an economic driver and a job source for communities across this country, that's a whole different conversation. . . .

I think what has happened in this pandemic is that all three of those groups have had to respond [to] or have been impacted by the decisions that are being made and all of them are being affected by the crisis. . . . That's forcing those decisions to happen. . . . In my experience, if you look at those three things as three points on a triangle, you can only ever work within two of them and the third is left to feel the consequences of the changes. But we have a moment here where everyone is in this together in a way that they never have been before.

– Community organization panelist

Throughout our examination of the response to the pandemic, these different populations arose repeatedly. In some cases, it was because specific actions to reduce infection risk largely focused on one population at the expense of the needs of the others. In many cases, it was because rapid responses in an effort to contain the toll of COVID-19 focused on two primary groups—the justice system itself and justice-involved populations—and did not consider as explicitly how those changes would affect victims of crime. And in a few cases, changes made were valuable across all three populations, suggesting the possibility of finding broadly beneficial paths toward a more effective, more efficient, and fairer justice system for the United States as a whole.

About This Report

This report presents the results of workshops focusing on the response to the COVID-19 pandemic across the criminal justice system. The information and insights provided by our participants are the backbone of this discussion, and throughout this report, we include many direct quotes to illustrate many of the experiences and key lessons learned in the voices of those who experienced them directly. We supplemented the workshop insights with a review of as much published material as possible on the response to the pandemic by the U.S. justice system in an effort to develop this report as an "in-progress stock-taking" for the justice system response to the COVID-19 pandemic. Because the workshops were held at the end of September 2020 and because the research and analysis were done primarily in October and November 2020, the circumstances described reflect conditions as they were at that time. Our analysis was ending just as case rates and community spread of COVID-19 were again increasing in the final months of the year and just before efforts to begin vaccination were beginning.

This report is organized such that readers with interests in a specific part of the justice system have the option of reading only the chapters of interest, while the entirety of the report is relevant to more–broadly focused readers who are interested in public safety, criminal legal system reform, and the justice system's ability to adapt to large-scale disruptions in the social and physical environments.

Chapter Two presents an overview of the COVID-19 pandemic in the United States and frames the sometimes very different circumstances and conditions faced by different criminal justice agencies across the country. Chapters Three through Seven present in-depth examinations of each component of the justice system—law enforcement, courts, institutional corrections, community corrections, and victim services providers—drawing on discussions from individual workshops and the insights of other workshops relevant to the sector. Because there were both commonalities and key differences among the sectors, there is some repetition across the chapters discussing each sector's response to the pandemic. Chapter Eight concludes by summarizing common challenges and innovations across sectors, key research and evaluation needs, and the potential for lessons learned to support broader innovation in the justice system going forward. Appendix A lists the names and affiliations of our panelists and interviewees.

CHAPTER TWO

The Varied Challenges to the U.S. Justice System Posed by the COVID-19 Pandemic

The outlines of how the justice system functions in the United States are understood relatively broadly. Law enforcement agencies investigate crime and arrest the suspected perpetrators of crimes; they also conduct other crime-prevention initiatives. Suspects are transferred to the courts, where they are charged and their cases are resolved through dismissals, pleas to charges filed, or trial proceedings. Suspects who are found guilty (which is most often determined through plea bargaining, but sometimes through trial) are sentenced for their crimes. Depending on their sentence, they are transferred to the corrections system either for incarceration in a jail or prison or for supervision in the community corrections system on probation (or—after completion of a sentence in custody—on parole). The steps and connections among these three main components—law enforcement, the courts, and corrections—are shown in the center of Figure 2.1. The functioning of the system creates what researchers and practitioners—including participants in our workshops—often describe as a flow of people through the system; an individual accused of a crime passes through the different steps with the relevant actions taken and decisions made in sequence.

Although it is frequently thought of as a purely governmental function, effective and efficient criminal justice depends on and involves a variety of actors and organizations beyond police, courts, and corrections agencies. The public plays a role as a participant in community policing and in reporting crime to law enforcement. Individuals or entities affected by crime have multiple roles in—and, in some states, a constitutional right to participate in—the justice process for the individuals accused. Some organizations associated with government and some nongovernmental organizations (NGOs) exist to assist, compensate, and counsel victims of crime in an effort to meet their needs. Other service-providing agencies are key players for justice-involved individuals, providing them with substance abuse treatment, counseling, education, and other services during their time in custody, under community supervision, or in reentry to reduce the chance that they will offend in the future.

Although the justice system often is viewed as a single river of people flowing from arrest to the corrections system, it is much more complex in reality. There are people whose charges were dropped or were acquitted at trial, and there are even more options: Depending on the context and the programs that are available, other paths might be available to divert people from that central flow. For example, there is prearrest diversion to treatment for substance abuse or mental health issues, diversion to specialty courts that serve specific populations or deal with specific types of offenses, or diversion to alternatives to incarceration later in the process. In some cases, intervention outside the criminal justice system might be better suited to address specific problems, and options have been developed to reduce the rate of growth

Figure 2.1
The Criminal Justice System

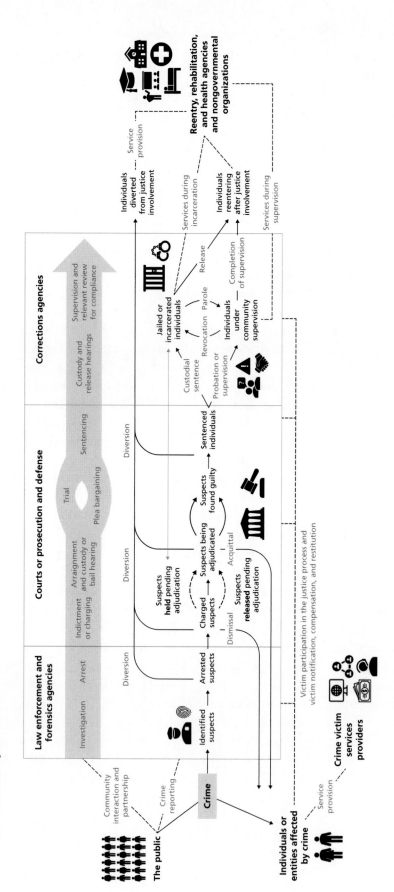

of the significant portion of the U.S. population under some form of correctional custody or supervision.

A National Justice System Built of Many Individual Justice Systems

Although the outline in the previous section generally reflects the operation of the criminal justice system in the United States, the U.S. justice system is not a single system. Rather, it is hundreds of individual systems built locally and operating *similarly*, although by no means *identically*.

There are more than 18,000 law enforcement organizations in the United States, some of which have thousands of officers and many more of which have only a few. Some serve urban areas that might be geographically compact but population-dense, while others serve rural areas where many fewer people live in much larger jurisdictions. Court systems in different states have different administrative and management structures, which means that legal options that might be available in one state could be off the table in another. Corrections systems in different areas might have very different constraints on how they can manage their populations in custody and under supervision. How these agencies—and the service providers on which they depend—are funded also can vary. Some agencies are funded from line items in state or local budgets, some are supported by specific tax revenues, and others rely on fees paid by people filing cases in courts, paying fines, or paying the costs of their own correctional involvement.

Each individual justice system also exists in its own context. Some types of crime that are a major concern in one area might not be an issue in another. The relationship between justice agencies and the communities they serve might be very strong in one city but strained to the breaking point elsewhere. Although correctional populations are significant nationwide, some areas had focused on reforming corrections and reducing the number of individuals in custody or under supervision before the COVID-19 pandemic. These local contexts, along with the differences in local policy, legal, and funding frameworks, had different effects nationally—enabling or constraining police, court decisionmaking, and what corrections agencies could do in response to the pandemic.

Because this diversity shapes how individual systems *could* respond, it also shapes the broader relevance of lessons learned from how agencies in different areas *did* respond. As a result, to successfully identify lessons that are broadly useful, we must recognize how the individual circumstances and challenges of the justice systems in different areas might have affected their response to the pandemic.

A National Pandemic Built of Many Individual Local Epidemics

Although the COVID-19 pandemic is a global pandemic and although it affected the entire United States, it was not the same everywhere at all times. From its local points of introduction, the virus spread through neighborhoods and towns at different rates. Some areas had superspreader events, where a large number of people were infected at the same time, which increased the transmission of disease in the area. Where those events drew attendees from outside the area or even the state, they advanced the spread of the virus in many locations near simultaneously.[1] This reality meant that how and when COVID-19 affected specific states and locales varied considerably, and the circumstances to which criminal justice and associated agencies had to respond similarly varied.

Washington State and New York City were the epicenters of the initial phase of the pandemic. They endured early spring spikes in case counts and had to wrestle with the effects on their governmental, health, local economic, and criminal justice systems. Spikes in infection and disease burden occurred later in states in the South and Midwest, putting the majority of the summer burden of the pandemic in those regions. In fall 2020, still other areas were driving national numbers, with states in the Northern Midwest enduring rapidly increasing infection rates. By late fall and early winter 2020, COVID-19 had spread near uniformly across the country.

Figure 2.2 shows the overall variation in the intensity of the pandemic nationally (with states shaded according to the total fatalities per 100,000 residents in each state through the end of September 2020). However, the dynamics of the pandemic (e.g., when the disease hit, how hard it hit) were very different in different areas. Case curves for a selection of states around the country are shown around the edges of the map and illustrate the strikingly different experiences in different states. These case curves span from early March to the beginning of October 2020, before the much larger fall and winter spikes occurred. For example, at the time these data were collected, Florida and New York had similar overall fatality rates—the states have the same shade on the map—but the phasing of their experiences with COVID-19 were very different, with New York's spike occurring much earlier in time.

The variability in experiencing the pandemic goes much deeper than the differences between states. Within states, different counties or even neighborhoods could have very different experiences, with hotspots of infection and spread occurring in different areas over time. And within counties or neighborhoods, the nature of COVID-19 meant that the burden fell disproportionately on different communities, with the elderly (who often are concentrated in nursing homes or other care facilities) and minority communities suffering more acutely from the health effects of infection. In a preview of the challenges that will be the focus of later chapters of this report, populations in the criminal justice system—in institutional corrections in particular—also were hit hard because those populations are heavily made up of minority individuals, people with health conditions that make them vulnerable to COVID-19, and aging individuals.

Different State and Local Approaches to Protecting Public Health

Local responses to the pandemic also varied considerably. Because there was not a unified public health response that was driven from the national level, different states, cities, and

---

[1]   Examples of superspreader events . . . included Mardi Gras celebrations in Louisiana with more than 1 million attendees, an international professional conference held in Boston, Massachusetts, with approximately 175 attendees, and a funeral in Albany, Georgia, with more than 100 attendees. . . . In the weeks after these events, amplifications in the host locations contributed to increasing U.S. case counts (Anne Schuchat, "Public Health Response to the Initiation and Spread of Pandemic COVID-19 in the United States, February 24–April 21, 2020," *Morbidity and Mortality Weekly Report*, Vol. 69, No. 18, May 8, 2020, p. 553).

Later events associated with significant spread of COVID-19 included the Sturgis Motorcycle Rally in Sturgis, South Dakota.

Figure 2.2
Deaths and Infection Profiles Show a National Pandemic of Distinct Local Epidemics

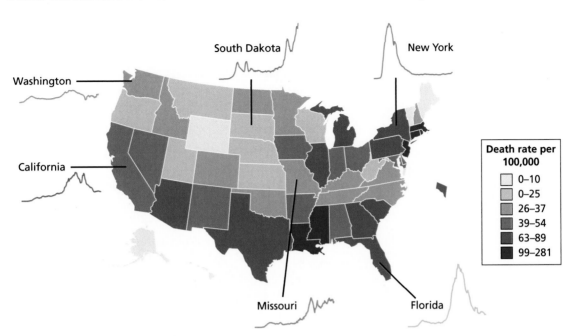

SOURCES: The color of each state shows total deaths per 100,000 residents as of October 2, 2020. Data on deaths per 100,000 residents are from Centers for Disease Control and Prevention, "COVID Data Tracker: United States COVID-19 Cases and Deaths by State," webpage, undated. State infection profiles were calculated from new positive cases reported in the COVID Tracking Project data set (The COVID Tracking Project, "The Data," data set, updated October 2, 2020). Values are seven-day averages of new positive cases per 100,000 residents (except for the first six days, which are averages of the previous N days of data available) as of October 2, 2020.

localities made their own decisions about what steps should be taken to control the disease, and these different jurisdictions did so at markedly different speeds.[2] The palette of options available to decisionmakers was the same—closure of certain types of businesses, closure of schools, restrictions of gatherings or events, stay-at-home orders, mandates or recommendations to wear face masks, and so on—but what measures those decisionmakers chose to use in a particular state or city ended up being quite different.

Figure 2.3 shows individual timelines for the implementation of different measures at the state level, illustrating the variation across the United States. The timelines are based on data collected and published by Thomas Hale and colleagues and Christopher Adolph and colleagues.[3] To provide an additional demonstration of the variation in approach from state to state, Figure 2.4 shows the full set of policies in six states that correspond to those in Figure 2.2. When we look at the full complement of measures taken by individual states, we

---

[2]   Haffajee and Mello, 2020, characterized this as "the dark side of federalism: it encourages a patchwork response to epidemics" (Rebecca L. Haffajee and Michelle M. Mello, "Thinking Globally, Acting Locally—The U.S. Response to COVID-19," *New England Journal of Medicine*, Vol. 382, No. 22, May 28, 2020, p. 2).

[3]   Thomas Hale, Anna Petherick, Toby Phillips, Sam Webster, Beatriz Kira, Noam Angrist, and Lucy Dixon, "Coronavirus Government Response Tracker," University of Oxford, Blavatnik School of Government webpage, undated; Christopher Adolph, Kenya Amano, Bree Bang-Jensen, Nancy Fullman, Beatrice Magistro, Grace Reinke, and John Wilkerson, "Governor Partisanship Explains the Adoption of Statewide Mandates to Wear Face Coverings," *medRxiv*, September 2, 2020.

see that they differ not only in the timing of particular measures (which is shown across all states in Figure 2.3) but also in the mix of measures that they chose to use at all.

In general, the darker shades correspond to more-severe requirements, while areas with no color represent where no measures were taken or no data were available. The figures do not include localities within states whose requirements might have been more stringent. In terms of closing schools, which is shown in purple in Figures 2.3 and 2.4, the darkest shade indicates that all levels of schools were required to close. The middle shade indicates that some levels or categories of schools were required to close (e.g., only high schools, only public schools), and the lightest shade indicates that schools were recommended to close. For closing workplaces, which is shown in blue, the darkest shade indicates that all businesses except those that were deemed essential (e.g., grocery stores, doctors' offices) were required to close, or work-from-home requirements were put in place. The middle shade indicates that some sectors or categories of workplaces were required to close (or work-from-home requirements were put in place), and the lightest shade indicates that workplaces were recommended to close or that there were work-from-home recommendations. The darkest shade of teal in the figure indicates that there was a requirement to cancel public events, while the lighter shade indicates a recommendation to cancel public events. For restricting gatherings, which is shown in green, the darkest shade indicates restrictions on gatherings of ten people or fewer. The second-darkest shade indicates restrictions on gatherings of 11–100 people, while the next-lightest shade indicates restrictions on gatherings of 101–1,000 people. The lightest shade indicates restrictions on very large gatherings (e.g., gatherings of more than 1,000 people).

In the second half of the figure, the darkest shade of lime green indicates that there was a requirement to close public transport, while the lighter shade indicates a recommendation to close or prohibit most citizens from using public transport. In terms of stay-at-home requirements, which is shown in yellow, the darkest shade indicates a requirement for people to stay at home, with minimal exceptions (e.g., people are allowed to leave once per week, or only one person can leave at a time). The middle shade indicates a requirement for people to stay at home, with exceptions for daily exercise, grocery shopping, and essential trips. The lightest shade indicates a recommendation for people to stay at home. The darker shade of orange indicates that internal movement restrictions are in place in that state, while the lighter shade indicates a recommendation not to travel between regions or cities. For mask mandates, which are shown in red, the darkest shade indicates that the use of masks or cloth face coverings by the public is required in indoor spaces and in outdoor settings where social distancing is not possible. The middle shade indicates a broader mask mandate, requiring the use of masks or cloth face coverings by the public indoors or in enclosed spaces, including while waiting in line to enter indoor spaces and on shared transportation. The lighter shade means that a limited mask mandate is in place with fairly limited scope to the public (i.e., in shared transportation services, certain types of stores, or in specified settings, such as large gatherings where social distancing is not possible).

Beyond state-level differences, in many cases, there were differences in policy approaches taken at the local level (e.g., single cities making their own decisions about public health measures). As a result, a police department or corrections agency operating near the border of one state—or even the border between their city and their neighboring city or county—could have been operating under a very different framework of public health rules or recommendations, even though the level of threat from the virus, which is unaffected by purely political divisions on a map, might have been the same in both locations.

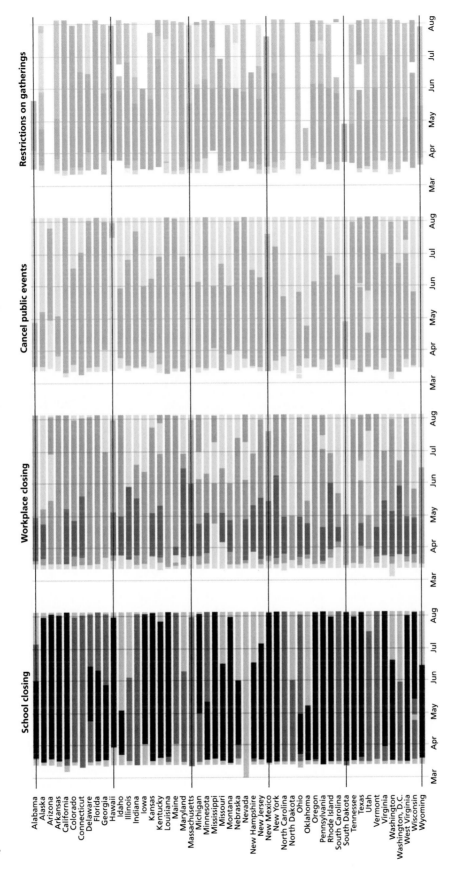

Figure 2.3
Implementation of Public Health Measures at the State Level Across the United States, March–August 2020

Figure 2.3—Continued

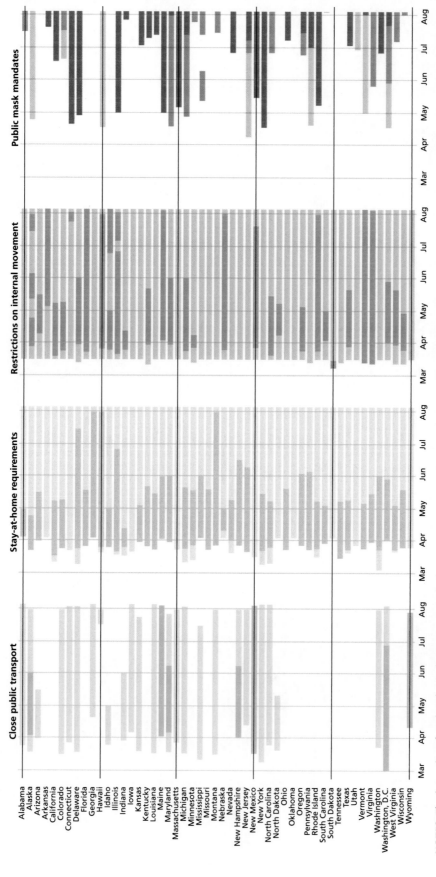

NOTES: The intensity of each color indicates progressively more-stringent implementation of measures (e.g., from a recommendation to a requirement). Data on all measures except mask mandates are from Hale et al., undated. Data on mask mandates are from Adolph et al., 2020.

Figure 2.4
Variation in Public Health Policy Implementation at the State Level, Selected States, March–August 2020

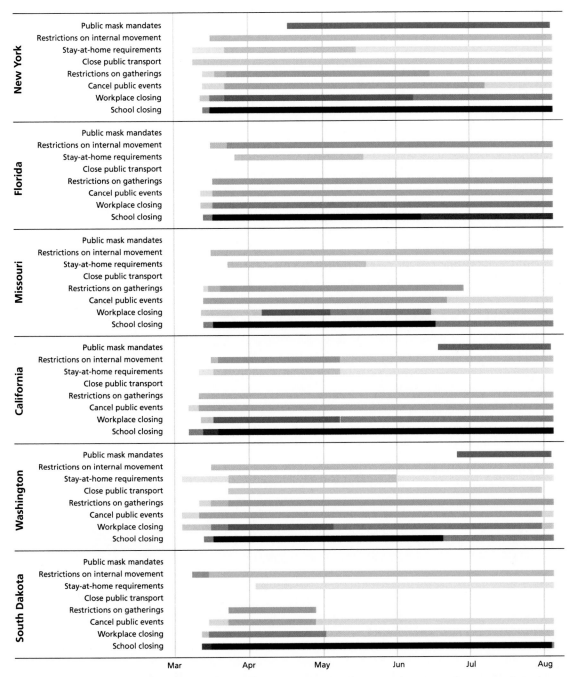

NOTES: The intensity of each color indicates progressively more-stringent implementation of measures (e.g., the darker orange bands indicate that internal movement restrictions are in place, while the lighter orange bands indicate that it is recommended not to travel between regions or cities). White areas indicate that no measures or data were available. Data on all measures except mask mandates are from Hale et al., undated. Data on mask mandates are from Adolph et al., 2020.

Different Effects of the COVID-19 Pandemic on Crime and Service Demand

The pandemic and the measures taken to control it would be expected to have an effect on crime. Changes in the nature of crime—and other behaviors, such as substance use—would be expected to shift the needs of individuals served by social and crime victim service agencies. As a result, understanding how the criminal justice system and its associated agencies responded to the pandemic requires exploring how the pandemic altered both the demands on the system and the environment in which agencies were operating.

Since the beginning of the pandemic, there have been multiple efforts to assess how crime shifted.[4] Different analyses reached different conclusions about both overall effects and effects on individual crime types. According to the discussions across our panels, which included law enforcement representatives, court practitioners, service providers, and community represen-tatives, it would appear that those differences likely resulted from differences in *when* data were collected (because effects on reported crime appeared to be quite different early in the pandemic versus later)[5] and where they were collected (because both the pandemic and the approach to addressing it differed significantly from place to place).[6] In spite of what appears to be a relatively safe conclusion that shifts in crime during the pandemic varied in different environments, some broader conclusions can be drawn to provide context for understanding the system's response to the pandemic.

Overall Calls for Service Are Down

Both in published work and in the discussions of our law enforcement and other panels, we found that calls for service to police for all reasons were down during the period preceding our workshops. In the first wave of IACP and GMU data, which were collected in April 2020,

---

[4]   Matthew P. J. Ashby, "Initial Evidence on the Relationship Between the Coronavirus Pandemic and Crime in the United States," *Crime Science*, Vol. 9, No. 6, 2020; John H. Boman IV and Owen Gallupe, "Has COVID-19 Changed Crime? Crime Rates in the United States During the Pandemic," *American Journal of Criminal Justice*, Vol. 45, 2020; George Mohler, Andrea L. Bertozzi, Jeremy Carter, Martin B. Short, Daniel Sledge, George E. Tita, Craig D. Uchida, and P. Jeffrey Brantingham, "Impact of Social Distancing During COVID-19 Pandemic on Crime in Los Angeles and India-napolis," *Journal of Criminal Justice*, Vol. 68, May–June 2020; Police Executive Research Forum (PERF), "How Has the COVID-19 Pandemic Impacted Crime Rates?" *PERF Daily COVID-19 Report*, May 12, 2020b; PERF, "PERF Analysis Reveals a Spike in Some Violent Crimes This Year," *PERF Critical Issues*, webpage, November 18, 2020f; Richard Rosenfeld and Ernesto Lopez, *Pandemic, Social Unrest, and Crime in U.S. Cities*, Washington, D.C.: Council on Criminal Justice, National Commission on COVID-19 and Criminal Justice, July 2020.

[5]   For example, some service providers saw drops in calls for service in the first few months of the COVID-19 pandemic, which then rebounded either to similar or higher levels than were observed before the pandemic.

[6]   Some of our participants reported increases in certain crimes in their jurisdictions, while others reported decreases in those same crime categories. This sort of variation also was observed by others. For example, in data collected by the International Association of Chiefs of Police (IACP) and the Center for Evidence-Based Crime Policy at George Mason University (GMU) in a questionnaire sent to a large number of police departments, significant percentages of respondents reported trends in different directions for the same crime type (Cynthia Lum, Carl Maupin, and Megan Stoltz, *The Impact of COVID-19 on Law Enforcement Agencies (Wave 2)*, Washington, D.C.: International Association of Chiefs of Police and the Center for Evidence-Based Crime Policy at George Mason University, June 25, 2020b). This and other surveys that were conducted during the pandemic faced challenges in that their response rates were sometimes low and the samples were not representative of all U.S. criminal justice agencies. We therefore draw on these types of survey results descriptively and, as a rule, do not report exact percentages calculated from their respondent populations. In this second wave of data collection, which closed on May 25, 2020, IACP and GMU distributed surveys to approximately 5,800 different police agencies. Of those surveys, 1,141 unique responses were returned that were sufficiently complete and able to be used, for approximately a 20-percent response rate. Other efforts saw significant place-to-place variation (e.g., Mohler et al., 2020).

the majority of agencies saw reduced calls for service.[7] Surveys of 9-1-1 operators from public safety answering points (PSAPs) show a similar finding.[8] Panelists and some researchers in the literature have ascribed this drop to a major reduction in minor crimes that generally are committed by juveniles in groups, because there are fewer opportunities for such offenses under stay-at-home conditions, although that likely varied between and within jurisdictions.[9] Although considering the sum of all calls for service together combines vastly different crimes, from murder to petty property crimes, it is a measure that reflects the scale of demand for law enforcement response. In addition, a theme we heard in multiple panel discussions is that fewer calls for service might mean less crime overall, but it also might mean less *reported* crime. For example, a community organization panelist argued that one factor that reduced calls to police was concern about the risk of exposure to COVID-19 for those who did so or for people who were arrested and brought into the system.

Our crime that's associated with juveniles . . . seems to be ticking down. As our calls for services dropped off, our officers had more time to virtually connect . . . with community members. And we're hearing a theme, from certainly the older members of our community that they're really focused on keeping their kids home, which we think might be connected to what we're seeing as far as lower crime rates with respect to our juvenile population.

– Law enforcement operations panelist

Increases in Violent Crime Have Been a Major Challenge in Some Areas

A prominent concern in our panels was an increase in violent crime during the pandemic, particularly in some large cities. In their analysis of data from 27 cities, Rosenfeld and Lopez found statistically significant year-over-year increases in both homicide (53 percent higher than in 2019) and aggravated assault (14 percent higher than in 2019).[10] In some large cities, the spikes in homicide have approached murder rates (i.e., homicides per 100,000 residents) seen during earlier eras of widespread violence.[11] In other areas, large percentage increases have occurred in smaller base rates of homicide, meaning that the increase in the rate per 100,000 residents is not as large in absolute terms.

---

[7]   Cynthia Lum, Carl Maupin, and Megan Stoltz, *The Impact of COVID-19 on Law Enforcement Agencies (Wave 1)*, Washington, D.C.: International Association of Chiefs of Police and the Center for Evidence-Based Crime Policy at George Mason University, April 13, 2020a. In this first wave of data collection, which closed on April 3, 2020, IACP and GMU distributed 6,402 surveys to approximately 5,800 different law enforcement entities in the United States and Canada. The response rate was estimated at 17 percent. The authors estimated missing responses at 5 percent or less.

[8]   National Emergency Number Association, *How 9-1-1 Is Changing in a COVID-19 World: 9-1-1 and COVID-19 Report Series*, Alexandria, Va., May 8, 2020.

[9]   Boman and Gallupe, 2020.

[10]   Rosenfeld and Lopez, 2020.

[11]   For example, projected 2020 homicide rates in the five cities with the highest expected rates—St. Louis (90.4 per 100,000 residents), Baltimore (55.8), Detroit (47.6), New Orleans (46.4), and Cleveland (41.3)—are similar to some of the highest rates observed in high-homicide cities in the late 1980s and 1990s. (Compare rates reported in Jeff Asher, "Murders Are Rising. Blaming a Party Doesn't Add Up." *New York Times*, September 28, 2020, with those in Pamela K. Lattimore, James Trudeau, K. Jack Riley, Jordan Leiter, and Steven Edwards, *Homicide in Eight U.S. Cities: Trends, Context, and Policy Implications—An Intramural Research Project*, Washington, D.C.: National Institute of Justice, December 1997.)

However, like in other observations of crime shifts during this period, significant local variation appears to apply for violence. In their data collection, IACP and GMU saw almost half of respondents reporting decreases in violent incidents, with a much smaller percentage reporting increases.[12] There was similar variation among law enforcement participants in our panels, with some reporting decreases in violent crime and others reporting increases.

> Our rates of violent crime are [stable]—we've been at historic lows in [our city]—but we're pretty much flat in comparison to last year.
>
> – Law enforcement operations panelist
>
> Our calls for service are down about 22 percent from last year, but it's kind of interesting because certain categories like assault with weapon [are] up 26 percent.
>
> – Law enforcement operations panelist
>
> And during this time, the crime continues—and in my county, we've had a real spike in violent crime. As of the end of August . . . we'd filed as many murder cases in 2020 as we had in all of 2019.
>
> – Court system panelist

Domestic and Family Abuse Appeared to Increase Under Stay-at-Home Orders

Because isolation or quarantine forced families or groups living together to stay home for extended periods, concerns among advocates and justice practitioners about the potential for increased intimate partner, domestic, and family violence and all forms of child abuse were widely reported very early in the COVID-19 pandemic.[13] Since the beginning of the pandemic, analyses of crime data that attempted to measure global effects—particularly for domestic violence—have produced conflicting results, with some analyses showing increases and others showing changes in rates that are in line with seasonal variation in victimization.[14] In the IACP and GMU data on calls for service reported by police departments, there were indications of geographic variation in calls to police for domestic and family violence. The IACP and GMU questionnaire asked about all domestic incidents, both violent and nonviolent, and, of their group of respondents, about two in five reported an increase in calls, about two in five reported a stable number, and about one in five reported a decrease in calls.[15] Among our law enforcement and victim services panelists, there also were indicators of significant variation

---

[12]   Lum, Maupin, and Stoltz, 2020b. See also PERF, 2020f.

[13]   PERF, "Changes in Domestic Violence Calls, and the Police Response, in the COVID Environment," *PERF Daily COVID-19 Report*, April 3, 2020a.

[14]   For analyses showing increases, see Boman and Gallupe, 2020; J. Andrew Hansen and Gabrielle L. Lory, "Rural Victimization and Policing During the COVID-19 Pandemic," *American Journal of Criminal Justice*, Vol. 45, July 17, 2020; Emily Leslie and Riley Wilson, "Sheltering in Place and Domestic Violence: Evidence from Calls for Service During COVID-19," *Journal of Public Economics*, Vol. 189, September 2020, p. 104241; Mohler et al., 2020; and National Emergency Number Association, 2020.

For analyses showing rates in line with seasonal variation, see Jennifer M. Reingle Gonzalez, Rebecca Molsberry, Jonathan Maskaly, and Katelyn K. Jetelina, "Trends in Family Violence Are Not Causally Associated with COVID-19 Stay-at-Home Orders: A Commentary on Piquero et al.," *American Journal of Criminal Justice*, October 7, 2020.

[15]   Lum, Maupin, and Stoltz, 2020b.

across jurisdictions, with some seeing increases, some seeing stable numbers, and some seeing decreases in domestic and family violence calls.

Both the literature and the discussions in our panel suggested a variety of reasons why reporting to police might go down, even if victimization was increasing. Prominent among those reasons are concerns that the pandemic would be a barrier to reporting, with victims uncertain about the nature of the response from police and others. Another important consideration is the absence of exposure to mandatory reporters in schools or to doctors who would be in a position to detect abuse in children and trigger a response. Figure 2.5 shows a map of the status of schools across the United States as of early December 2020. For many districts, instruction is online or only partially in person, reducing teachers' opportunity to detect and respond to abuse.

> I think a huge factor that we also can't discount is the fact that there's been a reduction in mandatory reporting from mandatory reporters on things like domestic violence, child abuse, because people haven't been going to school, they haven't been interacting [with people who might report to police].
>
> – Law enforcement operations panelist

Figure 2.5
School Operating Models

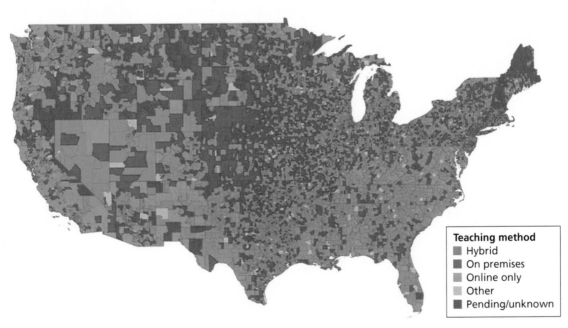

SOURCE: Adapted from MCH Strategic Data, "COVID-19 IMPACT: School District Status Updates for Fall 2020," webpage, as of December 6, 2020.
NOTE: Data are compiled from public federal, state, and local school district information and media updates.

> Calls to police [about domestic violence] are really variable across the country. And many places you had folks say, "I never felt safe calling the police. I definitely don't feel safe calling them now." And calls went down. In other places, police did a lot of community-based outreach and we saw calls go up.
>
> – Victim services panelist
>
> Thinking about maybe why victims are not reporting, I don't for a moment believe that there is less victimization occurring. I actually think given the factors we know that are related to victimization, particularly chronic male unemployment, I think many women might be challenged to seek out services at this time: less access to a vehicle, more control by the male partner, particularly if they're both involved in a lockdown. I also think some women might think that some services might be best saved for people with COVID . . . particularly hospital services, they may be both fearful to utilize hospital services, but they might also think that should be for the people who are sick right now.
>
> – Victim services panelist

Other analyses focused on calls to helplines for domestic and other forms of violence. In some cases, scholarly and journalistic analyses that showed stable numbers of or reductions in calls to police for such offenses as domestic violence, assault, and rape also showed increases in calls to domestic violence helplines.[16] But the number of calls to helplines had a delay before they began increasing, and in some cases, the number of calls decreased early in the pandemic.

> Within a couple of months, we saw the increase . . . in calls to our hotline. Interestingly enough . . . there wasn't too much of an increase in police reports, compared to what we were hearing in other areas in [the] state or across the country.
>
> – Victim services panelist

Significant drops in calls were observed for some other helplines, particularly those relating to child abuse. Those reductions are largely viewed as attributable to victims' reduced contact with mandated reporters of abuse in school and other settings, given pandemic-control efforts.[17] The general consensus of the participants in our panels who were directly involved in providing support to crime victims or in supporting organizations that do was that both calls to hotlines and demand for services had increased, and in some cases substantially, by the time our workshops were held in September 2020.

---

[16]   Susan B. Sorenson, Laura Sinko, and Richard A. Berk, "The Endemic Amid the Pandemic: Seeking Help for Violence Against Women in the Initial Phases of COVID-19," fact sheet, Philadelphia, Pa.: Ortner Center on Violence & Abuse, University of Pennsylvania, undated; James Grant and Kierra Sam, "Police, Advocates Say COVID-19 Pandemic Is Fueling Spike in Domestic Violence Cases," 12News, October 23, 2020.

[17]   Samantha Schmidt, "The Centers Helping Child Abuse Victims Have Seen 40,000 Fewer Kids Amid the Pandemic," *Washington Post*, August 19, 2020.

> Looking across the domestic violence field nationwide, generally demand for services, including shelter, was up. Over 160 cities, counties, or states reported at least double-digit increases in hotline calls, police calls, visits to helplines, or even homicides.
>
> – Victim services panelist

> [Our national hotline] has seen not only increase in calls, but disturbingly a significant increase in calls from children and adolescents. And so I want you to think about victims of intimate partner violence, child sexual assault, child abuse, physical abuse, who [because of stay-at-home orders] are literally stuck at the scene of the crime with the person who is harming them.
>
> – Victim services panelist

In addition, the pandemic itself was cited as a tool of abuse, particularly in domestic violence and family victimization situations. As part of a pattern of abuse, individuals used access to health insurance or safety measures and victims' fear of COVID-19 as tools of control and violence, increasing their ability to threaten victims and reducing victims' ability to seek help.

> The national domestic violence hotline reported a 15-percent increase in their contacts in April as compared to April 2019. About 10 percent of folks cited COVID-19 specifically as a condition of the abuse. . . . Perpetrators tearing up her insurance card, perpetrators throwing away all the hand sanitizer, perpetrators saying, "If you leave me, you're going to get COVID-19, I'm going to report you to child welfare.'" [There are] lots of ways that COVID just became another tool of abuse . . . it really can exacerbate abuse that is there because it's a tool of abuse. Because isolation itself is a tool of abuse. . . . And so many survivors just felt like [they] don't have any options.
>
> – Victim services panelist

Beyond more-recent observations of increases in helpline calls, participants also noted—for both domestic violence cases and family abuse—apparent increases in *severity* in the calls that they were receiving. Whether because the people involved delayed calling for assistance because of concerns about contracting COVID-19 or because pandemic stresses were intensifying abuse, the levels of violence observed seemed to be increasing. When service providers receive more calls in which callers are at greater risk, there is a greater demand on them to respond more rapidly and more effectively.

> For all those reasons, we see domestic violence and there've been some reports of increased severity, more-severe injuries or more homicides.
>
> – Victim services panelist

> So compared to March 2020 and March 2019, we saw an almost 40-percent increase in crisis cases [that is, cases in which safety concerns are so severe that they require immediate action] coming through the hotline. [The call could be from a] victim or survivor or someone who's supporting them. It could be a service provider. It could be law enforcement calling with an immediate need for that survivor. So that might be shelter. It might be someone trying to leave a dangerous situation, it could be immediate transportation to get from where they are to a safe place.
>
> – Victim services panelist

Shifts in Property Crime Are Aligned with Shifts in Public Behavior

Perhaps because citizens spent more of their time in their homes, a reduction in residential burglaries was observed in many analyses. Changes in the timing of crime also occurred, reflecting changes in individual behavior.[18] Unlike the decrease in burglary, some areas saw increases in theft of and from vehicles, which were used less during lockdown periods. According to a May 2020 news report,

> Despite silent streets and nearly nonexistent traffic, vehicle larcenies shot up 63 percent in New York and nearly 17 percent in Los Angeles from January 1 through mid-May, compared with the same period last year. . . . In Austin, Texas, . . . the total number of auto thefts in April spiked about 50 percent, and burglaries to vehicles were up 2 percent from April 2019.[19]

In their analysis of multiple cities' data, Rosenfeld and Lopez found a 25-percent decrease in residential burglaries.[20]

> Traditionally we'd see more residential burglaries during the day when people are not at home and you'd see commercial and business burglaries at night. Those two things might've been flipped because of the changing and dynamics of where people are and when they're there.
>
> – Law enforcement operations panelist

Pandemic-Related Online Fraud and Abuse, Particularly Targeting the Elderly and Children, Was a Concern

Even before the pandemic hit the United States in earnest, data suggested that individuals in the United States were experiencing more fraud in 2020 compared with in 2019, with some of that fraud capitalizing on fear of the virus. According to one analysis,

> A review of data from the Federal Trade Commission shows that reports of most types of fraud grew significantly in the first three months of 2020 in comparison to the same time period in 2019. Differences between fraud experiences based on age are considered. Older

---

[18]   Mohler et al., 2020.

[19]   "Vehicle Theft in L.A. Up 17% During COVID-19 Pandemic," *KTLA 5 News*, May 25, 2020.

[20]   Rosenfeld and Lopez, 2020.

persons lost much more to fraud than younger persons, and far more in 2020 than 2019. In addition, they reported being targeted more often for certain types of cybercrime (i.e., tech support scams).[21]

These trends held up through the pandemic, with data released by the Federal Trade Commission (FTC) later in 2020 showing significant incidence of fraud related to COVID-19 and stimulus payments and that affected individuals across a range of ages but with larger financial impact for older victims.[22] This was consistent with the experience of our panelists. Law enforcement participants reported increases in scams related to COVID-19 in their jurisdictions, and victim services participants reported very dramatic increases in calls for assistance in resolving identify theft and other crimes.

> We've seen an [uptick] in COVID scams especially early on . . . but overall crime is down in our jurisdiction quite a bit.
>
> – Law enforcement operations panelist
>
> [With respect to fraud and identity crime,] we have actually seen a swift and significant increase in the demand for our services, our one-on-one contact center services are up about 20 or 25 percent. And, as far as our web-based or web traffic and web-based services . . . when the stay-at-home orders started being issued . . . we saw about nine months' worth of web traffic come through our servers in about three weeks.
>
> People [had] a lot of cases around the [Internal Revenue Service] stimulus checks not being received and an inability to get unemployment insurance benefits at the state level because these folks were victims of identity crimes previously [and a] thief had already taken advantage of using their credentials. Just to give you some context, unemployment ID theft has been around for years, [but] we had about 14 cases back in 2019, we've had 510 this year. So that's a 3,500-percent increase.
>
> – Victim services panelist

Available data also have substantiated a significant increase in online threats to children, with many schools moving to virtual modes and youth spending longer periods online during the pandemic. Compared with the number of tipline reports received in April 2019, the National Center for Missing and Exploited Children received a more-than-fourfold increase in reports of children being abused online in April 2020.[23] As the pandemic continued, the overall rate remained higher than in 2019: Between January and the end of September 2020, reports of online enticement were nearly double the rate seen in 2019, and tipline reports of online abuse were more than 60 percent higher (18.4 million reports in 2020 versus 11.3 million

---

[21] Brian K. Payne, "Criminals Work from Home During Pandemics Too: A Public Health Approach to Respond to Fraud and Crimes Against Those 50 and Above," *American Journal of Criminal Justice*, Vol. 45, 2020, p. 563.

[22] See publicly reported FTC data in FTC, "FTC COVID-19 and Stimulus Reports: Age and Fraud," Tableau Public, data set, June 11, 2020, updated December 4, 2020a; and FTC, "FTC COVID-19 and Stimulus Reports: Map," Tableau Public, data set, June 11, 2020, updated December 4, 2020b.

[23] Fernando Alfonso III, "The Pandemic Is Causing an Exponential Rise in the Online Exploitation of Children, Experts Say," CNN, May 25, 2020.

in 2019).[24] Threats to children include sexual exploitation (e.g., individuals seeking to entice youth to share sexually explicit content) and the resharing of explicit and abusive content.

There Were Concerning Increases in Pandemic-Associated Hate Crime

Because of the national rhetoric about China and the pandemic, concerns have been raised about hate crimes aimed at the Asian community.[25] Surveys of Asian-American youth indicated that one in four Asian young people "have personally experienced anti-Asian hate amid the COVID-19 pandemic."[26] Some academic efforts to assess the level of hate crime occurring during the pandemic saw similar effects: For example, a survey conducted by researchers at Florida State University indicated that 16 percent of Asian survey respondents reported that they had been a victim of a hate crime between March and May 2020.[27] The increase in incidents prompted some police departments to take specific action in response.[28] Although there are concerns that existing efforts to collect data on hate crimes have significant limitations, hate crime data reported by the Federal Bureau of Investigation (FBI) showed increases in 2019, even before the pandemic.[29]

> [Coupled with the national political rhetoric,] the pandemic appears to be associated with a slight uptick, if not a big uptick, we don't know yet, in anti-Asian hate crime. . . reported by Asian-Americans to an online hate crime reporting database.
>
> – Community organization panelist
>
> [In the Asian community,] advocates themselves are concerned about going out in public. Race-biased hate crime, threats, and harassment are escalating. Also, some advocates are articulating that some domestic and sexual violence survivors they work with are reporting putting up with more harassment and sexual abuse at jobs than they normally would have.
>
> – Community organization panelist

---

[24] Brenna O'Donnell, "COVID-19 and Missing & Exploited Children," *National Center for Missing and Exploited Children* blog, July 16, 2020, updated October 20, 2020.

[25] Anti-Defamation League, "Reports of Anti-Asian Assaults, Harassment and Hate Crimes Rise as Coronavirus Spreads," *ADL Blog*, June 18, 2020; Angela R. Gover, Shannon B. Harper, and Lynn Langton, "Anti-Asian Hate Crime During the COVID-19 Pandemic: Exploring the Reproduction of Inequality," *American Journal of Criminal Justice*, Vol. 45, 2020; Hannah Tessler, Meera Choi, and Grace Kao, "The Anxiety of Being Asian American: Hate Crimes and Negative Biases During the COVID-19 Pandemic," *American Journal of Criminal Justice*, Vol. 45, 2020.

[26] Catherine Park, "1 in 4 Young Asian Americans Experienced Anti-Asian Hate Amid COVID-19," *FOX 5 News*, October 5, 2020.

[27] Brendan Lantz and Marin R. Wenger, *Bias and Hate Crime Victimization During the COVID-19 Pandemic*, Tallahassee, Fla.: Florida State University Center for Criminology and Public Policy Research, May 2020.

[28] Taylor Romine, "NYPD Creates Asian Hate Crime Task Force After Spike in Anti-Asian Attacks During COVID-19 Pandemic," CNN, August 18, 2020.

[29] "U.S. Hate Crime Highest in More Than a Decade—FBI," *BBC News*, November 17, 2020.

There Were Fewer Traffic Accidents and Less Traffic Enforcement

Because compliance with stay-at-home orders would be expected to reduce the time spent driving, decreases in traffic accidents (to which law enforcement generally respond to assist) would be expected. IACP and GMU's data call showed decreases in crashes and fatalities in the majority of departments, and literature analyses showed the same.[30]

As part of efforts to decrease contact with the public (which we discuss in more detail in Chapter Three), police reduced some traffic-enforcement activities, which would free them up for other tasks and responsibilities.[31] However, as related by one of our panelists, some citizens expected a greater reduction than departments pursued.

> [The] unrealistic expectations of folks was that we would stop enforcing certain laws. For some strange reason, people thought that if all my traffic officers were at testing sites [directing traffic there] that we were not going to be out on the highways, enforcing speeding laws or [driving under the influence (DUI)] laws. So they were kind of upset when they found out we were still out writing speeding tickets and still taking DUIs to jail.
>
> – Law enforcement management panelist

Calls to Police About Individuals in Mental Health Distress Increased Significantly

The demands of the pandemic caused stress across the population. Those demands could be even more consequential for individuals with preexisting mental health conditions that limited their resilience. Furthermore, in an effort to control COVID-19 transmission and protect staff members, many mental health treatment centers on which people might have relied before the pandemic changed their practices, became more difficult to access, or temporarily shut down.

> It's been mentioned . . . that [law enforcement] mental health response to those who have a mental health crisis certainly has shifted. In some cases, it may have slowed down and then seen a direct increase, especially with interruption to social service providers or mental health workers or medication impacting and getting a "slingshot effect."
>
> – Law enforcement operations panelist

These realities led to a situation in which there were increases in calls requiring police to respond to people in mental health distress at the same time as protests were occurring that were demanding less criminal justice and police involvement in such situations. In their data collection, IACP and GMU found that nearly half of departments reported increases in calls for service that were related to individuals in mental health distress,[32] which is similar to the

---

[30] Lum, Maupin, and Stoltz, 2020b; Stephen R. Barnes, Louis-Philippe Beland, Jason Huh, and Dongwoo Kim, *The Effect of COVID-19 Lockdown on Mobility and Traffic Accidents: Evidence from Louisiana*, Essen, Germany: Global Labor Organization, GLO Discussion Paper Series 616, 2020.

[31] Later in the pandemic, some departments returned to more-standard levels of traffic enforcement (see discussion in PERF, *PERF Daily COVID-19 Report*, September 16, 2020e).

[32] Lum, Maupin, and Stoltz, 2020b.

findings in a survey of PSAPs across the country.[33] Participants in our law enforcement panel also indicated major increases in these types of calls. Although it was a challenging shift in workload, one of our victim services panelists highlighted that these sorts of calls are an opportunity to identify victimization that might not be reported to law enforcement generally, creating a chance to help people who otherwise would fall through the cracks.

> In all of our sites, urban [and] rural sites, we saw increases in noncriminal crisis calls for law enforcement. And then once [officers] respond or victim service personnel get involved, realizing that those people were also victims of crime, but what they were initially reporting was a noncriminal crisis need. That's how it initially presented . . . but there really were victimization issues happening underneath the surface. . . . [As a result,] a lot of our sites [told] us that they were finding victimization that would have never been . . . reported to police [before the pandemic].
>
> – Victim services panelist

Drug, Alcohol, and Substance Abuse Have Shifted During the Pandemic

Although drug, alcohol, and substance abuse is not solely a criminal justice issue, it is clear that pandemic-imposed changes on people's lives and livelihoods also have changed consumption patterns for drugs and alcohol. For example, survey studies have tracked increases in alcohol consumption and negative consequences of alcohol use.[34] Surveys that looked at substance use more broadly also noted increases,[35] while still other survey efforts flagged increases.[36] Responses by service and treatment providers to reduce risk to staff and clients—coupled with fear of the virus on the part of individuals needing treatment—have affected access to substance abuse care during the pandemic.[37] Publicly available data have tracked significant increases in overdose deaths during the COVID-19 pandemic.[38] These concerns matched points raised by our panelists, including observations of increased opioid use in particular.

---

[33] National Emergency Number Association, 2020.

[34] Michael S. Pollard, Joan S. Tucker, and Harold D. Green, Jr., "Changes in Adult Alcohol Use and Consequences During the COVID-19 Pandemic in the U.S.," *JAMA Network Open*, Vol. 3, No. 9, 2020.

[35] Mark É. Czeisler, Rashon I. Lane, Emiko Petrosky, Joshua F. Wiley, Aleta Christensen, Rashid Njai, Matthew D. Weaver, Rebecca Robbins, Elise R. Facer-Childs, Laura K. Barger, Charles A. Czeisler, Mark E. Howard, and Shantha M. W. Rajaratnam, "Mental Health, Substance Use, and Suicidal Ideation During the COVID-19 Pandemic—United States, June 24–30, 2020," *Morbidity and Mortality Weekly Report*, Vol. 69, No. 32, August 14, 2020.

[36] In their analysis of multiple cities' data, Rosenfeld and Lopez found a 41-percent decrease in drug offense rates, although because such effects were deprioritized by many law enforcement organizations during the pandemic, crime data would appear to be less valuable in this case (Rosenfeld and Lopez, 2020).

[37] See, for example, discussion in Alexandra M. Mellis, Marc N. Potenza, and Jessica N. Hulsey, "COVID-19-Related Treatment Service Disruptions Among People with Single- and Polysubstance Use Concerns," *Journal of Substance Abuse Treatment*, Vol. 121, February 2021; and Tyler S. Oesterle, Bhanuprakash Kolla, Cameron J. Risma, Scott A. Breitinger, Daniela B. Rakocevic, Larissa L. Loukianova, Daniel K. Hall-Flavin, Melanie T. Gentry, Teresa A. Rummans, Mohit Chauhan, and Mark S. Gold, "Substance Use Disorders and Telehealth in the COVID-19 Pandemic Era: A New Outlook," *Mayo Clinic Proceedings*, Vol. 95, No. 12, December 2020.

[38] Josh Katz, Abby Goodnough, and Margot Sanger-Katz, "In Shadow of Pandemic, U.S. Drug Overdose Deaths Resurge to Record," *New York Times*, July 15, 2020; Mike Stobbe and Adrian Sainz, "Pandemic Could Be Contributing to Spike in U.S. Overdose Deaths," *Washington Post*, November 10, 2020.

> With this pandemic, what we've seen is that overdose rates across the country have sky-rocketed. A lot of the data hasn't come in yet, but the data that we *have* seen is very ugly. And so this pandemic has come in the midst of an epidemic, a nationwide epidemic of opioid use and overdoses.
>
> – Community corrections panelist
>
> Our drug market and our gang activity demonstrated that it was a pandemic and recession-proof.
>
> – Law enforcement operations panelist

Beyond the public health effects of the pandemic, the shift in drug use (coupled with changes in enforcement behavior) has had consequences for other criminal justice agencies' workloads. For example, participants in our panels from crime labs in particular emphasized a much greater requirement for postmortem toxicology, given increases in overdoses of opioids in particular.

> Postmortem toxicology is now through the roof because of the impact that a lot of these opioids and so forth have had with overdoses that [are] up.
>
> – Law enforcement operations panelist

Conclusions: Varied Justice Needs During the Pandemic Era

Considering the effects of the pandemic on the justice system requires dealing with a great deal of heterogeneity. The criminal justice system is not the same across the United States, and the circumstances of the pandemic that these individual systems were dealing with differed as well. Differences in how individual states or localities responded to the pandemic had implications for their respective justice systems. For example, an area that effectively locked down likely saw different patterns of reported crime than an area that made no attempt to do so. Those differences would pass to local justice agencies and organizations to deal with, and their challenges would be dominated by the local infectious environment, changes in crime and victimization associated with trying to reduce infection risk, or some combination thereof.

> We're really struggling right now with . . . this increase, this kind of spike in cases. How do we ease courts back that might already have been wanting to start jury trials? . . . We're in the process of . . . issuing some new guidance on the criteria that courts should use before they move ahead with the jury trial. Some really very difficult questions.
>
> – Court system panelist
>
> But I fear that, not just with the court system, but with our entire country . . . we don't have the patience to outlast this, and that we think we know what works and maybe we don't know as much as we think we know.
>
> – Court system panelist

In responding to these challenges, our participants noted the importance of assumptions about how long the crisis would last and the ability of both justice agencies and the country as a whole to endure what was required to weather it. For some, dealing with the COVID-19 pandemic required them to discard an initial assumption that the virus would pass quickly. Others had assumed from the start that this would be a longer-term challenge. But, in either case, a long-term view requires justice agencies to consider how the demands they face might ebb or flow over time. As of this writing, some areas faced intensive infection rates that receded only to increase again as control efforts were relaxed. Other areas that initially might have been able to view the COVID-19 pandemic as a problem affecting only other parts of the country are now enduring some of the most-intense levels of disease and infection yet observed. The reality that COVID-19 will be with us for some time requires both adaptability—agencies that thought that the threat to them had passed might have to respond again—and endurance.

CHAPTER THREE

Law Enforcement Agencies, Forensic Laboratories, and Crime-Prevention Initiatives

Law enforcement agencies are the first element of the criminal justice system and are responsible for managing and responding to crime in the jurisdiction that they are charged to protect (see Figure 3.1). Police officers respond to calls for service and engage in proactive activities that are intended to reduce crime and respond to community concerns. The relationship between law enforcement and the public they serve is a critical component; a strong relationship can enable problem-solving and effective response to crime. The activities of law enforcement are the primary driver of flows of people into the remainder of the justice system. Arrests drive in-custody populations as a result of pretrial detention and the eventual incarceration of individuals convicted of crimes. Other activities, such as the issuance of citations and traffic enforcement, can require individuals to come to court for hearings or pay associated fines.

Figure 3.1
Law Enforcement and Forensics Agencies

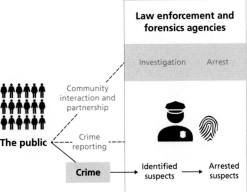

Police officers have significant discretion in the actions they can take in responding to criminal behavior. Although some offenses, particularly violent crimes, always result in the arrest of a suspect, less serious offenses might or might not result in arrest. Law enforcement agencies might have relationships with partner service agencies that provide options for pre-arrest diversion of individuals whose criminal behavior is driven by other issues—for example, substance abuse or mental health challenges—and where linking them to a treatment provider might be a more effective response than justice system intervention.

A patrol officer might come into contact with a large number of people in the course of their daily activities—responding to calls for service at businesses or homes, making traffic stops, or attending a community meeting or neighborhood watch group. In the COVID-19 pandemic, that level of interaction creates substantial risk—for the officer as an individual, for the police agency, and for the spread of the virus within the community. If arrests are made, officers bring individuals to jail in enclosed vehicles, creating greater opportunity for spread of the virus among all involved. Given concerns about transmission in jails, prisons, and court settings, law enforcement decisions about the arrest of individuals was a major lever for trying to reduce COVID-19 risk elsewhere in the system.

Forensic laboratories—which, depending on the area, might be directly connected to law enforcement or might be independent—support the investigation of crime. They do not have as large a public footprint as a police agency, although forensic examiners do deploy to crime scenes and testify in court proceedings. Much of their face-to-face interaction is with law enforcement because police officers and detectives bring evidence to the laboratory for analysis. As described by participants in our workshops, forensic laboratories might support other technical elements of policing, including managing field analytic devices, such as breathalyzers for testing drivers for alcohol. Staff in forensic labs specialize in different types of analyses—e.g., fingerprint analysis, DNA analysis, or firearms ballistics—with their expertise supporting the utility of their work and testimony in criminal trials. As a result, although the smaller numbers of staff might reduce the risk of contracting COVID-19, the capacity of a forensic lab for specific kinds of investigative analyses could depend on a relatively small number of staff members, making the functioning of the lab vulnerable to the spread of infectious disease.

Although police are the first criminal justice practitioners most people think of as responders to crime and actors to prevent future crime, there are a variety of other organizations—social service agencies and NGOs among them—that also play important roles. For example, as part of collaborative prevention efforts, groups composed of police, community organizations, and social service agencies use focused deterrence to address violence, drug use, and other crime concerns. Among other roles, NGOs seek to intervene in cycles of violence, reducing the likelihood that a victim of violence or their peers will retaliate against those who are thought to be responsible.

> First and foremost, even though we were going through a pandemic, people still expected us to continue to go out and reduce crime. And we've actually still been able to do a pretty good job.
>
> – Law enforcement management panelist

What "doing a good job" meant for police during this period depended on how the conditions of the pandemic affected crime and need in an area. As we explored in Chapter Two, different areas of the country experienced different combinations of changes, including shifts in violent crime, domestic and family violence, and mental health–related calls for service. Agencies had to shift their activities to respond to the changed needs experienced in their jurisdictions. Some departments moved staff and resources to cover the increase in mental health–related calls. Others allocated new resources, including funding provided by federal pandemic response legislation, to increase capacity to respond to increased numbers of domestic and family violence calls.[1] Members of law enforcement also have observed that, during the pandemic, public safety and public health are no longer separable in the same way they might previously have been, requiring them to broaden their thinking about what "doing a good job" means in these circumstances.[2]

> Emotionally disturbed person–type calls are up almost 40 percent, and we've actually been pouring extra resources into having more crisis intervention officers available to handle those types of calls.
>
> – Law enforcement operations panelist

Like in other components of the criminal justice system, planning efforts for a pandemic were conducted in the law enforcement community in response to the spread of avian influenza in the early 2000s. During a pandemic, law enforcement has a role it can play in supporting the efficacy of public health directives. This role can include the enforcement of directives intended to reduce risk in public locations (e.g., business closures, individual mask-wearing, distancing), more-targeted enforcement of quarantine orders for ill individuals, and such supporting roles as assisting in securing health facilities or testing centers.[3] However, as we described in Chapter Two, the measures a state or locality took in response to the pandemic varied widely, so the context in which a law enforcement agency was operating could differ markedly from one area to another. If an area responded aggressively to COVID-19, then the police might have many tasks supporting public health. If the public health response in their jurisdiction was limited or weak, police might have nothing relevant to do to help manage public health risk. Because of the inconsistency in responses across the United States, law enforcement in areas that are attractive to tourists faced a particularly complex environment, where they had to deal not only with the local response but also with visitors coming from areas that might have adopted very different response strategies. Some departments that found themselves in such situations were hit hard by the disease.

---

[1]   Dylan McGuinness, "Houston to Spend $6.2M in COVID-19 Funds to Expand HPD Domestic Abuse Teams," *Houston Chronicle*, November 9, 2020.

[2]   For example, according to one police chief, "Our motto here is that we are balancing public safety with public health, for the first time we are aligning public health and public safety, and that they're not separable at this point. In fact, they're inseparable" (RaShall Brackney, chief, Charlottesville Police Department, in Vera Institute of Justice, "COVID-19 and Policing Webinar," video, YouTube, April 17, 2020b).

[3]   Edward P. Richards, Katherine C. Rathbun, Corina Solé Brito, and Andrea Luna, *The Role of Law Enforcement in Public Health Emergencies: Special Considerations for an All-Hazards Approach*, Washington, D.C.: U.S. Department of Justice, Bureau of Justice Assistance and Police Executive Research Forum, September 2006.

> When things started opening up here and they weren't open up in other states, we started seeing an increase in a number of people who were coming not only just to visit [our state], but were also coming to visit [our jurisdiction in particular]. Well, it wasn't long before we saw the number of cases for members of the department really starts to explode. And we [ended up with 10 percent of the department positive] . . . it hit us pretty hard. It almost totally wiped out [the ability of] certain sections of the department [to function with so many officers out sick].
>
> – Law enforcement management panelist

The political divide around COVID-19 and the response to the pandemic, coupled with widespread racial justice protests triggered by the killing of George Floyd, made law enforcement support for the public health response to the pandemic difficult in many jurisdictions. Some law enforcement departments explicitly and publicly rejected the enforcement of public health measures,[4] and in one broadly reported case even prohibited the use of face masks by officers to protect themselves.[5] Other departments took more-measured approaches. According to discussions in our panel and press reports, the reasons behind departments' decisions varied. Some agencies and groups of agencies resisted becoming involved in public health efforts out of concern that it would not be productive, and others sought alternative approaches to contribute to public health efforts that were viewed as less potentially problematic given national protests and scrutiny of police.

The fact that law enforcement's potential to contribute to efforts to respond to the pandemic in many cities or regions was so fraught should not have been a surprise. Earlier efforts to prepare law enforcement for a pandemic emphasized community trust and strong relationships as critical for the ability to respond. According to one report, "bridges [between police and the community, built *before* the high-pressure situation of a pandemic] will greatly enhance all department efforts that involve the community and will ensure that the relationships necessary to support an effective and coordinated response to a public health emergency are in place."[6] Because the pandemic occurred simultaneously with the protests and in a political environment that further fractured relationships between many police agencies and portions of the public, the foundations of those police-community bridges were significantly weakened in many jurisdictions at a point when they would have been particularly valuable.

---

[4]   Maurice Chammah, "The Rise of the Anti-Lockdown Sheriffs," The Marshall Project, May 18, 2020; "Law Enforcement Agencies Refuse to Enforce Mask Orders," *Herald-Star*, July 27, 2020.

[5]   Neuman, 2020.

[6]   Richards et al., 2006, p. 17.

> Just like any other crisis, if those relationships did not exist with the community prior to the crisis, we weren't going to start building them after the crisis hit. So, for those of us that had positive, productive relationships with our community stakeholders before COVID, I think we're doing fine. . . . They know that we continue to look out for their best interests. And I think that agencies that didn't have those same relationships are probably having a much harder time right now.
>
> – Law enforcement operations panelist
>
> Overall trust in police and government has absolutely been eroded throughout this process. People are not sure who to trust anymore.
>
> – Community organization panelist

From the beginning of the pandemic, uncertainty surrounding COVID-19 and national chaos around such issues as the availability of protective equipment complicated police departments' planning.[7] Our panelists described vastly different assumptions about the likely duration of the outbreak. Some based their planning on an assumption that the COVID-19 pandemic would be a long-term crisis for the country, while others initially believed that it would be a shorter-term disruption. The assumption that was made affected planning, and other constraints shaped what steps departments could take, regardless of their planning assumptions.

> I don't think any of us thought that this was going to be a short-term type of event, as of course it turned out it isn't.
>
> – Law enforcement operations panelist
>
> If we would have known ahead of time, how long the pandemic was going to last, then we would have made some more-strategic plans. I think all going into this, we perhaps thought it was temporary, that things would quell, treatments would be found. Had I known from the beginning that we were in it for the long haul, certainly it would have altered plans.
>
> – Law enforcement operations panelist
>
> From the crime lab perspective, the initial reaction was [asking] "How are we supposed to keep operating as normal? Is this just a temporary thing?" Just trying to kind of figure everything out. And the laboratory management realized very quickly that we had to still operate as best as we could to give the service to our stakeholders while trying to manage [all of the challenges related to the pandemic].
>
> – Law enforcement operations panelist

Because of the pace of the pandemic and the pressures on law enforcement organizations, building a clear and complete picture of how seriously the pandemic has affected police departments and other agencies involved in crime prevention and investigation has not been possible. The National Police Foundation developed a tool that agencies can use to report percentages

---

7   Rosa Brooks and Christy Lopez, *Policing in a Time of Pandemic: Recommendations for Law Enforcement*, Washington, D.C.: Georgetown Law Innovative Policing Program and Edmond J. Safra Center for Ethics, April 10, 2020, p. 11.

of officers exposed, diagnosed, and unable to work because of COVID-19. The tool has been used in national-level analyses,[8] although at the time of this writing, those data reflected only slightly more than 600 agencies, and it was not clear how representative those agencies were of the full population of police departments.[9] IACP and GMU's information collection, which was done in May 2020, asked agencies to report how large an effect COVID-19 had had on their agencies. Although the representativeness of that sample also is unclear, the responses showed relatively modest impacts on average, with less than one-tenth of agencies reporting that 5 percent or more of their officers were on sick leave as a result of COVID-19. More than half of agencies reported no noticeable officer sick leave because of COVID-19.[10]

It is clear, however, that COVID-19 hit some departments hard.[11] During different stages of the pandemic, there were examples of entire smaller departments testing positive for the virus or having to be quarantined because of exposure,[12] requiring other agencies to step in to backfill policing in their jurisdictions. Similarly, cases were reported of police leadership becoming infected, which challenged departments to continue operations when key commanders had to recover or quarantine.[13]

> We had fully 10 percent of our patrol force be infected. . . . And on top of that we had one detective pass away as a result of COVID. We have two that have yet to come back because they have tremendous upper respiratory issues. . . . And then the others . . . are absolutely fine.
>
> – Law enforcement management panelist

At the time of this writing, estimates of the number of law enforcement officers who have lost their lives as a result of COVID-19 range from approximately 156 to nearly 282 among 28 and 34 different states and territories.[14] Figure 3.2 shows the 24 states listed by the National Law Enforcement Officers Memorial Fund (NLEOMF) in its roll call of officers lost to COVID-19. COVID-19 has claimed the lives of more law enforcement officers than all other on-duty causes combined, and there is concern that, by the end of the pandemic, it

---

[8]   National Commission on COVID-19 and Criminal Justice, *Recommendations for Response and Future Readiness: Interim Commission Report*, Washington, D.C.: Council on Criminal Justice, October 2020a, p. 23.

[9]   The National Police Foundation, "Coronavirus (COVID-19): Resources for Law Enforcement—COVID-19 Law Enforcement Impact Dashboard (Data from Impact Survey 2 & 3)," webpage, undated.

[10]   Lum, Maupin, and Stoltz, 2020b, p. 2.

[11]   For a review, see Christine Lehmann, "COVID Biggest Cause of Police Deaths This Year," WebMD, October 12, 2020.

[12]   The smaller department in East Texas had all five of its employees test positive (Stephanie Frazier, "Sheriff's Office Providing Backup After Entire East Texas Police Department Tests Positive for Virus," *KLTV News*, July 29, 2020). See also Bethany Freudenthal, "Most Staff at Sunland Park Police Department in Quarantine, County and State Officials Helping," *Las Cruces Sun News*, June 19, 2020; C. J. LeMaster, "As COVID-19 Forces Closure of Edwards Police Dept., 3OYS Explores Other Agencies' Pandemic Policies," *WLBT News*, June 19, 2020.

[13]   For example, see Timothy Bella, "A GOP Sheriff Vowed Not to Enforce Arizona's Coronavirus Restrictions. Now He's Tested Positive," *Washington Post*, June 18, 2020; and Ramon Antonio Vargas, "After High-Ranking NOPD Officer Contracts Coronavirus, Union Calls on Department to Test All Cops," *NOLA.com*, June 25, 2020.

[14]   Respectively, National Law Enforcement Officers Memorial Fund, undated; and Fraternal Order of Police, 2020.

Figure 3.2
States That Have Lost Law Enforcement Officers to COVID-19, as of November 2020

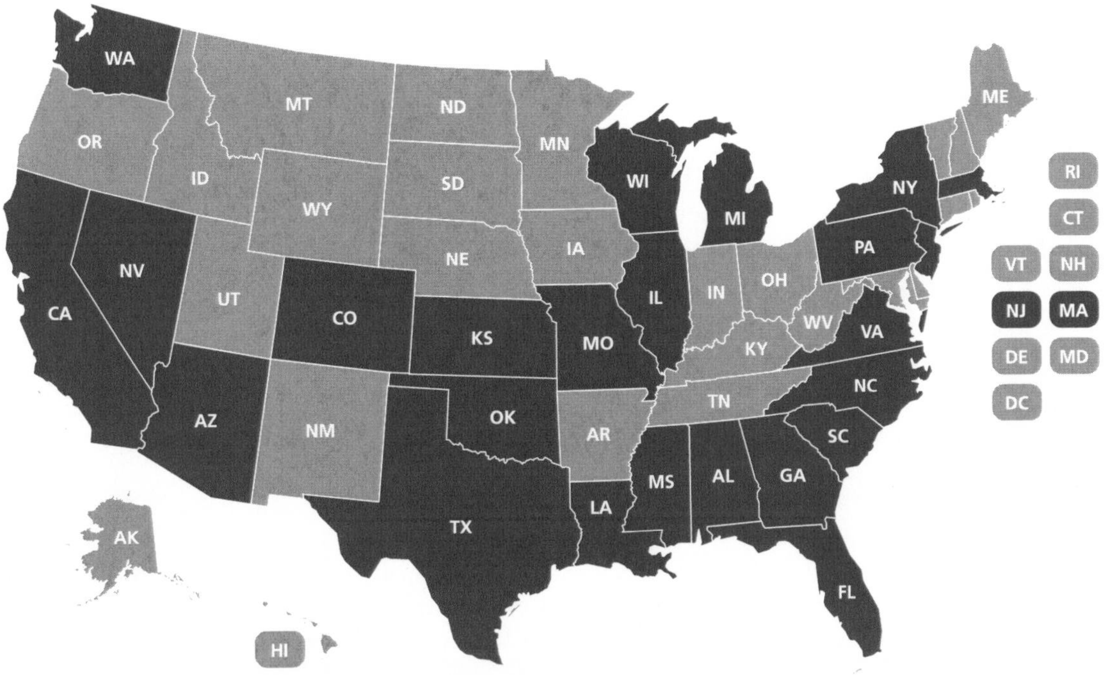

SOURCE: Adapted from National Law Enforcement Officers Memorial Fund, undated.
NOTE: States shaded in red designate those that have lost at least one officer.

might surpass the September 11, 2001, terrorist attacks (9/11) in the number of officers killed as a result.[15]

Further complicating the effects of COVID-19 on police and other crime-prevention practitioners, it is clear that some individuals infected by the disease have long-term debilitating symptoms. Although this issue was raised in the context of our law enforcement discussions, it is the reality for *all* criminal justice practitioners infected with COVID-19, and in fact, for *everyone* who has contracted the disease. As a result, although some police officers and others might recover with few ill effects, for others, COVID-19 infection could be a disabling or even career-ending event. The potential for long-term health effects and permanent disabilities also suggests parallels with the 9/11 experience, where large numbers of responders experienced long-term, debilitating, and eventually fatal health consequences of the exposures they experienced during response operations. That possibility means that the health effects of COVID-19 on criminal justice practitioners are not only an issue of individuals losing their lives today; there is the potential for long-term costs to individuals and their departments if disabilities associated with infection persist. This concern shaped the discussion in our law enforcement and other panels and increased the complexity of questions surrounding the protection of officers during the pandemic.

---

[15] Christopher Ingraham, "COVID-19 Has Killed More Police Officers This Year Than All Other Causes Combined, Data Shows," *Washington Post*, September 2, 2020.

> We also don't know the long-term health consequences of COVID. For instance, there seems to be some lasting consequences on heart health, which we already know is a big concern in the law enforcement community. So we don't know whether survivor benefit claims will be lasting [for] decades.
>
> – Law enforcement operations panelist

In response to the risk posed by COVID-19 to both police officers and the public more broadly as a result of law enforcement action, many agencies acted to make significant changes in the early stages of the pandemic. These adjustments affected agencies' outward-facing interactions and their internal management activities.[16] In the initial months of the pandemic, several efforts were carried out that sought to poll different groups of law enforcement agencies about the nature of these adjustments.[17] In our panels, which were held approximately six months into the pandemic, panelists discussed changes that had been made and reflected on how those adaptations worked, the path forward for policing during the pandemic using lessons from the first waves of the disease, and preparations for future events.[18]

> I think . . . COVID-19 . . . is going to change permanently how we do a lot of things in law enforcement, as well as just general business and how we communicate with other stakeholders, law enforcement partners, as well as the community. So it's created a new normal in a sense.
>
> – Law enforcement management panelist

---

[16] Major practitioner organizations provided guides with recommended operational changes using Centers for Disease Control and Prevention (CDC) and other guidelines for infection reduction and control, including such groups as the IACP (IACP, "Organizational Readiness: Ensuring Your Agency Is Prepared for COVID-19," webpage, March 26, 2020a).

[17] In the following discussion, we draw on survey results produced by multiple different entities. In most cases, because of the reality of the COVID-19 pandemic, the response rates to such surveys were sometimes low and the samples were not representative of all law enforcement agencies in the United States. We therefore draw on their results descriptively and, as a rule, do not report exact percentages calculated from their respondent populations.

[18] Simultaneous with our effort, two reports of the National Commission on COVID-19 and Criminal Justice were released. The initial report, which was released while our panels were being held, included top-level recommendations on protective measures, limiting contact and custody, support for officers, clear communication, and the strategic allocation of resources (National Commission on COVID-19 and Criminal Justice, 2020a, pp. 23–25).

Key Findings from Law Enforcement's Response to the COVID-19 Pandemic

- Many police departments adjusted their strategies for crime prevention and enforcement to limit officer contact with the public and reduce the flow of people into the justice system.

- In some cases, departments increased their use of nonarrest approaches, including the use of citations as an alternative to arrest. In others, departments merely deferred arrest until after the public health crisis improves, building a backlog of to-be-arrested individuals who will have to go through the system in the future.

- Some departments made significant shifts to virtual service delivery. Although some departments had taken steps toward virtual service delivery before the pandemic, it pushed the changes and increased public receptiveness to online and virtual police response.

- Public communication and community policing were very difficult during the pandemic, but departments had success using such virtual platforms as Facebook Live or Zoom. Reaching some groups required alternative methods, including direct mail.

- Community crime-prevention and violence-interruption efforts were much more difficult because limiting face-to-face contact and restricted entry to hospitals hurt their efforts to connect with crime victims.

- Protecting officer health and safety and, by extension, agency operational capacity required changes to staffing models (e.g., staff cohorts, or an exclusive group of staff that works the same shift), changes in procedures, and the use of protective equipment. In some cases, departments had difficulties with staff compliance with the use of protective equipment, which reduced its effective risk reduction.

- Some forensic labs were able to transition rapidly to significantly distributed work models, although agencies that had not invested in technology (e.g., those that were still dependent on paper files) had more difficulty.

- Operating in pandemic conditions and concerns about bringing exposure home to their families were significant stressors and mental health challenges for law enforcement staff. In response, some agencies implemented new mental health support and intervention resources, including remote counseling options.

- The national environment and conditions created by the criminal justice reform protests made law enforcement involvement in public health initiatives very problematic. Although police can have a role in such situations, doing so effectively requires a high level of trust between police and the public. In many areas, law enforcement resisted a role in direct pandemic response, limiting the contribution it could make to helping manage risk to the country. However, in some cases, police taking a more educational role was viewed as productive.

- Decisions made by other parts of the justice system and by social services agencies significantly affected law enforcement, including increasing demands to respond to individuals in mental health crisis, which were exacerbated by the pandemic.

- As a result of the economic consequences of the COVID-19 pandemic, police agencies are facing reductions in budget. Such cuts—although they are seemingly in agreement with the calls during protests to defund the police—will create additional issues for the remainder of the pandemic and during the recovery period.

Making Major Strategy Changes to Protect Officers and the Public

In an effort to limit the infection of law enforcement officers and to reduce the flow of individuals into the justice system, many police departments made substantial changes to how they did business. These changes were focused on meeting public expectations for safety and crime response while responding to the changed risk environment.

I actually think [public expectations have] *increased* because they want the same type of service and the same type of relationship, but for a while they didn't even want to be in the same room because of the concerns that they had with the virus.

– Law enforcement management panelist

[Looking across agencies,] I've seen the key challenges change over time, even in the past few months, initially the biggest challenges was how to maintain sufficient levels of service to the community while minimizing risk of officers' exposure [to] the disease. Any interaction with the public puts them at heightened risk. And so agencies were trying to minimize that as much as possible while still serving the public. But officer safety was definitely the first priority. And then as the pandemic evolved, the challenges did too.

– Law enforcement management panelist

Police Services Were Delivered Virtually Before and During the Pandemic

An immediate action taken by some departments was to close police facilities to entry by the public in an effort to prevent the introduction and spread of the virus.[19] Although many police services do not involve people coming to the station (e.g., in the same way that almost all court activities customarily do), some services do, meaning that the protective actions resulted in a backlog of needs that will have to be worked through over time.

---

[19] Brooks and Lopez, 2020, p. 11; Wesley G. Jennings and Nicholas M. Perez, "The Immediate Impact of COVID-19 on Law Enforcement in the United States," *American Journal of Criminal Justice*, Vol. 45, 2020.

> We closed our front lobby for several weeks until the pandemic at least slowed down a bit. So we're looking at backlogs now of fingerprinting for alcohol pouring permits. As the election comes closer, we are having a huge uptake in firearms fingerprinting. And again, those are backlogged probably through the first of the year already. So we're looking at some alternate ways to work with that perhaps, extending hours opening up on weekends, but again, we're staff limited.
>
> – Law enforcement operations panelist

To further cut down on contact between officers and the public, many police departments made significant changes in how they handled calls for service. Traditionally, calls to police would be answered in person by an officer. Some departments reduced the types of calls to which they would respond, requiring response to more-minor incidents to be done over the phone or online.[20]

> Our goal from the beginning was to keep everybody distant from not only each other, but also with the community members as much as practical.
>
> – Law enforcement operations panelist

In both of our law enforcement panels, participants emphasized that the transition from in-person response to online or telephone options has been important for reducing risk. However, similar to technological initiatives that were taken elsewhere in the criminal justice system, this transition was not something that was started during the pandemic. In some areas, there already had been initiatives that attempted to move toward alternative reporting and response options, but with only modest success—because the public felt that, to paraphrase one of our panelists, "they were paying for police response, and should get it." The risk associated with contracting COVID-19 prompted many to reevaluate their opinions, and the addition of other technology helped: According to some panelists, the addition of videoconferencing to these services—so that members of the public could see the officer who was taking their report rather than submitting a web form or talking to someone on the phone—aided acceptance. One of our panelists estimated that, when the pandemic was particularly intense in their area, the department was responding to approximately 40 percent of their calls for service virtually.

---

[20] In the first wave of the IACP and GMU survey, which was done in March 2020, the majority of agencies had made some changes to their policies for handling calls for service, with about three-quarters doing some via technology. In their second survey wave (which was done in May 2020), the result was similar, with nearly three-quarters responding to at least 10 percent of calls for service virtually and about one-quarter of agencies handling more than 30 percent that way (Lum, Maupin, and Stoltz, 2020a; Lum, Maupin, and Stoltz, 2020b). Other data calls from agencies in single states received similar feedback (John Shjarback and Obed Magny, *Policing During the Pandemic: California Officers' Experiences*, Sacramento, Calif., June 2020).

> When COVID hit, we made it very clear that if it was a report-only call, we were not dispatching officers to take those calls. And we told them, you can either do it online yourself; you can call our mobile report center, and they would take it over the phone; or they could do videoconferencing. To date, we've taken over 2,500 calls over the phone through our remote report center, and now people have gotten used to it. We may not ever shut that down again, that in turn has freed up our officers to spend more time out on the street, doing crime-related matters, doing more-proactive policing.
>
> – Law enforcement management panelist
>
> One of the things that really helped us—was we started doing videoconferencing with people so they actually see a police officer taking their report. So that kind of calmed their fears some without actually having an officer respond to take the report.
>
> – Law enforcement management panelist

Virtual-interaction options are not just about how police deal with less serious crimes. Criminal investigations of serious crimes can involve considerable numbers of interviews of witnesses or suspects.[21] Departments have added distance to such interactions and used technology to reduce infection risk.[22] According to a review by the Marshall Project, some departments are doing interviews and interrogations outside, some are conducting interviews at a distance in larger rooms, and some are using videoconferencing from adjacent rooms.[23]

> The other significant challenge was how to respond to calls for service . . . appearing in person to handle a call and dealing with phone calls to switching to online reporting, basically just how we conduct our business, how investigators would conduct their business of interviewing a potential victims, witnesses, and suspects.
>
> – Law enforcement management panelist

Public Interaction and Community Policing Were Challenging Under Pandemic Conditions
An initial casualty of the COVID-19 pandemic was public interaction and community policing events, even as tensions between police and some communities make those types of collab-

---

[21]   There were questions about whether pandemic measures, such as broad mask-wearing, would affect the ability to investigate crimes. Such concerns were similar to concerns that mask-wearing in court could affect the judicial process. At least one of our participants indicated that that had not been a major problem: "Identifying suspects in a masked environment? . . . [W]e found that suspects that didn't care what state statute had to say about putting a gun in somebody's face and robbing them also didn't care about what our mask order said. And so we found that many of these people were out there committing violent crimes without a mask. And we thank them for that because we were able to identify them just as we would in other cases."

[22]   See, for example, examples in PERF, *PERF Daily COVID-19 Report*, May 21, 2020c.

[23]   The distance required in COVID-19 response measures might reinforce ongoing changes in interrogation approaches. According to one report, "Cops were historically trained to invade someone's physical space to increase their anxiety, said Dave Thompson, vice president of operations at Wicklander [a consultant and training provider on interrogation]. 'That style was hopefully already beginning to be eradicated, but what's happening with COVID is accelerating that,' he said" (Eli Hager, "Your Zoom Interrogation Is About to Start," The Marshall Project, July 20, 2020).

oration and trust-building efforts all the more important.[24] For example, in a scan of changes made early in the pandemic, Jennings and Perez summarized that

> [a]cross the U.S., various community-oriented policing and outreach initiatives have been cancelled or modified due to the close proximity between officers and members of the public. . . . Due to social distancing guidelines, officers are being required to spend more time in their patrol cars and interact with community members less. . . . In the Metropolitan Police Department in Washington, D.C., community activities such as "Coffee with a Cop" and community member walks with the Chief have been put on hold indefinitely. . . . To prevent their police-community relationships from fracturing in Washington, D.C., the police have held community meetings via conference call instead of in-person.[25]

Of the departments that responded to the initial IACP and GMU questionnaire on law enforcement adaptations to the pandemic, approximately three-quarters had reduced their community policing activities.[26] In the IACP and GMU's later data collection, that fraction dropped somewhat but remained substantial.[27] Panelists in our workshops echoed the same concerns and challenges, and expressed reservations about whether the hiatus in interaction would pose longer-term problems.

> Communication with the public became a considerable challenge. I think my agency along with many, many other agencies across the United States has tried fervently to keep open channels of communication, whether it be different kinds of public events, meetings, et cetera. . . . [O]f course, with shelter-in-place rules limiting interactions and gathering, staff [were] presented [with] a significant challenge with trying to continue to build on relationships, as well as trying to improve relationships, especially with groups that we tend to lack trust with and [with which we] have some challenges.
>
> – Law enforcement management panelist

Multiple members of our panels discussed technological substitutes, including virtual meetings with citizens or with particular groups, taking the place of traditional community meetings.

> As far as the public, we were already pretty good with Facebook. And so we would have what I call these Teddy Roosevelt fireside chats, where we'd go [on] Facebook Live, where people could ask any question they wanted about how we responded to COVID, what the status was for our agency, as far as the people being infected and so forth. That worked really pretty well to get that information out.
>
> – Law enforcement management panelist

---

[24] David Montgomery, "COVID-19 Curbs Community Policing at a Time of Diminishing Trust," *PEW Stateline* blog, October 1, 2020.

[25] Jennings and Perez, 2020, p. 694.

[26] Lum, Maupin, and Stoltz, 2020a.

[27] Lum, Maupin, and Stoltz, 2020b.

> [I do] regularly scheduled Zoom meetings with members of our business community, key community leaders, community of faith leaders, even our elected officials who still aren't meeting face to face, keeping [them] plugged in on what's been going on in our community through Zoom.
>
> – Law enforcement management panelist

In some cases, departments had transitioned to making much more data available in an effort to meet community needs when they could not interact face to face.

> We have 150 community watch groups within our city, and now they want more information and they want to be able to disseminate more information. So we've gotten more requests. We've put a lot of it on our open data portal so that they can just go pull their own stuff. But . . . maintaining that has created an issue [for us].
>
> – Law enforcement management panelist

However, multiple participants from different areas of the country were realistic about the limits of technology for building long-term relationships and solving difficult community challenges. In addition, echoing concerns raised by other justice system panelists about the effects of digital divides on the viability of virtual justice during the pandemic, some described having to reach people through other means. For example, although outreach to younger audiences might work better through technology than even some in-person modes, older residents in a jurisdiction might not use such sources of information and might have to be reached in other ways—perhaps through direct mail.

> That deep engagement, having conversations with our residents and talking about long-term issues has really been back-burnered, and that's something that we really want to get back on as quickly as possible.
>
> – Law enforcement operations panelist
>
> As you know, there's different strata of public. One of our closest partners are elderly folks that do not go on Facebook, would never think about Zoom, and don't even do phone conferences. So we actually went backward and some of our places where it was heavy with elderly population who still wanted to know what was going on with the police department. We would actually go back to snail mail. It's like "somebody get some stamps"—like who, whoever went to the post office in the last five years [to get] stamps? We bought lots of stamps and we sent that information out.
>
> – Law enforcement management panelist

Community-Based Crime-Prevention Interventions

For crime-prevention efforts where police are not the central actors, the constraints required to manage COVID-19 risk have been a major challenge. Community-based violence-interruption efforts generally rely on significant face-to-face interaction among outreach workers, victims, community members, and potential perpetrators in an attempt to halt cycles of violence. Focused deterrence initiatives or group violence-reduction interventions similarly depend on bringing community organizations and actors together to intervene with groups of individuals who are at risk of perpetrating violence. Limitations and restrictions that were intended to reduce the spread of the virus, and the simple fear of person-to-person contact reducing the willingness of people and groups to meet, can be a major barrier to the initiation and success of such efforts.

Interventions that bring social services and counseling capabilities to bear on problems of substance abuse, violence, or juvenile criminality can include many different players and significant in-person contact for service provision and support. In considering the increase in violent crime that has been observed in some cities since the beginning of the pandemic, the difficulties faced by these initiatives have been flagged as a cause: "Los Angeles Police Chief Michel Moore [said that] among COVID-19's negative impacts . . . was how it had barred violence prevention workers from visiting the bedsides of gunshot patients, compromising their ability to help interrupt the cycle of retaliatory shootings."[28] To the extent that these constraints limit the capability of groups, there is the potential for the significant increase in violence observed in some jurisdictions (which we discussed in Chapter Two) to compound, reinforcing the breakdown in public safety. In these cases, the strains on police-community trust during the pandemic have the potential to significantly affect effectiveness.[29]

> What we found in our work is that post-COVID we've seen . . . an increase in violent crime in [our city]. We are seeing police being disengaged, and community outreach organizations struggling to deal with the demand. But the violence has continued to increase. And so there's a need to engage people around victimization in these communities yet it's at a time when distrust may be at an all-time high.
>
> – Community organization panelist

Access to patients in hospitals, where initial relationships supporting some interventions are built, has been limited to reduce COVID-19 transmission (intervention personnel are considered visitors to the patients). Programs have had to adapt to add other connection options and have had to rely on virtual connections, although there are concerns that they are less effective than face-to-face meetings. As a result, some hospitals are seeking to resume in-person meetings.[30]

---

[28] Jennifer Mascia, "Pushed Out of Hospitals by COVID, Anti-Violence Programs Try to Adapt," The Trace, October 5, 2020.

[29] These concerns echo similar points made regarding law enforcement participation in targeted violence intervention and countering violent extremism or terrorism prevention interventions that often also are collaborations with public health, counseling, and other service agencies (see discussion in Brian A. Jackson, Ashley L. Rhoades, Jordan R. Reimer, Natasha Lander, Katherine Costello, and Sina Beaghley, *Practical Terrorism Prevention: Reexamining U.S. National Approaches to Addressing the Threat of Ideologically Motivated Violence*, Homeland Security Operational Analysis Center operated by the RAND Corporation, RR-2647-DHS, 2019).

[30] Mascia, 2020.

It's worked best when we've had nurses working inside of the hospital that directly provide the information of the victims to our community partners, but that can only happen when there's consent. And it's been very difficult to get consent under the COVID restrictions and that's something we're still working through. . . . We think [that the amount of activity in hospital-based violence intervention has] gone down by around 80 percent. So we've had a very difficult time getting to people.

– Community organization panelist

The biggest challenge that they've faced is figuring out how to do mediations, provide wraparound services, and community street outreach–based interventions with the restrictions of COVID-19 in place.

– Community organization panelist

Similar problems were encountered by NGO staff working in nonhospital contexts, but also where face-to-face contact was a critical contributor to their effectiveness. According to Altheimer, Duda-Banwar, and Schreck,

> Societal restrictions imposed due to COVID-19 have posed challenges for violence street outreach workers. On one hand, intense face-to-face interaction with their clients places them at direct risk of COVID-19 infection. On the other hand, societal restrictions imposed in response to COVID-19 may make it nearly impossible for them to carry out work-related tasks. Further, it is unlikely that many of the non-profit organizations through which street outreach workers operate have the resources to provide support for sophisticated video conferencing technology. The conflict between job requirements and the necessity of social distancing contributes to higher stress levels among street outreach workers.[31]

In a case study of one such program, Altheimer, Duda-Banwar, and Schreck indicated that the changes in both the hospital and community contexts have made it more difficult to persuade individuals to participate in programs that are intended to reduce violence and crime. In addition, the study argues that other demands related to the pandemic on service-providing organizations have reduced their ability to support programming, and constraints in PPE availability and volunteer willingness to work under pandemic conditions have hurt their ability to deliver programs to those who need them.[32] To the extent that other types of violence-reduction efforts (e.g., more–broadly focused deterrence efforts) need to bring together community actors, service providers, and others with at-risk individuals, constraints for infection prevention can be a major barrier.

---

[31] Irshad Altheimer, Janelle Duda-Banwar, and Christopher J. Schreck, "The Impact of Covid-19 on Community-Based Violence Interventions," *American Journal of Criminal Justice*, Vol. 45, 2020, p. 811.

[32] Altheimer, Duda-Banwar, and Schreck, 2020.

The street outreach teams in [our city] have been experimenting with Zoom calls. Of course, there are privacy issues around that when it comes to violent victimization. They've been experimenting with other types of conference calls. They've been trying to meet people in the community and provide them with PPE while they meet them. And so it's . . . a work in progress.

– Community organization panelist

Arrests Were Reduced to Limit the Population Brought into the Justice System

Although some changes were focused on reducing or eliminating contact with members of the public, the nature of the law enforcement role required that policing could not stop completely. However, interaction between a police officer and a member of the public was not risk-free for either party. Furthermore, anyone taken into custody under arrest would have to be transported to and held in jail, increasing the risk of disease spread within the corrections system. As a result, many police departments made significant changes in their policies for how they carried out enforcement actions. Such changes were made in an effort to protect officer safety and public health. In some cases, the changes were forced by policy changes elsewhere in the justice system—i.e., changes in the types of individuals the local jail would accept into custody—which we discuss in greater detail later in this chapter and in other chapters. In our community organization panel, a participant argued that alternatives to arrest were important in maintaining community members' willingness to call police for help, given fears of exposure to COVID-19 in the justice system.

In some cases, these changes to reduce arrests kept someone who normally would have been brought into the justice system out of it permanently (e.g., in an interaction where an arrest normally would have been made but no action was taken at all). In other cases, the change deferred action (e.g., by issuing a notice to appear, formally arresting someone but not filing charges and taking them into custody), which meant that the change was creating a backlog of actions to be taken that the system will have to address at a later date.

Pretty much for any misdemeanor case other than DUI and other than domestic violence, which are cases [in which we] were required to make a physical arrest, if we could issue a promise to appear we would do so. Just anything that we can do to limit our interactions with people, to limit the number of people that we were incarcerating. We just had to really tell our officers to use the best discretion they could.

– Law enforcement operations panelist

Anecdotally, I've heard of people seeing a violent crime or seeing some concerning situation and refraining from wanting to call the police, because the fear is that being taken into custody is a greater risk than what they're facing at that moment of time due to exposure of COVID.

– Community organization panelist

Available data from the IACP and GMU survey of 1,000 to 1,500 police departments indicated that approximately three-quarters had "provided their officers with formal guidance to reduce their use of physical arrests for minor offenses."[33] A similar percentage of respondents across their two waves of data collection indicated that their jails had put limits on who would be accepted for custody. Somewhat fewer (slightly more than half of departments) indicated that they had limited proactive enforcement activities and traffic stops.[34]

> The way that we performed our daily activities significantly changed. Our chief was not shy about telling our patrol officers that we shouldn't be pulling over cars unless there was a real legitimate need to do so [and to] just use a lot of discretion for issuing citations.
>
> – Law enforcement operations panelist
>
> We went . . . looking for more-discretionary ways to deal with crimes. A lot of citations were handed out. A lot of warnings were handed out rather than arrest. Only those arrests that were of a violent nature, serious misdemeanor nature, were actually physically taken into custody.
>
> – Law enforcement operations panelist

In most cases, departments used alternatives to arrest, such as issuing citations, summons, or promises to appear at a later date,[35] although some departments issued warnings for some minor crimes. The National Association of Pretrial Services Agencies fielded a questionnaire from April to the end of May 2020.[36] An increased use of cite-and-release practices and summons was reported by about half of their respondents, but reports of reduced custodial arrests overall was more common. Other areas stopped executing certain warrants.[37] Most changes in practice were tied to the nature of the offense and the availability of alternative approaches or sanctions. For example, in an Arizona county,

> [t]he County Attorney urged all local law enforcement agencies to discontinue arrests for simple possession of drugs for personal use, crimes that are non-violent and non-dangerous. We suggested seizure of evidence in such cases, then either deflecting the individual directly to treatment, or simply waiting until the end of the health crisis to make an arrest.[38]

---

[33] Lum, Maupin, and Stoltz, 2020a.

[34] Analyses using data collected from departments within single states produced similar results (e.g., Shjarback and Magny, 2020).

[35] National Conference of State Legislatures, "Criminal Justice System Responses to COVID-19," webpage, November 16, 2020.

[36] The survey and its results are described in National Partnership for Pretrial Justice, "COVID-19 Sparks 'Unprecedented' Pretrial Reforms, Survey Shows," webpage, undated. Although the 197 respondents to the survey covered 40 states and the District of Columbia, the respondents were not a representative sample of agencies across the country (i.e., the National Association of Pretrial Services Agencies described its results as "purely anecdotal evidence"). As a result, we do not report percentages of the respondents, but instead note measures as more common and less common.

[37] See, for example, Buncombe County Justice Services Department, *Buncombe County Fact Sheet: On Addressing COVID-19 in Our Local Justice System*, undated.

[38] Amelia Cramer, "How Interagency Trust Can Foster an Optimal Jail Response to COVID-19," MacArthur Foundation Safety and Justice Challenge blog, April 8, 2020.

Panelists on both our law enforcement and community organization panels also indicated that the need to reduce arrests has resulted in increased use of diversion and deflection programs by their departments.

In some cases, special-jurisdiction law enforcement organizations, such as university police, had different challenges in reducing enforcement (e.g., responding to college parties where there could be significant spread of disease) but also had other options available to them in response, including sanctions from the university that could be much swifter and more certain than those pursued through the judicial process.

> If they're a violent offender or state-mandated to be arrested and incarcerated, they are going [to jail]. Otherwise right now, people are being referred or they're going through expanded diversion and deflection programs. . . . I would say that that's been a positive outcome, we're finding that, at least in the short term, our folks are not re-offending and are being diverted into treatment alternatives and other things that we may not necessarily have done [before].
>
> – Law enforcement management panelist
>
> I work with a lot of good law enforcement. And what we are seeing is a lot of agencies are hiring counselors or looking to hire counselors. . . . We also do a lot of training, a [crisis intervention team] youth training with school resource officers. So we're seeing a slowdown in the pipeline from a youth going into detention centers here locally, which is good.
>
> – Community organization panelist

All of these changes resulted in very significant reductions in some areas' jail populations, supporting COVID-19 risk-mitigation efforts there (we discuss these efforts further in Chapter Five).

As we discussed earlier, the choices of approach for addressing minor offenses in particular have significant consequences for how the effects of the pandemic on this part of the justice system will evolve over time. If, as suggested earlier in Cramer, 2020, and by one of our panelists from institutional corrections, arrests are still planned but are deferred until a later date when the health risks are lower, a backlog of to-be-arrested individuals will accumulate over time. Greater use of citations will create a pool of individuals with future court dates, or with fines that must be paid to address their infractions. The use of diversion and other approaches, however, would not result in pressure building in this part of the justice system that must be worked through over time, after the risk of the COVID-19 pandemic recedes.

> When COVID started, we knew that this was going to cause some problems. So we immediately reached out to our district attorney's office and the other law enforcement agencies in the county, and we reduced the number of crimes that would be charged. So basically, it's not that nothing will be done. They're treating all of the nonviolent misdemeanor crimes on a "to-be" basis. So the officers out on the streets are still, in so many words, making the arrest, but they don't get to actually file the charges. They'll do it on a "to-be" basis. *Currently, last count I was informed was somewhere around 5,000 cases waiting "to be filed" once we give them the green light that they can go back and finish what they started doing back in March.*
>
> – Institutional corrections panelist

Beyond overarching choices about whether specific types of offenses would result in arrest, decisions were being made at a lower level regarding managing risk in specific investigative activities—e.g., whether it was worth taking the risk of suspect interviews for a particular crime—and about the use of such technologies as breathalyzers for evaluating whether someone was driving under the influence. Breathalyzers were a particular concern, given the need for someone to blow into the testing device, which, if they were infected, could spread COVID-19 to the officer or others.

> We had to make some difficult choices in what cases we would interview suspects and what cases we wouldn't. So we decided, murder cases, sex crime cases, those cases went without saying that we were still going to conduct interviews of suspects arrested for those crimes. Domestic violence cases, as well. As far as property crimes, it was a judgment call.
>
> – Law enforcement operations panelist
>
> Obviously doing a breath test where you're blowing out air is a risky thing to do with COVID. So we worked with our [state occupational safety agency] creating some additional safety guidelines for performing breath alcohol tests. I will say that since April, we have seen about a 30-percent reduction in evidential breath tests across the state due to less enforcement in that area I think. We've also seen a little bit of an uptick in blood draws.
>
> – Law enforcement management panelist

However, as was the case for other responses to the pandemic, there were differences from place to place in how police agencies responded. Not all departments made big changes in practices or viewed the changes they did make as significant diversions from normal operations.

> From a police-specific perspective, when all this started, we made the decision fairly quickly to try to maintain as many of the operations that we had before COVID during the pandemic. . . . The only things that we stopped were in-person community meetings . . . that we restarted in July, and we reduced the proactive service of minor misdemeanor arrest warrants.
>
> – Law enforcement management panelist

Safely Managing a Police Agency in a Pandemic

Because policing activities had to continue in spite of the pandemic, police agencies had to find ways to continue to operate and to do so as safely as possible under the circumstances. Like other organizations, agencies needed information and guidance about how to do so. Our participants indicated that their main sources for information on COVID-19 risks were CDC and their local public health agency, and that remaining in sync with the guidance from both was critical, although having different entities providing different guidance could be challenging. Multiple participants commended their state and local public health agencies for their efforts to regularly communicate and keep the department up to date on the evolving situation. That guidance enabled departments to make choices about which processes to move into the virtual space, what steps to take to protect staff who still had contact with the public, and how to adapt such internal activities as recruiting and training to the realities of the pandemic environment.

> It's still trying to run a police department. It's still trying to hire people virtually through Microsoft Teams or Zoom, and still trying to get those pieces moving. We can't just stand still. So we have to keep moving forward with training and hiring.
>
> – Law enforcement management panelist

Virtualizing Agency Management and Operations

In addition to trying to virtualize as many of their interactions with the public as possible, law enforcement agencies used virtual tools to minimize COVID-19 risk in their internal processes. A frequently cited example was shift roll-call briefings, which, under normal circumstances, would bring together all the officers on the shift for information-sharing. Although some agencies kept roll calls in person but moved them outdoors, many others eliminated the in-person briefing and substituted virtual communications.[39] Participants in our panels indicated that some agencies went to telephone roll calls, while others used video options that are now more available and familiar to staff.

> One of the things we really focused on was . . . internal communication. I did a lot of videos and a lot of Zoom meetings with members of our department to continue to keep them connected and to continue to keep them informed.
>
> – Law enforcement management panelist

Agencies, and forensic labs in particular, also made major changes to allow staff to work from home for some portion of their time. Having staff be able to do work while not physically present helped support social distancing, which is particularly necessary in areas where it is difficult to separate staff because of building designs. Just as many other private-sector agencies discovered, videoconferencing tools could maintain a level of connectivity for tasks that

---

[39] Brooks and Lopez, 2020, p. 11; Jennings and Perez, 2020; Shjarback and Magny, 2020.

required multiple people to collaborate, although the organization had previously assumed that in-person collaboration was essential.

> We've kind of ended on our current situation where we expect people to spend about 75 percent of their time here in the lab, performing the casework, and then they can go home and do all their administrative work at home. We got laptops and [virtual private networks (VPNs)] for each of the analysts. We already had shifted toward a mostly paperless system in many places. So we continued, we kind of finished a lot of that so people could do technical reviews of data at home. Everything was on a shared drive off of a server. So we were able to get that done within about two weeks of when this started.
>
> – Law enforcement management panelist

However, the ease of adding work-from-home options varied considerably, even across the agencies that participated in our panels. It was particularly difficult for organizations whose existing technology infrastructure was limited or where continued reliance on paper-based processes made it hard to disperse operations and staff.

> We were definitely behind the curve in relation to how we could get other work done internally with our civilian staff and how we can best utilize technology. . . . It was something that we'd always talked about but never really planned for. . . . We're just reaching out to other cities, looking for model policies, as far as management of time, work, task, assignment, and management, things that we never really considered when we were all in person before.
>
> – Law enforcement operations panelist
>
> What we have found is that, and we knew this, we still have an overabundance of relying on paper records. . . . We've bought these lockboxes so that people can take case files home with them . . . so that they can do some case review at home. But we really have started moving toward seeing what steps we can take to minimize some of the paper.
>
> – Law enforcement management panelist
>
> For some labs, it was really easy for them to start working from home because they were just able to VPN in and get to all of their software. But other laboratories didn't have that. So they were having to work with their [information technology (IT)] folks to get VPN access for all these people who all of a sudden needed it right now and had never had that. Some of that was actually taken from lab budgets, which was unexpected.
>
> – Law enforcement operations panelist

The pandemic also increased pressure to complete already planned technology upgrades that could enable other risk-reduction options, and to develop approaches to enable key staff—notably 9-1-1 call-takers and emergency services dispatchers—who are normally co-located in locations that are vulnerable to spread of infection. According to one source,

National 911 groups will explore how operators could field calls from home, heads of the National Emergency Number Association (NENA) and National Association of State 911 Administrators (NASNA) said in interviews last week. Operators began working remotely in Alexandria, Virginia, when the coronavirus struck the U.S. Most public safety answering points (PSAPs) don't allow that, despite widespread safety concerns of having call takers working near each other indoors.[40]

> We have worked with our laboratory information management system vendor and we're getting a little closer to implementing a pre-log system where law enforcement can just enter the [necessary] information [about their evidence submission] prior to coming to the lab. And that's one of those things that had been on the back burner that we've been talking about and talking about and working on very incrementally, that all of a sudden it's like, "All right, we've got to get this done, let's move."
>
> – Law enforcement management panelist

Among our participants whose departments had made significant shifts to virtual operations, they reported seeing benefits that went far beyond COVID-19 risk reduction. Virtual meetings meant that no one had to spend time traveling to meet, which made things easier for police, other agencies' staff, and community members. Virtual connectivity meant that the police department was more accessible for more of the time, and that police potentially had more information at their fingertips to inform people when they called. When those connections involved criminal justice data systems—which were known for their security requirements and, as a result, accessibility and usability limitations to protect data—participants were impressed by how quickly technical change happened.

> The other thing we realized is [about] our virtual meetings. I don't know for quite some time [whether] we will go back to actual in-person meetings. We're even doing our monthly CompStat meeting virtually and having our partners, instead of trying to travel down here to the station, they're logging on to Zoom or whatever virtual meeting platform [we] are using, and we're doing our monthly crime report meetings. Everything has become more convenient by going virtual.
>
> – Law enforcement management panelist
>
> All of a sudden there have been some incredible breakthroughs in technology, between criminal justice information systems that, in the past, you would never have been able to remote into because of firewalls and security concerns. And we've been able to overcome that because of the stay-at-home order and just the necessity. So I don't think there'll be another snow day, where we're actually closing the government like we have in the past.
>
> – Law enforcement management panelist

---

[40] Adam Bender, "COVID-19 Could Change Views Toward Remote 911 Operators," *Communications Daily*, June 15, 2020.

Law enforcement and forensics laboratory staff also have benefited from the virtualization that has been done elsewhere in the justice system, notably in the courts. By minimizing travel time for staff, video testimony has increased efficiency, particularly for forensic examiners. On the police side, participants indicated that the fact that it is much easier for police officers to appear in court virtually is a major benefit. Court appearances might be scheduled during periods when an officer is not on duty, and the ease of remote appearance has reduced the number of cases where officers did not appear when summoned.

> If you're working for a city laboratory, or in a county, you might have a quick drive to court. For other states, you may have a four-hour drive to get to court and you may have a 15-minute testimony, or you may sit on the bench all day long and never actually get called, or have the case dismissed. So having this ability for the forensic scientist to be able to continue to do their work and then pop off to do their testimony and then get back to it has been actually something that's quite positive.
>
> – Law enforcement operations panelist
>
> I think that justice is served on both ends [with virtual appearances], where we have our police officers fulfilling their duty and showing up in court more often and, and where court isn't . . . more of a burden than it should be for people who are experiencing hard times.
>
> – Law enforcement operations panelist

Protecting Officer Health and the Ability of Law Enforcement Agencies to Operate

Many of the policy changes made to allow for the virtual delivery of police services were motivated primarily by officer safety concerns; minimizing contacts reduced the probability of an officer encountering a carrier of COVID-19. However, because such contacts could not be eliminated, a variety of other steps were taken by departments in an effort to protect both staff and the functioning of the police agency from infection or disruption from the quarantines required after exposure. These steps included making adjustments to policing approaches, trying to implement medical management efforts, providing PPE to staff, sharing infection data, and developing staffing models to limit overall risk to the agency, even if some staff were infected.

> Sometimes employees are fearful of contracting COVID or sometimes they're the opposite extreme. They're not fearful at all of contracting it, they're invincible, they can do their thing.
>
> – Law enforcement management panelist

Distanced Policing

When officers did need to respond to a scene in person, they changed the way they responded in an effort to reduce risk to themselves and others. Strategies included the now-familiar approach of seeking to keep distance between people and stay outside in well-ventilated areas, and sometimes "using technology in person" (i.e., officers would use their phones to communicate even while they were on scene to observe what was happening). Some other departments used novel technologies—e.g., unmanned aerial vehicles or drones—for public communication while avoiding close contact.[41] Other examples of response strategies included single-officer response to calls with back-up standing off, which is counter to the assumption that there is greater safety when multiple officers respond to a call together.[42]

> We did what we referred to . . . as *doorway triage*. So we would actually have our dispatchers ask to talk to the complainants when they would call in, and the ones we couldn't kind of farm out to a phone conversation, we'd say, "Why don't you come outside to talk to us" so that. . . . If one of our officers was inadvertently infected and he didn't know that he was infected, we weren't infecting that family. We made that very clear. And then same thing goes that if we had an infected family, then they could come out. And so we were limiting [the risk of] that conversation.
>
> – Law enforcement management panelist
>
> As far as policing goes, as police officers we're used to walking into a room, recognizing a threat, knowing what the problem is and solving the problem and moving on. COVID has presented an almost . . . blind threat. We have to treat everybody as if they're infected, but still try to build those relationships . . . where you build that rapport very quickly, but yet still maintaining a distance and maintaining a healthy workforce.
>
> – Law enforcement management panelist
>
> [Beyond taking calls completely over the phone,] patrol officers would sometimes use their phone to minimize contact—they still may go to the scene and either observe what's going on or try to have some distance [by communicating with people there by phone]. But we try to do as much as we could over the phone.
>
> – Law enforcement operations panelist

Staff Health-Management Efforts

Beyond limiting the risk of infection, agencies took steps to manage the potential risk for staff by making changes to policies and medical screening practices. Participants in our workshops described steps that included establishing a medical unit that was in charge of managing any potential exposures to personnel and making decisions about quarantine and isolation.[43] Another department represented on our panel met that need—and took the burden off of station commanders for managing officer health—by using a supplemental safety officer program in which staff were pulled from their regular duty assignments and devoted to responding to exposure and coordinating testing for officers. Testing availability for officers was a concern, particularly early in the pandemic, that complicated agency management efforts. In their

---

[41]   Kristine Phillips, "Police Agencies Are Using Drones to Enforce Stay-at-Home Orders, Raising Concerns Among Civil Rights Groups," *USA Today*, May 3, 2020. In a discussion in our community organization panel, participants raised concerns about the potential for these new technologies, which were deployed for good reason during the pandemic, to become more normalized and used in ways that increase agencies' surveillance capabilities after the pandemic, and the associated civil rights and civil liberties concerns.

[42]   Jeremiah P. Johnson, "Police Response to COVID-19: Innovation and Diffusion by a Policy Community of Practitioner-Scholars," *Police Forum*, Vol. 29, No. 1, April 2020.

[43]   Sets of guidelines were produced to help support agency decisionmaking in the event that an officer was exposed to the virus (IACP, "Law Enforcement Officer Exposure to COVID-19," webpage, April 15, 2020c).

data collection from law enforcement in California, Shjarback and Magny indicated that less than half of their respondents said that their agency had made it easy for officers to get tested.[44]

> Testing [availability for officers was a problem as well]. . . . We had officers that would get some type of symptom and we didn't know if it was COVID or not. . . . For several weeks, that was quite a challenge to have to quarantine an officer just because we couldn't find adequate testing, just because of the hotspot [in our] area.
>
> – Law enforcement operations panelist

Departments also sought to make it easier for staff to stay away from work if they felt ill, particularly given limitations in testing capability. Such strategies included pushing people to stay home if they were unsure whether they were sick and expanding sick leave availability to make that possible without cost to the officers.[45]

> We were very careful about how we brought people to work. Everyone has to take their temperature every single day before they entered the building. We were very, very liberal with people saying, "You know, I just don't feel well," *go home, go home, go home.*
>
> – Law enforcement operations panelist
>
> We did opt to offer unlimited [personal time off] for any type of COVID-related illness or quarantine. We used quite a bit of that. We've had a few officers contract COVID and we've had, for instance, one officer whose wife works in a health care facility and she tested positive, then he had to go on quarantine for 14 days. So we have a small department and those types of issues can really have an effect on day-to-day personnel.
>
> – Law enforcement operations panelist

Challenges with Personal Protective Equipment

In the panel discussion, participants noted concerns about the uncertain long-term health effects of COVID-19 and made the analogy to the long-term effects of 9/11 response operations on the individuals involved. The possibility for COVID-19 to result in enduring heart and other consequences made providing individual officers with the equipment they needed to prevent infection (and the importance of using it properly) about preventing acute illness not only in the short term but also, for some, in the very long term. Although there were reports of shortages of such PPE as gloves and face masks early in the pandemic, the multidepartment data sources that are available suggest that extreme shortages were comparatively uncommon. In the IACP and GMU data, the majority of agencies that responded indicated that officers had PPE available, even in the first wave of data collection in March 2020. Although only about half of agencies rated their "ability to provide for PPE to their officers," as either good or excellent, more than half had provided protective equipment and also "tasked their first-line

---

[44] Shjarback and Magny, 2020.

[45] In the California survey, most respondents indicated that their departments had been "flexible in allowing officers to self-quarantine" (Shjarback and Magny, 2020, p. 6).

supervisors with regularly inspecting, monitoring, and supervising the use of PPE."[46] By the second wave of data collection in May, only a small percentage of agencies reported PPE availability problems, and an even greater percentage of respondents had tasked supervisors with supervising PPE use.[47]

Policies around PPE use also varied from department to department. At one extreme, there was an example of a department that publicly *prohibited* its staff from wearing respiratory protection while on duty.[48] According to an unscientific poll conducted by the publication *Police1* of responders in general (although most respondents were police), a high percentage of departments had a policy that required officers to wear masks when interacting with the public. A lower percentage required mask-wearing inside department buildings or in vehicles with two or more people. The majority of departments were issuing masks to staff, although often only for frontline staff. A significant percentage of the respondents were skeptical of masks and were concerned about their ability to communicate with the public while masked, but a larger portion thought that wearing a mask improved public perception about their department.[49] A separate survey of PSAP staff indicated that "use of—and even access to—face coverings and other protective equipment in PSAPs is inconsistent."[50] About half of respondents said that their PSAPs were mandating masks but that mask use is complex when their main task is telephone communication.

But even if staff were provided with masks and their managers were tasked with monitoring their use, it was not certain that officers would wear them. As was the case in the responses to 9/11,[51] there have been public reports of officers being unwilling to wear respiratory protection.[52] Echoing those reports, several of our panelists emphasized that, at least in some departments, it has been difficult to get officers to use respiratory protection that would reduce their chance of being infected by COVID-19.

> One of the major challenges that we had was convincing a bunch of young men and women, who typically have an alpha mentality, that they have to take care of themselves, and they have to take care of the people around them. And that wearing a mask—even though it might not be the sexiest thing or the most attractive thing—is still productive for keeping our workforce . . . healthy.
>
> – Law enforcement management panelist

---

[46] Lum, Maupin, and Stoltz, 2020a, p. 2.

[47] Lum, Maupin, and Stoltz, 2020b, p. 3.

[48] Neuman, 2020.

[49] Greg Friese, "Face Masks: Here's What Cops, Firefighters, Medics and COs Have to Say About Use, Policy and Effectiveness," *Police1*, July 31, 2020.

[50] National Emergency Number Association, 2020, p. 2.

[51] See discussion in Brian A. Jackson, D. J. Peterson, James T. Bartis, Tom LaTourrette, Irene T. Brahmakulam, Ari Houser, and Jerry M. Sollinger, *Protecting Emergency Responders: Lessons Learned from Terrorist Attacks*, Santa Monica, Calif.: RAND Corporation, CF-176-OSTP, 2002.

[52] For example, see the following sources from two different geographic extremes: Michaela Winberg, "Some Philly Police Aren't Wearing Masks, and the City Won't Enforce the Rule," Billy Penn newsletter, June 30, 2020; and Emily Elena Dugdale, "They Got the Memos, But LA Cops Still Aren't Wearing Masks," *LAist*, July 6, 2020.

> I'm not sure if others have faced this as . . . one of the things that we've experienced was just getting officers to comply and get used to using the PPE . . . it's been somewhat of a challenge to get officers to comply. Lots of . . . in the field reminders from supervisors going on calls and ensuring that it's happening. But initially that was one of the sticking points.
>
> – Law enforcement operations panelist
>
> One of the challenges is . . . getting officers to wear a mask and certainly to wear a mask when they're in the police department because they feel like it's home.
>
> – Law enforcement management panelist

In considering mask use in their departments, participants speculated that, for both good and ill, staff compliance with mask use had affected the infection rates they observed in their departments.

> Telling some of these young officers that they needed to also wear a mask and they needed to show leadership [or] it'd be kind of difficult for us to go out and enforce a mask ordinance . . . became somewhat of an issue. *And I think that's somewhat contributed to the number of positive cases that we ended up having here in the department.*
>
> – Law enforcement management panelist
>
> Our chief was very early on in mandating masks to employees before it became kind of socially acceptable. And we've just held true to that. And *we've been pretty successful in that we've only had one or two confirmed cases within our organization of [several hundred] employees.*
>
> – Law enforcement management panelist

When considering strategies to remedy the issue, participants suggested that messaging about protective measures should come either from police union representatives (where that was applicable) or from midlevel officers, on the assumption that the message would be more-enthusiastically received from those sources than from higher leadership.

> [If an officer hears from his sergeant,] "Hey, this is why we have to do it. This is the thought process" [rather than from the chief,] they're more likely to go along with it. It's just finding that communication line to say, this is why we have to do it at the end of the day. It's really just good leadership explaining why you're making decisions, why these processes [are in place,] and at the end, I don't care who gets credit for it. I just don't want my whole agency being sick.
>
> – Law enforcement management panelist

In an effort to reduce the logistical burden and costs associated with PPE, one participant who had contact with multiple law enforcement departments indicated that some departments were experimenting with reusable respiratory protection that could be decontaminated as a substitute for disposable N-95 or other types of face masks.

Providing COVID-19 Infection Data to Police as a Staff Protection Measure

In an effort to protect officers from exposure to COVID-19, some departments also had "dispatchers seek to screen for COVID-19 exposure or symptoms during calls" for service to inform the officers who would be sent to the scene.[53] Others, including some departments that were represented on our panel, received exposure information from state health departments and tracked it in their dispatch system to automatically alert officers.[54]

> Our state health department . . . does give us the addresses of residences or locations within the city where somebody has tested positive. But I know that not every state health department has been that forthcoming.
>
> – Law enforcement operations panelist
>
> The other thing was for us . . . what we do is we enter into our dispatch system every day where the infections are, what apartment building it is, what address it is and what name it is. And obviously there's some privacy concerns there, but we felt that public safety trumps privacy . . . knowing that just gave the cops, a nice peace of mind knowing that when they came in, they could go into a building, they knew there were people in there, in fact, so . . . even going in the elevator, they had a heightened situational awareness.
>
> – Law enforcement management panelist

Health agencies are allowed to share individually identifiable information with law enforcement and others under federal regulations as part of managing a public health emergency like that posed by COVID-19. However, given the current environment, their doing so has been controversial in some instances.[55] State laws and regulations also might restrict information-sharing. Available information indicates that this type of information has been shared in the majority of states as part of the response to the pandemic: Associated Press reporting from May 2020 stated that "public officials in at least two-thirds of states are sharing the addresses of people who tested positive with first responders—from police officers to firefighters to EMTs. . . . [And] at least ten of those states also share the patients' names."[56] However, in some states, law enforcement was not given access to data, even after pursing the issue in court. For example, Illinois police departments sued their local health department to

---

[53] Brooks and Lopez, 2020, p. 11.

[54] For example, the Tennessee Health Department was providing names and addresses of individuals who tested positive for the virus to law enforcement (Anita Wadhwani, "State Health Department Gives Names, Addresses of Tennesseans with COVID-19 to Law Enforcement," *Chattanooga Times Free Press*, May 8, 2020).

In Minnesota, the governor signed an executive order providing case data to 9-1-1 dispatch centers (Marielle Mohs, "Coronavirus in MN: Gov. Walz Signs Executive Order Giving COVID Case Data to 911 Dispatch Centers," *WCCO CBS Minnesota*, April 11, 2020).

[55] US Department of Health and Human Services, Office for Civil Rights, *COVID-19 and HIPAA: Disclosures to Law Enforcement, Paramedics, Other First Responders and Public Health Authorities*, Washington, D.C., undated. See also Association of State and Territorial Health Officials, "Public Health and Information Sharing Toolkit: Authorities and Limitations in Sharing Information Between Public Health Agencies and Law Enforcement," webpage, undated.

[56] Kimberlee Kruesi, "COVID-19 Data Sharing with Law Enforcement Sparks Concern," Associated Press, May 19, 2020.

access infection information but the appeals court ruled that they were not entitled to do so.[57] In other states, sharing was halted after the initial period of the pandemic, after law enforcement departments addressed PPE shortages.[58]

Even in instances where sharing is legal and appropriate, civil-society groups raised some concerns about the potential consequences. Those concerns included questions about whether individuals who had tested positive would receive equal protection by law enforcement, whether the data would be further shared with other agencies (e.g., for immigration enforcement) and would therefore potentially reduce the willingness of people to seek testing, or whether sharing the data would further undermine strained relationships between communities and police.[59] There also were reports of data breaches that might have compromised case information provided to law enforcement.[60]

Using Different Staffing Models to Minimize Department-Level Risk

As the examples of small departments—where the infection of the majority of staff or the need to quarantine after exposure shut down operations—demonstrate, the COVID-19 pandemic has had major effects on the functioning of some law enforcement agencies.[61] For crime labs, staff specialization could mean that laboratory functioning for particular types of testing depends on a very small number of staff. In that case, losing only a few people to illness or quarantine could cause specific parts of the lab's work to stop completely.

> If you have a small lab where maybe only two or three people can do a particular type of testing, you wanted to try to keep those people as far away from one another as you could, in case one person goes down, then you don't have both people sick and they can't do a particular type of test.
>
> – Law enforcement operations panelist

Some organizations, including police departments, laboratories, and PSAPs, faced staffing shortfalls even before the pandemic.[62] Concerns about the risk of contracting COVID-19 also led to additional attrition in some departments, with officers choosing to retire or resign out of concern for their and their families' health.

---

[57]   Charles Keeshan, "Court: Police Have No Right to COVID-19 Patients' Names, Addresses," *Daily Herald*, June 28, 2020.

[58]   Laken Bowles, "Tennessee Will Stop Providing COVID-19 Patient Data to Law Enforcement, First Responders," *News Channel 5 Nashville*, May 27, 2020.

[59]   Kruesi, 2020.

[60]   "FBI Investigating COVID-19 Data Breach in South Dakota," Associated Press, August 21, 2020.

[61]   In a particularly compelling example, an officer involved in a multiagency enforcement operation tested positive, exposing tens of other officers to the virus and requiring their quarantine ("Law Enforcement Officer Tests Positive for COVID-19, Exposes 41 APD Employees," *KOB 4 News*, April 19, 2020).

[62]   National Emergency Number Association, 2020.

> We are understanding because the . . . [nearby] department went through quite a bit of attrition when COVID hit. A lot of deputies decided that was not the job for them. They had quite a bit of folks resign early on, which has [hurt the capacity of our corrections department] just due to . . . staffing.
>
> – Law enforcement operations panelist

In an effort to manage the risk to department operations, one common response was to develop alternative staffing models and shift structures to reduce the chance of large portions of staff being exposed or infected simultaneously. Early in the pandemic, about three-quarters of respondents to IACP and GMU's questionnaire indicated that their agency had plans to deal with large numbers of officers being affected by COVID-19, and a little less than three-quarters rated their agency's ability to "manage exposed officers" as excellent or good.[63]

> We went through a handful of different shift work schedules, where we'd split each section in half and split the lab in half. And then some come in really early in the morning, some work later hours, just so if a section did have a positive case come through, we would decrease the amount of risk for shutting down the entire laboratory, which is what we are worried about.
>
> – Law enforcement management panelist
>
> We made doomsday plans for what . . . the department [is] going to look like if we lose 10 percent of the workforce, 20 percent, all the way down to 80 percent, and it is just shuffling schedules and making sure that we have our most core functions working. Thankfully that didn't become necessary. . . . It was manageable, [but] I guess that the lesson that we learned was just plan for the worst.
>
> – Law enforcement operations panelist

Most approaches to managing agency-level risk focused on creating cohorts of staff who worked together but did not interact, so if one cohort was exposed, the other could continue to work. In an example provided by a police department contact from an agency from the Western half of the country, staff was split into four cohorts, with two covering a 14-day period with officers working 12-hour shifts (seven days per cohort) while the other two cohorts isolated for 14 days. Participants in our panels described similar arrangements, with groups of staff (both sworn and civilian) rotating into and out of the office to limit risk to the entire workforce, similar to the examples in published analyses of law enforcement adaptations to the pandemic.[64]

---

[63] Lum, Maupin, and Stoltz, 2020a, p. 2.

[64] Jennings and Perez, 2020.

> So we shifted very quickly from [our standard schedule] . . . to 12 hour tours where they work two days, two 12-hour days back to back. And they were off for six days and we just did the math and said, all right, well, if we can get them in for two tours, they're off for six, they're in another two and they're off another six. Well, that equals 14 [if a shift was exposed and needed to quarantine]. And we . . . very carefully [follow] the CDC guidelines, because you don't want to deviate too far from that.
>
> – Law enforcement management panelist
>
> We basically went on a platooning system and every bureau, every facility may have some different nuance, but essentially you only had half of the workforce at work at any given time. . . . In patrol, we put all the detectives and administrative support staff on a patrol schedule. So they were all working with one half of the week or the other with cleaning days in the middle. And that type of adjustment was effective, but it was substantial.
>
> – Law enforcement operations panelist

According to one panelist, agencies made more–fine-grained adjustments to limit the risk of individual transmission, including going from teams of two officers in cars (who would therefore be exposed to one another for long periods in a confined environment) to single-officer cars.[65] According to a panelist who was involved with multiple law enforcement agencies, where decisionmakers still felt that two officers per car were needed for physical safety, such measures as fixing officer assignments for longer periods (so the same officers would be riding together, limiting close exposure to others) and the frequent decontamination of vehicles were used.

After taking all the steps they could to reduce the risk, departments prepared to detect and respond to staffing challenges. In one department represented on our panel, the agency developed a near–real-time dashboard for staffing at different stations (within a large metropolitan department) to make it possible to react quickly to staffing constraints within individual pieces of the agency. According to another panelist, in other areas, this role was reportedly taken on at the regional level by intelligence fusion centers that collected daily data on staffing numbers, infections, and quarantines among staff at both law enforcement and other emergency responder agencies to help manage workload and ensure continuity of response operations.

Although platooning and other models for breaking up the workforce and limiting overall agency risk worked well for larger departments, particularly those with the flexibility to move staff from investigative or other functions to supplement building multiple separate patrol platoons, these strategies were much tougher for smaller and rural departments.[66] In building staffing cohorts, it is much harder to create multiple split cohorts when you have a handful of officers total, and there is much less margin for error in the event that an infection or exposure event occurs.

---

[65] Other agencies reportedly separated even training officers and trainees into separate cars to reduce exposure (Johnson, 2020).

[66] Hansen and Lory, 2020.

> We're a smaller department, which brought some unique challenges. We're 41 sworn. So [while larger departments could move units around to the street,] we really moved more toward reciprocal agreements with some of our local agencies surrounding those to ensure that we had adequate [staff] coverage.
>
> – Law enforcement operations panelist

Physical Infrastructure Challenges Limited Protective Approaches

In a theme that was common across all justice agencies, the nature of law enforcement physical infrastructure—police stations, dispatch centers, and other facilities—limited what could be done to reduce infection risk when staff still had to work in person. Many buildings are old and do not have good ventilation systems, and many put staff members in close proximity to one another. Those limitations forced the pursuit of other strategies; when there was not available space for risk management, staff could not work in person.

> Early on, we realized that a lot of what we thought would work, *definitely* didn't [work]. We stood up, for example, our emergency operation center with the fire department and quickly realized that traditional setting for social distancing did not work out very well. [So] we did end up making use of a virtual technology.
>
> – Law enforcement operations panelist

> With our staff, we have some areas where it's really not easy to spread out and have that kind of distancing within the laboratory. And so we have allowed for significant schedule flexibility for staff. They do have to do a lot of their lab work in the laboratory. It's only some administrative things that they are able to do either telework or at off hours by themselves, but when they were having these flexible schedules, they had to have a buddy so that no one was working in the lab by themselves.
>
> – Law enforcement management panelist

> One of the things we're exploring is the communications dispatch system. It's a big one because . . . call takers and dispatchers are all confined in a very small area by the nature of their work. . . . Because of the very, very small area they're in, if one gets sick, you could lose the entire shift. And then what do you do?
>
> – Law enforcement management panelist

> We've got some pretty old facilities here that our folks are in, which caused us some concerns with the air filtration system. And then also being able to distance our folks with the buildings being kind of old. So that, that became somewhat of a challenge for us too.
>
> – Law enforcement management panelist

Mental Health and Stress Management Are Critical

Although the focus to this point has been on officer and staff physical health, stress and mental health were flagged as a critically important concern as well. The circumstances surrounding the COVID-19 pandemic and the risk of getting infected; the risk of bringing the virus home to at-risk family members;[67] and the stresses of losing family, colleagues, friends, or others to the disease have added stress to an already stressful occupation. The effect of the national protests focused on law enforcement and criminal justice also cannot be ignored, combined with the risks associated with COVID-19 circulating in the community. At the same time, pandemic demands on departments have made it more difficult for individuals to manage stress: One participant on our panels reported that, as of our workshop dates in September 2020, there had been no vacations approved in their department for months, setting up a "recipe for burnout."

> I know officers who haven't seen their families in months because they're staying, living separately from them to protect them.
>
> – Law enforcement management panelist
>
> [The officers are also dealing with what] we called a guilt by occupation . . . family members were afraid to let people know they were related to a cop . . . [and] with some of the young recruits, they're getting a lot of pressure about "Why are you in this field?" You know, you just started, let's get out before somebody gets hurt.
>
> – Law enforcement management panelist

Similarly, uncertainty around the risk of different activities and, as we learned more about COVID-19, changes in guidance were cited by our panel members as sources of added stress for staff. Although such a dynamic is unavoidable as scientists and public health experts learn more about the effectiveness of different measures, feeling that guidance and rules are changing frequently is still challenging for personnel.

> Certainly at the beginning of this whole time of pandemic, it seemed like the instructions and the guidance that we were being given for how to work safely was changing. I mean, not only daily, but sometimes like 15 minutes after you give guidance, something comes in that's different. It causes confusion. It makes people more stressed out and anxious. . . . It's stressful for you, stressful for everyone.
>
> – Law enforcement management panelist

Just as schools being closed and other consequences of the pandemic have affected a large portion of the country's workforce, they affected criminal justice workers. In addition to work stress, law enforcement officers, civilian staff, and forensics practitioners had to manage challenges in child care, such as being put in the role of technical support for online schooling, and other demands. Individual officers faced and continue to face different circumstances; for example, an officer whose spouse is sheltering at home might have very different pressures

---

[67]   In an effort to address the stress associated with an officer's potential to bring the virus home to their family when they were exposed and had to isolate, some departments are providing alternative lodging. However, doing so substitutes the stressor of family isolation for health concerns. See, for example, Richard Winton, Matt Hamilton, and Benjamin Oreskes, "LAPD Has Quarantine Site for Officers: Biltmore Hotel in Downtown L.A.," *Los Angeles Times*, April 15, 2020.

than one whose partner is also in an essential occupation and must continue to work through the pandemic.[68]

> And that was one of the things we started seeing, a significant increase in officers coming into counseling because of problems with what was happening with our schools. The teachers really didn't know how to do remote teaching, the kids weren't used to dealing with remote teaching, and the parents were unsure how to help. So it was creating these ongoing conflicts within the family.
>
> – Law enforcement management panelist

Panelists described actions that departments were taking to try to address or reduce these stressors on staff. Although some of the changes in work scheduling were intended to reduce COVID-19 risk to agencies, the increases in flexibility and the ability for some staff to work from home helped manage family stresses. Other steps included seeking out alternative approaches to manage child care issues for staff with young children.

> The YMCA was very helpful to offer first responder child care. So that helped us bridge that gap.
>
> – Law enforcement operations panelist
>
> We also worked hard communicating with our staff, letting them know the information that we had at that time. Moving into the kind of . . . challenges that it created for the lab is the same as you'd expect in terms of just continuing to get all the testing that was needed to get done completed while still juggling the staff shortages that we had at different times, whether that was through different quarantines or people having to deal with their children and no schools and things like that. So we just worked to try and come up with new ways and give them a lot more flexibility with their scheduling.
>
> – Law enforcement management panelist

Given the confluence of stresses staff were dealing with during the pandemic, there was an expanded need for mental health support for officers and other staff. As has been observed for the general population, there are concerns about how emergency responder populations are seeking to deal with the stresses they are under and the longer-term consequences of coping mechanisms.

> We have increased officer anxiety, increased trauma [among officers] that's being triggered. We have increased unhealthy coping, like alcohol and pain pills and [other coping mechanisms].
>
> – Law enforcement management panelist

---

[68] In their questionnaires, which were sent to officers in California, Shjarback and Magny, 2020, reported that many officers reported challenges with children in remote education, issues related to child care, and challenges when they had spouses who were also essential workers.

The need for increased mental health support has manifested in increases in calls to helplines and in resources within departments. According to one source, two helplines that are focused on law enforcement, Cop2Cop, at Rutgers University, and Copline, based in Freehold, said they have recorded recent increases. Cop2Cop reported 2,718 more calls and other messages during the first eight months of the year, compared to the same period in 2019, while Copline logged a 74 percent increase in calls."[69] Panelists indicated that there had been very large percentage increases in requests for counseling from within-department resources. Participants in our panels described their departments providing various resources to their staff, ramping up peer support options and employee assistance, connecting with community chaplains as an additional source of counsel, and exploring other mechanisms to better respond to mental health needs and improve the resilience of their staff to stress.[70] Other departments were seeking out ways for leadership to show appreciation for staff efforts. As is the case for other responses to the pandemic, however, many of these options are easier for larger and better-resourced departments than small ones with relatively few officers and a much narrower variety of options to provide support.

> [The] first [resource we distributed] was about dealing with the pandemic, then dealing with the quarantine. And then, talking about how to balance one family member being out in the community and the other having to homeschool and the different stressors there.
>
> – Law enforcement management panelist
>
> We've poured a lot of resources into [responding to staff mental health]. We kind of basically took a lot of our peer support and other services and just really expanded it and checked in as much as possible with all the officers on the patrol squad.
>
> – Law enforcement operations panelist
>
> Agencies [need to] have a good [employee assistance program] that officers know is going to be confidential . . . where they feel that the process is legitimate and truly respectful of their privacy. We started, in addition to our employee assistance program or in conjunction with it, a peer support program as well. And again, the same has to apply: There [have] to be rules of confidentiality that the officers know are respected.
>
> – Law enforcement operations panelist

In an effort to better meet officers' needs, participants in our panels described alternative mechanisms for delivering mental health support to officers, including pursuing virtual models to deliver telehealth counseling. Although some had positive views of such options,

---

[69]   Blake Nelson, "More Law Enforcement Officers Calling Helplines as Protests and Coronavirus Pandemic Add Stress to Stressful Job," Officer.com, September 10, 2020.

[70]   Alternative sources for counseling and private discussions of work stresses could be critical for rural departments, where mental health providers might be fewer and less accessible.

Although their data were collected in the first quarter of the pandemic (May 2020), more than half of Shjarback and Magny's respondents disagreed or strongly disagreed with the statement "My agency is taking active steps to maintain officers' mental health during this crisis," suggesting that a focus on officer mental health might not be equal across departments (Shjarback and Magny, 2020, p. 6). IACP and GMU did not have similar questions in their data collection.

panelists indicated that some officers were more comfortable doing in-person counseling sessions, and for individuals in severe distress, virtual options would not be good enough to meet clinical needs.

> The other thing we wanted to look at was how to deliver mental health services. So what we did there is provide a variety of options. We still were willing to do in-person mental health counseling, obviously sanitizing and masks and distance and stuff. But then we also found a series of telehealth sites where they could get on. And [they were] pretty well secured and we didn't have to worry about breaching confidentiality. So we really tried to give all the officers and the family members options, depending on what they were comfortable [with]. Surprisingly, we had a lot of officers [who wanted] to still keep coming in on a face-to-face basis. They felt a little more comfortable there.
>
> – Law enforcement management panelist
>
> Let's just say we had a suicidal officer, you are not going to do a telehealth session with that individual. I'm going to meet face to face with that individual in a private confidential office setting. But then you try to put in place things to minimize the risk of that in-person activity.
>
> – Law enforcement management panelist

Recruiting and Training Virtually

Because training programs—both initial academy training and in-service training efforts—bring together many people from different areas and locations, the suspension of training activities was an early reaction to the pandemic.[71] It was certainly not universal, however. In their data collections, IACP and GMU reported that only about one-third of responding departments had done so, and more than half were still continuing recruitment and hiring, necessitating the training of new recruits, although some had longer-than-expected timelines because of the practicalities of doing so during the pandemic.[72] For departments that had pre-existing staff shortages, halting recruitment and hiring was difficult, particularly because some departments had staff leave and because pandemic conditions have made recruitment more challenging for others.[73] But continuing business as usual has risks.

> This is a very challenging question because I know like at [our department], at the police academy, we continued on with our recruit classes, right? Because the show must go on, the community must be protected and served. And then it only took one person who was positive to infect most of the class and shut down the whole academy. And so I think there's going to be a tension there between trying to meet the demands of the community and trying to minimize risks and look out for the well-being of your employees.
>
> – Law enforcement management panelist

---

[71] Brooks and Lopez, 2020, p. 11.

[72] Lum, Maupin, and Stoltz, 2020a.

[73] National Emergency Number Association, 2020.

As was the case for other departmental functions, agencies that had existing technology investments that supported virtualizing parts of their recruitment and training options had an easier time.

> We had shifted to more of an online recruiting platform prior to the pandemic, so that was very helpful for us. We struggle immensely with recruitment as it is. So, we're having difficulty figuring out [whether current challenges are] pandemic-related or social unrest–related. Fortunately, that was one of the areas where we were doing a lot of things online.
>
> – Law enforcement management panelist

Others worked to move the process online, and in their data collection, IACP and GMU reported that agencies were seeking to provide online alternatives to in-person training (where the fraction of reporting departments increased between their two waves of data collection).[74] A smaller number of agencies were using hybrid approaches that combined online and in-person elements. In some cases, our panelists expected these alternative approaches to persist after the pandemic because of the advantages in cost and flexibility they provide.

> The state academy was closed for a time. They're now open again. But they've cut about 80 hours of hands-on training specifically with defensive tactics and training scenarios out of their instruction. So we are now trying to pick that up as we're hoping to get officers on the street that are trained and have good practical hands-on experience. And so far, that's being done by trying to reduce the number of people in training together. So doing some defensive tactics trainings with an instructor, everybody's got masks on and just some small groups.
>
> – Law enforcement management panelist
>
> What I would anticipate in the future—clinically and nonclinical training—is that that [virtual access] would expand. . . . I don't think that the in-person [activities] will go away. You know, it will at some point come back, but I don't think that the telehealth or the virtual trainings or the whatever will ever go away, because it's a viable option, especially when you think about the defunding issues right now in cities.
>
> – Law enforcement management panelist
>
> [Our] training folks . . . had to come up with some ways of teaching online. I was worried about what it would look like having watched my kid in virtual school, where it was a disaster. But they did a really good job of coming up with teaching topics and then activities that somebody went to do. . . . And I think that, although they don't think that they should get rid of all in-person training now, they see that something that they had said before could not be done, can be done. We have jurisdictions [in remote areas of the state], where it's really difficult for them to [travel for] training, and so I think that it's going to provide a really great opportunity to have choices, instead of necessarily replacing the way that we used to do things.
>
> – Law enforcement management panelist

---

[74] Lum, Maupin, and Stoltz, 2020a; Lum, Maupin, and Stoltz, 2020b.

However, among our panelists, there were concerns about the effectiveness of online training models, particularly for new recruit academy training. Furthermore, for advanced training for leaders (including such examples as the FBI Academy) or other complex training requiring scenario-based exercises, such as de-escalation courses, there were questions about whether online models could provide the most-important elements of such programs. Some of the training that would respond to concerns raised in the national protests—including de-escalation and other training to reduce use of force—is among the most difficult to successfully deliver virtually.

> They were doing a lot of this virtual stuff and they were, to be blunt, very weak in [some] skills when they tried to apply them out into the streets. So a lot of departments had to do remedial training quicker, like within a month or two, once they hit the streets. So I think those critical things we have to do hands on.
>
> – Law enforcement management panelist
>
> [For command-level training from places like the FBI Academy,] we are certainly feeling it here in our inability to provide that kind of experience and the relationship-building that occurs in person. I don't know if we could replicate that with virtual training. But it's certainly something that we're missing right now.
>
> – Law enforcement management panelist

Pandemic Policing, Public Health Enforcement, and Public Education

In our workshops, the role of law enforcement in contributing to managing the pandemic was a central topic, and one in which the experiences of participants differed considerably based on the area of the country they policed and the local landscape of the pandemic. Practitioners from areas that had been intensely affected and had given police central roles had considerably different experiences from those in areas that had been less affected at that point in time or in areas that had adopted much weaker public health strategies. Early in the pandemic, analyses examined the variety of roles that law enforcement were taking in different areas of the country:

> The police are often tasked with communicating voluntary measures, such as social distancing, and mandatory measures, such as quarantines and mandatory lockdowns, and the consequences for violations. For example, Phoenix [police department] officers were assigned to go to local businesses to explain the statewide orders and educate staff about safety measures. This may also involve communicating the value of compliance with these measures for the common good and reassuring frightened residents.

> In the immediate aftermath of the pandemic, the Los Angeles Police Department . . . shifted many detectives and other personnel to daily patrol in highly visible areas, while the Los Angeles County Sheriff's Department . . . assigned deputies from more specialized units to work in crowded public areas, such as grocery stores, to help maintain public order. . . . In Santa Cruz County (California), the Sheriff's office created a specialized Compliance Contact Team where deputies were specifically reassigned to recreational areas in the county,

such as beaches and parks, to find social gatherings of groups and direct individuals to disperse.[75]

Other organizations provided guides for law enforcement authorities in enforcing public health orders and compliance with such measures as quarantine.[76]

In the data collected by both IACP and GMU and Shjarback and Magny, respondents cited some of these activities, including increasing presence at grocery stores and smaller percentages of officers becoming actively involved in enforcing public health measures. As discussed previously, some law enforcement organizations publicly rejected roles in public health enforcement measures,[77] while others were more actively enforcing compliance with public health disease control efforts.[78] There also have been publicly reported examples of police having to enforce quarantine orders in some areas.[79] In some cases, the pandemic led public safety and law enforcement organizations to take on very different roles: "If you would have told me that my agency [a PSAP] would be the one managing self-quarantine registries, hot-meal-delivery registries and complaints about people not complying with the mayor's business order, I would have said, 'No, that's not really an appropriate place for our PSAP [to be involved].'"[80]

Among the participants in our panel, the roles that had been played by law enforcement differed considerably. There were some departments that had an active role in enforcement, and others adopted more of an educational posture with regard to public health infractions. In some areas, even if police did enforce measures, prosecuting attorneys did not plan to prosecute for violations of them, although participants did note having other types of recourse (e.g., to other state agencies) in situations where there was serious and continuing noncompliance.

---

[75] Jennings and Perez, 2020, pp. 695 and 694, respectively.

[76] IACP, "COVID-19 Public Health Protections," webpage, April 1, 2020b.

[77] Because mask-wearing was infused with such political context early in the pandemic, law enforcement organizations in multiple parts of the country rejected roles in the enforcement of universal mask orders. See James Kust, "These Wisconsin Sheriffs Say They Won't Enforce Gov. Tony Evers' Statewide Mask Order," *TMJ 4 News*, July 31, 2020; "Law Enforcement Agencies Refuse to Enforce Mask Orders," 2020; and Alexandra Yoon-Hendricks and Michael McGough, "Sacramento Sheriff, Other Capital Agencies Won't Enforce Newsom's Mask Order. Here's Why," *Sacramento Bee*, June 19, 2020, updated June 20, 2020.

[78] For example, see Stephanie Farr, "N.J. Has Charged More Than 1,700 for Violating Stay-at-Home Orders but Just a Handful of Citations Have Been Issued in Pa.," *Philadelphia Inquirer*, April 21, 2020.

[79] Adrian Mojica, "Police: Man Who Tested Positive for COVID-19 Charged with Escape for Leaving Quarantine," *WZTV Nashville*, May 10, 2020.

[80] Donny Jackson, "COVID-19 Could Have Lasting Impacts on 911 Practices, Speakers Say," IWCE's Urgent Communications, April 6, 2020.

We also had an issue early on with trying to keep up with all the emergency orders. They were changing, a lot of times they were vague and ambiguous. We were looking for what our authority was in this. We really didn't want to go with a very heavy handed . . . enforcement manner, but just knowing what our authority was if we got backed into a corner. Most of this ended up falling on our state partners, so we would pass those complaints over to state police and they finally stood up some frameworks for dealing with that.

– Law enforcement operations panelist

We did have to enforce . . . stay-at-home orders. We did have to enforce mask orders. . . . The only remedy available to us until our city commission and the county commission put a few ordinances into effect was arrest. And so we were very hesitant to arrest people for not wearing masks. And so we relied very heavily on issuing verbal warnings until we got a civil citation program in place to issue civil citations instead. . . . We did reach an agreement with our state attorney's office that the state attorney's office would not prosecute for curfew violations. And so if we needed to take care of a problem then and there, we would make the arrest knowing full well that the problem was solved that night, and that we wouldn't be putting any further resources into prosecution there.

– Law enforcement operations panelist

In addition to the state taking a very proactive stance on [social distancing and mask-wearing,] our city, our mayor, also put out stay-at-home orders and instituted social-distancing policies. So right off the bat, we were working with members of our community. We would get calls from individuals concerned about mask wearing . . . gatherings were also very high on the radar. So we had to figure out right away how to work with our community members to get them to comply. We haven't had one arrest related to failure to comply [with] either the city's orders or the state's orders.

– Law enforcement operations panelist

For police roles in supporting the public health response to the pandemic, the differences in policy that existed from place to place were a major challenge. Some of the differences in how measures were implemented were ascribed by our participants to vagueness in the executive orders that guided responses to the pandemic (e.g., within a state, an order shutting down nonessential businesses but providing no definition of what was essential would leave law enforcement to wade into a political debate by defining it for themselves, which often would result in different definitions than those used in the city or county next door). Many of the orders were litigated from a variety of perspectives, which increased uncertainty in the absence of clear judicial guidance.[81] Members of our community organization panel agreed with the

---

[81]   See discussion in Michael D. White and Henry F. Fradella, "Policing a Pandemic: Stay-at-Home Orders and What They Mean for the Police," *American Journal of Criminal Justice*, Vol. 45, 2020. Furthermore,

> [t]he United States Supreme Court, in a divided decision, has turned away a challenge to state authority to impose general public health restrictions that did not exempt religious institutions. While most state and federal courts have also rejected challenges to public health orders, an unprecedented number of courts have sided with the challengers and substituted the courts' judgment on public health safety measures for that of the state or local public authorities (Edward P. Richards, "A Historical Review of the State Police Powers and Their Relevance to the COVID-19 Pandemic of 2020," *Journal of National Security Law & Policy*, Vol. 11, No. 1, October 19, 2020, p. 83).

views expressed by law enforcement panelists that the lack of clarity and consistency was a major challenge.

> We also had to make sure that we were careful, because we're a tourist town, with having too much close contact with people. You know, people come to town, especially people who didn't want to wear masks, refuse to wear a mask, but they want to stop and they want to ask you directions, or they want to stop and ask you about different historical monuments and the officers—rightfully so—were very nervous about that, about getting too close to people without them wearing a mask [but they were also concerned about perceptions that they were being] rude or disrespectful to people.
>
> – Law enforcement management panelist

> But one of the other challenges that we had was *slowly we became not just . . . social-distancing police, but we also became the mask-enforcement police.* The mask-enforcement thing was something that became pretty political for us. Because at the time the mask . . . mandate came down, we were the first [in our state] to implement a mandatory face-covering law. That kind of put us at odds with the state as a whole, the county, surrounding law enforcement agencies. And then we started getting into this back and forth with people who were saying, "Well, the governor says that I don't have to wear a mask, but now you're saying that I do have to wear a mask. I'm just going to follow the governor's orders and I'm not going to follow your order." So we actually handled it pretty well. We made it a point to really focus in on education [rather than] enforcement and it actually worked pretty well for us.
>
> – Law enforcement management panelist

> I think the biggest challenge at the beginning of this was just working in the gray space, working where things weren't clearly defined. We had stay-at-home orders issued by the governor relatively early on in mid-March and immediately it fell [to] the law enforcement to decide how to enforce it, when to enforce it, and what the exceptions were.
>
> – Law enforcement operations panelist

> We had to make a kind of a judgment call [about whether a particular type of store was] critical or not. Obviously it was very political. We . . . were hoping the governor would say they are, they aren't and would take the burden off of us, but he . . . essentially kicked it back to the local county sheriffs and said, "You do whatever you want. You decide." So in [the county next to us], they said, they're not essential. And they went about basically citing . . . store owners and shutting them down. In [our county,] we made the other call, that they were, and so we left them alone. And that made half the population angry and half the population glad that we made that decision.
>
> – Law enforcement operations panelist

> A lot of [the governors' orders] were guidance to local actors. Some of them, in our estimation, pushed the problem back to local jurisdictions or jails instead of [taking] a holistic response. So that was a challenge.
>
> – Community organization panelist

The ambiguity and lack of clarity were particularly problematic given the national environment around policing, making some departments reticent to take steps that would be viewed as overreaching their legitimate authorities and hesitant to take actions that would reinforce views of police as responding excessively. They also viewed perceptions of police and the national political environment as constraints on their ability to participate in responses involving some communities or vulnerable populations. An example cited was non-English-speaking populations, where there were concerns about immigration enforcement that would make an initiative focused on COVID-19 that involved law enforcement less effective than one where police were not prominently involved.

> We have a state mandate for mask-wearing. And so . . . there's pressure for the law enforcement officers like at a grocery stores to follow up on mask compliance . . . And, that became kind of a problem in light of all the negative attitudes toward law enforcement, because what's the officer going to do to this little old lady? Trip her and Tase her to get her to wear a mask? So that became an issue.
>
> – Law enforcement management panelist
>
> There was a lot of ambiguity and lack of clarity in law enforcement's role in enforcing public health orders. As some of you have already alluded to, things like enforcing social distancing orders or mask mandates, law enforcement was really stuck between a rock and a hard place as to whether or not they would actually take enforcement action.
>
> – Law enforcement management panelist
>
> This region of the country is very large in chicken processing. So we have a number of national and international processing plants here in the region. And we have a large migrant and also non-native-speaking population here. And we started noticing a lot of them were getting sick. They were contracting and then spreading COVID-19. So a grassroots campaign was started with a vulnerable populations group. Initially, we were very much a part of that group. We were present in helping people to avail themselves of testing. And then we had to back off because of the issues related to social unrest.
>
> – Law enforcement operations panelist

Members of our panel cited examples of alternative models for enforcing public health measures that took police out of the issue. For example, some cities have begun to use environmental health inspectors as "mask ambassadors" to improve compliance with health-protection measures.[82] Others cited departments using privately hired security officers to remove police from an enforcement role. Although it is a potentially realistic path given current circumstances, such a strategy limits the contribution that law enforcement agencies can make to safeguarding public safety during pandemic conditions.

---

[82] Alison Kuznitz, "Mask Ambassadors Will Soon Help Charlotte Area Residents Follow COVID-19 Rules," WBTV, August 6, 2020.

Looking at enforcement approaches [of public health orders], I know there were a number of places where they did go to citations at the outset. I know some states looked at having public health agencies operate more of the enforcement. So I think getting that clear at the outset [is important] as well, so that when you're issuing an executive order, there's already guidance and clarity around how enforcement is going to be carried out and what the approach will be.

– Law enforcement operations panelist

One of the things that's been really beneficial for us is our city manager has slowly taken us out of the mask-enforcement business. We've created what we call city deputies. There are city employees [who are] actually deputized to go out and enforce that city ordinance. They can actually go out and write a citation for a violation of the ordinance, which frees up my folks and really keeps us out of being in the middle of a controversy as far as whether or not somebody is wearing a mask.

– Law enforcement management panelist

Members of our community organization panel in some cases agreed with some law enforcement panelists that direct police involvement, given the current environment and broader concerns, might not be a productive role.[83]

Our city took the [Coronavirus Aid, Relief, and Economic Security (CARES)] Act funding and paid the police overtime to do additional enforcement of social-distancing requirements, which I think was a bad idea because [that] criminalizes [noncompliant behavior], and I think that there are some questions about how to enforce aspects of the social-distancing requirements, everything from masks to crowd sizes to which businesses can be opened and so forth.

– Community organization panelist

I think it's absolutely right that we have to think of this in context with the protests. Very early on, protest policing and surveillance measures often took on the vernacular of public health . . . and what we found is the relationship—even the perceived relationship—between law enforcement and public health was undermining trust in public health initiatives.

– Community organization panelist

In efforts to play more-educational roles with respect to public health measures, some departments adopted nontraditional communication strategies. In previous sections, we discussed the use of COVID-19 infection data for officer safety purposes, but some departments developed ways to provide geographic information about disease burden to the public in an

---

[83] In a Vera Institute discussion of this issue, Brandon del Pozo, former chief of police in Burlington, Vermont, put it this way:

> I think the opportunity here is to see how far we can get by *brokering* these rules instead of *enforcing* them. . . . Health has what are called in the law, police powers, if you look at public health's authority it's a police authority, but it's not a legal authority as an end in itself, it's the authority to achieve a public health end . . . we're in the same boat of using laws to empower us to achieve public safety, not to enforce them as ends in themselves (Vera Institute of Justice, 2020b).

effort to educate them about the value of protection and social-distancing measures. The Marshall Project examined several such efforts in different cities, highlighting both the value of such initiatives and the privacy concerns they raise.[84] In our community organization panels, there was a discussion about concerns with these sort of technologies as examples of the broader trend toward providing more surveillance capability to local police and about how their use during the pandemic might shape their use afterward.

> We actually used a similar format we use for hotspotting—so the same way we . . . track crime metrics [on crime maps,] we started using the hotspots for infections. . . . Obviously there were some privacy concerns with respect to having this information, but [we] weren't using anyone's name or anything. We're just . . . point[ing] to a specific neighborhood . . . and saying like, "That place is red hot." And . . . we could also use that to do the proactive information-sharing with asking people to social distance. [We could] say, "Look, you're in a very, very challenging area right now where their cases are piling on day after day after day, you need to be extra special careful." So I think you can weave that into the whole aspect of information-sharing. . . . So when you show them something, an illustration on paper, to say, "Look at your neighborhood, look at your street. You really, really need to be careful here because you're seeing an uptick in cases."
>
> – Law enforcement management panelist

Just as the protests were raising concerns about equity in traditional policing activities and use of force, concerns were raised about how law enforcement agencies in different areas were enforcing public health directives and whether they were being enforced fairly in different communities.[85] Analyses in the press flagged these concerns: "Comprehensive data does not yet exist on how police are enforcing stay-at-home and social distancing orders. But a small group of early tallies showing a stark divide along racial lines has prompted concern from advocates and lawmakers who say police may be taking a harsher tact toward people of color."[86] There were particular concerns raised by civil-society groups in New York City that pandemic-related public health measures were being disproportionately enforced in minority communities. According to one source, "more than 80 percent of social distancing violation summonses—tickets which require court appearances and can lead to arrest warrants—were issued to black or Latinx people during the span between March 16 and May 5, despite the fact that those groups constitute just half the city's total population."[87]

---

[84] Simone Weichselbaum, "Have COVID-19? Cops May Have Your Neighborhood on a 'Heat Map,'" The Marshall Project, June 9, 2020.

[85] Members of our community organization panel cited disparate enforcement as a major issue and a challenge to the legitimacy of police activities through the pandemic.

[86] Justin Jouvenal and Michael Brice-Saddler, "Social Distancing Enforcement Is Ramping Up. So Is Concern That Black and Latino Residents May Face Harsher Treatment," *Washington Post*, May 10, 2020.

[87] R. J. Vogt, " Racial Disparity Spurs Challenge to NYPD COVID Policing," Law360, May 31, 2020.

Law Enforcement Was Affected by Other Justice System Components' Responses to the COVID-19 Pandemic

In our law enforcement panels, the connectivity of the different components of the justice system—and the effects that strategies related to the pandemic that were adopted in other components had on police—was prominent. Participants expressed some frustration with other components closing down while police had to keep performing their roles and with how their shutdowns affected the ability of law enforcement to be effective. Officers were concerned about the implications of the courts being largely closed down; that meant that the decision of an officer to arrest someone and take them into custody might result in the person being incarcerated for an indefinite period before having their day in court.

> We see some of these businesses and other government entities . . . that still haven't figured out how to reopen and get along with business while all of us on this call pretty much had to continue our operations without any break at all.
>
> – Law enforcement operations panelist
>
> People [were] sitting in jail for [an extended period] before they were able to have their day in court. And that's just not fundamentally what the role that police officers should be put into is to take someone's freedom away . . . without any type of judicial review, other than a paper review of the probable cause statement or something very minimal like that. So I think it erodes the public trust in the whole system.
>
> – Law enforcement operations panelist

Because police are the most outward-facing of the justice system agencies, it makes sense that they would be significantly affected by changes made in courts, corrections, and other agencies. Law enforcement had to manage new requirements regarding infection-control measures in courts or jails, which complicated their efforts to continue to function. But it was not just traditional justice agencies.[88] Panelists also noted the responses of social service agencies and service providers as a challenge—those agencies' partial or complete shutdowns to manage COVID-19 risk hamstrung diversion efforts and the use of alternatives to incarceration at a time when having those options available is increasingly important. Changes in policy by some parts of the justice system meant that arrestees had to be taken to different facilities, and sometimes much farther than usual, to be processed, which burdened police officers.

> [Other external agencies that are not operating create cracks in the system. For example,] social services—trying to reach out to them, we were getting very, very much delayed responses and continued to get delayed responses in situations that are critical for their presence. So that continues to be a struggle.
>
> – Law enforcement operations panelist

---

[88] In fairness to their partners, some participants noted unintended positive outcomes from their approaches (e.g., a crime lab participant mentioned that the halt in court cases gave staff time to clear a substantial backlog of work, and a law enforcement panelist described how they redeployed staff who normally would have been working the courts to supplement their force elsewhere).

Even if some panelists were frustrated with how the choices made by other parts of the justice system affected them, there was still a strong message that different agencies in the system have to work together and that it is not effective to point fingers elsewhere.

> [What was critical was] recognizing the different roles that people had and never, *never* letting people play the health officer against the sheriff or the governor against the sheriff, just never buying into that conflict. Whenever the media or some politician would try to draw us into that, we would always just sidestep it and say, "[Y]ou know, we're all in this pandemic together, everybody's affected professionally and personally, and we will only get through it if we work together."
>
> – Law enforcement operations panelist

In some cases, police departments relied directly on other agencies for very tangible support. In both of our panels, participants spoke about coordinating stocks of PPE and sanitization supplies with other public safety agencies (e.g., their local fire department) and forming reciprocal agreements with other regional law enforcement agencies to share supplies when availability was limited. According to one panelist with knowledge about multiple law enforcement departments, knowledge-sharing with fire and emergency medical services (EMS) on such topics as vehicle and equipment decontamination also supported some departments' efforts.

> Some of the significant adjustments I've seen are more collaboration and more partnerships. People have had to rely on each other and work together. And that includes everything from the more obvious solutions of partnering with an agency in your local jurisdiction [or] a neighboring agency to more-creative relationships like leveraging local distilleries for hand sanitizer [or] partnering with organizations outside of the criminal justice realm.
>
> – Law enforcement operations panelist

Panelists spoke about instances in which police departments played roles to take pressure off of other parts of the justice system (notably, using mobile technology to resolve warrants in the field to clear pressure on the courts). However, they also discussed situations where better connections among agencies could have helped. One of the shifts in crime that was flagged by panelists and reported in the press was a significant increase in mental health–related calls. The pandemic increased stress for the entire population, and likely was more difficult for individuals with preexisting mental health challenges. To protect their staff, many service providers had to reduce operations, which made it more difficult to serve individuals in need (see Chapters Six and Seven for a related discussion). Panelists on both our law enforcement and community organization panels noted that cuts by service providers meant that people who went into crisis and could not get care had to be dealt with by police. Panelists also noted the potential value of better links between medical providers and law enforcement, so that in police contacts with the public they could provide information on the best ways to seek care while minimizing potential spread of the virus.

> We have police actually, either with a tablet or with their iPhones, going to homeless [people] in the parks, connecting with the magistrate, [and] clearing warrants out in the park [or] going to the homeless shelter and doing it.
>
> – Court system panelist
>
> I think the transmission, a lot of it [happened] because we were sending people to the hospital. [We should] talk to the hospitals in advance and say, "When people call us, what do we want to tell them?" You know, people call the police for all kinds of things. They may even call when they don't necessarily have a need for service, but they're asking for information. So to have that all . . . married up together in a real concise way, I think that that's something I would definitely want to do going forward.
>
> – Law enforcement operations panelist
>
> Effectively, what happened here was . . . on top of the courts being just turned off, every social service [agency] also kind of turned off. . . . We've seen . . . mental health [calls significantly] up, but overall we've seen crime go down . . . that's kind of a weird juxtaposition because, I think you would think these things would move together, but they're moving apart in this situation.
>
> – Law enforcement operations panelist
>
> COVID is definitely limiting access to the help that people need. So the [mental health] crisis centers were unable to be utilized because they were closed down [because of] COVID. And what we know is when we don't have access to that kind of care, it normally ends up in a criminal issue. So we are very concerned about that.
>
> – Community organization panelist

Funding and Defunding During the Pandemic

The COVID-19 pandemic has had massive economic consequences for the United States, and those consequences are affecting municipal budgets via reductions in tax revenue, decreased local economic activity, and the need for unplanned expenditures. Although some areas have tried to insulate public safety budgets from the cuts, police departments are not immune.[89]

> [We would have] made those investments a little bit differently, starting to write policy for the long haul . . . the way we decon[taminate] our cars even, those types of budgeting for that. . . . Some of that I missed, I'm going to have to rearrange some funds to account for decontamination and those types of things that just really carry a lot of expense that I hadn't planned for.
>
> – Law enforcement operations panelist

These fiscal dynamics are occurring simultaneously with national protests, part of which included the argument that police budgets should be reduced to enable more-robust funding of non–criminal justice approaches to crime and public safety concerns. But the options for real-

---

[89] Allan Smith, "Police Departments Face One-Two Punch: Defund Protests and Coronavirus," *NBC News*, June 28, 2020.

location might be limited in a reality of smaller budgets overall. A survey done by the National League of Cities that was released in May 2020 projected that more than "one-third of the three million city employees in the nation may be subject to furloughs, layoffs and pay cuts," and more than half of their respondents expected their police departments to be "significantly impacted."[90] Data, including responses to questionnaires distributed by PERF[91] and as part of the IACP and GMU data-collection effort,[92] that have been collected directly from groups of police leaders also have noted expectations of significantly reduced budgets. Furloughs and layoffs have already begun in some agencies.

> The mayor has declared furloughs for all civilians across the city [including the police department]. That includes the doctors who are supposed to work 24/7. So we continue to need to work 24/7, but without getting paid for that, we have to do the same amount of work, even though we will be furloughed and not receive the compensation for that work. So there's also uncertainty because layoffs may be coming.
>
> – Law enforcement management panelist
>
> There have been labs that have already started furloughs and layoffs, and that obviously adds to stress as well.
>
> – Law enforcement operations panelist

The shift in budget expectations was quite sudden in some areas, going from expectations of high revenue to a need to cut very rapidly.

> COVID hit not just at a time of a very strong economy nationally, but especially here locally. The last thing that we were thinking about here was making budget cuts, which is what we're looking at now. We were actually . . . asking for budget enhancements because we had all this extra money that we had no idea what to do with. And so you just always have to be ready for that, for that possibility that great budget that you have overnight may or may not be there. And you better have contingency plans to plan for manpower, to plan for doing more with less, even if it doesn't seem that way.
>
> – Law enforcement operations panelist

Our participants also indicated that, in some cases, the shift in funding has hit some programs that provide alternatives to criminal justice involvement, cutting directly against the goals of police reform efforts.

---

[90] Anita Yadavalli, Christiana K. McFarland, and Spencer Wagner, *What COVID-19 Means for City Finances*, Washington, D.C.: National League of Cities, May 2020, pp. 4, 13, respectively.

[91] PERF, *PERF Daily COVID-19 Report*, August 3, 2020d.

[92] Lum, Maupin, and Stoltz, 2020b.

> Since the pandemic has started up here robustly over the spring, we haven't been able to fund [co-responders to overdose incidents that connect individuals to treatment]. And we also haven't been able to get our resources out to folks who have overdosed. So it was very, very problematic at the moment.
>
> – Law enforcement operations panelist

The role that police did or did not play in COVID-19 response efforts could become a factor in future funding decisions. For example, in one state, funding applications for expenses related to the pandemic ask for information to support requests "on how your entity demonstrated enforcement efforts" as part of the pandemic response.[93]

Taking Stock and Moving Forward

In considering the path forward through the remainder of the pandemic and preparation for future public health crises, a key transition for departments was considering COVID-19 not as a wave that would pass rapidly but instead as something that had to be considered in planning for the longer term. That transition required planning not only for PPE or disinfection to continue but also about how alternative modes of policing might need to remain a part of U.S. law enforcement for some time.

> In dealing with our stakeholders and dealing with some of these other issues, we're starting to incorporate long-range planning with COVID components indefinitely. We were trying to find workarounds, and that seemed to be an exercise in futility at best. So we're planning for the long haul now, which I think has reduced some stress and has helped us make some appropriate investments for the future.
>
> – Law enforcement operations panelist

Having made that transition to thinking over the longer term, panelists saw the potential for law enforcement to make a greater contribution to public health efforts going forward. Although the complex environment around the pandemic might make such contributions difficult in the short term, with sufficient efforts to restore trust and build stronger relationships, panelists believed that there were significant contributions police could make to protecting not just public safety but also public health.

---

[93] Jens Gould, "State to Scrutinize Local COVID Enforcement as Part of Aid Decisions," *Santa Fe New Mexican*, July 28, 2020.

I think it's incumbent upon public officials and, in particular, law enforcement leaders to get tied in with public health to issue calming statements and guidance for the public. And regardless of where things are on a national narrative, I still firmly believe that most people look to law enforcement as being a calming factor and a guiding light. And I think, if we suffer through another pandemic or see this resurgence, it's important for all law enforcement leaders to get right out in front right away and work with their elected officials to send a solid message that is linear and focused. So everyone is on the same page. And I think that'll do a lot to prevent conspiracy theories and other things that seem to have besieged us over this past year.

– Law enforcement management panelist

Taking a longer-term view also requires keeping the uncertainties around the health effects of COVID-19 as part of the consideration. What those risks are and the extent of their effects is a major unknown in terms of the effect of the pandemic on police. Because law enforcement officers still have to be in contact with members of the public, and because of variation in the use of such measures as respiratory protection to reduce the chance of infection, the numbers of current officers who might have long-term consequences from COVID-19 exposure is unknown. Those unknowns reinforce concerns about law enforcement officer safety and wellness on such issues as fitness and health maintenance, stress management, and mental health. Existing initiatives to address these challenges might be even more important as the pandemic continues and after it has passed.

Different departments are treating COVID-19 infection differently, and those differences will have consequences for the individuals affected, their departments, and the country. Some departments are treating any COVID-19 infection as presumed to have occurred on duty, and others are not. In the first case, costs associated with long-term disability or death would be borne by worker's compensation and other benefits. In the latter case, at least initially, the costs would be borne by the individual alone. Changes have been made to federal legislation that make officers who are disabled or killed by COVID-19 automatically eligible for some federal benefits, creating another potential source of compensation.[94] But the costs of exposure could be significant, regardless of who eventually bears those costs.

Not every agency is giving their first responders the presumption that they contracted COVID on duty. [In my jurisdiction,] we are. We stress the importance of reporting any exposure to our employees, and reporting the exposure immediately. And we are treating them as on-duty injuries, which is really to the benefit of the employee, because if problems come up later on down the line that we can't foresee now, the officer did what he or she was supposed to do in reporting it. And it's on the books as a workers' comp[ensation] claim, but that's a big gray area for many other jurisdictions that are not affording their employees the same latitude.

– Law enforcement operations panelist

---

[94] Bureau of Justice Assistance, Public Safety Officers' Benefits Program, "About PSOB," webpage, undated; Ingraham, 2020.

The long-term cost of treating the 9/11 responders has been considerable, and, over time, it became a contentious political issue at the national level. Depending on how common and serious the long-term effects of COVID-19 end up being, there might be many more responders affected, even if the individual consequences end up being less severe. The differences in how areas are treating infection create the potential for the issue to play out differently across the country, with the effects treated as a duty-related disability in some areas and not in others. Furthermore, the specific decisions made by departments regarding protection and the potentially available evidence of officers' compliance with those decisions could affect whether an individual claim for compensation is successful.[95]

Promising Practices from the COVID-19 Pandemic Response

In considering the future state of the justice system, the following adaptations and innovations made during the pandemic seemed to our panelists to be valuable to preserve:

- **Maintaining virtual access to the courts:** Participants saw major advantages in making court appearances virtual for criminal justice practitioners (including forensic examiners and police officers) and citizens. The option was viewed as reducing costs for everyone when resource constraints likely will affect both government organizations and individuals.

- **Maintaining remote work options and schedule flexibility:** Although remote work options and schedule flexibility were driven by the necessity of minimizing the risk of transmitting the virus, panelists viewed such options as valuable for improving staff morale and retention in the long term. As a result, like in many private-sector firms, flexible schedules and remote work options were viewed as something to maintain in the longer term.

- **Continuing the use of virtual calls for service and alternative ways to efficiently meet the public's needs:** The use of web-based reporting and nontraditional responses to some crimes have been explored by some agencies as a cost-saving measure for some time. The pandemic pushed the adoption of these modes, but their value to the public and likely significant resource constraints are arguments for maintaining them.

- **Using virtual connectivity and new IT platforms to support leadership and community situational awareness:** In panel discussions, participants noted the value of law enforcement leaders being able to connect remotely and get information about what was going on. They thought it was useful in responding to questions from political leaders or the public. In addition, providing more data resources on department websites was noted as a strategy to strengthen communication when staff were not connecting with people in person. Both appear valuable to maintain.

---

[95] In some areas, occupational safety and health regulatory agencies have cited some law enforcement organizations for not sufficiently protecting their staff from infection (Nashelly Chavez and Lori A. Carter, "Santa Rosa Police Department Fined $32,000 Over Workplace Coronavirus Outbreak, Detective's Death," *The Press Democrat*, September 22, 2020).

We really hope that the things that have served us well and that [serve] society well after, after COVID, are here to stay, you think about people who are impoverished and they're, arrested, cited, and they have to make court appearances. If these people have jobs, they could lose their job for having to make that court appearance. Whereas now, if they can, if they could show up to court remotely for a traffic ticket for a misdemeanor charge. I think that's a net positive for society.

– Law enforcement operations panelist

It's a lot easier for laboratories to make these types of [flexible work schedule] changes . . . but what I do believe we'll find here in the long run is by providing our [staff] more flexibility to kind of set work schedules and by setting them up with work-from-home environments, I do think that that's going to increase morale and decrease burnout . . . that I do think it'll help our retention. And we've kind of set a price tag at every time we have an opening, it roughly costs our agency about $300,000 per opening for by the time you get someone else new in there, get them trained because there's long training periods. It can take sometimes one to two years to get someone to 100 percent up on board. So by decreasing turnover, I think that'll give future savings.

– Law enforcement management panelist

Pandemic Pressure as a Driver of Broader Criminal Justice Innovation

Because the pandemic and national protests focusing on equity in criminal justice occurred at the same time, it is nearly impossible to fully separate their effects. Nowhere is that more difficult than in considering how the pressures put on law enforcement by the pandemic and the changes made in response might shape future innovation and reform efforts. A major element of the protests has been calls to defund the police. Although for many, that slogan is an argument for the reallocation of public safety resources rather than a desire to punitively cut police budgets,[96] the reality of the economic fallout from the pandemic means that many police departments will face cuts because money has just gone away rather than there being a policy debate about whether and how pre-pandemic levels of funding should be divided between police and alternative approaches to solving public safety problems.[97]

The best arguments I've ever heard for defunding police came from police because time and again, they'd walk into court and say, "I can't be a social worker. I can't be a counselor. I can't be this." So stop doing it then, and we should give the money to people who can.

—Community organization panelist

---

[96] Michael J. D. Vermeer, Dulani Woods, and Brian A. Jackson, *Would Law Enforcement Leaders Support Defunding the Police? Probably—If Communities Ask Police to Solve Fewer Problems*, Santa Monica, Calif.: RAND Corporation, PE-A108-1, 2020.

[97] Rebecca Rainey and Maya King, "Defund the Police? It's Already Happening Thanks to the COVID-19 Budget Crunch," *Politico*, August 15, 2020.

> [Given all the additional pressures of the pandemic,] it's time to take a serious look at law enforcement's roles in communities because law enforcement, much like our school teachers, have been handed a whole lot of problems that are better handled by other agencies and other service sectors.
>
> —Community organization panelist

In spite of the fact that calls to change how policing is done must face the reality of tighter resources to implement change, the pressures of the pandemic on police and other agencies that support law enforcement activities could contribute to moving the sector forward in ways that previously were not seen as viable. At the minimum, the major shifts made in response to the pandemic broke through organizational inertia, which can be a major barrier to innovation and change in some agencies.

> The people who've been around a while who said, "Well, we can't do it that way cause we've never done it [that way]. We've always done it this other way." It's kind of pushed that out the window because it's forced them to think outside the box. So that challenge actually has helped us kind of move forward in some of our technology use.
>
> – Law enforcement operations panelist

One of the themes related to larger future changes that came through in our panels was the value of public communication and transparency. It has long been appreciated that it is valuable for police agencies to communicate effectively, explain their policies and actions, and be open when there are challenges that must be resolved. However, the COVID-19 pandemic provided yet another demonstration of the value of transparency in extreme circumstances, supporting departments' efforts to continue their core public safety missions and help protect the public from a very different hazard.

> [To fight misinformation,] we have to open ourselves up to be able to have those honest conversations and be willing to answer questions when they come to us. So it's really just being completely transparent as to why we're doing that, which isn't a bad leadership principle to begin with.
>
> – Law enforcement management panelist

The push provided by agencies' COVID-19 responses could contribute most to efforts to reduce the use of arrest and leverage diversion options as alternatives to always bringing people into the criminal justice system. Panelists cited greater use of diversion as a strategy to deal with jails not accepting people at the same rate during the pandemic, and multiple panelists cited the potential for limits in the use of arrest being carried forward, potentially fundamentally changing how police agencies do business. Although there have been arguments that police could arrest less while maintaining crime control and achieve better overall societal outcomes, the pandemic forced a broad experiment in doing so that is unlikely to have been conducted otherwise.

About two years ago, we implemented a civil citation program for marijuana posses-sion and a few other low-level felonies and city ordinance violations. And, of course, the knee-jerk reaction was . . . "Uh we're going to see increases in crime." Just the exact opposite has happened. We're again at record lows this year. 2020 is going to be an outlier because of COVID, but the same thing with the civil citations played out last year and the year before that's playing out now. We're making less arrests—we've made 50 percent less arrests—and our part one crimes year to date are down about 22 percent. So, we're just not seeing the connection that many of us assume would be there by making less arrests.

– Law enforcement operations panelist

I was trying to push my department more toward a philosophy of arrest as a last resort, except for mandatory arrests. And it was an uphill climb with them. We were making steady progress, but this has really pushed it forward. . . . I think that some of those officers who thought crime would just go off the chain if we did that are seeing it dif-ferently now. So that's, that's been helpful in that philosophical change for our agency.

– Law enforcement operations panelist

However, other panelists were cautious about considering such policy changes. Noting the unique circumstances of the pandemic, they were less willing to conclude that these strate-gies have not had negative effects on crime and victimization. This assessment highlights the need for research and evaluation efforts to measure the effects of the changes that have been made and support arguments for their continuation.

Policy Development and Evaluation Needs to Better Inform Decisions in Both the Short and Longer Terms

In the response to the COVID-19 pandemic, changes have been made in policing practices that are major diversions from usual practice, and research and evaluation efforts can support both assessments of effects to understand the full consequences of the pandemic and deter-minations about what lessons should be taken forward. Because some of the changes made to address public health threats also could be responsive to calls for reform, that need for assess-ment is even more critical.[98] In our panels, participants emphasized the need to collect data and measure outcomes; otherwise, the opportunity to persuade policymakers and the public to preserve beneficial practices might be lost in skepticism regarding their value or a gravitational pull toward business as usual when the pandemic recedes.

---

[98] See, for example, Kevin J. Strom, Andre Richards, and Renée J. Mitchell, *Defund the Police? How to Chart a Path For-ward with Evidence and Data*, Washington, D.C.: RTI International, July 22, 2020; and Vermeer, Woods, and Jackson, 2020.

> There's a great potential to find out what works and what doesn't in many of these cases. . . . So many of the things that from a research perspective, we've been asking [about] for dozens of years: Does this work? We have the unfortunate opportunity to really use this as an experiment, to really find out, what drives crime, what helps reduce crime? How do police actions actually influence crime? How does early parole and all these different things, how do they really impact crime rates? . . . We might be surprised by some of the answers, and I think we might be surprised how crime has shifted and how people respond to these different circumstances.
>
> – Law enforcement operations panelist

Once the short-term pressure of the pandemic lets up, there are policy recommendations and changes that have arisen in response that can be assessed through a deeper look at history. For example, recommendations have been put forward for agencies to "constantly maintain their inventories of PPE, including masks, gloves, gowns, eye-wear, and hand sanitizer,"[99] to ensure that, in the future, departments are not bedeviled by shortages like those experienced in early 2020. Although PPE availability was clearly a challenge in the early months of the pandemic, history—specifically, the post-9/11 period, when departments devoted considerable resources to buying PPE because of concerns about unconventional terrorism; that PPE expired unused—can help flesh out the pitfalls and challenges of achieving the goals of safety and response effectiveness.

> The only problem with tying [current lessons] to a future pandemic is that we don't know if what we learned in this one is going to directly translate to the next one.
>
> – Law enforcement operations panelist

Beyond questions of logistics design, however, the actions taken by police agencies to respond to the COVID-19 pandemic suggest multiple research and evaluation needs. As suggested in the quote above, the shock of the pandemic can provide the opportunity to look at questions apart from how the justice system responded, including questions about the nature of crime and how criminological theories of behavior hold up under very different circumstances. However, in terms of considering preparedness for future pandemics and the assessment of the national response to this one, the most-pressing questions focus on what was done and how it worked:

- What explains the differences from place to place in how crime and victimization changed during the pandemic?
- What have been the effects of nonarrest policies and actions taken in response to lower-level crimes during the pandemic? Do initially positive perceptions that there have not been increases in crime hold up over the longer term?
- How has the level of community trust and the public perception of the legitimacy of police departments affected their ability to contribute to managing COVID-19? Have

---

[99] Jennings and Perez, 2020, p. 698.

more-trusted departments been more effective or been provided with access to sensitive data or other resources to enable pandemic response? Are there other roles that law enforcement could productively play in public health response?

- How can areas better plan for future pandemics to limit the conflicts and imprecision in public health orders (e.g., what businesses were classified as essential, what level of enforcement by police is appropriate or useful) that made law enforcement participation in managing the crisis more difficult and controversial? Can a consensus be reached around definitions and categories to make it possible to respond more quickly, collaboratively, and effectively to future outbreaks?

- Are there more-effective ways to address the increase in mental health calls that has been observed during the pandemic, and how might alternative models inform consideration of police reform efforts? Can other models for mental health and substance abuse services (including addressing increasing overdoses) better respond to these needs?

- How effective have virtual models to recruit, select, and train new staff and officers been? Over time, how do the skills and capabilities of officers who went to the academy in cyberspace differ from those of officers who were trained in person?

- How satisfied has the public been with the provision of virtual police services during the pandemic, and how much have those alternative models saved departmental resources?

- Did digital divides among different groups in the public affect the effectiveness of communication and other strategies? Were alternatives used by departments that encountered such problems effective?

- How can law enforcement officers be better protected from infection risks during large-scale outbreaks, including increasing their compliance with the use of available protective equipment?

- What is the extent of the long-term physical and mental health consequences of COVID-19 for law enforcement officers? How has the pandemic affected officer suicide, which was a significant concern before the pandemic?

- What have been the effects of alternative work schedules and models on staff and law enforcement agencies, and how should those effects shape the decision to continue them over the longer term?

- What technologies are needed to support more law enforcement practitioners in flexible work models (e.g., systems to better enable dispatchers to work remotely)?

- What should be measured to better assess the effects of pandemic restrictions on alternative approaches, such as violence-reduction interventions, and assess the effectiveness of efforts to create virtual options for generally relationship-intensive face-to-face interventions?

- Given likely funding constraints on departments going forward, what are the implications of the types of programs and initiatives that will be cut? How do such cuts interact with reform efforts arguing for the reallocation of resources from police budgets?

Answers to all of these questions will contribute to moving beyond general lessons learned, such as departments' need for better plans for future events, and getting to a more practical understanding of how to build those plans according to the extent to which different strategies and measures were effective during the COVID-19 pandemic.

CHAPTER FOUR

The Court System

The court system is the central component in the criminal justice process and receives the flow of individuals arrested or cited by police. The role of the courts is to act as a constitutional check on the power of police and protect the rights of the accused; make a judgment of guilt or innocence; and determine an appropriate sentence through the combined efforts of the prosecution, defense counsel, judges, and others. The flow of individuals into the courts can be lessened by diversion out of the system or to alternative court processes that focus on specific concerns, such as addiction, mental health, or veterans issues, but the remainder of cases are resolved through the traditional processes of arraignment, resolution through plea bargain or trial adjudication, and sentencing to correctional custody or supervision.

Figure 4.1
The Courts: Prosecution and Defense

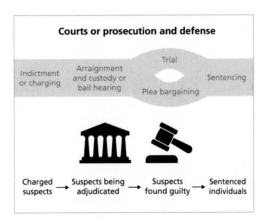

During the process, courts make decisions about whether individuals stay in custody or are released before trial (often with the posting of money bail). These decisions are driven by concerns about whether the person poses a danger and whether they will appear at a future court date. Court activities and timelines—particularly when defendants are held in custody because they cannot pay bail—are shaped by the requirement to protect an individual's right to a speedy trial and not spend an excessive amount of time detained before having their day in court.

The flow of individuals through the court system—some of whom are held in custody in jail settings, while some are released before trial—involves considerable numbers of people and therefore poses a risk of COVID-19 transmission. However, the accused are only a fraction of the people involved in courts. Employees of the court system include judges, administrative employees, and security staff, and cases have associated prosecutors, defense counsel, witnesses, forensic examiners, and citizens summoned to serve on grand and trial juries. The involvement of all of these individuals, and the fact that multiple cases are heard in a major courthouse simultaneously, mean that the courthouse is a point where people from different places come together to do the justice system's business.

Individuals who are affected by the crimes at issue have rights—and in some cases, these rights are protected by state law, their state's constitution, or the U.S. Constitution—to observe and participate in the process. Other activities bring people to the courthouse for access to justice, including seeking protection orders, solving civil disputes, and handling other administrative matters. Courts also are largely open to the public, and there is a constitutional imperative for them to remain so, because the actions of the courts should be open to public scrutiny as a protection of individual rights and a check on government power.

> The courts are likely the largest convener of people . . . in [our state]. . . . On a typical day in our courthouses, we require or bring in . . . 1 percent of our [state's] population, and a large percentage of those people do not have a choice about whether to attend, because we've ordered them to appear. . . . We have an obligation not only to those people, but to the rest of the country to get it right, because if we don't get it right, we can set the whole community, state, [and] country back.
>
> – Court system panelist

The many different people with reasons to come to the courts make this part of the justice system very vulnerable to infectious disease; more people together in one place means that the probability that someone will bring the virus with them is higher, and the potential consequences if it is passed on to others are higher as well. As a result, many courts changed how they performed their functions—in some cases, putting key parts of their functioning on hold to reduce the risk of transmission—to protect the ability of courts to function and to reduce the risk of a court creating a spike in infection more broadly.

Like the other parts of the justice system, the courts have a potential role to play in direct response to the pandemic, to the extent that criminal justice action and legal intervention become part of supporting actions to protect public health. The workshop we conducted on this topic focused on how courts responded to the challenges created by the pandemic. We did not focus on the courts' role in rendering judgments *related to* the pandemic, either broadly (e.g., ruling on the legality of public health measures) or individually (e.g., adjudicating the cases of individuals who violated those orders). As was the case for other branches of the justice system, previous public health events, including the H1N1 influenza outbreak in spring 2009 and the introduction of Ebola into the United States in 2014, led to efforts to define and describe the structure for court actions during a pandemic before the COVID-19 pandemic began. In 2016, a task force managed by the National Center for State Courts and the State Justice Institute published a benchbook laying out those legal frameworks.[1] However, it

---

[1]   National Center for State Courts, *Preparing for a Pandemic: An Emergency Response Benchbook and Operational Guidebook for State Court Judges and Administrators*, Williamsburg, Va., 2016.

should be noted that, reflecting the contentious national political environment surrounding the COVID-19 pandemic, legal action in multiple states targeted the authorities of state and local officials to enforce public health measures, placing some courts in the position of rendering judgment on the authorities and capabilities of other parts of government to respond to the pandemic.[2]

To reduce the risk of spreading COVID-19, court systems took several steps—some of which represent major changes from how court systems have historically functioned. Some of these changes have had significant effects on the capacity of court processes. The measures that were possible for a court system varied by jurisdiction because differences in administrative structures, legal frameworks, and other factors constrained what actions could be taken in some parts of the country. Different types of courts also had different constraints; what is practical and effective for a trial versus an appellate court, for the specialty courts that are key in diversion processes, and for other courts can be quite different.

> We cannot go back to doing things we did before, otherwise you do have this choice between safety and the justice system working . . . you don't have to pick one or the other, you can do both . . . we can have the safety and a running court system.
>
> —Court system panelist
>
> Doing both is what we absolutely have to do, but doing both looks different depending on where you are.
>
> —Court system panelist

At the time of our workshop discussions, at which point the country was more than six months into the pandemic, courts were exploring alternative approaches in an effort to increase court throughput and relieve stresses that were created by earlier infection-control measures. In doing so, participants emphasized that efforts must seek to restore functioning without sacrificing safety, because although ensuring that people accused of crimes can have their day in court in a timely way is critical, justice cannot be done if the safety of the participants in the process is compromised. As a result, doing so is not a return to business as usual, but is instead a search for new approaches that build on what has been learned to get to a court system that can operate more resiliently under the threat of infectious disease. Even then, there was concern about what would happen if and when cases started to increase again, as they did within weeks of our discussion. This reality emphasized that considering the changes made is relevant for the longer term and determining what further adaptations will be required for the next phases of the pandemic.

---

[2] The environment surrounding COVID-19 response—which included communicated threats to public health officials and, subsequent to our workshop, arrests disrupting an alleged terrorist plot to kidnap a state public official motivated by a view that the enforcement of public health measures constituted sufficient justification for violence—is an inescapable element of the context in which the justice system responded to the pandemic (see Michelle M. Mello, Jeremy A. Greene, and Joshua M. Sharfstein, "Attacks on Public Health Officials During COVID-19," *JAMA*, Vol. 324, No. 8, 2020; and Criminal complaint, *United States v. Fox, Croft, Garbin, Franks, Harris, and Caserta*, case 1:20-MJ-416-SJB, W.D. Mich., October 6, 2020). Although it was not a major focus in our workshop, one participant described efforts early in the pandemic to reassure judges that any orders would originate in the department of public health and that, according to the panelist, "they did not have the responsibility for issuing either an isolation or quarantine order, should that be a request of them." However, they would have the responsibility to respond if individuals did not follow orders issued by public health authorities.

Key Findings from the Court System's Response to the COVID-19 Pandemic

- Because of significant concern about virus transmission at courts, which are major conveners of people drawn from across wide jurisdictions, many court processes were initially stopped to reduce the risk of transmission.

- Courts were central in reducing populations in other parts of the justice system, including by reducing pretrial detention, limiting issuance of warrants, and facilitating release of individuals from custody where appropriate.

- To restart operations, some courts made significant shifts to virtual models for many types of proceedings and services. That has worked very well and has been viewed as providing benefits to both justice agencies and individuals who must appear. As a result, it is a potential practice to continue after COVID-19 has receded.

- Limitations in bandwidth, connectivity, and available technology make it difficult for some individuals or organizations to participate in virtual court processes. To address concerns about these digital divides, systems had to develop such approaches as loaning technology or providing other ways to join virtual proceedings.

- Virtual proceedings raised concerns about public access to courts and transparency. Some courts responded by streaming proceedings widely on the internet. However, that approach raised different concerns about the effect on participants in proceedings.

- Because virtual hearings are viewed as inappropriate by many for serious felonies and other cases requiring a jury trial, large backlogs of unresolved cases have formed in many court systems, raising concerns about the rights of the accused. This has led to efforts to develop safe approaches to resume in-person proceedings.

- Although some areas have resumed jury trials, e.g., in alternative locations where physical distancing is possible or in alternative courtroom arrangements, capacity is still limited.

- Court systems likely will have major backlogs of cases to address even after the COVID-19 pandemic recedes, requiring additional innovation to more rapidly resolve cases.

- Because of pressure on the funding streams on which some courts depend to operate, including filing fees or specific tax revenues, these systems face resource constraints and have had to reduce staff. These constraints could make resolving court backlogs even more challenging.

- Court systems had major concerns about the safety of staff in older, sometimes crowded court facilities. Protecting court staff with high risk of COVID-19 complications was a driver for closing courthouses and seeking alternative ways to operate.

Initial Responses: Reducing the Flow of People and Cases into the Courts as Much as Possible

In the initial response to the COVID-19 pandemic, courts took steps to manage the potential for infection within court facilities to protect their staff and others involved in justice proceedings and reduce the risk for outbreaks in other parts of the system, specifically jails and prisons. These efforts were informed by earlier efforts, including the response to the H1N1 outbreak, during which planning had occurred around social distancing, sanitation, and the use of technology for virtual operations.[3]

Reducing the Potential for Disease Transmission at Court

After the outbreak, the initial reaction of many court systems was to limit entry to the courthouse, which was analogous to the closure of other public locations, and to halt most or all in-person court operations.[4] Varied approaches were used to enable court business to continue without members of the public and staff having physical access to the building (e.g., dropboxes for filings, electronic submissions and e-signatures, telecommuting models for staff, remote access).[5] In some cases, access to court buildings was maintained, but only for essential personnel or for limited populations and with the required health screenings associated with entry to many locations or with involvement in interpersonal activities during the pandemic.[6]

> [With respect to prioritization of cases,] there are certain priorities imposed by our state constitution. There are certain priorities imposed by statute. There are certain priorities imposed by rule, by administrative order, by custom and practice, and [by] our Supreme Court.
>
> – Court system panelist

Because of their critical time sensitivity, specific types of essential court services were exempted from the halts in proceedings. According to an early review of such orders, which was done by the National Center for State Courts, those services comprised (1) "the protection of vulnerable people, such as elders, children and those who suffer from disabilities;" (2) "preliminary hearings, bail hearings and arraignments for criminal defendants;" (3) "hearings related to quarantine orders and other public health–related matters;" (4) "protection

---

[3] Julie Marie Baldwin, John M. Eassey, and Erika J. Brooke, "Court Operations During the COVID-19 Pandemic," *American Journal of Criminal Justice*, Vol. 45, 2020.

[4] The National Center for State Courts lists these two measures as among the five most-common steps taken in response to the COVID-19 pandemic by state-level court systems (National Center for State Courts, "Coronavirus and the Courts," webpage, undated a). In a convenience sample of approximately 200 respondents, the National Association of Pretrial Services Agencies found that essentially all of the respondents had postponed court hearings (National Partnership for Pretrial Justice, undated). See also Baldwin, Eassey, and Brooke, 2020.

[5] See, for example, Supreme Court of Arizona Plan B Workgroup, "Guidelines for Arizona Courts: Court Emergency Needs Checklist to Work Remotely, September 1, 2020b; Office of Victim Advocate, "COVID-19 Guidance," webpage, undated.

[6] National Conference of State Legislatures, 2020. See also, for example, Jana Hrdinova, Douglas A. Berman, Mark E. Pauley, and Dexter Ridgway, *Documenting the Challenges (and Documents) as Ohio Courts Respond to COVID-19*, Columbus, Ohio: Ohio State University, Moritz College of Law, Drug Enforcement and Policy Center, 2020.

orders for women and others who fear for their safety;" and (5) the issuance of warrants and other support to law enforcement operations.[7] Echoing the importance of those court services, Chuka Emezue highlighted the halt of court operations for these issues as a serious problem in some areas:

> Family court and Family Justice Center proceedings have also ground to a halt, slowing down filing and sentencing procedures. This is a crucial impediment, as orders of protection through the family court are a vital resource for survivors seeking to hold their abusers accountable, especially those in underserved areas.[8]

Other pandemic-related access-to-justice needs have been noted where court shutdowns and case prioritization might be a concern. These issues include landlord-tenant disputes, employment-related concerns, and other civil issues.[9]

Because of the cancellation of proceedings and limits on what hearings and proceedings can be held, courts automatically issued continuances,[10] and granted extensions on many court deadlines, including extending time to pay fines and fees.[11] Some courts suspended the collection of fines and fees entirely, both as a protective measure and as a reflection of the economic challenges created by the pandemic. In addition, according to some of our panelists, courts suspended the issuance of warrants for the nonpayment of fees and nonappearance, eliminating that flow of individuals into the courts and corrections system.[12] Reflecting the prioritization of protecting vulnerable populations, courts in some areas provided automatic extensions of restraining orders or orders of protection.[13]

For courts that maintained in-person operations, the types of measures taken to reduce risk are also familiar. For example,

> [s]ome courts that have continued in-person practices fully or in a limited capacity but have restricted the number of individuals permitted in shared space, implemented social distancing, required the use of masks, and provided disinfectant. However, these measures might be best thought of [as] enhancements to existing practices. They do not alter how the courts actually operate, for example, how they convene, communicate, process cases, and protect private information.[14]

---

[7]   National Center for State Courts, "The Evolving Nature of 'Essential Services' and 'Urgent Matters,'" webpage, undated b.

[8]   Chuka Emezue, "Digital or Digitally Delivered Responses to Domestic and Intimate Partner Violence During COVID-19," *JMIR Public Health Surveillance*, Vol. 6, No. 3, July–September 2020.

[9]   American Bar Association, Task Force on Legal Needs Arising out of the 2020 Pandemic, *Summary Report: Survey Regarding Legal Needs Arising from the COVID-19 Pandemic*, Chicago, Il., May 2020.

[10]   Hrdinova et al., 2020.

[11]   National Conference of State Legislatures, 2020.

[12]   In addition, see Laurie Dudgeon's comments in Council on Criminal Justice, "Facing COVID-19 in the Courts," video, YouTube, April 16, 2020a; and Hrdinova et al., 2020.

[13]   Storm Ervin and Sara Batomski, "We Need to Do More to Support Victims of Domestic Violence During the Pandemic," *Urban Wire* blog, April 21, 2020.

[14]   Baldwin et al., 2020, p. 747.

However, whether for court systems that continued in-person activities or those that are in the process of resuming them, there was wide variation across the country at both the state and local levels on the measures that were thought to be required for safe public access to court facilities. Figure 4.2 shows state-by-state variation in requirements for mask-wearing and temperature checks before entry into courts.

Because jury trials involve significant groups of individuals and extended contact among those individuals, their suspension was a recommended practice for limiting the spread of COVID-19.[15] According to panelists, because this could significantly extend the timeline that an accused individual had to wait before trial, suspending jury trials often required courts to suspend speedy trial requirements.

> There's a huge tension, obviously, between defendants who've been sitting in custody . . . who have not had a court appearance in six months now since the beginning of [the COVID-19 pandemic] . . . and no trial in sight.
>
> – Court system panelist

Figure 4.2
Variation in State-Level Requirements to Physically Enter Courthouses, as of August 2020

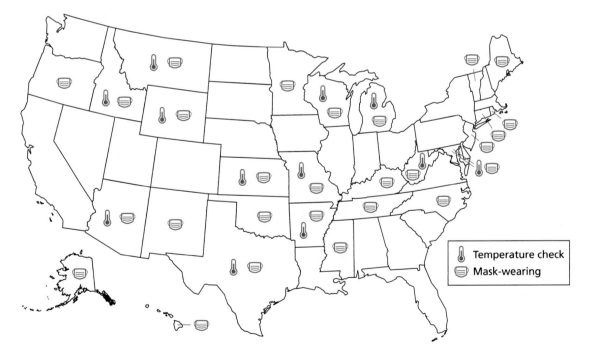

SOURCE: Data are from National Center for State Courts, undated a.

---

[15] National Conference of State Legislatures, 2020. The National Center for State Courts lists the suspension of jury trials as one of the five most-common steps taken in response to the COVID-19 pandemic by state-level court systems (National Center for State Courts, undated a).

Whether an area chose to suspend jury trials—and, if so, for how long—also varied considerably across the country. Figure 4.3 shows individual jury trial restriction timelines for the states and Washington, D.C., from the beginning of the pandemic to early October 2020, illustrating the diversity in approach across the country, with some states restricting them for a relatively short period while others shut down for a long (and, in some cases, indefinite) period.

Beyond reducing access to court buildings and implementing safety procedures for entry, court systems took several steps to further protect staff members and plan to continue court operations if staff members were directly affected by COVID-19 (either because they were infected or if they had to quarantine) or had to care for others who were affected. These protective measures included policies for the use of PPE within court buildings, planning for and retrofitting workspaces for social distancing, and the installation of barriers and dividers to reduce the risk of exposure. To maintain the ability to continue court operations in the event of an outbreak among the staff, specific measures were implemented, including dividing staff into cohorts and limiting in-person presence to a single cohort at a time to limit the potential need to quarantine the entire workforce; pursuing agreements with nearby court systems to share staff in the event that one court was seriously affected; and planning for long-term operations with reduced workforce levels.[16]

> [Another strategy] is siloed team staffing where we've asked the courts to split the staff where some are working remotely, others are at the courthouse. And so in the event that somebody does become infected, that court can continue to operate.
>
> – Court system panelist

Court Actions to Reduce COVID-19 Risk Elsewhere in the Justice System

Although halting cases coming into the courts reduced the population that could potentially be exposed there, many of the actions taken in this part of the justice system—whether by prosecutors, defense counsel and public defenders, judges, or others—were focused on limiting the flow of people into jails (e.g., during pretrial detention) or into prisons to serve custodial sentences. Moving through the stages of the process, we explore changes in charging decisions, changes in warrants, reductions in pretrial detention, settlements of pending cases, and issues related to in-custody individuals.

Changes in Charging Decisions

In many areas, regardless of whether arrests were still being made, prosecutors declined to file charges for categories of low-level offenses. As a result of controversy surrounding the enforcement of public health measures, there also were examples of prosecutors declining to file charges for arrests related to violations of mask-wearing or social-distancing orders.[17] In some cases, areas delayed the filing of charges, which reduced the immediate entrance of those

---

[16] See, for example, guidance from New Jersey State Bar Association, *Notice to the Bar and Public: COVID-19—Update on Court Operations During "Phase 2.5" of the Supreme Court's Post-Pandemic Plan*, New Brunswick, N.J., September 22, 2020b; and the Wisconsin Courts COVID-19 Task Force, *Chief Justice's Wisconsin Courts COVID-19 Task Force: Final Report*, Madison, Wisc., May 2020.

[17] Some examples are cited in Brennan Center for Justice, *Prosecutors Responses to COVID-19*, Washington, D.C., March 27, 2020, updated July 15, 2020.

Figure 4.3
Variation in State-Level Prohibition of In-Person Jury Trials, as of October 2020

SOURCE: Data are from National Center for State Courts, undated a.

individuals into the justice system but created a pre-charging backlog that would have to be addressed at a future date.[18]

Changes in Warrants

Numerous areas noted that they stopped issuing warrants for nonpayment of fines and for failure to appear at a court hearing. Some areas also converted or suspended existing warrants.[19]

Reducing Pretrial Detention

Areas significantly reduced pretrial detention by increasing release without bail which limited jail populations. Early in the pandemic, California went to a zero-bail schedule across its court system in an effort to relieve stress on jail populations, driven in part because of limits in judges' situational awareness about whether jails could accept individuals safely;[20] corrections agencies had to focus their efforts on developing approaches to keep COVID-19 out of their facilities or limit its effects if it was introduced.[21] According to one source, initiatives elsewhere involved collaboration between court actors to reduce risk:

> We talked about the Sheriff's Department Jail commander preparing a list of pre-trial detainees who had committed non-violent non-dangerous crimes, such as repeated shoplifting or simple drug possession for personal use, who had remained in jail simply due to inability to pay bail. Our Public Defender then led a review of that list on behalf of all the defense attorneys representing individuals on the list. And our County Attorney agreed to file joint motions along with the Public Defender, asking the Criminal Presiding Judge to remove bail as a condition for release, which the judge has granted.[22]

Similar efforts were described by others in different regions of the country.[23] In descriptions of this approach, representatives in more than one area of the country pointed out the conflict between policies and laws designed to protect crime victims and the flexibility in using pretrial release to reduce COVID-19 risk. These sorts of constraints were cited in Arizona, where pretrial release motions for individuals accused of crimes with statutory victims had to include specific victim-protection elements,[24] and in Pennsylvania, where the issue was framed in terms of balancing the needs of the victim and the rights of someone still presumed innocent in the eyes of the law.[25]

---

[18] In an example from Buncombe County, North Carolina, which published a list of the varied steps taken to reduce jail populations, the authors indicated that the county "*delayed* or stopped filing on non-violent charges (low level)" (Buncombe County Justice Services Department, undated; emphasis added).

[19] Buncombe County Justice Services Department, undated, p. 3.

[20] The National Commission on COVID-19 and Criminal Justice also mentioned the need for situational awareness about the status of the pandemic within the justice system to inform decisions (National Commission on COVID-19 and Criminal Justice, *Experience to Action: Reshaping Criminal Justice After COVID-19*, Washington, D.C.: Council on Criminal Justice, December 2020b, p. 30).

[21] Comments from Tani Cantil-Sakauye, California Supreme Court Chief Justice, in Council on Criminal Justice, 2020a.

[22] Cramer, 2020.

[23] Comments from Keir Bradford-Grey, chief defender, Defender Association of Philadelphia, in Council on Criminal Justice, 2020a.

[24] Cramer, 2020.

[25] Comments from Keir Bradford-Grey in Council on Criminal Justice, 2020a.

Settling Pending Cases

To reduce pressure in the system, focused efforts were made to resolve pending cases, generally prioritizing individuals who were in custody. Many of these cases involved plea bargaining. According to Baldwin, Eassey, and Brooke:

> There has been an increase in plea bargains during the pandemic due to COVID-19 risks and system concerns. While this can be both advantageous for the court and defendant, there is a concern that defendants may feel pressured to plead guilty to stay out of jail due to their health concerns amid the COVID-19 pandemic.[26]

In a Council on Criminal Justice Roundtable in April 2020, chief defender Keir Bradford-Grey from Philadelphia, Pennsylvania, noted that the risk of infection in custody could mean that the plea is viewed as being provided "under duress."[27] If the risk did mean that pleas were viewed as compromised, the case resolution might not stand up in a later appeal. In spite of the desire to resolve larger numbers of cases through pleas, our panelists noted a problem: Without the threat of a trial, the incentives for the prosecution and defense to reach a deal were significantly reduced, making it tougher to settle.

More broadly, some assessments framed individual defendants' risk of COVID-19 exposure (e.g., for an elderly or otherwise vulnerable individual) during incarceration as another factor that needed to be considered in decisionmaking at all stages, from pretrial detention through sentencing.[28]

> The plea bargaining system depends on defendants and everybody believing that, if you don't take this offer, we're going to take you to trial and things will get worse. Right now I'm not sure that we have that credible threat [of a trial occurring].
>
> – Court system panelist

Review and Release of In-Custody Individuals

In some areas, beyond efforts to not reincarcerate for minor or technical probation violations, initiatives were created to release people who were already in custody for these reasons.[29] Some of these efforts focused on individuals in custody in vulnerable populations who were more likely to have serious complications from COVID-19. According to our panelists, the desire to reduce jail and prison populations through review and release created workload issues for courts; there were large numbers of bail motions and compassionate release motions filed on the part of currently incarcerated individuals.[30]

---

[26] Baldwin, Eassey, and Brooke, 2020, p. 752.

[27] Comments from Keir Bradford-Grey in Council on Criminal Justice, 2020a.

[28] Crystal Watson, Kelsey Lane Warmbrod, Rachel A. Vahey, Anita Cicero, Thomas V. Inglesby, Chris Beyrer, Leonard Rubenstein, Gabriel Eber, Carolyn Sufrin, Henri Garrison-Desany, Lauren Dayton, and Rachel Strodel, *COVID-19 and the U.S. Criminal Justice System: Evidence for Public Health Measures to Reduce Risk*, Baltimore, Md.: Johns Hopkins Center for Health Security, 2020, p. 17.

[29] Comments from Keir Bradford-Grey in Council on Criminal Justice, 2020a.

[30] See also American Bar Association Task Force on Legal Needs Arising out of the 2020 Pandemic, 2020.

All of these strategies—from changing charging strategies, court bail decisions, shifts in plea bargaining, or release strategies for existing populations—emphasize how connectivity among different elements of the justice system is needed to effectively manage risks where the actions of one part of the system are designed to have an effect elsewhere. Decisionmakers need to know the state of conditions in the corrections system to make balanced risk trade-offs in the courts, which also could inform law enforcement's arrest decisions.

> A lot of times courts have good data, but it may not be timely. We seem to always be a month or two behind. . . . I think we're going to need to be more real time. There's a lot of focus on electronic dashboards, business intelligence, and all that. And, if there was ever a time we would need it, I think this is really the time for that kind of thing.
>
> – Court system panelist

Although many of these efforts reduced jail populations significantly (some participants in our panel reported double-digit percentage reductions in jail populations, which enabled corrections agencies to take further steps to reduce risk), their application was far from universal. In a survey fielded from April to the end of May 2020, the National Association of Pretrial Services Agencies sought to identify steps being taken in the courts and in other parts of the justice system to reduce COVID-19 risk.[31] Across the respondents to this survey, the use of increased pretrial release or release on personal recognizance was common, with fewer respondents indicating that there had been increased release from jail for individuals who were already sentenced or releases before first appearances. About half of the respondents cited reductions in total numbers of criminal complaint filings.[32] Increases in case dismissals, increases in diversion, and reductions in fine or fee amounts were much less common. In addition, successes in reducing jail populations were sometimes short-lived, with populations gradually creeping back up as the pandemic wore on and arrests and other policies reverted.[33]

Beyond the efforts to control the flow of people through the courts on the criminal side, decisions that had been made on other pandemic issues were noted by our panel as important to consider. Some national and state policies that were aimed at protecting individuals during the pandemic—notably, the moratorium on eviction proceedings[34]—also had an effect in reducing the number of new cases in courts in areas where they were put into place. However, as one participant on our court panel put it, echoing the metaphor of a flow of cases moving through the system, they expected that dam to break when the measures expired and to wash over the court system.

---

[31] The survey and its results are described in National Partnership for Pretrial Justice, undated. Although the 197 respondents to the survey covered 40 states and the District of Columbia, the respondents were not a representative sample of agencies across the country (i.e., the National Association of Pretrial Services Agencies described its results as "purely anecdotal evidence"). As a result, we do not report percentages of the respondents here, but flag measures as more common and less common.

[32] National Partnership for Pretrial Justice, undated.

[33] See Jasmine Heiss, Oliver Hinds, Eital Schattner-Elmaleh, and James Wallace-Lee, *The Scale of the COVID-19–Related Jail Population Decline*, Brooklyn, N.Y.: Vera Institute of Justice, August 2020, for a review of populations across the country.

[34] See National Center for State Courts, undated a, for summary data on states with eviction moratoria.

> In evictions, for example, a tsunami of cases . . . are going to come [when] our governor's stay goes away. Those are building up, and that avalanche is going to hit, and we need to be ready.
>
> – Court system panelist

A Shift to Virtual Court Operations to Keep Staff and the Public Safe

Beyond efforts to reduce the flow of cases and individuals into the system, one of the most-dramatic shifts in the court system in response to the COVID-19 pandemic was a rapid and expansive move to virtual operations.[35] Pre-pandemic use of technology for virtual court proceedings was viewed as a promising and potentially efficiency-enhancing approach, although there was significant concern about whether justice outcomes would differ between virtual and in-person proceedings. Before the pandemic, relatively modest progress had been made in using virtual technologies because of concerns about outcomes and a view that the criminal justice system is technologically conservative and therefore comparatively slow to innovate.[36] With the arrival of the COVID-19 pandemic, those barriers vanished in a matter of months, if not weeks. Members of our panel described technology implementations that were driven by necessity being completed faster than anything they had seen in their professional careers. Although holding proceedings virtually was the most recognized shift in operations, the ability of court infrastructure functions—e.g., case filing, evidence management—to be done outside court buildings also was critical. Systems that allowed remote access enabled some court staff to work from home and enabled distributed operations that did not require presence in the courthouse. Connecting court employees to such systems helped courts implement alternative ways of assisting people at a distance, which was not unlike the innovations made by police in the use of electronic means of reporting crime or police response via video calls.

> Fortunately, we did already have electronic filing for all of our case types as well as remote access for most of our judiciary. We were really dealing with just a few judges who didn't . . . so that really helped us out a lot.
>
> – Court system panelist

---

[35] Blake Candler, "Court Adaptations During COVID-19 in the World's Two Largest Democracies," *SSRN*, May 24, 2020; Hrdinova et al., 2020.

[36] See, for example, Gail S. Goodman, Ann E. Tobey, Jennifer M. Batterman-Faunce, Holly K. Orcutt, Sherry Thomas, Cheryl M. Shapiro, and Toby Sachsenmaier, "Face-to-Face Confrontation: Effects of Closed-Circuit Technology on Children's Eyewitness Testimony and Jurors' Decisions," *Law and Human Behavior*, Vol. 22, 1998; Camille Gourdet, Amanda R. Witwer, Lynn Langton, Duren Banks, Michael G. Planty, Dulani Woods, and Brian A. Jackson, *Court Appearances in Criminal Proceedings Through Telepresence: Identifying Research and Practice Needs to Preserve Fairness While Leveraging New Technology*, Santa Monica, Calif.: RAND Corporation, RR-3222-NIJ, 2020; Carol L. Krafka and Molly Johnson, *Electronic Media Coverage of Federal Civil Proceedings: An Evaluation of the Pilot Program in Six District Courts and Two Courts of Appeals*, Washington, D.C.: Federal Judicial Center, 1994; Shari Seidman Diamond, Locke E. Bowman, Manyee Wong, and Matthew M. Patton, "Efficiency and Cost: The Impact of Videoconferenced Hearings on Bail Decisions," *Journal of Criminal Law and Criminology*, Vol. 100, No. 3, 2010, pp. 869–902.

> A couple of things that we have done with technology is we have used live chat for self-help and traffic department matters, and we have been routing phone calls to court laptops, given to employees that are away from the courthouse. And we expect that to endure after the COVID crisis is over.
>
> – Court system panelist

In an effort to get the court system functioning again, the transition to virtual hearings was focused and extremely fast. Courts that had made investments in technology were able to pivot more rapidly.[37] For example, a panel member pointed out that some rural court systems had made such investments in response to the challenge of the large areas they served. In this case, that challenge became a source of advantage because the court system already had telepresence systems in place. Moving all types of proceedings to the virtual space was not possible in many jurisdictions, but there was a push to do as much as possible virtually to keep cases moving through the courts.[38] Such actions as ensuring access for individuals in need of protection orders and other court services were a driver to make courts accessible in person during the pandemic. However, as the pandemic continued, some participants reported an increasing drive to move activity onto telepresence platforms.[39]

> [In our area,] there's a presumption of virtual hearings and only if somebody insists on an in-person hearing [is one held in person]. This varies tremendously around the country, [however.]
>
> – Court system panelist

In addition to navigating the new technology, some courts had to address practical concerns that had not arisen when all business was done in person. For example, one participant mentioned the need to issue new administrative orders and determine how to manage parties' contact information to enable virtual proceedings.

> We've used the virtual platforms . . . for protection orders so that domestic violence victims could still access the courts. It was very important to me to tell the public that the institutions of public safety and justice were still open, even though everything was different.
>
> – Court system panelist

Although many jurisdictions are holding different types of court proceedings virtually—e.g., preliminary hearings, arraignments, depositions, status hearings—only a small

---

[37] See, for example, Laurie Dudgeon's comments in Council on Criminal Justice, 2020a.

[38] Baldwin, Eassey, and Brooke, 2020.

[39] Forthcoming PCJNI research discusses this shift to virtual court proceedings for dispute resolution (Amanda R. Witwer, Lynn Langton, Duren Banks, Dulani Woods, Michael J. D. Vermeer, and Brian A. Jackson, *Online Dispute Resolution: Perspectives to Support Successful Implementation and Outcomes in Court Proceedings*, Santa Monica, Calif.: RAND Corporation, RR-A108-9, forthcoming).

number are attempting to hold jury trials virtually. There are concerns about virtual jury trials, particularly for criminal offenses where the accused's liberty is a risk, which we will discuss in the next section. There are fewer concerns about the ability to hold virtual jury trials for civil matters.[40] Some states are pursuing virtual jury trials for criminal offenses (e.g., Texas)[41] and civil cases (e.g., Florida).[42] At the time of this writing, some other states were developing guidelines or were exploring virtual jury trials.[43] In some states, consent is required for a virtual trial, while in others, consent is required only when a jailable criminal offense is at issue. The Texas court system published a report detailing its jury trial efforts during the pandemic. It concluded that virtual jury trials could be done effectively, although "courts trying virtual jury trials needed a technically savvy bailiff to assist prospective jurors with technical issues during check-in, trial, and deliberation . . . [and] the courts needed to take extra time during the juror check-in process to provide this assistance."[44]

Benefits of Court Virtualization

These efforts achieved their main benefit for many court systems: cutting in-person activity and reducing infection risk, with participants in our panel reporting that their systems had completed hundreds, thousands, or even 1 million hours of proceedings since resuming operations in virtual space.[45] Panel members also cited other beneficial outcomes of the shift, some of which were unexpected. For specific types of courts or cases that were well suited to virtual adjudication, some participants cited *increases* in efficiency. These include improvements overall and more-narrow efficiency gains in parts of the process (e.g., the time it took for participants to find and adjourn to a separate room for a sidebar versus being able to use a virtual breakout room with the click of a mouse). Virtualization also enabled new staffing approaches to increase capacity and balance caseloads among courts.

> Now that everything is remote, we can use retired judges. We can use judges that aren't so busy [in different regions of the state,] who were all connected. And so they could pick up the slack in places that are [busy], that are really overwhelmed with a backlog. . . . And especially if it's judges who are currently working and already getting paid, it doesn't cost the local jurisdiction anything to put that visiting judge to work remotely.
>
> – Court system panelist

---

[40] Zack Needles, "Law.com Trendspotter: Virtual Civil Jury Trials Are Definitely Divisive—and Likely Inevitable," *Law.com*, September 13, 2020.

[41] David Lee, "Texas Judge Holds First Virtual Jury Trial in Criminal Case," Courthouse News Service, August 11, 2020.

[42] Janna Adelstein, "Courts Continue to Adapt to COVID-19," Brennan Center for Justice, September 10, 2020.

[43] Thomas P. Boyd, State Court Administrator, Michigan Supreme Court, "Virtual Jury Trials," memorandum to all judges, Lansing, Mich., July 20, 2020; Shelly Bradbury, "Colorado Courts Catapulted Online Amid Coronavirus Pandemic," *Denver Post*, August 16, 2020; Carl Smith, "All Rise: Virtual Court Is Now in Session," *Governing.com*, September 16, 2020.

[44] David Slayton, *Jury Trials During the COVID-19 Pandemic: Observations and Recommendations*, Austin, Tex.: Office of Court Administration, August 28, 2020, p. 17.

[45] For example, see John Nevin, "Michigan's Justice System Reaches 1 Million Hours of Zoom Hearings," Lansing, Mich.: Michigan Courts News Release, September 17, 2020.

Virtual proceedings also have advantages for many of the participants involved.[46] Practitioners in cases involving children argued that being able to interact with child victims or witnesses virtually—where the child can stay in a comfortable environment—is better than bringing them into an intimidating court building.[47] Virtual proceedings also make it easier for litigants to be present in court; travel time and long waits in a courthouse for a case to be called for a short hearing can essentially be eliminated. One participant in our panel said that in some types of cases, "the number of defaults has kind of flipped—where defaults used to be perhaps 80 percent, now they're more like 20 percent because people can appear remotely." As a result, according to this panelist, cases can be decided "on the merits as opposed to because somebody was skittish or can't get time away from work to appear."

There's a lot of advantage with some of the remote appearance, advantage to litigants, the speed and cost of their cases. And just the convenience: Rather than taking a half a day [of] work off to go down and have a 15 minute [meeting] at the courthouse, they're able to dial in and go from their phone potentially, and make that appearance [during a short break in their workday]. That's a fantastic thing that I never thought I'd ever seen in my lifetime.

– Court system panelist

There's been a big uptick in courts allowing video teleconferences, particularly for non-trial appearances, which there's no reason that shouldn't have been allowed before the pandemic, like why you have to go into court and sit there for six hours for a 30-second hearing where your lawyer just picks a new date.

– Community organization panelist

Beyond the intended reduction in the risk of COVID-19 infection, participants cited other security benefits of virtualization. For example, avoiding having to transport incarcerated individuals from jails simplifies security and reduces other risks (and cuts associated costs).[48]

Challenges of Court Virtualization

Although virtual models were needed to continue court operations during the COVID-19 pandemic, there were significant questions about the appropriateness of such models for different types of proceedings, which we discuss in more detail in the next section. Beyond the base concern about whether true justice *can* be virtual,[49] participants in our courts panel discussed some safety concerns for court staff as a result of the shift to virtual operations. Like other workers in distributed work models, court staff had to deal with the practicalities of working at home, managing children in online school, and managing other stresses of the pandemic. All of these concerns have the potential to increase stress and threaten mental health. Virtual

---

[46]   See discussion in Gourdet et al., 2020.

[47]   Allie Reed and Madison Alder, "Virtual Hearings Put Children, Abuse Victims at Ease in Court," *Bloomberg Law*, July 23, 2020.

[48]   See also Hrdinova et al., 2020.

[49]   See Gourdet et al., 2020, for a review of concerns about court proceedings via telepresence technologies.

models also had practical challenges, including how to deal with sealed orders (which are generally done in hard copy), situations in which lawyers in a case might have key files locked in commercial buildings that were closed as a result of the pandemic, and how to sufficiently verify participants' identities virtually.

Members of the panel also emphasized some issues that are more unique to criminal justice practitioners, including the national climate and, to paraphrase a panelist, the "conversation to right racial injustices from the past," the justice system's roles in those injustices, and job-specific stresses mixing work and home life (e.g., a sex-crimes prosecutor working at home potentially risks exposing their family to the disturbing images and evidence associated with such crimes).

> One of my concerns is isolation among the judges, particularly rural judges. [Under normal circumstances,] one of their biggest challenges is being isolated. And I think the COVID experience has enhanced that not only for rural judges, but for Metro judges as well. And . . . that this cuts across probably all walks of society, among my peers, among clerks of court, everybody is talking about their isolation and the impact [it] has on their jobs and their health.
>
> – Court system panelist

Digital Divides Among Court Staff and Members of the Public

Although court systems that already had upgraded technology had a head start in adapting to the pandemic, digital divides hurt the ability of some systems to move proceedings and court processes into the virtual space. Some participants reported that their workforces were not initially equipped for virtual operation. According to one panelist, "I've had prosecutors call me and say they had to go out and buy five laptops for her assistants because they didn't [have one at home]." Some systems had limited video technology at the beginning of the pandemic, meaning that such adaptations as having incarcerated individuals join hearings virtually were initially not viable.

> It's created just a huge host of issues for [individuals] who were detained. It took weeks to figure out how to get computers into the jail so that we could actually see them [and they could see others involved in their proceedings]. So somebody would get arrested, they would go and have an [audio only] virtual hearing. . . . They would get charged, [and] the person would never have seen their lawyer, the courtroom, the judge or anybody. Then we started to get video hearings, as everyone got used to the technology and it became available.
>
> – Court system panelist

Different participants in the justice process—e.g., judges; prosecutors; defense counsel, including public defenders—might have been at very different levels of technical sophistication at the outset of the pandemic, creating different capacities to adapt to the new virtual circumstances.[50] Some of those systems made up that distance very rapidly. According to a

---

[50] Comments from Keir Bradford-Grey in Council on Criminal Justice, 2020a.

Florida state attorney, "I do think there has been a silver lining at least for our operations. Necessity has forced our hand. We have a three-year strategic plan and we wanted our office to be paperless by the end of next year and we went paperless in a matter of three weeks because we had to learn how to work remotely."[51]

> In February of last year, I didn't know what Zoom was. By the end of March, we had 246 courts up and running with Zoom. That's just a pace that's unbelievable. I like to say that "we really didn't close our courts, we just shifted to a virtual environment."
>
> – Court system panelist

In addition, simple infrastructure constraints in some geographic areas, given the differential availability of high-speed, high-bandwidth internet access, meant that court staff's ability to work remotely was significantly affected by where they lived.

> We also have a digital divide with the staff. Some of them do not have high-bandwidth [internet] at home, so . . . that [does] disadvantage them from the opportunity to telecommute. I think it's sort of a rural justice issue . . . we went ahead . . . to offer the Zoom licensing [to all our staff], but we found that it doesn't work very well [for staff in] very remote areas.
>
> – Court system panelist

While one digital divide affecting court staff created logistical challenges, broader digital divides among members of the public were major concerns for the fairness and constitutional acceptability of virtual processes. A recent review of the trend to virtualization emphasized that, although this is certainly an issue for *individuals* (e.g., someone who must appear as a witness in a proceeding), there are similar concerns for *organizations* as well: "Interested parties are also apt to confront technical or logistical issues. Indigent defendants and witnesses, small or solo law firms, and smaller or rural counties are likely to have issues with consistent access to high-speed internet."[52] In addition to internet access, hardware access is a concern, as is the likelihood that not all individuals with a need to participate in court proceedings will have high-capability computers or mobile devices. Even if hardware is available, whatever software platform is used could create compatibility or usability issues that make it difficult for some individuals. There are specific concerns about whether the elderly or self-represented litigants will be able to participate in virtual proceedings, but similar arguments would apply to individuals facing socioeconomic challenges (which could have become more common and more serious because of the economic dislocation of the pandemic).[53] Addressing these concerns requires courts to provide alternative approaches for access to virtual justice.

---

[51]   Comments from Melissa Nelson, state attorney, Florida's 4th Judicial Circuit, in Council on Criminal Justice, 2020a.

[52]   Brandon Marc Draper, "And Justice for None: How COVID-19 Is Crippling the Criminal Jury Right," *Boston College Law Review*, Vol. 62, No. 9, E. Supp. I.-1, 2020, p. I.-8.

[53]   New Yorkers for Responsible Lending, "Implementation of Virtual Court Appearances in Nonessential Matters," letter to Judge Lawrence K. Marks, New York, April 15, 2020.

> In order to accommodate people who did not have remote technology, they put a set of kiosks on the first and second floor of the courthouse where no elevators were. . . . It has worked remarkably well, no issues. So basically people can join from home if they want, or if they don't have access, then they can come to the courthouse and appear remotely from the courthouse.
>
> – Court system panelist

These digital divide issues have raised particular concerns about the acceptability of virtual jury trials. Accused individuals are supposed to be judged by a jury of their peers, and if technology access prevents parts of the population from serving, it is a concern for the representativeness of the jury pool. Resolving these concerns requires courts to actively bridge these divides, including asking prospective jurors whether they have technical or other problems that would prevent their serving on a virtual jury; providing technology if needed; and, potentially, providing connectivity capability. Some have characterized these requirements as similar to reimbursing juror transportation expenses to the courthouse to remove barriers to physical participation on in-person juries.[54]

> The [State] Supreme Court will only allow remote jury trials to occur as long [as] all of the potential and selected jurors are provided access to technology. So basically the way it happens is whenever the normal summons goes out, there's actually a questionnaire that goes out with it that asks them about their access to technology, as well as their availability to participate in a quiet and remote room. . . . If they respond back that they don't have access to technology, we actually provide [it] to them. What we've been using is an iPad with cell service and also Wi-Fi, but our anticipation is they'll use a cell service, and—at least so far—that has worked remarkably well. I'm assuming there's going to be situations where that won't work well because cell service doesn't work well everywhere. It does point to the need for broadband everywhere.
>
> – Court system panelist

Public Access and Unintended Consequences

Court proceedings, and particularly criminal proceedings, are supposed to be open to the public because public trial is a critical check on government and is therefore a mechanism to safeguard individual rights. The transition from proceedings held in a courthouse, where a motivated member of the public could come and observe, to those held in the virtual realm has the potential to eliminate that access and therefore raise questions about whether such proceedings pass constitutional muster. Civil-society actors who are concerned with the implications of reduced access have gone "so far as to call it a transparency nightmare."[55] In response to the need for transparency, several court systems have moved to either livestream proceedings online or to post videos after the fact.[56]

---

[54] Supreme Court of Arizona Plan B Workgroup, "Minimizing the Digital Divide During Jury Selection," memorandum, July 30, 2020a.

[55] Candler, 2020, p. 6.

[56] National Conference of State Legislatures, 2020.

> Public access has been really important to us because, if you go virtual and the public would normally be able to watch proceedings in a courtroom, if they can't get into the court building, how do they watch? So . . . now we stream all of our court proceedings on YouTube. . . . [Users] can just . . . click on a link and watch live proceedings.
>
> – Court system panelist

Although streaming clearly eliminates the reduced transparency of an otherwise closed online courtroom,[57] it swings the pendulum to the other extreme, making essentially *all* court proceedings immediately available to anyone, with a very low barrier to access. When assessed only against an ideal of government transparency, that shift could be viewed as positive. However, because of the sensitivity of the issues that individuals go to the courts to resolve—e.g., in divorce adjudication, family law matters, victim testimony during criminal trials and sentencing proceedings—the privacy interests of the participants must be considered. Although those court hearings were open to the public before the COVID-19 pandemic, the requirement to go to the courthouse and attend in person limited the potential invasion of participants' privacy even during a formally open, public proceeding.

> [Transparency is] a great thing on the one hand, but then on the glass-half-full side, what about proceedings [like] domestic violence, child abuse, especially courts that might not need to be public? . . . What might we need to change to protect the privacy in those cases, but also to protect the need for public access?
>
> – Court system panelist
>
> Having an open parole hearing as opposed to a closed one where victims aren't allowed to participate and the public can't attend, there's a tremendous discrepancy in decision-making on similar cases, because the pressure that a commissioned panel feels has been [the] same as a jurist would feel because you're getting scrutinized. [If] you make one mistake, or it's not even a mistake, it's your best judgment, and it didn't work out, but that is immediately remembered, not the 99 decisions you make that are correct. And the same thing would happen with public bail hearings . . . if that were to continue after this [pandemic] slows down, I think that would be a serious detriment to the system. And it would cause much more incarceration than we're currently seeing. . . . And I would be concerned if that becomes the norm.
>
> – Community corrections panelist

Furthermore, the accessibility of virtual court proceedings has raised concerns about the safety of witnesses involved in trials: "District Attorney Larry Krasner said . . . livestreaming criminal trial proceedings over YouTube made it possible for any viewer to surreptitiously record witness testimony for nefarious purposes, with little hope of accountability."[58] The

---

[57] Sometimes, courtrooms are deliberately closed, even during in-person proceedings, to protect the safety or identity of witnesses, victims, or defendants. Such an action is taken deliberatively, after weighing the need for closure and the value of transparency. The mass adoption of virtual proceedings had the potential to render all proceedings closed simply as a result of the technology used rather than as a result of an intentional choice on the part of the judge and parties involved.

[58] Matt Fair, "Witnesses Not Safe with Livestreamed Trials, Philly DA Says," Law360, September 14, 2020.

broad dissemination of victims' participation in trials might broadcast individuals' descriptions of traumatic events of serious personal harm, potentially further victimizing them. In response to this concern, some governmental victim advocates have requested courts to not livestream "criminal and civil protection order proceedings, release hearings, or other hearings in which the court anticipates testimony or other evidence concerning the victim," "affording the victim [or] witness an opportunity to proceed via a pseudonym in any technology assisted hearing," and not publicly releasing recordings involving victims without their prior review.[59]

Beyond concerns about witnesses and victims, observers have argued that streaming trials is potentially unfair even to the accused, regardless of whether they are found guilty. It risks creating additional "digital punishment" as a result of broadcasting images of those involved, the full content of the proceedings, and their archiving for an indefinite period.[60] It is also the case that broadcasting proceedings is particularly dissonant with the goals of problem-solving courts, whose actions straddle the boundary between adjudication and treatment. Broad public dissemination of the proceedings of such courts has the potential to seriously undermine their value as alternatives to standard criminal justice processes.

> People already suffer collateral consequences for the rest of their lives based on a conviction. And it's possible to record these [virtual hearings and trials] and it can impact on people's ability to get employment and to get housing. And it can brutally impact on people's families, especially their children. I think there's a very big difference between the idea that individuals of the public who really want to take trouble to come in and listen, and people who might be poking around looking for something titillating.
>
> – Community corrections panelist
>
> On the privacy issue, one area that hasn't been mentioned are the problem-solving courts, mental health courts, drug courts, veterans courts. There, the privacy of the participants really helps their recovery and so how do you reconcile that? That's, that's a big issue that we're struggling with and don't have an answer.
>
> – Court system panelist

[59] Jennifer Storm, Joyce Lukima, Julie Bancroft, Meg Garvin, Diane Menio, Natasha McGlynn, Angelis Padilla, Karen C. Buck, Laura Vega, Karen Hinkle, and Carline Menapace, "Victim Advocates Request Changes to Procedures in Philadelphia Courts," Philadelphia, Pa.: Office of Victim Advocate, September 15, 2020.

Although the intensity of privacy questions surrounding the streaming of court proceedings is new, a participant in our courts panel argued that managing those issues is not dissimilar from what courts must do to protect victim and other information in court records:

On privacy . . . I think the answer to that may be a stratified approach as opposed to a one-size-fits-all approach. . . . It needs to be nuanced. How do you deal with victim information . . . in family court matters, how do you deal with sensitive information and children of . . . tender years? But we deal with that in terms of our electronic filings already, so to me, this is a timeworn issue. In a new format to be sure, and it's harder, but I think there's some opportunities there. But there's definitely some risk and some downside along the way.

[60] Sarah Esther Lageson, "The Perils of 'Zoom Justice,'" *The Crime Report*, September 1, 2020.

Concerns About the Acceptability of Virtual Models Resulting in Case Backlogs and Leading to the Resumption or Expansion of In-Person Proceedings

Although many virtual options for court proceedings have been valuable for continuing court operations during the COVID-19 pandemic, they are not the same as in-person judicial processes. Distance can limit the ability to do some tasks efficiently; for example, our panelists noted issues with sharing documents appropriately during proceedings or with having private conferences between individuals involved in the process. Participants in our workshop also argued that there are key elements of court proceedings that are nearly impossible to conduct when the people involved are connected only by technology, including defense counsel building rapport with clients. That lack of connection was viewed as particularly problematic for specialty and treatment courts, and the requirements to safeguard participant treatment data also meant that those courts' virtual systems had to be compliant with regulations for protecting personal health information.[61]

> So in problem-solving courts, we've found supervision is key. And so we have been absent for a while. It's hard to supervise individuals and to give them that bimonthly, if not monthly, kind of check in. And so there have been some issues with compliance. And so how do we do that and monitor that during this time?
>
> – Court system panelist

Beyond basic technological limitations, there have been broader concerns about virtual jury trials in particular—concerns that the virtual environment risks the perceived legitimacy of the judicial process itself and about whether virtual proceedings are appropriate in cases in which individuals' liberty interests are at stake. Our participants were not convinced that virtual proceedings had the same gravity and, therefore, the same legitimacy for victims, witnesses, and the defendants involved.

> This time, this year has really propelled the courts into the technology age, and the courts have never historically embraced technology in a big way. But my imagination stops at the point where a person might be losing [their liberty] over Zoom . . . there's something about being in the courtroom that makes the gravity of the situation real.
>
> – Court system panelist

---

[61]   Baldwin, Eassey, and Brooke, 2020.

> So we have had cases where people have been arrested—and it makes it very uncomfortable to be honest—people have been arrested, they plead, they get the presentence process, they get sentenced and they've never actually been to court. They've never met their lawyer in person. They've never met the judge in person. Some of them aren't even by video. . . . Is it necessary? Yes, obviously, but we have to recognize that some of these innovations are great and how quickly they came into being is great. . . . [But] we're talking about a fundamental realignment of our system . . . [and while] a lot of these innovations, I think that are great for the system, so to speak, but may not be great for the human beings involved in the system, the litigants.
>
> – Court system panelist

Some of the objections to virtual jury trials, even with the participants' consent, are related to whether such trials truly meet the requirement for the accused to be able to confront their accusers. Other concerns are related to the unknown; for example, whether outcomes from virtual proceedings will be different from those conducted in person, even if we do not know the exact reason why the outcomes differ. For example, one participant related that, anecdotally, sentences in virtual proceedings seem to be diverging from those in similar cases that are adjudicated in person. Others have concerns about whether the virtual environment affords the same opportunity for participants to read the body language of the accused, lawyers, witnesses, and jurors (although some have argued that the close-up, face-front view of witnesses and ease of reviewing evidence provided by virtualization could be superior to the in-person experience).[62]

The experience with some early efforts at virtual jury trials has made other court participants wary. In a law review bringing together multiple different experiences with virtual juries, Draper summarizes:

> In practice, the limited results from virtual proceedings have been troubling. A study conducted by New York University's Civil Jury Project notably found that the jurors had issues with focusing over a long period of time. One juror's Zoom crashed twice. Another expressed concern that the lack of juror bonding could impact deliberations. In a civil summary jury trial conducted in Collin County, Texas, one juror left to take a phone call. During another civil trial, jurors appeared to sleep, exercise, or tend to their children. Thus far in the pandemic, hackers have interrupted and caused delays by uploading pornographic images and obscene language in both criminal and civil Zoom hearings.[63]

Increasing Case Backlogs

Because of the cessation of jury trials in many areas, cases are accumulating in large backlogs. Participants in our panel described pending case numbers that amounted to multiple years' worth of trial capacity, even under ideal circumstances. These backlogs are growing in spite of efforts to reduce the flow into the system and, in some cases, the backlogs represent individuals who are held in custody and waiting for trial at some unknown time in the future. Although

---

[62] Carl Smith, 2020.

[63] Draper, 2020, p. I.-8.

speedy trial requirements might be suspended, at some point they will be reimposed, and the stakes for addressing the backlog will increase. However, as we observed for other effects of the pandemic, the extent of backlog growth differs from place to place. In an effort to gather some data on the extent of backlogs, the National Center for State Courts queried state court systems. Eleven court systems provided data suggesting that backlogs were not growing rapidly in some areas, although the small sample size made it impossible to reach general conclusions.[64]

> We have an enormous backlog of felony cases. We normally carry about 2,500 at any time of pending unresolved cases. We now have 6,000 and another thousand cases that I could file tomorrow if they gave me a date for people to appear in court. So that's a tremendous problem.
>
> – Court system panelist
>
> The problem is we don't have capacity. You know, even if we're assuming that we're at full capacity to do all these jury trials that we have queued up, it's going to take a long time to do it. And we're not at full capacity.
>
> – Court system panelist

The idea expressed by multiple panelists is that these cases are accumulating behind the choke point of jury trial suspension like water building behind a dam, and the number of cases is getting to a point of serious concern. Although our focus is on criminal justice and criminal courts, the issue of case backlogs is a concern for the civil justice system. Similar comments have been made regarding pandemic-related civil issues that have been deferred because of court closures and case prioritization, with some also using metaphors of a coming "surge," "flood," or "tidal wave of need."[65] For both components of the court system, the increasing numbers increase the pressure to find ways to continue to adjudicate cases in the system.

> You can analyze this all day long, but your numbers are going to be overwhelming. We cannot get out of this situation unless we relieve the pressure behind the dam—or else the whole thing is going to break.
>
> – Court system panelist

Seeking to Resume In-Person Proceedings While Protecting Staff and Public Health

The growing pressure of the backlog is the main driver of court systems seeking to resume in-person operations.[66] Many court systems are seeking to develop approaches that would allow

---

[64]   National Center for State Courts, "New Data Shed Light on Pandemic-Related Backlogs," webpage, undated c.

[65]   American Bar Association Task Force on Legal Needs Arising out of the 2020 Pandemic, 2020.

[66]   Others have argued for a continued delay, even if backlogs grow, out of concern that fairness in *criminal* trials cannot be assured under circumstances in which infection risk is sufficiently managed. For example, one bar association argued that the challenges in doing both are "insurmountable" and that trials should continue to be delayed. However, core in their argument—and similar to the reasoning behind steps taken in other parts of the system—is the idea that the continued delay will not be excessive: "The experts believe a vaccine may be available by the end of 2020 or early 2021. The [New Jersey State Bar Association] strongly urges the Judiciary to continue the pause on criminal jury trials for the time being"

the resumption of in-person jury trials even with the enduring risk of COVID-19 spread. One panelist reported that, in their state, almost all of the county-level courts had developed plans for resuming in-person operations, and half of those had plans to resume in-person jury trials. Panelists from courts that are seeking a path to do so were all acutely cognizant of the risks. In developing their strategies, participants emphasized the importance of collaboration with local public health authorities and other medical experts (for example, a participant cited close collaboration with a local medical school in developing their strategies). Caution is warranted: Both on our panel and in public news reporting, there were examples of incidents where individuals brought COVID-19 into the courtroom, exposing everyone involved in the process.[67]

> [Given the numbers involved, if] we screw it up . . . we've got a huge spike of cases. And so I think we have to err on the side of caution in protecting the health and safety of the public . . . and that requires us to find other ways to deal with our due process and constitutional requirements.
>
> – Court system panelist

The risk is not just to the public. Multiple panelists pointed out that the judiciary employs significant numbers of people with added risk from COVID-19 complications, including the elderly and those from minority groups, which poses added concern for risk management. To manage the potential for stress and mental health consequences related to reopening, participants emphasized that communication is critical because staff understanding and assessment of the steps being taken will affect stress levels.

> It's very important to be as transparent as possible with respect to [what the court is doing], because the justice partners, the lawyers, the staff, the jury, the public, they don't really understand what operations has to do to manage the daily workings of a court.
>
> – Court system panelist
>
> It's really been tremendous to see some of the leadership on the part of the presiding judges, court administrators, clerks of court. These folks have been, I think, pretty courageous. Some of them, You know, coming back after sickness, coming right back to court, working on site, and I think I've also seen probably the highest level of collaboration ever.
>
> – Court system panelist

That communication is also critical for jurors, because their willingness to come in and serve is necessary for the resumption of in-person proceedings. Jurors' stress level is also a

---

(New Jersey State Bar Association, *Report of the Committee on the Resumption of Jury Trials of the New Jersey State Bar Association Pandemic Task Force: Part Two*, New Brunswick, N.J., September 2, 2020a, p. 6).

[67] Christopher Damien, "Man Tests Positive for COVID-19 During Trial; Attorneys Say Court Isn't Protecting Public," *Desert Sun*, August 14, 2020; Freddy Monares, "Bozeman Attorneys Quarantining After Defendant Tests Positive," *Bozeman Daily Chronicle*, July 10, 2020; "Wake County Closes Courtroom After Defendant Shows Up with COVID-19," *WRAL.com*, June 16, 2020, updated June 17, 2020.

concern for trial outcomes. There are concerns that virtual juries will not serve their roles appropriately, and similar concerns have been raised regarding jurors who are uncomfortable and afraid because of perceived infection risk.[68] Like concerns about the digital divide for the representativeness of virtual juries, concerns also are raised about whether fear of infection will make in-person juries less representative. A participant whose system had resumed in-person proceedings indicated that they had not seen a large increase in no-shows, and the resulting jury pools still appeared to be representative of the community. However, monitoring the issue to ensure that those positive trends continue is important. Progress in most areas is very slow. One panelist said, "We've only done six jury trials since March and that's a real concern. So while we've proven that we could slow down, we haven't proven yet that we can get back to speed." After our workshop, reporting indicated that some jurisdictions are having difficulties, with juror concern about COVID-19 leading to summons nonresponse that is limiting the ability to hold jury trials.[69]

> One of the things that really impressed me and still continues to impress me is the response of jurors to the call of duty. We early on recommended that we make sure that we inform the jurors of what we're doing to keep them safe as they come and do their civic duty. Reactions [have] been incredible, particularly the smaller counties where we have a good turnout anyway, we're looking at very few no-shows. We have a very liberal policy in regard to deferments. And the jurors are commenting afterward that in many instances they felt safer in the courthouse than they did in their local grocery store.
>
> – Court system panelist

Infrastructure Challenges Complicate Safe Resumption

To address the risk from a virus that is transmitted through contact and the air, the core responses are separating people to limit contact, sanitizing surfaces, limiting the concentration of infectious droplets in the air, and ventilating or filtering to reduce airborne transmission. Implementing these measures can be a challenge, especially for court facilities that were constructed many years ago; that, in the words of one of our panelists, were built with the goal of "how many can we get into one room or one building" in mind; and that might not have had their heating and cooling systems upgraded for some time. Panelists talked about efforts to add plexiglass dividers in courtrooms, improve air handling or quality,[70] add signage and markings to encourage (or force) distancing, and other measures,[71] but the most frequently cited challenge was simple real estate—i.e., having enough space in court facilities to separate people enough for safety. These space constraints significantly affected the convening of

---

[68] Draper, 2020.

[69] Dave Collins, "Jury Duty? No Thanks, Say Many, Forcing Trials to Be Delayed," Associated Press, November 22, 2020.

[70] Some areas have defined baseline requirements for ventilation capability before courts can reopen: "If adequate filtration devices cannot be obtained for every courtroom [or] jury room, the county should utilize only those rooms that are sufficiently equipped with filtration devices and reduce court calendars to accommodate the reduced number of courtrooms" (Wisconsin Courts COVID-19 Task Force, 2020, pp. 10–11).

[71] For a discussion of federal court modifications in different areas of the country, see United States Courts, "As Courts Restore Operations, COVID-19 Creates a New Normal," news release, August 20, 2020b.

criminal grand juries, which involve more people than trial juries. Space constraints also have determined what cases can be held in which courtroom: One participant described a process of inventorying their area's available courtrooms to recalculate maximum occupancies under COVID-19 control measures, and space constraints meant that there were very few rooms that could handle large multiparty or multidefendant trials. And it is not just space constraints in courtrooms: Some processes—notably, jury selection—can involve even higher concentrations or larger numbers of people and, therefore, require even more space to manage infection risk.

> Very, very few of our courthouses have space in them to actually do the jury selection process . . . which means the limits and capacity going forward are going to be significant.
>
> – Court system panelist
>
> So our court has permitted people to start having a limited number of jury trials in October, pending the health situation and the resurgence of the virus—but . . . it's going to look very different. With our jury trials [under these circumstances], no one sits where they sat before. Jury's not in the jury box, witnesses [are] probably not in the witness stand because they've had to move closer to the jury, jury can't deliberate in a jury room. The public probably can't watch from [where they would normally] because now the jury is seated there, the courtroom is flipped around backward. It just looks really different, and the question is what does that mean for due process and for the whole process generally?
>
> – Court system panelist

These space constraints have resulted in courts seeking alternative locations where physically distanced court proceedings can more easily take place. This strategy echoes historical practices: During the 1918 influenza pandemic, some courts reportedly held hearings outdoors to address the same concerns about distancing and ventilation that are bedeviling today's court administrators.[72] Participants in our panel cited several examples of courts holding trials and other steps of the court process in alternative locations to allow distancing, but they also cited challenges. Key barriers included cost (because many alternative sites have to be rented), managing the security of the courtroom and the custodial security of defendants away from the court facility infrastructure, information technology and network capacity, and the logistics of cleaning and sanitization.[73]

> We're seeing some of the rural counties are using like a community center. We've heard about empty office buildings or hotel space. I know it sounds kind of crazy. The one consideration would be court security because we would certainly want screening there as well.
>
> – Court system panelist

---

[72] Draper, 2020.

[73] Another panelist suggested that "bringing the courts into the community" through using alternative sites, such as community centers or school facilities, could have unexpected benefits. By making them more accessible and connected to the area they are serving, the argument was that legitimacy and trust could be bolstered.

Concerns About Other Risk-Reduction Measures at Trial

In plans for court reopening and holding jury trials in particular, other noninfrastructure modes of risk reduction were discussed, including the screening and mask-wearing requirements summarized in Figure 4.2. Different participants indicated that their courts have had varied success with such measures, noting that, because the measures are connected to local public health strategies for controlling COVID-19, they are affected by the inconsistency of such strategies across the country. For example, although some indicated that universal mask-wearing has not been an issue in their areas, others reported a different experience.

Participants were not unanimous regarding whether these other safety measures, including masks and distance, could be used without affecting the trial process and outcomes. Mask-wearing was discussed most, and similar concerns about individuals being able to read body language and judge veracity in the virtual environment were raised regarding masked trial participants. Suspect identification was a specific point where universal mask-wearing posed problems. Such concerns go beyond masks: Concerns also have been raised about whether having a jury spread out to reduce infection risk will result in them being so far away from lawyers, witnesses, and the accused that similar concerns apply.

> [If] witnesses [are] in masks, one of the things is jurors can't size up the facial expressions of the person, and [if] lawyers [are] wearing masks and the jurors can't [assess their behavior either], and [if] jurors [are] wearing masks during *voir dire* or during the case. . . . [the lawyers] can't see their reactions. So there's that whole issue with masks.
>
> – Court system panelist

The success of infection control measures and the ability to resume in-person trials relies not only on what courts do but also on what other parts of the system do. Managing infection risk in jail facilities is a particular concern, given the possibility of a defendant bringing COVID-19 from an infected jail into the courtroom.

> Clients who are in custody, being brought in [to the jails] off the streets . . . and the jails don't have the capacity to test them. They're brought over to court with a van full of other people every day. The marshals are extremely worried, cause they're the ones who are sitting right next to them and transporting them.
>
> – Court system panelist

Planning for Long-Term Capacity Constraints for In-Person Jury Trials

Even if courts take steps to use alternative sites and resume in-person jury trials, participants in our workshop emphasized that those measures were unlikely to enable the same throughput that was possible before the pandemic. One panelist estimated the reconstitution of 30 percent of pre-pandemic capacity as a realistic scenario. Even with reduced case flows into the system, that level of capacity would not be sufficient to stop the backlog from increasing.

> If you already have [a significant] backlog and you can only do a third of [the number of jury trials] you were doing before, again, do the math, we're going to continue to build the backlog.
>
> – Court system panelist

Other strategies can help improve efficiency, notably by keeping as many steps as possible in the process of jury trials in the virtual space. Participants cited examples of doing jury summons, questionnaires, and steps of the *voir dire* process remotely. In this strategy, risk exposure is minimized because the larger group of prospective jurors is winnowed to the final jury virtually, and the court has to manage the logistics of risk reduction only for the smaller, seated jury.[74] Conducting steps that require larger groups—and therefore larger spaces to safely convene in person safely—remotely also minimizes the logistical costs associated with alternative sites. Some participants indicated that rule changes could make holding jury trials more straightforward, including reducing the ability of lawyers to reject judges without cause or limiting the number of preemptory strikes against jurors to reduce the size of the pool that must be called.

> We have a software system where jurors can now be summoned, but they don't have to come to court. The idea is to keep people away from the court if possible, but if they want to come in [they can]. And we certainly do have litigants and lawyers and potential jurors who don't have access to technology who have come in the court, but we have an online process where we can hardship a juror. If they are ready to do their service, to complete questionnaires online so that the lawyers and the court can have some advanced review of the prospective *voir dire*.
>
> – Court system panelist

But even when in-person juries are as efficient as possible, participants emphasized that they will have to be viewed as a scarce resource for some time, and therefore must be conserved as much as possible for the cases that really require them. As a result, as many cases as possible will have to be heard in the virtual space or capacity will be exhausted. This will require continuing case prioritization for in-person action using criteria that are similar to those discussed for prioritizing action in virtual proceedings. According to the Wisconsin Courts COVID-19 Task Force, "[i]t is recommended that when establishing the policy, the following factors are taken into consideration: the nature of the cases; the extent to which the cases involve liberty

---

[74] Wisconsin Courts COVID-19 Task Force, 2020, includes a more extensive list of steps:

It is recommended that the court consider the following strategies to reduce the number of people required to report for jury selection: utilize preselection questionnaires as part of *voir dire* to reduce the number of jurors needed in the courtroom; preselect jurors (commonly referred to as a paper selection) so only the empaneled jurors report to the courtroom; conduct *voir dire* in sessions based on the number of jurors that can be socially distanced in the courtroom; conduct *voir dire* virtually in full or in part to reduce the number of jurors reporting to the courtroom; utilize in-person and virtual *voir dire* simultaneously (in-person in the courtroom virtually broadcasted to another room[s] with the rest of the jurors); to preserve space for *voir dire*, broadcast jury selection and limit or eliminate spectators in the courtroom; utilize six-person juries upon stipulation to cut the number of jurors needed in half; give priority to "strikes for cause" based on juror health and safety concerns (p. 17).

interests; the extent to which cases have time limit requirements; and cases with victim rights interests."[75] There will still be the need to resolve many cases through other means—primarily plea bargaining, but potentially also dismissing less serious cases—to ensure that serious cases have a jury to hear them.

> One thing that we've been saying is we need to do everything we can remotely in every case type that can be done remotely, so those things that must be done in person can occur in person. If everything goes back to normal and every family law case and every status conference in a civil case and everything else goes back to the courthouse, we're not going to have capacity to deal with the criminal matters that need to be done in person.
>
> – Court system panelist

Participants made similar arguments for the civil side: for example, according to one participant, a settlement judge telling parties that if they are going to a jury "this better be good because the jurors are not [going to be happy] coming in here just to hear a dispute over 50 or 100 dollars" might provide a strong push to reach a pretrial settlement.

> [But] it better be worth it, because we're bringing people in and we're assuring them— without really the ability to do that—that everything's going to be fine. And so when they sit there and hear [the case], it better be something that's important.
>
> —Court system panelist
>
> So meanwhile, how do I do [thousands of] felony cases when we've done six trials in the last six months? I don't know, other than it's a lot of plea bargaining, and a lot of dismissals . . . with the idea of preserving the capacity of our court to handle the most serious things so that when we do bring the jurors in, it is for a murder trial, it is for a sexual assault. This is for something that's very, very serious.
>
> —Court system panelist

Pandemic Effects on Court Funding and Pressures for Even More Change and Innovation

Because of the interconnectivity of the criminal justice system, some of the measures designed to reduce COVID-19 case counts have created different pressures on court systems, most directly for systems that are funded by fees and fines paid as a result of the justice process. Efforts to reduce cases coming into the court system reduce funding coming into the system in lockstep, choking off resources that could be useful for responding to the pandemic in other ways and potentially creating additional capacity constraints.

---

[75] Wisconsin Courts COVID-19 Task Force, 2020, p 18. See also, for example, Supreme Court of the State of Arizona, *COVID-19 Continuity of Court Operations During a Public Health Emergency Workgroup Best Practice Recommendations*, Phoenix, Ariz., May 1, 2020.

> It's not talked about much, but I think there's been a huge revenue hit on courts . . . when traffic filings and [other filings] are down 40 or 50 percent in a lot of these jurisdictions and those monies are used, not just to fund the courts, but also parts of law enforcement and victim services that's sort of another dimension.
>
> – Court system panelist

Even for courts that are not funded directly from fees and fines, the effects of the pandemic have created financial pressures, including requirements to cut budgets as local tax revenues have dropped precipitously. Participants argued that, if the courts are going to keep functioning, there will have to be changes in policy, and they are actively seeking relief from states and the federal government to "keep justice going."

> We're almost all sales tax–funded. All of a sudden we went from an even budget to [a] $150 million hole . . . my office was looking at a $9 million cut in the next biennium.
>
> – Court system panelist

The funding pressures have required staffing cuts in some systems, which will only reinforce the capacity constraints that are producing case backlogs and pressure. Tellingly, a panelist from one court system described their situation as "fortunate" because they had enough staff departures and retirements to stay within their reduced budget. It was not that they were not having to manage with less staff; instead, they had not had to go through the dislocation of implementing furloughs, salary cuts, or other measures (which had been necessary elsewhere in their state). These financial pressures have caused some systems to consider significant changes in policy, including large increases in pretrial diversion, changes in prosecutorial strategies, and other alternative approaches to reduce the pressure in the system and to stay within their pandemic-reduced budgets.

> We're hearing from some jurisdictions, depending on how they are funded in their state, that a few offices have even had to consider closing down because they can't afford to keep staff on based on their particular funding structure.
>
> – Court system panelist

Taking Stock and Looking Forward

In responding to the COVID-19 pandemic, many of the initial steps taken by the court system—like those elsewhere in the criminal justice system and in the country writ large—would have been well matched to a scenario in which the pandemic was a short-term event. Halting operations and building case backlogs for a few weeks would have created challenges, but a relatively rapid return to baseline functioning could have worked the backlog through the system. Because the pandemic is a longer-term crisis—and one that is shaped by the nature of the responses taken to manage its initial phases—court systems were required to consider alternative approaches to reconstitute functioning while managing ongoing infection risk. That planning must contend with the large case backlogs that are accumulating at different points in the system, along with potential future waves on both the criminal and civil sides related to the pandemic and its aftershocks. Identifying and maintaining efficiency enhancements that are being adopted might be critical not only for relieving the pressures that have built in the system since March, but also in dealing with the pressures to come.[76]

> We can manage safety, but we can't eliminate risk until that big medical breakthrough comes through for COVID-19 that we all hope will come.
>
> – Court system panelist

Promising Practices from the COVID-19 Pandemic Response

When we look across the changes made in court systems, we find a variety of changes that appeared to be valuable both in terms of strengthening the system to address future challenges and because they could be more broadly beneficial. Our panelists emphasized the following practices:

- **Maintaining virtual access to the courts:** The ability of individuals to attend court remotely not only improves efficiency but also appears to have improved access to justice by making it easier and less costly for individuals to participate. Although digital divide concerns—which might increase because of the economic effects of the pandemic—must be resolved, the value of virtual options appears to be considerable.
- **Maintaining remote and paperless work processes for courts:** Even before the pandemic, courts were pursuing paperless processes and other improvements in information technology. Although models that allowed easy work from home were valuable in the pandemic, they also would improve efficiency after the pandemic.
- **Continuing virtual elements of in-person processes:** Although a return to traditional in-person jury trials is a priority, maintaining virtual components wherever possible—in jury selection and *voir dire*—would increase efficiency and make jury service less burdensome.
- **Maintaining routine virtual connectivity between courts and corrections agencies:** In both the courts and corrections panels, participants noted the high value of bringing individuals to court virtually because it increased safety for all and cut costs involved with prisoner transportation and security at court.

---

[76] See, for example, discussion in Tania Sourdin, Bin Li, and Donna Marie McNamara, "Court Innovations and Access to Justice in Times of Crisis," *Health Policy and Technology*, Vol. 9, No. 4, December 2020.

> I think [virtual connection] is something that in the long run will be an option that people will take to at least for the preliminary stages of *voir dire*, which would include answering the summons, reporting in, doing hardships, and perhaps doing question-naires . . . And I think in terms of customer service for our public, they'll like that, and I think we're going to be having that for the long run to reduce the amount of time that people spend at the courthouse as a juror.
>
> – Court system panelist

> It strikes me as pretty remarkable that the same companies that are charging incarcer-ated people $15 a minute for videoconferencing have never found a way to install vid-eoconference software in probation and parole offices or in courthouses. Clearly there's a capability here, it's just a lack of willingness and intent. But we're starting to see that shift and that should be the standard going forward to drastically minimize every single person's need to physically interact with the system's machinations.
>
> – Community organization panelist

Pandemic Pressure as a Driver of Broader Criminal Justice Innovation

The pandemic has stimulated rapid innovation in the court system. When they described the changes that have been made in the use of virtual technologies and court approaches, multiple members of our panel expressed shock at the pace and scope of change. But because those changes have not been enough to maintain the functioning of the system, and because of the accumulating pressure of case backlogs, participants argued that the pandemic might be a catalyst for even more significant change. Some participants were quite blunt, stating that, if further changes are not made, the accumulating pressures might "break the system" in funda-mental ways.

> I think the biggest issue is [that] the capacity of the courts to operate at the level they did before is not going to be there until this is behind us. And then the backlog will take years or decades to dig out of, unless we provide some creative way to dispose of the cases that are in the system.
>
> – Court system panelist

Out of practical necessity, some court systems are exploring the significant expansion of alternatives to avoid putting everyone through the criminal justice process. For example, one court system panelist described a new initiative to *significantly* increase the diversion of individ-uals accused of their first felony to NGOs for intervention outside the traditional justice pro-cess. The savings from doing so are intended to forestall the need to make significant personnel cuts to balance their budget. In the jurisdiction the panelist described, this diversion effort is going to be supported by a government-funded victim compensation fund because restitution sometimes is a factor that makes diversion more difficult. Without alternatives to prosecution, a point might be reached where cases—particularly cases in which the individuals involved do not have a long, violent history—are dismissed to reduce the pressure.

> One way that I think that we can achieve both an investment in the community and reduce the footprint of the criminal justice system—and reduce the pressure behind the dam [from the growing backlog of cases] that threatens to swamp the whole thing—is to do a lot more diversion. And that's where the prosecutor has a particular super-power, which is prosecutorial discretion.
>
> – Court system panelist

These approaches, which were forced on the system so that it could weather the pandemic, do not represent new ideas. Programs for the diversion of individuals out of the justice system and initiatives to reduce the use of traditional punishment-focused approaches to all crime have been experimented with and used in different jurisdictions for many years. Such initiatives often encounter pushback, because of concerns that they are "too soft" on people who have committed serious crimes or adherence to the belief that retributive approaches deter future offending. Although such objections clearly still exist—our participants described encountering them during their efforts to respond to the pandemic—the backlogs and pressures on the system have created a policy alignment between the rapid expansion of such programs and the logistical survival imperatives of the justice system. Furthermore, many of these programs have been assessed to be at least as effective as incarceration (if not more so) for responding to crime.

> I also know that there's an awful lot of people in our community who just don't want anything to change at all. And that's the pushback that I'm getting, but things are going to change and we're going to have to involve the community more. And we're going to have to reduce the load of the court so that the court can handle the most serious, violent cases that have arisen in our community.
>
> – Court system panelist

The context of pressures for justice reform also loom large and reflect the complexity of the national environment. Although much of the focus of protests has been on law enforcement, issues regarding systemic racism in judicial processes are prominent as well. Participants in our panel noted that this environment is both a stressor for court staff and a key factor to consider in planning for how the courts should function after the pandemic is no longer the primary driver of decisionmaking. Many of the goals of the Black Lives Matter movement, including increased alternatives to traditional criminal justice action and less involvement of the system in people's lives, are in relatively close alignment with the practical needs of courts during the pandemic—specifically, increased diversion, less prosecution, and seeking to reduce the number of cases entering the courts in the first place. This reality suggests that the pressure of the pandemic could be the stimulus for further, broader innovation; to quote Michigan Chief Justice Bridget McCormack, "[the] pandemic was not the disruption [the courts] wanted, but it might be the disruption we needed to transform."[77]

---

[77] Michigan Justice for All Task Force, "Chief Justice Tells Congress of Michigan's Virtual Court Successes," No. 3, September 2020.

Policy Development and Evaluation Needs to Better Inform Decisions in Both the Short and Longer Terms

Discussions among the court panelists also highlighted multiple issues that merit focused efforts at policy development (for short-term needs) and longer-term research and evaluation. In the former case, the driver is for better informing the actions to manage pandemic risk, many of which are being developed independently in different systems across the country. Three short-term priorities flagged by participants were

- identifying sets of alternative facilities where jury trials could be held in the community and coordinating all relevant stakeholders needed to do so
- soliciting local community input on case prioritization to ensure that community views are reflected in which cases are allocated scarce court resources and acted on in backlog-reduction efforts
- developing resources to educate court system stakeholders about Health Insurance Portability and Accountability Act (HIPAA) requirements regarding the sharing of COVID-19 case information during the pandemic.

When we consider the longer term—including decisions to continue using the promising practices discussed in the previous sections—we find a significant need for evaluation research. Panelists were clear that, although the outcomes of these efforts appear to be positive now, the ability to maintain them beyond the immediate needs created by the pandemic will require evidence that they are indeed beneficial. Research must also take into account the significant variation that exists among court systems at all levels, even between counties in the same state. Panelists argued that courts were unlikely to be able to do all of this assessment themselves, in part because of the demands the backlog will place on systems after the pandemic. Collaboration with researchers to fill that gap would be beneficial.

> We need research now and on lots of different areas. . . . One is around what efficiencies have been gained from doing things through technology, that because of to the degree we look to go back to normal, whatever that is, what are we going to retain from this? What are we going to toss? And the efficiency piece needs to be a big part of that conversation. [But] equally as important is what's the impact on procedural fairness and actual due process fairness. And . . . I'm not aware of any real research that's going on with that.
>
> – Court system panelist

Although performing some of the analysis and evaluation that is needed might be possible with data that are already collected, some will almost certainly rely on ephemeral data that might not be recorded anywhere if they are not captured now. For example, tracking different individuals who went through combinations of virtual and in-person processes, changes in diversion or specialty court practices to address the pandemic, and so on will be needed to explain differences in outcomes. If those data are not collected soon, the opportunity to assess some of the changes made in the courts might be lost. The budgetary effects from the pandemic on court systems might make such evaluation more difficult, with remaining staff and resources stretched to manage day-to-day business.

At some point in the next few months, hopefully several months, maybe it's six or nine months, we're going to start to lose the opportunity to research that because we're going to start moving back to normal. So now is the time to do that research.

– Court system panelist

One of the hard parts about this is we're trying to leverage our resources in order to make cases go. There isn't a lot of backfill with regard to data collection. We do our best to do what we [are] already ordered to do or what we're required to provide. And that's a lot, but . . . in light of the pandemic, it's going to make it more difficult because frankly our budgets are shrinking . . . as a practical reality.

– Court system panelist

The following questions, the answers to which would inform post-pandemic decision-making, came out of the panel discussion:

- Have remote-appearance options reduced failure-to-appear rates?
- Has the significant reduction in pretrial detention and money bail had an effect on appearance rates?
- Can the effects of the pandemic on plea bargaining behavior and outcomes be identified and measured? Can concerns about the potential coerciveness of COVID-19 in correctional facilities (i.e., increasing bargaining power of prosecution) be distinguished from ways that the push to reduce jail and prison populations might lead to a greater desire to reach agreement rapidly?
- Do victims of crime have a different perception of whether justice is served in remote hearings and proceedings?
- How do jurors perceive the experience of serving on a virtual jury?
- If virtual juries are used, are there issues maintaining the representativeness of the jury pool?
- In virtual proceedings, do outcomes differ from those of in-person court processes on measurable factors, such as bail, sentences, or other outcomes? If there are differences, do they arise from the medium itself or from differences in participant behavior (e.g., attentiveness to proceedings by jurors, how well judges can control the room in virtual versus physical space)?
- Can the positive effects of virtual proceedings on litigants—in easier access, lower costs, and other factors—be quantified? If costs are lower, is access to justice increased?
- How has the shift to virtual proceedings affected self-represented litigants?
- Are there safety or mental health issues with judges and other staff from remote work models?
- Can the effects of streaming or broadcasting court proceedings online be measured to allow for the weighing of broader access versus greater exposure for both victims, defendants, and other parties?
- Is there a measurable effect on case outcomes of trial participants being socially distanced or wearing face coverings?

- Could online dispute-resolution processes be applied in the criminal area to help reduce the backlog while maintaining procedural justice?[78]
- How have the mechanisms through which court systems are funded affected their ability to respond to and operate through the pandemic?
- Does the potential for integrating virtual technology into future court operations suggest a need to revisit court design and security standards?

Research efforts that are focused on these questions could provide a broader understanding of the effects of the substantial adoption of virtual technologies in particular and inform decisions for court technology and policy going forward.

---

[78] See, for example, Nevin, 2020; and Witwer et al., forthcoming.

CHAPTER FIVE

Institutional Corrections: Prisons, Jails, and Other Custodial Facilities

When individuals are sentenced to time in custody as a result of conviction, or when they are being held before having their day in court, they spend that time in a correctional facility—e.g., prisons, jails, or other custodial facilities (Figure 5.1). Many of these facilities are operated by government departments of corrections at the federal, state, county, or local level, but others are operated by commercial providers that incarcerate people under contract to the government. Correctional institutions have relatively less control than other parts of the justice system over the flows of people into and out of their custody, which is driven most significantly by prosecutorial and court decisions about charges and sentences. However, some agencies can set acceptance criteria for the types of individuals that can be brought to them. In addition, some agencies have direct roles in parole and release processes that can either speed up or constrain the release of people from custody to the community.

Figure 5.1
Corrections Agencies

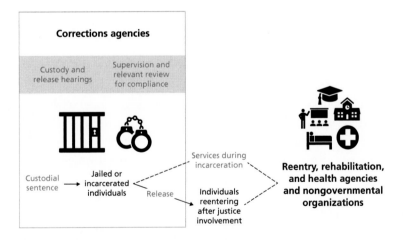

> In most cases, our correctional leaders don't have control over the front door. In most cases, that's a court system. And the back door, in most cases, that's a parole system with [its] own sets of decisionmakers.
>
> – Institutional corrections panelist

Beyond the simple flow in and out of this part of the system, flows within institutional corrections are critical. For example, restrictions on the movement of individuals from jails to prisons or among facilities with different levels of security can constrain options for responding to disease risk and other issues. Our participants emphasized that being aware of those internal flows also was important for fully understanding the effect of the pandemic on the system. During the pandemic, decisions by parts of the corrections system (e.g., prisons) had impacts on jails or other facilities, such as transitional housing sites.

> Everything in the criminal justice system is like flowing bodies of water. People come from the courts, they got convicted. They're housed in local jails. They're declared state ready. They get delivered to reception centers. From there they're processed then delivered to general confinement facilities. From general confinement facilities, they may start off as max, moved to medium eventually, with lower security to minimum, released to the community.
>
> – Institutional corrections panelist

The realities of the correctional environment meant that the spread of COVID-19 within the walls of custodial facilities was—and remains—a major concern.[1] For example,

- much of what these agencies do is inside by definition, so strategies like those adopted in other parts of the justice system to move activities outside are relevant only to a limited extent
- the population density inside some correctional facilities is very high. The scale of incarceration in the United States means that many facilities operate at or above their designed capacity, and even their designed capacity houses many individuals in high-density arrangements, such as multiperson cells or dormitories, which creates significant risk for the spread of disease. The spread of COVID-19 in carceral situations was found to be more than twice as fast as for the nation overall.[2]
- because of the populations incarcerated and the length of sentences, a significant percentage of correctional populations fall into high-risk groups for more-serious consequences from COVID-19 infection—e.g., elderly individuals; people with preexisting health conditions; and members of minority groups, who have higher average fatality rates from COVID-19.[3] Incarcerated individuals who suffer from mental health and behavioral disorders might resist compliance with infection-control procedures, which complicates efforts to contain the spread of disease within a facility.
- standard prison practices frequently involve close contact and interaction among residents and staff. According to one source,

---

[1]   Kimberly Kindy, "Inside the Deadliest Federal Prison, the Seeping Coronavirus Creates Fear and Danger," *Washington Post*, April 10, 2020; Andre G. Montoya-Barthelemy, Charles D. Lee, Dave R. Cundiff, and Eric B. Smith, "COVID-19 and the Correctional Environment: The American Prison as a Focal Point for Public Health," *American Journal of Preventive Medicine*, Vol. 58, No. 6, June 2020; Meghan A. Novisky, Chelsey S. Narvey, and Daniel C. Semenza, "Institutional Responses to the COVID-19 Pandemic in American Prisons," *Victims and Offenders*, Vol. 15, Nos. 7–8, 2020.

[2]   Watson et al., 2020.

[3]   Watson et al., 2020.

[s]ocial distancing guidelines to combat COVID-19 aren't as effective in the prison community. The common areas, fluctuating population, mandatory physical interactions (such as strip searches, pat downs . . . shakedowns [and other security practices, such as breaking up fights and cell extractions]), and inherently confined spaces are obstacles to health and wellness.[4]

Standard practice also includes the frequent movement of staff, who could introduce infection to a facility or carry it from the incarcerated population to the community.

If a jail or prison is an older building with antiquated ventilation systems and if it is tightly limited in the space that is available and the number of people who have to be housed there, options of distancing and infection control also might be very limited.

> We are what we call a "facilities-challenged jail," built over 30 years ago, it's falling apart.
>
> – Law enforcement management panelist
>
> Early on, we kept hearing talk about, "You need to socially distance your inmates." Well, I was always asking, how do you socially distance, [thousands of] people in a fixed concrete footprint? So everybody came up with the idea that we will make them sleep head to toe, head to toe. Well, my argument was always that the majority of these folks are here because they don't follow rules. If they followed rules, they probably wouldn't be here."
>
> – Institutional corrections panelist
>
> If you're at a hundred percent capacity or above, [and] you have an outbreak, there is nothing you can do. You can't quarantine people, you're stuck. If you have a little bit of breathing room, there's a lot of things you can do to help manage an outbreak and keep people safe, both inmates and staff.
>
> – Institutional corrections panelist

As was the case for other components of the justice system, past concern about pandemic influenza and other diseases prompted some preparedness efforts in institutional corrections systems, but the extent of preparedness varied from system to system.[5] Examinations of corrections operations during the pandemic discussed preparedness concerns, including that "correctional health services have often been left out of the epidemic preparedness planning undertaken at the local, state, and federal levels."[6]

---

[4] TaLisa J. Carter, "COVID-19 in the Common Area: The Pandemic Is Reinforcing the Interconnected Nature of Corrections," *Urban Wire* blog, June 16, 2020.

[5] Baldwin, Eassey, and Brooke, 2020.

[6] Emily A. Wang, Bruce Western, Emily P. Backes, and Julie Schuck, eds., *Decarcerating Correctional Facilities During COVID-19: Advancing Health, Equity, and Safety*, Washington, D.C.: The National Academies Press, 2020, p. 1-2.

> We're fortunate to have a really good relationship at the sheriff's office with correctional health and public health. And we were already on the process of [a] hepatitis vaccination program. So, we already had chicken pox protocols in place for whenever we had chicken pox outbreaks in our jails and . . . we had dealt with the AIDS outbreak and the SARS outbreaks. So we had a lot of policies already in place.
>
> – Institutional corrections panelist
>
> We leveraged our experience with pandemic preparation—swine influenza, pandemic flu—for purposes of managing our preparation at the outset of this coronavirus. In partnership with correctional health, we had done tabletop exercises and we presented our corrections plan to our local oversight agencies in February.
>
> – Institutional corrections panelist

As a result of differences in preparedness and magnified by the variation in the pandemic across the country over time,[7] different correctional systems responded very differently to the pandemic. Broad reviews of actions taken across the country show wide variation,[8] and examinations of the spread of responses echoed the conclusion that differences in response mirrored the fragmentation of the broader national response to the pandemic.[9]

Although not all correctional systems were equally affected by the pandemic,[10] the disease hit the corrections sector hard:[11]

> In some state prisons, three out of every four inmates have tested positive. In late April, over 70 percent of tested inmates in federal prisons had COVID-19. This spring, the rate of infection for prisoners was 5.5 times higher than that of the general public, and the COVID-19 death rate was three times higher. . . . Correctional facilities have become a leading source of community transmission in the U.S. Researchers estimate that one-in-six cases of COVID-19 in the state of Illinois can be traced back to the jail in Cook County,

---

[7]   See, for example, the discussion in Bryn Nelson and David B. Kaminsky, "A COVID-19 Crisis in U.S. Jails and Prisons," *Cancer Cytopathology*, Vol. 128, No. 8, August 2020.

[8]   See, for example, the data set built and maintained by the University of California, Los Angeles (UCLA) (University of California, Los Angeles, "UCLA Law: COVID-19 Behind Bars Data Project," webpage, undated) or individual assessments by the Marshall Project (The Marshall Project, "How Prisons in Each State Are Restricting Visits Due to Coronavirus," webpage, March 17, 2020, updated November 25, 2020a).

[9]   For example, "In many ways, the fragmented response of the country's state and federal correctional systems is symbolic of the broader approach to the pandemic throughout the United States as a whole" (Novisky, Narvey, and Semenza, 2020, p. 1247).

[10]   For example, in an analysis of prison system mortality, Schnepel identified 14 states with no reported deaths and "six states with COVID-19 mortality rates below what would be expected given the state mortality rates for specific sex, age, and race/ethnicity groups. Several other states, by contrast, exhibit mortality rates within prisons that are considerably higher than the adjusted state mortality rates" (Kevin T. Schnepel, *COVID-19 in U.S. State and Federal Prisons*, Washington, D.C.: Council on Criminal Justice, National Commission on COVID-19 and Criminal Justice, September 2020, p. 3).

[11]   Bill Chappell and Paige Pfleger, "73% of Inmates at an Ohio Prison Test Positive for Coronavirus," NPR, April 20, 2020; Brendan Saloner, Kalind Parish, Julie A. Ward, Grace DiLaura, and Sharon Dolovich, "COVID-19 Cases and Deaths in Federal and State Prisons," *JAMA*, Vol. 324, No. 6, 2020.

Chicago. Everyday movement of correctional staff and people entering and leaving jails contribute to transmission to and from correctional facilities and communities.[12]

Looking across the country, illness among residents of the corrections system varied over time and in intensity, but COVID-19 accounted for thousands of deaths and hundreds of thousands of cases to date (Figure 5.2). Efforts that have focused on specific populations—e.g., The Sentencing Project, which has tracked infections among juveniles in youth detention facilities—have reported cases in 38 different states and territories as of the end of October 2020.[13]

[In my county] we have the largest jail population in the state at the county level. And we, unfortunately, we also had the highest level of COVID cases. So it goes together. And it came on so fast.

– Institutional corrections panelist

We know that about 1,200 people have died so far in terms of incarcerated people and staff, the largest clusters of COVID continue to be jails and prisons, and we're continuing to struggle to find ways to kind of get a better response from the system.

– Community organization panelist

Because staff in custodial institutions—not just corrections officers or security staff but service providers and others as well—often work in proximity and contact with resident populations, they are at risk of being infected with or transmitting the virus. It is estimated that between 98 and 161 corrections officers and staff have died as a result of COVID-19 as of November 2020.[14] Figure 5.3 shows the distribution of staff fatalities across the country, emphasizing the broad effects of COVID-19 on this part of the criminal justice workforce. The numbers of corrections staff who have contracted the disease and who have had to quarantine as a result of exposure concerns are much higher, with consequences both for the morale and mental health of correctional staff and for the continued functioning of corrections institutions, which require sufficient numbers of people to maintain security and meet the needs of residents. As the pandemic continued into late 2020, some areas reportedly had to shut down entire facilities because of shortages of staff and the extent of outbreaks in the population.[15]

---

[12] Vikki Wachino, "Testimony of Vikki Wachino, CEO, Community Oriented Correctional Health Services to the National Commission on COVID-19 and Criminal Justice," testimony before the National Commission on COVID-19 and Criminal Justice, Washington, D.C., September 3, 2020, pp. 1–2. Other estimates place the mortality rate in prisons lower, but still significantly exceeding the rate for the general public (Schnepel, 2020).

[13] Josh Rovner, "COVID-19 in Juvenile Facilities," The Sentencing Project, webpage, December 4, 2020.

[14] The Marshall Project, 2020b; American Correctional Association, undated. Note that tabulations of corrections personnel lost to COVID-19 include both individuals working in corrections facilities and individuals involved in community supervision.

[15] Brendon Derr, Rebecca Griesbach, and Danya Issawi, "States Are Shutting Down Prisons as Guards Are Crippled By Covid-19," *New York Times*, January 1, 2021.

Figure 5.2
Cases of COVID-19 in Correctional Facilities, by State, March–September 2020

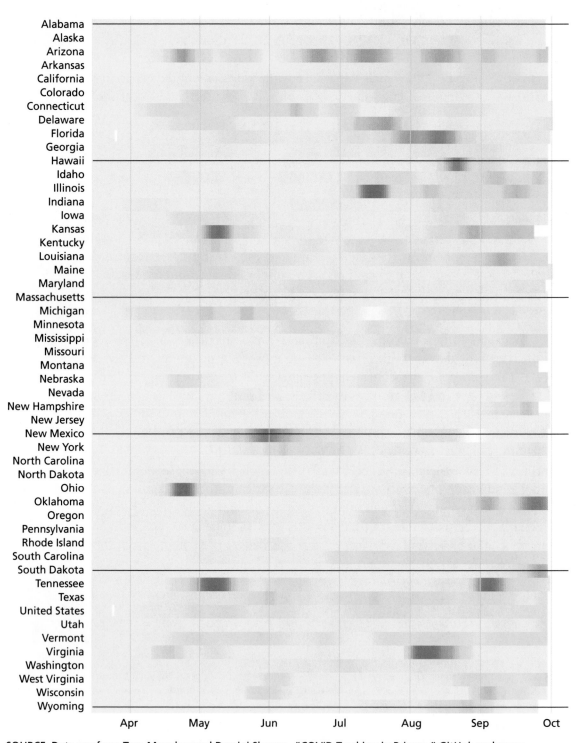

SOURCE: Data are from Tom Meagher and Damini Sharma, "COVID Tracking in Prisons," GitHub webpage, undated. See also The Marshall Project, 2020b.

Figure 5.3
Fatalities from COVID-19 Among Correctional Staff, by State, November 2020

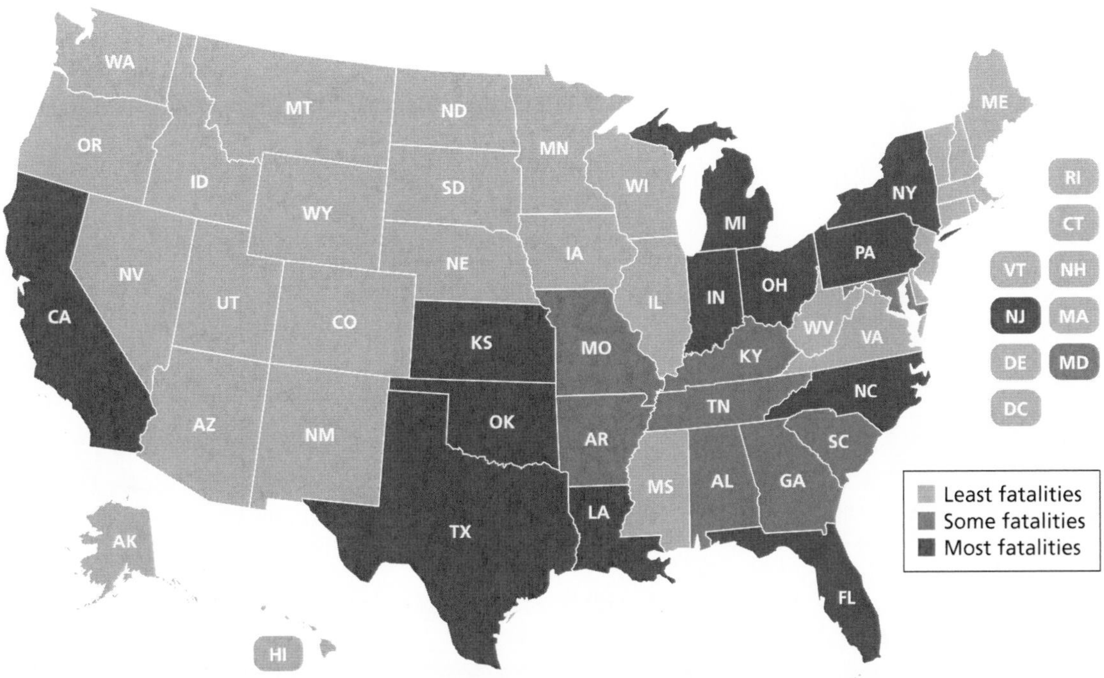

SOURCE: Data are from The Marshall Project, 2020b, and Officer Down Memorial Page, "Line of Duty Deaths by State," webpage, undated (for the District of Columbia).

> [More than one-third] of our uniform staff were out sick and for a variety of symptomatic or confirmed reasons. And testing was hard to come by.
>
> – Institutional corrections panelist
>
> Unfortunately the, the first sort of news of the outbreak was the death of one of our officers and the death of one of our inmates from COVID. So it really got everyone's attention locally very quickly.
>
> – Institutional corrections panelist

Given the combined effect of COVID-19 on corrections populations and, by extension, on the communities surrounding correctional facilities,[16] understanding the path of the pandemic within the institutional corrections system is important not just because of how it affected criminal justice, but also as a key piece of the puzzle for understanding its effects in the United States as a whole. As Era Laudermilk put it in a Vera Institute webinar on this early in the pandemic, "[t]his is a public health issue. If our jail is in a dire strait, then all of us are in a dire strait."[17] Using data published by the *New York Times*, Figure 5.4 shows the distribution

---

[16] A study from a large county jail estimated (for a period early in the pandemic through April 2020) that more than 15 percent of cases in the city were associated with people "cycling through" the jail (Watson et al., 2020, p. 12).

[17] Era Laudermilk, deputy of policy and strategic planning, Law Office of the Cook County Public Defender, in Vera Institute of Justice, "COVID-19 and Jail Releases Webinar," video, YouTube, April 17, 2020a.

Figure 5.4
Correctional Facility Outbreaks with the Highest Case Counts of COVID-19

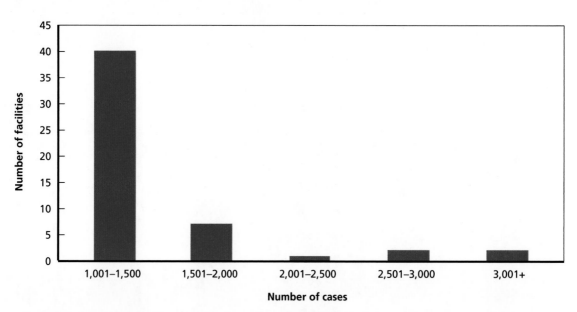

SOURCE: Data are from "Coronavirus in the U.S.: Latest Map and Case Count," *New York Times*, undated.

of the 52 correctional facilities with the largest reported outbreaks (broken down into groups of 500 cases), ranging from 40 facilities that had between 1,001 and 1,500 cases to two facilities with more than 3,000 infections. There also were more than 100 facilities with between 501 and 1,000 cases and more than 850 facilities that had between 50 and 500 cases of COVID-19 (not shown in the figure).

> Something like 40 of the 50 largest outbreaks of COVID in this country have been in correctional settings. So this not like, "Oh, this is a side population that happens to be infected." *This is the main driving part of this epidemic.* We've been frankly spanked by it. And it's not just the people who are incarcerated. It's the people who work there, the officers and their families, and their communities, and their connections there. So that's a huge problem that really has a lot of implications. And I think the first one is it's laid bare the vulnerability that we as a society have by creating this mass incarceration. And so I think hopefully this will, this is a wakeup call for us to kind of smarten up and say, "Gee, it's not really a good idea to put a lot of people behind bars."
>
> – Community corrections panelist

Reflecting a common thread across the justice agencies that participated in our panels, assumptions about the likely duration of the pandemic shaped thinking about how to respond and about the sustainability of actions that were taken. Suspending contacts and halting some operations to try to keep the virus out of institutions would have been much easier for a short-term wave of risk, which a significant part of national rhetoric regarding the pandemic argued would be the case. But as it became clear that it would be an extended crisis, existing agency models for operation with minimal staff—either as a protective measure or out of necessity because of ill staff members—were more difficult to sustain. Participants argued that the assumption that this would be a short-term crisis also affected staff willingness to remain committed to response measures in the long term.

> I think a lot of it is also how we frame it to our employees and as a country, for the most part everything was "it's going to be weeks, or it's only going to be a few more weeks or a few more months." And then people start to have that belief in their head. And now we're having like a COVID burnout in our employees because they're just tired of having to deal with this. And it was sold a certain way, so we have to kind of start framing it as a country, and especially as our different organizations that this is more of a marathon. It's not a sprint and it's going to be a continuous process.
>
> – Institutional corrections panelist
>
> [Because of staff losses to illness and quarantine,] we reached a phase of critical staffing and, [although we had to manage with reduced staff before for short events, such as snowstorms,] we *never* had to manage it for the duration of . . . this crisis. And I think that was a real learning experience for us because what we had been prepared for at that level of critical operations, wasn't robust enough to . . . be the playbook that could sustain us for three months of that level of operations. And so I think that was a real, you know, trial-by-fire lesson learned.
>
> – Institutional corrections panelist

Given the constraints under which the institutional corrections system operates, and because of intense concern regarding the vulnerability of incarcerated populations and the potential effect on public health of COVID-19 spread within corrections, a variety of actions were taken in an effort to reduce risk. In a complementary effort with those to reduce arrests and change court practices to cut flows of people into the justice system, jails and prisons took steps to reduce populations and made other significant changes that were designed to protect incarcerated populations and the staff involved in the corrections system from COVID-19.

Reducing Prison and Jail Populations to Reduce COVID-19 Risk

Although the corrections system has comparatively few levers to affect the numbers of people under its care, it does have some options. Beyond actions taken by law enforcement or courts to reduce the flow into institutional corrections, some correctional systems changed policies and practices that cut populations further, including at intake (which has implications for law enforcement strategies, as discussed in Chapter Three) and through release (which had consequences for community corrections and supervision agencies). In some cases, different decisions by different parts of the corrections system led to pressures building *within* the sector.

In statewide data assembled by the Prison Policy Initiative in June 2020, for states that reported separate numbers for jail and prison populations, the average reduction in the jail population was approximately 20 percent (ranging from a 3.7-percent increase in one state to more than a 40-percent reduction in another) but the reduction was less than 10 percent for

Key Findings from Institutional Corrections Agencies' Response to the COVID-19 Pandemic

- Corrections facilities are limited by the space they have, and facilities that were overcrowded before the pandemic had great difficulty controlling the spread of the virus. In concert with other parts of the system, institutional corrections agencies sought to reduce jail and prison populations to open up space and enable disease control. Less reliance on incarceration was one of the reforms called for during national protests, meaning that the COVID-19 response represented a broad-based experiment implementing that change on a national scale.

- Some facilities closed their doors to visitors and many types of nonsecurity staff, which reduced the chance of the virus entering facilities but hobbled many types of programming. Although such approaches were fine for short periods, as the pandemic wore on, they became more difficult to maintain.

- Shortages in testing and the difficulty of managing large-scale testing programs made it difficult to keep the virus out of facilities and manage outbreaks when they occurred. Facilities had to develop management strategies for isolation and quarantine of multiple populations to limit risk.

- Masks and hygiene practices were central components of many facilities' responses.

- Many institutions had difficulty managing public messaging regarding the situations within the facilities and the steps they were taking in response. Agencies that had provided their residents with tablets or other ways to communicate with family cited transparency benefits because inmates could give their families, counsel, and other audiences updates.

- Delivering health care in hard-hit facilities was difficult, particularly for agencies that relied on outside hospitals to provide advanced care to residents. COVID-19 control procedures made meeting residents' other care needs (e.g., for substance use disorders or mental health challenges) more difficult. Doing so was facilitated by virtual technologies for telecare.

- Correctional and service provider staff faced major stress and health concerns, both from the broader pandemic and the specifics of their occupational exposure. Strategies to protect staff included procedural measures and providing protective equipment, although agencies sometimes had issues with staff use of PPE.

- Institutional corrections agencies face funding pressures as a result of the effects of the pandemic on municipal and state budgets. There are concerns that those budget constraints will limit the ability of agencies to maintain the reduced density that has enabled infection-control strategies but that also could enable the system to improve performance and implement reforms going forward.

prison populations (ranging from 2 percent to just more than 37 percent).[18] Other analyses echo these findings, noting more-substantial decarceration in jails than in prisons.[19] Some early data suggest that the strategy was effective, likely in part because of the variety of other actions that were made easier by reducing populations. An analysis of population reductions and COVID-19 rates suggested that "those with greater reductions in population from early April to early July also had lower rates of COVID-19 infections," although conclusions were complicated by variation in testing and data reporting from facilities.[20] However, other analyses disagree that it has been enough.[21]

Agencies Acted to Reduce Flows of Individuals into Their Facilities

Actions taken by corrections agencies, including changes in acceptance criteria for local jails,[22] helped both reduce populations and drive shifts in practice by others in law enforcement and in other parts of the corrections system.[23]

> We immediately throttled back our booking acceptance criteria.
>
> — Law enforcement operations panelist
>
> We did stop the regional lockups [i.e., holding arrestees before arraignment for several jurisdictions] simply because they were bringing more people in. And when you run a jail like this, it's close quarters. We have everybody in here. . . . So to bring somebody in here for maybe a weekend, and then they go back to the courts on Monday morning and they get released [because the courts weren't charging people for many offenses]. We had to stop it because, only one in five were actually coming back [after being arraigned]. So I know that was an impact on the local police departments that we were reluctant to [hold people], but we really had to . . . [maintain] safety here.
>
> — Law enforcement management panelist
>
> A big, big hurdle we had was [our state] Department of Corrections not accepting the prisoners. They basically said, "Our doors are closed," yet ours remained open [in the jail]. So we've just been working to try to figure out the best way to get people out of our custody, just to keep that population down. The rules have changed a couple of times, which we're used to, but trying to make sure we're getting people tested and quarantined and held separately so that the prison system will accept them.
>
> — Institutional corrections panelist

---

[18]   Emily Widra and Dylan Hayre, *Failing Grades: States' Responses to COVID-19 in Jails & Prisons*, Northampton, Mass.: Prison Policy Initiative, June 25, 2020.

[19]   Kelly Servick, "Pandemic Inspires New Push to Shrink Jails and Prisons," *Science*, September 17, 2020.

[20]   Servick, 2020. Simulation studies using data from jails also provided support for the effectiveness of depopulation (Lisa B. Puglisi, Giovanni S. P. Malloy, Tyler D. Harvey, Margaret L. Brandeau, and Emily A. Wang, "Estimation of COVID-19 Basic Reproduction Ratio in a Large Urban Jail in the United States," *Annals of Epidemiology*, Vol. 53, January 2021).

[21]   Wang et al., 2020.

[22]   National Conference of State Legislatures, 2020.

[23]   See discussion in Council on Criminal Justice, "Corrections and COVID-19: Challenges and Strategies," video, YouTube, April 30, 2020b.

In a Council on Criminal Justice analysis, jail populations in a sample of 375 jails across 39 states were estimated to have been reduced by just more than 30 percent between January 1 and July 20, 2020.[24] The reduction in population seen in the Council on Criminal Justice data occurred in the first months of the pandemic (mid-March through mid-to-late April) and then populations slowly began to increase, although they remained well below pre-pandemic levels through late July, when the analysis ended. This pattern echoes some of the comments made by some of our participants. The Council on Criminal Justice analysis also concluded that the reduction in population was driven most by a reduction in admissions to jail (versus an increase in releases). The analysis found that rebooking rates were similar to pre-pandemic levels,[25] suggesting that the estimates may support further jail population reductions.[26] In some cases, these changes opened up significant space in local facilities, reducing the constraints of infrastructure and crowding on the ability to change management practices for infection control.

> In the Sheriff's department, through decreased arrests during the initial periods, [they] dropped their population without ever doing any targeted release. But that had impact. That gave us the room to shuffle people.
>
> – Institutional corrections panelist

Expediting Release Was Part of Decarceration Strategies

Reductions in the flow of new individuals into the correction system had the greatest effect for jails, which have a much more dynamic churn of individuals coming in and leaving than prison facilities. The other strategy for reducing populations is to let more people out. This was sometimes done for jails, but it was much more important as a mechanism for areas seeking to reduce prison populations.

> In the setting of this emergency, I think the jails had it a lot easier because arrests dropped dramatically across the country . . . and that has to do with, you know, policing practices and court practices. . . . But I think the prisons didn't have as much help on that front. Although the flow in slowed, the flow isn't that great in prisons and jails, of course, and so it didn't have that much impact on the total count.
>
> – Institutional corrections panelist

Significant numbers of people who fell into specific categories were released from prisons in many states and at the federal level.[27] For example, "[t]he Bureau of Prisons reported as of August that because of the risks related to COVID-19, more than 7,000 inmates have

---

[24] Anna Harvey, Orion Taylor, and Andrea Wang, *COVID-19, Jails, and Public Safety*, Washington, D.C.: Council on Criminal Justice, National Commission on COVID-19 and Criminal Justice, updated December 2020.

[25] Rebooking rates are similar, although not identical, to recidivism rates or reoffending rates.

[26] Harvey, Taylor, and Wang, 2020.

[27] There were also focused efforts to use more pathways for release for juveniles in custody (Molly Buchanan, Erin D. Castro, Mackenzie Kushner, and Marvin D. Krohn, "It's F**ing Chaos: COVID-19's Impact on Juvenile Delinquency and Juvenile Justice," *American Journal of Criminal Justice*, Vol. 45, No. 4, 2020).

been moved to home confinement for the COVID-19 pandemic."[28] Across states, UCLA's COVID-19 Behind Bars project tracked policies for release and identified categories used, including releasing individuals in prison for technical parole violations (which was uncommon across states and systems), individuals incarcerated for low-level or nonviolent crimes (which was common), individuals with relatively short periods left on their sentences (which was common), and members of vulnerable populations (which was common).[29]

> I also have the parole board here in [my state]. So we had to look at all the prisoners in prison who could possibly be paroled. And they were working overtime. We've been a parole board that uses teleconferencing to do interviews for a number of years, but still we were generating lists of prisoners that might be susceptible to COVID, sick prisoners, elderly prisoners. And we get all these people on their list, so the board could review them and possibly get them out.
>
> – Community corrections panelist
>
> We've worked really hard to do that so we can continue to make our paroles and continue to get people out. Like many, we've seen about a 10-percent decline in our prison population since the beginning of COVID. And that's been a good thing.
>
> – Institutional corrections panelist

The National Academies examination of decarceration in response to the COVID-19 pandemic went further, recommending that

> correctional officials in conjunction with public health authorities should take steps to assess the optimal population level of their facilities to adhere to public health guidelines during the pandemic, considering factors such as overcrowding, the physical design and conditions of their facilities, population turnover, health care capacity, and the health of the incarcerated population.[30]

The study went on to recommend that, if the population is currently above that level, officials should release people to reduce the population with a focus on vulnerable groups. Others echoed that recommendation.[31]

The practical process of releasing individuals from a facility became more complex because sending someone carrying COVID-19 out of a facility into the community would not serve public health even if it reduced the correctional population. This required quarantine processes before release and added to testing requirements (which, at various points, were stretched beyond capacity). Corrections agencies also did not want to send a healthy person out into a household that was infected either, adding another facet to release planning.

---

[28]   Watson et al., 2020, p. 12.

[29]   UCLA, undated. One of the recommendations of the National Commission on COVID-19 and Criminal Justice was to "expand emergency release mechanisms," particularly for vulnerable populations (National Commission on COVID-19 and Criminal Justice, 2020b, p. 21).

[30]   Wang et al., 2020, p. 91.

[31]   Watson et al., 2020, p. 17.

> We release anyone that's going to be released for that month . . . on the first of the month. We test all of our releasees . . . usually 14 to 20 days prior to the release. And then we isolate them if they're positive, so that hopefully their course will be done by the time of their release. If we do have a facility that goes on a quarantine close to release date, we will still test those persons. And then what ends up happening is we have to hold any positives until their true max-out date. And then if we can't, then we connect with our health department who will put them up in a hotel room for the remaining . . . total of ten days during their isolation period.
>
> – Institutional corrections panelist
>
> One of the things we started doing on the front end was we started collecting information from the individual who was being discharged to figure out where they were planning to go. And we were calling those residents to make sure that nobody in the home was symptomatic. Cause we want to make sure that we weren't sending healthy people to sick homes. And then also making sure that those people who were in the homes were prepared to be able to bring someone into the home, whether they were in the general population, quarantine, or isolation.
>
> – Institutional corrections panelist

Population reduction in both jails and prisons was sometimes complicated by pandemic-exacerbated bottlenecks in delivering programming, including shutdowns in some programs required before release reportedly stranding eligible parolees in custody early in the pandemic.[32] Current events also intervened, with arrests associated with protests putting upward pressure on jail populations even as they were being cut to reduce COVID-19 risk.[33]

> We've still been able to get people out [and through their prerelease programming], but as this thing wears on and on, it becomes more of a challenge, because we have to limit the number of prisoners that we have in a class. And so the sheer number of people we can get through the classes is reduced.
>
> – Institutional corrections panelist
>
> One of the issues though, was everything going on in [our city] with violence and national issues around race relations and things like that. So unfortunately we saw our population go right back up.
>
> – Institutional corrections panelist

---

[32] Beth Schwartzapfel, "COVID-19 Has Trapped Thousands of Parolees in Prison," *Slate*, May 7, 2020b.

[33] A panelist raised concerns that the use of different categories of individuals in pandemic-focused releases—e.g., distinctions drawn between individuals incarcerated for nonviolent crimes (who were therefore released) versus violent crimes (who were held through the pandemic)—had the potential to reinforce societal judgments about the relative value of people labeled as violent versus everyone else. Although such categorical decisionmaking likely was needed to move quickly to reduce populations (indeed, some correctional systems were criticized for not moving fast enough given the rapidly spreading pandemic), reinforcing a distinction between people more deserving of protection and others is fraught.

With more-rapid releases, the larger number of people coming out of correctional facilities strained reentry services providers and increased the complexity of reentry planning for institutional corrections staff. According to a CNN report,

> [t]he mass releases, according to government officials, lawyers and social service workers, have tested government safety nets and access to housing for many of these inmates. In normal times, there are hurdles to place inmates back into the community, but now, social service workers and government officials say, there are added factors complicating their re-entry, ranging from overcrowded housing shelters to families and landlords who won't accept prisoners because of concerns about contagion.[34]

These concerns—in addition to those about specific cases, such as the release of individuals suffering from serious mental illness or those who likely would become homeless when released—are discussed in more depth in Chapter Six.

Managing Entry to Facilities in an Effort to Keep the Virus Out

If policy changes significantly *reduced* the new resident population coming into facilities, it did not eliminate it entirely. And an operating correctional institution that was not accepting any new residents would still have some traffic in and out, including staff coming and going from the facility and critical inmate transport for required in-person court appearances or to get outside medical care. As a result, institutions had to manage risk from such flows. An element of that effort was health screening, which has become common in many contexts, including temperature screening and health assessment, and in accordance with health guidance that evolved over the course of the pandemic. In addition, other measures focused on isolating new arrivals and controlling flows of people as much as possible.

> We still do temperature checks and the standard health screening questions at entrances. And whenever we have somebody that has tested positive, we do a lot of contact tracing trying to go back and see who [they] were near, check with those individuals, [and] if they are symptomatic, we will test.
>
> – Law enforcement management panelist
>
> The guidance from either the CDC or the state health department, and then even the local health departments, sometimes contradicts each other. We've had situations here in [our state] where we have local public health departments that put down much more stringent requirements on us than perhaps the state has. And so we've had to try to work through those.
>
> – Institutional corrections panelist

---

[34] Kara Scannell, "Nowhere to Go: Some Inmates Freed Because of Coronavirus Are 'Scared to Leave,'" CNN, April 4, 2020.

The Limitations of Testing Meant That the Focus Had to Be on Intake Practices

Although testing for COVID-19 infection has improved, someone testing negative does not necessarily mean that they are disease-free. Because of the nature of the virus and the course of infection, using solely testing-based strategies for trying to keep COVID-19 out of a correctional facility is very difficult. As a result, although facilities do use testing upon intake as part of risk reduction—which is a path advocated by some outside the sector for the protection of corrections populations—several of our participants emphasized that new people coming into their facilities were generally quarantined for 14 days to reduce the chance that they would introduce COVID-19 to the general population. Although some advocacy groups and others have argued that quarantine amounted to the use of solitary confinement,[35] panelists with experience studying confinement practices emphasized how medical isolation should be implemented differently than punitive separation from the rest of the prison population (which we discuss in more detail in the Population Management section). In some facilities, that quarantine is reimposed if an inmate has to leave the facility (e.g., for an in-person court appearance). However, a panelist also cautioned that infrastructure and space constraints (which are tied to population levels in the facility) can hinder these strategies, and that there was a period where they were unable to maintain a full 14-day quarantine because space was insufficient.[36]

> There's a lot of advocates that say they want us to test every inmate upon intake. . . . I think a lot of people do not realize if they test negative on day one here at the jail, they could become positive at day four or five down the road further. It's not "I don't have it at all. I won't get it." You could be tested today and be asymptomatic and be negative on the test. But like I said, by the end of the week, you can be positive and it's something you can't test every single day for, number one, cost, and also just protocols on it. I don't know if everybody understands that in the general public either.
>
> – Law enforcement management panelist
>
> We actually created separate blocks with separate housing units for males and females where we can put them in for another 14 days and monitor their health before they went back to the larger population. And while they were there, they still had all the same things we had [for everyone else] . . . so that they weren't deprived of anything. We had no complaints from that. I think that was really instrumental in maintaining that COVID-free environment.
>
> – Law enforcement operations panelist

---

[35] See the discussion in Joseph Shapiro, "As COVID-19 Spreads in Prisons, Lockdowns Spark Fear of More Solitary Confinement," NPR, June 15, 2020.

[36] This quarantine approach was also described for juvenile facilities, although there were concerns about the potential mental health effects of 14-day medical isolation on young people (Buchanan et al., 2020).

> We do an initial rapid test on all incoming inmates, which we found out that those inmates without symptoms, that test is less accurate. . . . But we still run the test just to get an idea. They immediately go into a "new house quarantine," which we put every new house in an individual cell. We keep them in that individual cell for 14 days. Now that being said, we've had groups from the outside, challenge us in the public that that was inhumane punishment to take someone who was not worthy of being placed in administrative segregation in that type of cell. Though those arguments have some-what died down, every now and then it pops up.
>
> – Institutional corrections panelist
>
> We've had—because of population growth and no one getting out at certain points—to decrease the duration of in house quarantine. At one point in time, we could only quarantine new arrivals for seven days because we just ran out of space. . . . But when we took them out of that individual quarantine, we moved them—those that were safe to classify together—we moved them into a general population cell, so we kept some control over them. But, of course, we much rather keep that individual 14-day quaran-tine in place so that we had some level of comfort when we do put them in the general population.
>
> – Institutional corrections panelist

Reducing Other Flows of People Had Varied Consequences

Beyond new residents coming into a facility, other groups come and go from operating custo-dial institutions on a daily basis—staff, contractors, family members of inmates, teachers or medical professionals, and inmates themselves for security and other purposes. In a pandemic, each person coming and going becomes a potential introducer of the virus.[37] In response, facili-ties sought to limit movement as much as they could. In-person visits were halted.[38] Inmates stopped coming and going for nonemergency medical appointments or work programs. And facilities assessed who among their staff and contractors were essential (meaning that they would still come and go during the pandemic) versus nonessential.

> We stopped visitation and volunteers, work programs, education, court transport, and transfers, unless they were emergency medical or mental health or security reasons.
>
> – Institutional corrections panelist
>
> We stopped—I hate using this term *nonessential staff*—but we basically only kept the security staff and other staff in the facilities that were necessary for the immediate safe operation of the facility. So all our vocational instructors, all of our teachers, et cetera, all of our program, recreation leaders, they had to stay home. And we had to basically run a bare-bones operation.
>
> – Institutional corrections panelist

---

[37] Rita Rubin, "The Challenge of Preventing COVID-19 Spread in Correctional Facilities," *JAMA*, Vol. 323, No. 18, 2020.

[38] Buchanan et al., 2020.

> Not being able to physically sit in front of a health care provider, the way that they were used to (we are a very, very active jail as it relates to programs), so taking that huge shift where everyone had the shelter-in-place was definitely a difficult toll for all of the detainees who are used to going to school, going to programs, [a] lot of movement, moving to court. So it definitely was a big change.
>
> – Institutional corrections panelist
>
> One of the things we had to do is we had to really lock down the jail. We did that for probably about three months. [When I say] locked down, I'm not talking about so much about the inmates, just to the public: no visitation, no moms and dads and sons and daughters coming in to see their loved ones. No visitors, no volunteers, no vendors, unless they were providing critical infrastructure or critical services to us. So the jail was really kind of quiet.
>
> – Law enforcement management panelist

That hunkering down to try to keep COVID-19 out of facilities had a cost, even if it did reduce risk. On the services side, it meant that programs, such as counseling, vocational training, and others that were deemed nonessential, stopped. In juvenile detention contexts, concerns have been raised that options for the alternative delivery of education are insufficient, particularly for students with a wide variety of educational needs (e.g., in facilities with limited online connectivity and with specialized volunteers excluded for infection control, education reportedly sometimes constituted line staff distributing worksheets to resident youth).[39] Furthermore, the cessation of interfacility transfers cut off a path for accessing programs (e.g., moving someone to a different facility that had a program they needed) and managing security issues because separating inmates that had conflicts or caused other problems is one approach for keeping facilities safe.[40] As one of our participants put it, it led them to question the distinction drawn between essential and nonessential personnel because the contributions of many of the staff deemed nonessential delivered programming that, although not related to *security*, was very important for both keeping inmates productively engaged and the postrelease outcomes for residents. Although these staff might have been nonessential for a short-term emergency, the duration of the pandemic made that distinction problematic.

> One of the real impacts has been the inability to move people easily across these different institutions and these different programs because of the lockdown. Because . . . there's been an outbreak in one facility, but not in another. And so coming up with these overall improvements in testing and tracing and actually being able to track where the disease is, I think, [is] an important step to restoring some of the programs that have been so heavily damaged by this pandemic.
>
> – Community organization panelist

---

[39] Buchanan et al., 2020.

[40] Catherine D. Marcum, "American Corrections System Response to COVID-19: An Examination of the Procedures and Policies Used in Spring 2020," *American Journal of Criminal Justice*, Vol. 45, 2020.

We stopped basically all movement between correctional facilities, which is a fundamental way you maintain security. You separate inmates when things get hot, gang members, et cetera, and facilities were basically forced to deal with their individual problems for an extended length of time.

– Institutional corrections panelist

At least as far as staff goes, it tested our definition of what's essential versus nonessential employees . . . this has been going on since mid-March. *Even a "nonessential" function was there for a reason.* And how long can that be delayed? . . . Looking at the work in the various functions and the outcomes, what is it that we need to do to make sure that we're offering our services and fulfilling our roles in an acceptable manner?

– Institutional corrections panelist

However, the desire to limit risk while still achieving the goals of the system spurred some innovations, including the development of approaches for more socially distanced in-person visitation (which supported connections between residents and family members) and alternative ways of doing work release programs using technology and electronic monitoring that did not require individuals to return to the jail each night to sleep.[41]

We reconstituted . . . a work release program for sentenced individuals. . . . There are two forms of electronic monitoring that we stood up. Not everyone released in that program needs electronic monitoring, but there's a possibility for that both court-ordered and through the department of probation. . . . So that technology is being used and everyone is provided a cell phone who's in that work release program so that they can stay in contact [and] check-in with the community based organization that's supervising. In fact, they're provided some other equipment, [including] laptops . . . for them to search for both employment and education and other opportunities. And then some of the programming that they're doing as part of that work release program is then able to be done remotely, because in a traditional non-COVID setting, they would be coming in for meetings and for groups and other engagement. So we've utilized technology pretty quickly in the establishment of that work release program.

– Institutional corrections panelist

Because of the weather, we've been able to do all of our [family] visits outside, which was cool. Now it's starting to get cold. It started to get darker sooner. So we're basically transitioning. We got approval to use some of our inmate welfare dollars, and we're basically going to build like a dome—and so all of the detainees will be able to have in-person visitation in those spaces. The domes have been created for COVID-like things because of the air circulation's a little bit different, but it also allows us to meet our goals of trying to limit the amount of exposure any children could have coming into correctional settings.

– Institutional corrections panelist

---

41   National Commission on Correctional Health Care, "COVID-19 Weekly Roundtable For Law Enforcement and Correctional Health Care Webinar," blog post, March 20, 2020, updated May 15, 2020.

Altering Practices to Limit COVID-19 Transmission Within Facilities

Because strategies seeking to keep the virus out of facilities would never be perfect, managing the spread within facilities required significant changes in practices. Outbreaks that occurred where there was significant spread within correctional facilities show that business-as-usual corrections practices involved real risk. Panelists—some of whom were from agencies that had been very successful to that point managing risk in their systems—argued that there were templates and approaches for managing risk in infection-control practices used across different diseases. In implementing those templates, participants indicated that there had been a transition in some of their facilities to putting health care leaders in a more central or even a leading role in decisions.[42] However, doing so successfully required both policy change and implementation by staff in collaboration with incarcerated individuals.

> [A significant change was] the acknowledgment as part of the pandemic that we gave the reins with respect to certain operational and . . . more-traditional custody and security matters in terms of housing and movement and other things [to correctional health practitioners]. Really in partnership with correctional health, [we] gave them kind of the front seat on driving us to health and safety. And I think that is something that, while paramount in our operations in the pandemic, we can think more broadly about . . . both as it relates to how we're caring for and then meeting the needs of people in custody.
>
> – Institutional corrections panelist
>
> We leaned heavily on tried and true practices of infection control. Those of us who work in corrections, particularly in health and public health, are keenly aware that thinking about infectious diseases and corrections is not new. This is not our first rodeo. We've had plenty of other outbreaks and things that we deal with on a routine basis, including these novel viruses that come up from time to time.
>
> – Institutional corrections panelist
>
> We got tremendous cooperative response by and large from our population in custody to pretty severe changes, almost overnight. Limited movement, elimination of services, they weren't going to court, their cases weren't advancing. And all of the things that we would have expected would have caused an uprising [or] a resistance actually was pretty much the exact opposite. We were tremendously grateful for that level of understanding and working together.
>
> – Institutional corrections panelist

---

[42] Brie A. Williams, Cyrus Ahalt, David Cloud, Dallas Augustine, Leah Rorvig, and David Sears "Correctional Facilities in the Shadow of COVID-19: Unique Challenges and Proposed Solutions," *Health Affairs Blog*, March 26, 2020.

This is a significant change. In past PCJNI work, correctional medical leaders noted the issue of medical concerns being considered only after—and as lower priority than—security and population-management concerns. The level of threat from the COVID-19 pandemic shifted that in some places. See, for example, the discussion in Joe Russo, Dulani Woods, John S. Shaffer, and Brian A. Jackson, *Caring for Those in Custody: Identifying High-Priority Needs to Reduce Mortality in Correctional Facilities*, Santa Monica, Calif.: RAND Corporation, RR-1967-NIJ, 2017. Two of the highest-priority needs identified were "[t]o help ensure that health care issues receive the appropriate level of attention within an agency or facility, organizational structures should designate authority and autonomy to medical officials" and "[t]he inherent conflicts between security and medical objectives can make it challenging to deliver quality health care on a day-to-day basis. There is a need for collaborative approaches to overcome these obstacles" (p. 20).

Masks and Hygiene Measures Were Central Prevention Strategies for Many Facilities

Health guidance directed members of the public to wash their hands frequently, disinfect surfaces, and use face coverings to reduce respiratory transmission, and these measures were central in correctional institution approaches as well.[43] As was the case for other justice system agencies, there were reports of difficulties in getting supplies and protective equipment.[44] Participants on our panel indicated that, in their states, there was more difficulty among smaller correctional systems in getting the supplies they needed because the larger urban systems had standing contracts and greater access to resources. The issue of whether contract support to institutions—including medical providers working in facilities—could get needed PPE was raised because they did not have the same priority as the correctional system itself. Multiple organizations represented on our panels issued face masks to their residents comparatively early in the pandemic and indicated that uptake and use of masks by inmates was relatively smooth. A June 2020 cross-state analysis by the Prison Policy Initiative of public information provided by departments of corrections showed that the majority of states were providing masks to residents in their facilities.[45]

> And more focus has to be on our normal procedures, our normal infection control, which in jails and prisons, this is kind of what we do. And so we are good at it and we should be just continuously using our more universal precautions. A lot of these things weren't surprises, we've had places with measles outbreaks or Varicella outbreaks, it's very similar. It's just a bigger one in a sense. And it's affecting a lot more people.
>
> – Institutional corrections panelist
>
> We mandated mask-wearing for everybody in the jail, staff and inmates alike, and believe it or not, it went over pretty well. I probably had a harder time getting our officers to wear them than the inmates, and you might think it would go the other way, but I think the inmates kind of realized what was going on.
>
> – Law enforcement management panelist

Some Facilities Implemented Population Management Using Lower Density to Limit Spread

To limit the spread of COVID-19 within facilities, the options that were available for population management were tied intimately to the success—either before or during the pandemic—of reducing population and freeing up space.[46]

---

[43] A set of comprehensive policies was produced by the New York City Department of Corrections (which was seriously affected early in the pandemic) in Maura McNamara, "Correctional System Recommendations for Responding to COVID-19: A Toolkit," New York: New York City Department of Corrections, 2020.

[44] See, for example, discussion in Nelson and Kaminsky, 2020.

[45] Widra and Hayre, 2020.

[46] According to Supreme Court of Georgia Justice Michael Boggs,

> The real issue is not how many you're releasing from jail, it's what does that release allow you to do in that facility. Does that release allow you to reduce some of your staff, your nonessential staff, and get those folks out of that environment? Does it allow you to do medical quarantining in the county jail? Does it allow you to better and more efficiently engage in telehealth and telemedicine? (Council on Criminal Justice, 2020a)

One of the ways we were fortunate was our population had been declining in prior years and we had some space available to us which helped us establish COVID-positive housing units. In fact, one whole COVID positive facility. And so we were able to use that space effectively to separate the sick or the most critically sick from the other [residents].

– Institutional corrections panelist

Over the past couple of years with bond reform, we were able to drop our population down where we were seeing pretty regularly a constant flow of anywhere from 5,800 to 6,200 people. So that was a really sharp decrease, but that seemed to be our baseline. Once everything started kicking up in March, a lot of the stakeholders got together and a lot of community groups obviously [were] pushing to get as many people out of the jail as possible. So we did see a really drastic decrease in our population, which allowed us to take advantage of the landscape and start single-celling all the detainees so that we were able to socially distance people. Obviously I know everybody doesn't have the luxury of doing that. We, you know, we had to open up some old buildings that have been closed down for a long time but we were able to socially distance everyone, which was a huge, huge benefit for us.

– Institutional corrections panelist

Where systems had open space, they had many more options for managing populations and controlling the spread of the virus in the facility. According to a published description of efforts in an Arizona county,

Our jail is not a dorm style jail, it's predominantly a pod-style jail—typically with just a few individuals per cell. Due to previous reductions in the jail population, some space was available. Now, there is even more space, so it is possible for the Sheriff's correctional staff to have inmates practice social distancing and to set aside areas for quarantine and isolation as necessary.[47]

With additional releases for individuals accused of some categories of crimes, they were "able to use the extra space freed up in the jail to institute safe quarantine and separation areas, and as a result . . . have so far avoided a single case of COVID-19" in the jail.[48] Some facilities that did have dormitory-style portions emptied them as much as possible, enabling inmates to distance and limit contact with one another.[49] Others adopted cohorting strategies, grouping a set of staff and a set of residents together to reduce the chance of broader spread. According to Anne Precythe, director, Missouri Department of Corrections, "[p]art of our cohorting in our containment plan is making sure that housing units stay singular and that they're not mixing with other housing units and we have specific staff assigned to housing units so that we're not cross-contaminating across the whole facility."[50] Others adopted single-celling, reducing risk

---

[47] Cramer, 2020.

[48] Cramer, 2020.

[49] According to a participant in a COVID-19 Weekly Roundtable for Law Enforcement and Correctional Health Care Webinar (National Commission on Correctional Health Care, 2020).

[50] Council on Criminal Justice, 2020b.

even more.[51] Also, changes had to be made to recreation and meal service because both are times when large numbers of individuals could congregate.[52]

> Another really key thing I think they did earlier than a lot of places is they with the entire facility, grouped inmates in groups of four to six that you were assigned to group together. And like all of you, we have different kinds of facilities. So if you're in a cell facility, you mostly remained in cell, but you were let out of cell for group experiences only with your group. If it was dorm, you were bunked until you could get off the bunk with your group. I think that was a helpful strategy.
>
> – Institutional corrections panelist

Where there was space, facilities could separate people under preventive quarantine (e.g., when new people came into a facility), residents who were confirmed to be infected with COVID-19, residents who tested positive but who were potentially not sick, and individuals who had been exposed to positive or sick people but where it was still unsure whether they had caught the virus. Facilities could separate all these groups from the general population where possible. Where there was not space, potentially broader groupings had to be done, which reportedly meant, in some cases, that exposed residents who tested negative (although those who might become positive at a later point) might be quarantined with those who had already tested positive.[53] Managing all these separate populations made the already complex task of managing facilities even more difficult.

> To avoid mistakes of movement, we would admit [new individuals in custody who were exposed] and give officers lists of the people or even access into the electronic health record so that they could see these guys can't be moved. Don't take these guys to court. Don't expose people.
>
> – Institutional corrections panelist
>
> The way that we started housing people was we had isolation. We then had quarantine, which for us, we basically quarantined any unit that had one to two people come from that tier who tested positive or were symptomatic. Those sick people would go into isolation. And then the other members of the tier were on quarantine for at least 14 days or 14 days until after the last person was sick. [Other inmates were in] our general population.
>
> – Institutional corrections panelist

---

[51] Puglisi et al., 2021.

[52] Marcum, 2020.

[53] The effects of this grouping at the individual level on incarcerated individuals is described in Ko Bragg and Kate Sosin, "Inside the COVID Unit at the World's Largest Women's Prison," *PBS News Hour*, October 19, 2020.

> It's really just a full-time job, managing these housing categories and our business oper-
> ations. Custody has to constantly juggle [the] population because there's [only] so much
> open space. We have cohorts, we have medical observation, we have quarantines, we
> have temporary quarantines, we have quarantine cleared, and we had recovered hous-
> ing. And our observation and our quarantine housings are on a movement restriction.
>
> – Institutional corrections panelist

Advocates and analysts alike have raised concerns that space limitations might mean that individuals who are isolated for medical reasons are housed in the same types of isolation cells used for punitive solitary confinement. Given beliefs that solitary confinement can have strongly negative effects on individuals, they discussed concerns about the ethics of blurring the two:

> In some cases, carceral facilities do not have spaces appropriate for quarantining or isolating inmates who are ill or have been exposed to someone with COVID-19. In other facilities, the only usable spaces for quarantine or isolation are segregation cells that are typically used for solitary confinement. However, these spaces lack the medical capacity and supervision necessary for medical isolation. Solitary confinement is a punitive measure that severely restricts access to recreation and contact with friends and family, and there is little transparency in the process. Many incarcerated people will not report potential COVID-19 symptoms for fear of being placed in such a situation.[54]

Our panelists emphasized that, in some ways, resolving this problem is a problem of messaging—it is important to explain to residents the difference between punitive and public health isolation, the differences in practice between them, and the fact that it is medical staff that drive decisions for the latter.[55] Our participants also emphasized that it was incumbent on facilities to make medical isolation as minimally emotionally and socially isolating as possible by maintaining access to resources and connectivity through technology.

> [Yes, solitary confinement should be eliminated as a corrections practice, but] isolating
> someone for public health reasons or infection control is [not] the same thing. . . . The
> problem or the risk [in] supermax [solitary confinement] practices is architectural, but
> it's also the whole routine, the number of hours of lockdown, sensory deprivation,
> extreme social isolation. If you're keeping someone isolated to make sure they don't
> spread infection to people around them, you can physically isolate them, but not socially
> isolate them. You can provide activities. Technology allows us to do this. Some of you
> have mentioned that you're using this, which I think is excellent. So there's really a lot
> of opportunity to make sure that you are minimizing the harms.
>
> – Institutional corrections panelist

---

[54] Watson et al., 2020, p. 12.

[55] Watson et al., 2020, pp. 18–19.

For managing prison facilities in particular, the COVID-19 pandemic has been very challenging for sites that rely in part on inmate labor to function.

> We've been dealing . . . with a labor shortage of our inmates and . . . that's been one of our largest challenges. . . . And with the lower [numbers of] arrests of people for misdemeanors, we've seen less sentenced inmates come into our system. And so that's just been a real challenge. And the fact that we have all these housing categories to manage COVID, we have to sit there and decide, "All the recovered inmates can work on second shift, but all the quarantine cleared inmates have to work on day shifts" . . . the labor shortage with the inmates has definitely been a challenge.
>
> – Institutional corrections panelist
>
> We're spending a fortune on meals. Our detainee workers were primarily the ones working in our kitchen. Early on we saw some spikes happening because we were pulling from different living units. So we're trying to make sure that we avoid that moving forward, but all lunches are [delivered in] Styrofoam [packaging versus cafeteria style]. We're paying extra there, and we really need to come up with some type of a solution on how to reintroduce our detainee workforce so that we can just move forward, to save money, to allow people to work, but kind of just get back to normal.
>
> – Institutional corrections panelist
>
> Part of what we did [to address the labor needs inside the facility was] during the onset of the pandemic, we identified folks [in custody] who had tested positive and who had recovered from COVID. And we recruited those individuals to be our essential services workers, and that's what we called them. And we did an honorary lunch for groups of them at different facilities to recognize them for their service. And they were putting themselves on the line, just as our staff were putting themselves on the line, coming to work every day. And we thank them profusely for their contribution to enhancing sanitation and other services, [doing] laundry and other protocols that helped us keep running.
>
> – Institutional corrections panelist

COVID-19 Strained Correctional Health Care Delivery Systems

A major concern in the United States was the stress placed on hospitals and medical care professionals by cases of COVID-19, and providers of health services within correctional facilities faced the same issues. Functioning in many cases like self-contained towns or even cities, facilities had difficulty with testing for COVID-19, managing the care needs of residents, and delivering mental health and other services under pandemic conditions.

There Was High Demand for Testing and Difficulty Meeting the Need

Correctional facilities often did not have access to the testing capability that would have been ideal to manage infection risk, which was also a challenge in the country overall. Facilities had challenges with access to the number of tests they needed and how to best use the results given concerns about the specificity and selectivity of different types of COVID-19 tests.

> We had our initial infections and outbreaks very early on in March and April back when there really wasn't good testing available. And in fact there really weren't good guidelines available.
>
> – Institutional corrections panelist

Across our panel, some systems were doing broad testing of their populations, which participants described as extremely labor-intensive but useful,[56] and others adopted different testing strategies for cost and management reasons. In some cases, meeting testing capabilities required our panelists' systems to collaborate with other local partners that had technical facilities and staff to perform the laboratory component of the tests for the corrections system.[57] Reflecting these difficulties, a June 2020 cross-state examination by the Prison Policy Initiative showed that relatively few states were doing comprehensive testing across populations and staff.[58]

> We have a statewide testing order now. So we are doing about 25,000 tests a week, prisoners and staff, and it is a mammoth undertaking. And so it's mandatory testing for us. Anytime we have one, just one prisoner or one staff [member test] positive at an institution, [it] triggers testing for the whole institution. And then we test weekly until we can go [to] a 14-day period without any positive tests. And so we're doing that at like 21 facilities right now. And I will say, there's a lot of different schools of thought about mass testing. Should you do it? Shouldn't you do it? We were one of the very first states . . . to test our entire population. And that was important to us and it did benefit us because what we know obviously is the majority of people are asymptomatic and we found that out very quickly once we started testing and as we continue to test.
>
> – Institutional corrections panelist

> The importance of testing cannot be overstated. We had the experience where, in our first phase, you just didn't have the capabilities. The commercial labs couldn't handle the volume. Of course there were budget issues. After that initial phase, which was at least slowed down by these sort of conventional measures, the county was able to expand its own lab capacity by purchasing a trailer with COVID-specific testing. [So] we now do very aggressive testing. . . . Now, all [new arrivals] are tested at intake and held until their results are back. Surveillance of the facilities is voluntary, which wasn't my recommendation. I suggested randomized [testing], but [the decision was that] each month about 25 percent of the population is tested.
>
> – Institutional corrections panelist

---

[56] Other simulation studies have indicated that asymptomatic testing can be an effective approach, even with the shortcomings of the tests (Puglisi et al., 2021).

[57] Testing strategies might need to be adjusted, depending on the facility environment. A participant in a National Commission on Correctional Health Care panel discussion noted concerns about individuals who tested positive (e.g., in the case of broad testing efforts) being mistreated by other inmates, potentially requiring random sampling to inform management decisions without reporting results to individuals (National Commission on Correctional Health Care, 2020).

[58] Widra and Hayre, 2020.

Participants argued that more guidance is needed on using the results of population testing. The other core recommendation was that adding analytic capability—e.g., to a larger system's research unit—is valuable for tracking all of the tests and their results to support individual and population-level decisionmaking.

> We were not able to keep up with the demand for tests. So we had to rely on our community partners to try to get things done. . . . [W]e relied on them heavily to try to get testing done when it came to doing targeted testing [and] intake testing. We just couldn't keep up.
>
> – Institutional corrections panelist

> More point-of-care testing is going to be needed onsite, especially going into the winter season. So I'd like to see more guidance. . . . Everybody harps on, "does it have a 10 to 15 percent false negative rate or not, and you can't make housing decisions based on it." But the jails especially are going to have to base housing decisions off some of these point-of-care tests, despite that rate. . . . And [a] lot of our point-of-care testing has false negative rates, but everybody just wants to harp on this one, but yet they don't say you got a 5-percent rate on our rapid strep [test] also. I mean, there's a lot of things that we do every day in medicine that goes with that. And I'd like to see CDC and others push more to give guidance and things for corrections on that point of care in isolation. *Cause it's going to be a hard winter.*
>
> – Institutional corrections panelist

> When we started testing, we connected our research unit, which is very strong, to monitor everyone, keep track of them facility by facility so we had an accurate count . . . and that was the lesson going forward, "Don't rely on medical staff who are so swamped with everything else to be the numbers people that keep track of where the tests are, who's quarantined, how many results, et cetera."
>
> – Institutional corrections panelist

Emphasizing the benefits of a steady stream of information from broad testing, one of our participants indicated that, thanks to the availability of tests (and the fact that their positivity rate was low at that time), they were able to begin reopening the facility to visitors and others, which is valuable both for the residents' quality of life and to restart programming intended to help long-term outcomes.

> We're coming back with only a very, very small number of positives, even though [we've brought] back nonessential staff, delivering programming and visiting, et cetera. So we're monitoring a lot of different things and testing will tell us whether or not reinfection is happening.
>
> – Institutional corrections panelist

Care Delivery for COVID-19 Stretched Even Large Correctional System Medical Staffs

Concerns about the effectiveness of health care services for incarcerated populations were raised even before the pandemic because of the levels of mortality in corrections facilities and the increasing needs of aging and medically vulnerable populations in U.S. prisons in particular.[59] The COVID-19 pandemic stressed those systems even more.[60]

Because rapid intervention is key to stopping the spread of highly communicable diseases, elements of the health care approach adopted in some institutions sought to lower the barriers for residents to seek care. These approaches included reducing or eliminating medical co-pays for inmates.[61] In Figure 5.5, we summarize data collected in June 2020 (relatively early in the pandemic) by the Prison Policy Initiative on changes in co-pay policy by state. One of our participants described installing dedicated phones to contact the prison's health services to lower the barrier for residents to speak with a medical professional and providing such tools as soft thermometers to make it possible for inmates to better monitor their own health.

> We did put in place . . . telephone lines to give people in their housing unit direct access to our health care provider and clinicians. And then we . . . had those temperature-taking strips that you stick to your forehead and it takes your temperature. We distributed those to housing units so that people could take their own temperature. And so giving folks in custody back a little bit of autonomy and control over their health and their circumstance. I think was really valuable at a time of great crisis and something that we don't intend to take away as we move forward through this pandemic and onto the other side, because there is real value in that.
>
> – Institutional corrections panelist

Facilities that experienced significant outbreaks of COVID-19 were challenged by both infrastructure and medical staff capacity in delivering care. Participants in our workshops from large jail or prison systems with substantial organic health capability and strong connections to outside hospitals had many fewer difficulties.

> I attribute a lot of [the success in treating ill residents], not just to identifying and separating right away, but also providing the needed level of care in our outside hospitals. There was never a question. If somebody needed care, someone needed to go to an [intensive care unit], someone needed a ventilator. They got that. Some of them were on ventilators for weeks, and it was touch and go as to whether they would recover.
>
> – Institutional corrections panelist

Even in well-resourced hospitals served by health care contractors, some panelists reported challenges because of the way that priorities were set during periods when PPE and other supplies were scarce. Because health providers were not directly employed by the corrections department, they did not have the same priority for access to PPE as the corrections system itself, even though they were the people delivering services within the facility.

---

[59] Russo et al., 2017.

[60] For a historical review of challenges with health care delivery in prisons, see Susan M. Reverby, "Can There Be Acceptable Prison Health Care? Looking Back on the 1970s," *Public Health Reports*, Vol. 134, No. 1, 2019.

[61] Marcum, 2020; National Conference of State Legislatures, 2020; Watson et al., 2020.

Figure 5.5
Changes in Institutional Corrections Facilities' Medical Co-Pay Policies, as of June 2020

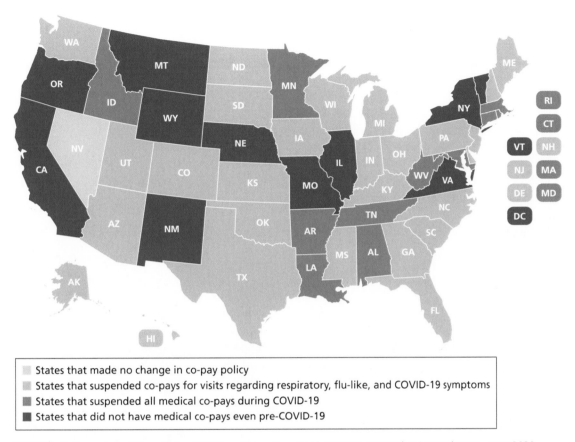

☐ States that made no change in co-pay policy
☐ States that suspended co-pays for visits regarding respiratory, flu-like, and COVID-19 symptoms
■ States that suspended all medical co-pays during COVID-19
■ States that did not have medical co-pays even pre-COVID-19

SOURCE: Data are from Prison Policy Initiative, "Responses to the COVID-19 Pandemic," webpage, June 2020.

> We utilized one of our spaces that did not typically house detainees . . . and set it up like a bunch of barracks. The health system was able to bring in some additional nursing staff and medical staff. We were able to put up a couple of different tents and basically operationalize that as being our isolation unit.
>
> – Institutional corrections panelist
>
> Maintaining staff has been a big challenge. For custody and then nursing staff we [were] challenged to find enough . . . even before COVID. And [now] nursing has been a huge challenge for us.
>
> – Institutional corrections panelist

In most facilities that are not as well equipped, the delivery of more-intensive care to resident patients requires transfer outside hospital facilities, with care delivery in the facility clinics limited to less serious issues.[62] As a result, connections with outside hospitals are critical.[63] Panelists across several of our workshops reported challenges in this area, particularly as outside hospitals were stressed by cases coming from the community. In some cases, the option available was telemedicine, allowing some level of care to be delivered without moving residents into the hospital. Specific concerns have been raised about the capacity of correctional systems to deliver care to older patients, given the increasing age of prison populations in particular.[64]

Looking back at what I would do differently, one of the things was our relationships with hospitals in the communities where we have prisons. It's kind of funny because normally, we're a cash cow [for hospitals]. We're providing a lot of [patients]—and it's not just the hospitals, but we're providing a lot to the communities that we live in. But in COVID, there was a lot of pushback from hospitals again, I think just because of the capacity and the ability to handle the high level of acuity that was coming in from the community. And then to put the prisoner population on top of that, there were a lot of challenges there.

– Institutional corrections panelist

Even though the CDC and our [state] identifies the rapid test as an acceptable test [in spite of concerns about false negatives,] we have hospital systems here who won't accept it. And so when we test inmates who are going out for procedures, for surgeries, we can't use that test. That can be problematic because the other tests that we do, the turnaround time is not immediate—sometimes it takes a few days or more. And when you're trying to get somebody to a medical appointment that doesn't work very well.

– Institutional corrections panelist

We peaked [at] 83 cases. . . . We had some hospitals [that] didn't want us to come. We do have a privatized medical provider [and they] actually use telemedicine. So a lot of cases we would normally take to the hospital, they did it over virtual and they treated the inmates here.

– Law enforcement management panelist

---

[62] Williams et al., 2020. Although reporting data were collected some time ago, a CDC survey done in 2012 indicated that "[f]or inpatient and outpatient medical, dental, and emergency care, most states delivered services using a combination of on-site and off-site care locations" (Karishma A. Chari, Alan E. Simon, Carol J. DeFrances, and Laura Maruschak, *National Survey of Prison Health Care: Selected Findings*, Washington, D.C.: U.S. Department of Health and Human Services, National Health Statistics Reports, No. 96, July 28, 2016, p. 1). However, a considerable number of facilities relied on offsite care for emergencies.

[63] Joseph Neff and Beth Schwartzapfel, "Infected, Incarcerated—and Coming to an ICU Near You?" The Marshall Project, April 16, 2020.

[64] Stephanie Grace Prost, Meghan A. Novisky, Leah Rorvig, Nick Zaller, and Brie Williams, "Prisons and COVID-19: A Desperate Call for Gerontological Expertise in Correctional Health Care," *Gerontologist*, Vol. 61, No. 1, February 2021.

> We really had to bridge a lot of gaps, and there [were] a lot of discussions between a sheriff department's responsibility to keep the community within the jail safe, and then the [hospital's responsibility] to keep the community within the hospital safe. And then how do we bridge those two gaps? . . . In some cases we sat with, with our prisoners for hours waiting for decisions to be made on either side. So we actually had to show them the data of "Hey, this is who we're arresting. This is why we're arresting them. This is where they're coming from" and how to have those conversations with different facets outside of law enforcement, specifically dealing with the health care profession. . . . It was to a point where we were taking prisoners and would have to sit outside in a tent because they wouldn't let them in the hospital for an extended period of time.
>
> – Law enforcement management panelist

In managing health operations (and other disease-prevention activities within the facility), multiple participants on our panel described stresses on leadership—both of medical branches and the overall correctional facility directors—that necessitated bringing in additional staff to share the logistical load of managing and delivering care.

> We already had a full hospital staff of somewhere around 350 medical employees inside the jail hospital/clinic. But we brought on an additional physician that was an infectious disease–type position. And she is actually overseeing our COVID response. In the beginning, the medical director, who oversees the jail hospital itself, was kind of doing two jobs. He was doing that part as well as the COVID response. So we brought on another physician, and a staff of about seven or eight, and her primary focus is COVID response and COVID practices . . . that just took a load off of the medical director from the hospital.
>
> – Institutional corrections panelist

Because the participants on our panels came from a selection of jail and prison systems, their experiences cover only a fraction of systems across the country. Furthermore, some participants were purposely selected because their systems had responded well to COVID-19, with the expectation that they would have useful lessons learned that would be relevant to others. As a result, the experiences of our participants might not fully reflect the experience of delivering health care to incarcerated populations across the country. In March 2020, building on work done related to standard care delivery in some facilities, the U.S. Commission on Civil Rights issued a public statement on the obligation to deliver adequate levels of care to incarcerated individuals during the pandemic.[65] Other public health analysts flagged broader concerns, and some assessments argued for a mandated "national set of basic standards of care for COVID-19 for [correctional] healthcare operations and [the] develop[ment] of strategies to ensure compliance" to ensure equitable care delivery across populations and systems in different areas.[66]

---

[65] United States Commission on Civil Rights, "The U.S. Commission on Civil Rights Calls for Adequate Healthcare in Prisons and Detention Centers During the COVID-19 Outbreak," press release, Washington, D.C., March 20, 2020.

[66] Watson et al., 2020, p. 20.

COVID-19 Procedures Complicated Delivering Treatment for Incarcerated Individuals' Mental Health and Substance Abuse Needs

The COVID-19 pandemic caused stress broadly among the public and public safety practitioners and also for incarcerated individuals.[67] Although our participants did not indicate that this stress resulted in an increase in suicide attempts in their facilities, it did increase demand for broader counseling and mental health services.

> [In our facility,] we haven't seen any real increase in suicidal attempts or ideation, but we have seen a general increase in people asking for mental health services so that's increased some. . . . And I think that the tie for that is more limitations on visitation and things like that.
>
> – Institutional corrections panelist
>
> We didn't see an explosion of mental health case[s] or attempted suicides. And I think it was just part of the phenomenon that we all have to get through this together.
>
> – Institutional corrections panelist

Participants noted challenges among staff in addressing these greater needs, including concerns about how to do so in culturally sensitive ways, and broader strategies to try to reduce stress in the population. The need for mental health staff to continue to report to work to help the population also created challenges for workforce management (which we discuss in greater detail later) because of concerns among staff about infection.

> A number of correctional facility chaplains [indicated] just not really feeling equipped to address some of these unique mental health needs that have emerged within the correctional facilities. [Asking] how do they address some of these issues in a way that is culturally competent and respects religious diversity . . . but also help to curb public health risk in the correctional facilities.
>
> – Community organizations panelist
>
> It was a particular challenge with our mental health workers who thought that they shouldn't have to come to work since other people were working from home. But our message to them was, "No, we need you here now more than even before, because our prisoners are under stress, they're anxious, they can't see their families, they're scared, and we need our mental health staff out, walking and talking and checking in on people."
>
> – Institutional corrections panelist

---

[67]   See, for example, discussion in Juliette Rihl, "'It Almost Broke Me': How the Pandemic Strains Mental Health at Pittsburgh's Jail," *The Crime Report*, September 16, 2020.

> And [as the pandemic wore on] we said change the channel on the TV, put on a movie because standing there for our staff and then for people in custody with three televisions going all day long, it was overwhelming. . . . I mean people need some space and because they aren't getting these interventions of family visits and engagement in a congregate way. And people were really appreciative. Um, our staff were appreciative of the suggestion, people in custody were like, "Yeah, let's watch a movie." We had like some archival sports . . . games that people wanted to watch that were legendary. And so we, we played those kinds of things on the television just to take everyone's mind somewhere else, even just for a little bit.
>
> – Institutional corrections panelist

For individuals with more-serious mental health issues, the added stress of the COVID-19 pandemic could make those processes more acute, and the pandemic emphasized the need to continue treatment. The Committee on Psychiatric Dimensions of Disaster and COVID-19 and the Council on Psychiatry and Law of the American Psychiatric Association (APA) developed guidance that argued that "the COVID-19 pandemic has exacerbated the systemic inequalities that lead to [people with mental illness] being treated differently than other prison populations."[68] Furthermore, "crowding and movement restrictions in jails and prisons may exacerbate mental illness leading to symptomatic exacerbation."[69] Beyond other measures that were helpful to all residents, APA argued for the need to, "where possible, modify mental health programming to conform with infection control measures (e.g., smaller groups for a shorter time in order to accommodate social distancing) rather than cancelling," and to "balance infection control measures (e.g., social distancing, group cancellations) with measures to maintain psychiatric stability, recognizing that in some cases the exacerbated mental illness may pose a greater threat than COVID-19."[70] Continuing to deliver treatment was complicated for facilities that classed involved staff as nonessential, and therefore excluded them from the facility for infection control.

The delivery of substance use interventions, which can involve supervised administration of medicines, was similarly complicated and required adaptation of standard practices. There are published descriptions of how some institutional correctional facilities adjusted their treatment protocols to continue to meet residents' needs under COVID-19 mitigation conditions.[71]

---

[68]   APA, *The Impact of COVID-19 on Incarcerated Persons with Mental Illness*, Washington, D.C., 2020, p. 2.

[69]   APA, 2020, p. 2.

[70]   APA, 2020, p. 3.

[71]   See, for example, Alexandra Duncan, Noah Sanders, Maria Schiff, and Tyler N. A. Winkelman, "Adaptations to Jail-Based Buprenorphine Treatment During the COVID-19 Pandemic," *Journal of Substance Abuse Treatment*, Vol. 121, February 2021.

About two-thirds of our inmates suffer from some sort of substance abuse. And . . . probably around 60 percent suffer from some sort of mental illness. And a lot of them have co-occurring disorders. Trying to handle that in a jail, in the middle of COVID, was challenging. We were lucky. We did a lot [with our] health care provider, dispensing medications on the unit floors (obviously taking security precautions) but working to make sure we could continue those services.

– Law enforcement management panelist

Virtually Linking into and out of Correctional Facilities

As was the case for other parts of the justice system, virtual connectivity—particularly videoconferencing—was noted by panelists as extremely useful for managing correctional institutions during the pandemic. In the most basic cases, these approaches involved reducing the cost of phone calls or video calls from centralized systems to reduce barriers to use.[72] Broader virtual modes provided alternative ways to deliver programming and care (providing a solution to the challenges discussed earlier) and substituted for visitation, which had been stopped to limit the introduction of COVID-19 into the facility.

We didn't have the ability to do video visits prior to the pandemic. And now we've done nearly 20,000 of them. We established family video visit capacity in a matter of weeks in March, but we weren't able to close [in-person] visits until late March. . . . We were having visits, contact visits in our jails, even after we'd had a staff member pass away.

– Institutional corrections panelist

[There are] a lot of possibilities [for virtual technology for] delivering academic education. We have many relationships with outside colleges. They're not coming in yet. We're looking to leverage our tablet technology, we've connected with a secure messaging [platform] so some of the professors can communicate directly with the population on assignments. We physically deliver the paperwork, they'll drop it off, et cetera, et cetera. So that kind of model can be expanded to provide college to facilities that are not proximate to a college.

– Institutional corrections panelist

Inmates having direct access to virtual platforms—e.g., personal tablets in their cells—was noted as particularly useful by participants in our panels. If residents had access in their cells, it limited the need for moving them around and therefore contributed to reducing infection risk within the facility. Multiple participants across different panels talked about the advantages of existing tablet programs or the rapid deployment of tablets. Participants whose facilities lacked tablet deployments lamented that reality, supporting their usefulness from the other perspective.

---

[72] National Conference of State Legislatures, 2020.

We were able to obtain . . . 900 tablets to give to the inmates, free of charge, and they can do . . . reentry [programming], educational, vocational training. Now they could do that with a tablet, they could do it in their cells, participate on those continuing education classes that we had to shut down [in person] because of the lock-in. They could also make more frequent phone calls, keeping them in touch with their loved ones outside, which took a lot of pressure off of us from the families that don't hear from anybody to help control the rumor mill and help us keep things in check.

– Law enforcement management panelist

One of the big initiatives was our tablet program. Fortunately, every one of our incarcerated individuals was provided a tablet free of charge a while ago, and we amplified the additional free services they can get on that. Free movies, free secure messages, free phone calls to some degree, by working with our providers. So that has helped significantly . . . as we move toward a new normal.

– Institutional corrections panelist

We had a whole plan to be rolling out tablets way before COVID happened, and then sure enough, we weren't able to roll them out—and then COVID happened and everything would have been so much easier if we had tablets.

– Institutional corrections panelist

These virtual connections potentially were most critical for maintaining connections with family members during periods when visitation was stopped, and they allowed direct access to entertainment and other programming to divert residents from the stress of pandemic circumstances.[73] Participants noted that this increased communication—directly from inmates to their families and others—helped control the spread of rumors about conditions within the facility that caused problems in some areas, given trust and other issues that could affect the credibility of official information released by facility leaders.[74]

From the jail perspective, one of the things that we did was we found ourselves in a great position. We had just implemented a tablet program in the jail. So we had approximately 200 tablets that were out there that we could message to the inmates. And that really paid dividends for us, because what that did was it minimized the amount of pressure we got from either lawyers, family members, calling or initiating court proceedings to get loved ones out of jail. . . . When we shut everything down [in the jail], as far as visits with attorneys, family, and everything, we utilize the video tablets to do video visitation. We brought in our medical staff, psychiatrists and doctors to do those visits on there, and we could bring them up into private areas to have that private consultation via video visitation. And so we were fortunate to have that option.

– Law enforcement operations panelist

---

[73] One multipanel participant emphasized the value of making these resources easy to get for reducing inmate frustration and reducing the chances for violence and unrest within facilities. Although we identified only one report of facility unrest associated with pandemic responses in U.S. facilities, there were other examples internationally (Watson et al., 2020, p. 12).

[74] The National Commission on COVID-19 and Criminal Justice echoed this need for additional "communication between correctional facilities, people in custody, their families, and counsel in order to share critical medical information" (National Commission on COVID-19 and Criminal Justice, 2020b, p. 33).

These changes also pushed models that had not been readily adopted in corrections—e.g., direct access by family members via the internet to connect with their family members. For security reasons and because of the business models of technology providers, some video visitation systems required family members to go to a central location to video into the facility. In addition to requiring travel (which potentially involved exposure) by the family members, such models made the centralized site they were forced to come to a potential node of COVID-19 transmission. As a result, some areas moved away from that model to a more distributed one.

> In our agency, [we] had *started* video visitation. We hadn't necessarily gone to rely solely on it, like we have needed to [during the pandemic]. But the other thing [the pandemic] pushed us to [was] . . . we also didn't want the family members coming [to] one centralized location [for video visits]. So that pushed us to accepting family members being able to [join a video] visit [from] a website or their phone. . . . [The pandemic] forced us to move a little quicker. We would have been apprehensive. We would have been thinking of all the reasons why we couldn't and this forced us to look at all the reasons why we should and could.
>
> – Institutional corrections panelist

Panelists from institutional corrections systems also emphasized the value of the transition to virtual models elsewhere in the justice system and the practical benefits that video hearings and other video contacts produced for facilities.

> The other big thing that I want to mention is videoconferencing. . . . We had luckily started this a couple years ago, but it really has increased in usage throughout the county . . . where now we don't have to take the inmates out to the courts. We have . . . rooms inside where we can set up videoconferencing. It's a win, win for us. We don't have to take them out. They don't have to go out to court where they may pick up COVID from somebody else in the lockups of the court. For the courts, we can schedule a little bit easier, and it's a huge public safety factor. For us, the inmates don't leave the jail. They're not going into the community. We don't have to worry about escape issues or anything like that, or even spreading the disease
>
> – Law enforcement management panelist

> We were able to work with the other stakeholders to implement video court hearing[s] so that we weren't transporting physically to court. It's great cause we don't have to put people on buses and take extra trips and use bullpens and things like that. But we still had to figure out a place where we could centralize court without just mimicking exactly what we would have been doing in the courthouses. So everyone was happy that we weren't moving people to court, but we still had to figure out . . . how to keep everybody socially distanced . . . so we brought in upward of 58 different laptops into one of our gymnasiums and . . . pulled in some of our staff from the courthouses to help us with security.
>
> – Institutional corrections panelist
>
> [Because we already had tablets deployed in the jail,] attorneys can also do visits on the tablets that makes it really nice. They don't have to come in. Our courts are working on virtual court appearance, that's coming into full swing, so that's helped a lot. The court operations and transportation, that's been an issue.
>
> – Institutional corrections panelist

Managing Corrections Staff Members' Safety and Health

Space was an issue for managing infection risk, and space in correctional institutions—housing and specialized functions, such as medical facilities—has to be staffed. Corrections departments have had challenges with staffing for many years because of the difficulty of the job, compensation, and stress.[75] In the COVID-19 pandemic environment, the potential for staff to become infected at work and bring the virus home to their families did not make the career more attractive.

> But I will say one of the biggest challenges in that is you can have all the space in the world. But if you don't have the staff to go and staff those units, then you know that you've got a big problem. And so I think for us people who run corrections departments across the country, one of the things way before COVID and continual conversations we have is about our staffing challenges.
>
> And those have been further exacerbated by COVID. So you lay an already existing problem of recruiting and retaining staff. Then you put COVID on top of that. And what COVID has done in terms of people being off for COVID-related illnesses has been a huge challenge for us.
>
> We were about to start an Academy, right when COVID hit and we have quarterly academies here in [our state]. So our goal is hire, roughly 200 in each quarterly Academy. And so the spring Academy was canceled. We ended up going partially virtual with a downsized summer Academy.
>
> – Institutional corrections panelist

---

[75] See discussion in Joe Russo, Dulani Woods, George B. Drake, and Brian A. Jackson, *Building a High-Quality Correctional Workforce: Identifying Challenges and Needs*, Santa Monica, Calif.: RAND Corporation, RR-2386-NIJ, 2018.

> Fortunately, the sheriff's office about a year ago started a really aggressive hiring campaign . . . so that helped us a lot. We recently had an Academy get hit hard by COVID. About half the Academy had to be recycled because they had a COVID outbreak in that class. So they had to change some of their procedures there and how they were doing their defensive tactics.
>
> – Institutional corrections panelist

Protecting Officer and Staff Health to Protect Institution Functioning

For existing staff to do their jobs, they needed to remain healthy. Facilities where large numbers of staff were either infected or had to quarantine had difficulty adjusting their operations.[76]

> [In terms of defining who was an essential worker,] *everybody* remained a critical worker and had to stay [working]. And I'm really glad that we did that because at our facilities that were very hard-hit with COVID where we had the majority of the population sick and we had a lot of staff out, we needed them to work the chow hall, and our staff did those things. We had to use staff from other areas of the department in nontraditional places. . . . So for us, it was really everybody had to be present and had to pitch in and do things that they weren't necessarily used to doing or things that weren't their job normally.
>
> – Institutional corrections panelist

For staff working during the pandemic, however, the risk of infection was real, and panel members raised the issue that corrections workers (both before and during the pandemic) are not given the same recognition and respect as other first responders. Contractors within facilities, whose activities might be no less critical than those of uniformed officers, face that challenge even more acutely.

> Just like the emergency responders that have been going to work every day, just like the people that deliver the *visible* services to the community, our staff are heroes as well. They just deliver the *invisible* services.
>
> – Institutional corrections panelist
>
> Public health collaborations have been key for us, both on the inmate care side, but also for staff-related care . . . everybody's worried about the virus, but they're in with the inmates on a day-to-day basis. There's a lot of concern and rightfully so and, right off the bat, we need to make sure that the jail staff is considered in that first responders number for when it comes time for testing and response or vaccinations or however it proceeds.
>
> – Institutional corrections panelist

---

[76] See, for example, Angie Jackson, "COVID-19 Cases Among Marquette Prison Staff Double in One Day," *Detroit Free Press*, October 15, 2020.

> We really need to think about, when we start talking about jails and prisons, is our contract services employees. My kitchen is contracted out. My commissary is contracted out. And while the jail staff . . . are considered public safety and we train them from the very beginning [that] when there's problems, you still have to show up . . . contract services folks come from a little different cloth. . . . Obviously we need them there. The food still has to go out. I think it's important that, because they're not technically our staff, we don't allow that to get lost in the mix.
>
> – Institutional corrections panelist

One example of the consequences of this disparity was that hazard or "pandemic pay"—i.e., incentives provided in some areas to reward critical staff who had to keep working—was not given to corrections staff or, in some cases, was given to some staff within the facility but not others.

> We just finally got our hazard pay through like a month ago, and it was a real challenge with the board of supervisors. For some reason, correctional health services got a large amount of hazard pay, but they didn't deem our detention staff working in facilities and our civilian staff to be at the same risk. And we've actually had three employees die, even though we'd had no inmates dying. . . . So I think that kind of finally opened their eyes and they're amending that.
>
> – Institutional corrections panelist

To protect workers during the pandemic, facilities adopted a variety of measures, including health screening, different work models, and issuing PPE.[77]

Health Screening
One goal of resident intake was to keep COVID-19 out of facilities, and, similarly, processes were put in place to screen staff members for symptoms before entry and to encourage staff who did not feel healthy to stay home.

> Of course, we sent all our nonessential staff home, but we still had the interactions with our security, nursing, medical staff that we had to deal with. So one of the things that we did was we created a call team, where we screened staff coming in symptom checks, temperature, that kind of thing. And we kept people out if they did not pass that screening.
>
> – Institutional corrections panelist
>
> We kind of had to change that mentality of our folks, especially our nursing staff and physicians, where you [may have the] sniffles [but] you still work.
>
> – Institutional corrections panelist

---

[77] Marcum, 2020.

Staffing Models

According to the discussion in our panels, there appeared to be less of a focus on cohorting staff and alternative staffing models to reduce the potential consequences of COVID-19 spread within the workforce than in other criminal justice organizations. However, there were examples of agencies that split their staff in two and worked separate days, made adjustments in scheduling, and rotated teams of staff that worked for 14-day stretches and then quarantined for a similar period at home.[78]

> Even here at headquarters, we only had half staff on duty any day. We had to alternate.
>
> – Institutional corrections panelist
>
> [We're] trying to come up with different types of schedules, to allow the staff to be tested onsite, those types of interventions, we're still working on that.
>
> – Institutional corrections panelist

Telework

Corrections organizations, like other congregate living facilities, are limited in the amount of staff that can telework. Facility security cannot be "phoned in." However, corrections organizations could facilitate telework for some staff, and participants in our panels talked about an increase in other types of schedule flexibility to address family obligations created by the pandemic.

> We had a lot of staff requesting to stay home for child care. Fortunately we're a critical employer. So our staff has to work with us and we have three shifts that they can work on, so if they have to stay home during the day, they can work on second shift.
>
> – Institutional corrections panelist
>
> [When we were not in the group that was physically in the office], we had to work from home. And I just think we're going to see a lot of continuation of that. It's an opportunity for our staff, and it's something that I think our organization is going to have to continue with.
>
> – Institutional corrections panelist
>
> I think one of the biggest changes we'll see in our organization is more use of teleworking. This pandemic kind of forced us to allow more of the staff to work from home. We were issuing laptops right and left, and . . . identifi[ed] employees who had the capability to work from home. I don't think some of that is [ever] going to go away. I think we're going to see more and more of our admin staff working from home at least two days a week. If not, a minimum of at least one day a week.
>
> – Institutional corrections panelist

---

[78]   This last 14-on/14-off strategy was discussed in the juvenile justice community, although there were concerns (which could be relevant to adult facilities as well) regarding the consequences of such rotations on continuity of programming for residents (Buchanan et al., 2020).

Personal Protective Equipment and Staff Health Management

A combination of respiratory protection, hygiene, and health monitoring (i.e., testing when it became more broadly available) were the main elements for maintaining the health of corrections staff in facilities. Although there were shortages of protective equipment early on, most of our panelists indicated that their systems had been able to get needed PPE (and they were frustrated by what they saw as misinformation that systems were not providing needed PPE). For some of our panelists, mask use by staff (and residents) was mandatory, and although some reported few problems, others indicated that there were problems with compliance. A June 2020 cross-state analysis by the Prison Policy Initiative of public information provided by departments of corrections showed that nearly all states were providing masks to all of the staff members in their facilities.[79] However, in an August assessment, the Prison Policy Initiative reported that 20 states did not require their use.[80] Echoing the concerns of some of our panelists, the report also cited concerns that mask-use policies were not uniformly followed. Implementing testing for employees was complicated in some cases by union resistance.

> We also mandated masks for all of our staff, which was a big step. And for our population, we provided as many as 12 [per inmate] from a lot of different sources. We also diverted several industry programs to produce PPE, not just for our jails, but for our entire state.
>
> – Institutional corrections panelist
>
> We had ample supplies of PPE. We had procured . . . surgical masks for the first time back [at] the beginning in February, we'd never procured those [before]. We had plenty of N95s on hand from our last pandemic for regular use, but the messaging [from some] that we didn't have supplies, that we weren't providing supplies, was a whole other bit of a challenge to our operations.
>
> – Institutional corrections panelist
>
> Unfortunately I think our staff have really shifted, where people seemed to be a little bit more on board in the beginning, right now we're having a hard time with that. It seems like we're in that struggle where they just don't want to do things because we're asking them to do it, and have forgotten about COVID and the importance of wearing masks. . . . So trying to get them a little bit more on board is something we're working on right now.
>
> – Institutional corrections panelist

---

[79] Widra and Hayre, 2020.

[80] Emily Widra and Tiana Herring, "Half of States Fail to Require Mask Use by Correctional Staff," *Prison Policy Initiative* blog, August 14, 2020.

> Your next problem of introduction of virus comes from staff and in [our county], we ran into union issues . . . they resisted any requirement to be tested. It's voluntary. So that creates a portal of potential reentry of the virus, and hence surveillance testing of the population will remain important in [that] model. In [another area,] they got the cooperation of the union and the staff are part of the universal testing model. And by the way, I should point out [that area] has been much more successful than [our county]. So that's, that's worth noting.
>
> – Institutional corrections panelist

Managing Stress and Mental Health

Although the physical health of correctional staff is a concern, stress and mental health were also major issues given the pressures of the pandemic. Stress on correctional staff was an enduring concern even before the pandemic, as reflected in higher death and suicide rates among staff than the general population.[81] Like other public safety practitioners, correctional staff have had to deal with the family and other stresses of the pandemic and the risks specific to their professional context. These stresses apply to both line workers within facilities and their leaders. In our panel, the primary approach for responding to staff stress concerns was increasing access to different models of counseling, peer, and employee support. According to a panelist with contact with multiple corrections agencies, this included leveraging counselors who might traditionally work with inmates to increase access for corrections officers. According to panelists, other strategies included seeking to expand connections with community chaplains to provide additional opportunities for staff to receive counsel and reduce stress and mental health issues.[82]

> I'm watching firsthand, our professional leaders . . . going through the fact that they've lost staff and residents to COVID-19. . . . I worry about the impact to them, their own mental health, their own emotional health. And what's going to happen as we continue to roll down this way. What does burnout look like and so on and so forth?
>
> – Institutional corrections panelist
>
> One of the biggest challenges, frankly, during this whole time has been just trying to still run the department and do all of the things that we're accustomed to doing and have to do, but [dealing with] COVID on top of that. Because COVID is just a full-time job for everybody.
>
> – Institutional corrections panelist

---

[81] See, for example, Dionne Hart, "Health Risks of Practicing Correctional Medicine," *AMA Journal of Ethics*, Vol. 21, No. 6, June 2019.

[82] Such alternative sources for counseling and private discussion of work stresses could be critical for rural facilities where mental health providers might be fewer and less accessible.

John Q. Average Worker has to go to work every day, wondering is he or she going to be exposed to something? Are they going to bring it home? And [are] they going to affect their parents or the young kids or anybody with a vulnerable condition? So I think regularly saying thank you to them, acknowledging the work that they did and putting them up there with everybody else as heroes that responded to a crisis because they had to, they had no choice.

– Institutional corrections panelist

We have . . . really invested in an in-house employee assistance program, led by our staff chaplain as the executive director of staff wellness. And we've brought on board both full-time and part-time, psychiatrists and counselors and, with partners in cities, other health and mental health and wellness . . . assistance programs for training and resources. [This was] opposed to what we had previously done, we had an [employee assistance program] vendor . . . [that was more] "distanced" in terms of its connectivity to the agency. I think . . . [the internal assistance resources are] something we will fight to maintain because we've gone through this horror and seen the value of that and the meaningfulness of that for staff, and . . . it was certainly valuable to have, and we're going fight to keep it.

– Institutional corrections panelist

Panelists also saw communication as an important component of managing staff stress.

We need to make sure that we're getting information out to those who work in the facility there at the same time, or even before it goes external. I mean nobody wants to be apprised of what's going on in their agency or their facility by watching the evening news, that seems disrespectful to their staff. That seems like a very simple concept, but when everything's flying at a hundred miles an hour, it's hard to remember that along with everything else that you have to do.

– Institutional corrections panelist

Cascading Effects of the Decisions of Other Justice System Components and Outside Entities

The efforts of other justice organizations that affected the flow of people—both positively and negatively—into the justice system have been discussed previously. However, among our correctional system panelists, the cascading effects of some of those decisions did raise concerns. Echoing points made by law enforcement, institutional corrections panelists noted that it was inappropriate for an individual officer's decision to arrest someone to lead to them being detained for a significant period without their day in court.

> Something that I think really needs to be talked about [is that], because so many sup-
> porting functions have shut down, my average length of stay is up. . . . We don't have as
> many people coming to jail, but when they come to jail, they're staying longer because
> they can't get into the courts. The courts are shut down. So, so my average length of
> stay . . . has increased by at least ten days.
>
> – Institutional corrections panelist

Their conclusion was supported by broader data from jails that were analyzed for the Council on Criminal Justice, which also showed an increase in average duration of stay across their population of jails of on the order of ten days.[83]

This issue of individuals in detention—and intense concerns about the safety and health of incarcerated populations—drove the most-significant external pressure on the corrections system that came up in our panel discussions. This pressure from outside advocates and other groups on the situation within facilities drove a significant need for communication and transparency in response. Among participants from our community organizations panel and from corrections organizations, there were significant differences in views about the level of transparency regarding systems' responses to the COVID-19 pandemic and the status of correctional populations.

> I think the overall impression . . . is that in many ways, the justice system reverted back
> to its worst instincts in terms of how it sees and treats incarcerated people and staff in
> terms of how it delivers a message to the public about what is or isn't happening. And
> the overall lack of transparency . . . has been a hurdle to system accountability for a long
> time.
>
> – Community organization panelist
>
> Another thing that's been important, just talking about things that have worked. We've
> tried to be very transparent throughout our COVID response, from the very beginning,
> we document all of our numbers, all of our everything we're doing and we put it on our
> website, and we communicate every night since this began, we send out a nightly staff
> message. And we also communicate not nightly, but very regularly through [messages
> to] prisoner[s]. And so we're trying to be as transparent as we can.
>
> – Institutional corrections panelist
>
> So much of this is about communication. Communication with the health care provider,
> communication with our own staff, and communication with the detainees. . . . We
> started sending out daily bulletins to the detainees about [how] visitation has been
> changed or changes in the court system, just so that people could feel more educated,
> informed, more sense of control about what's going on in the world.
>
> – Institutional corrections panelist

Although external oversight and advocacy are important for catalyzing system change, practitioner participants expressed frustration—they saw the conditions in facilities being mis-

---

[83] Harvey, Taylor, and Wang, 2020, p. 17.

characterized as part of legal efforts focused on gaining individuals' release, even as systems were involved in their own efforts to decarcerate many of their residents. As discussed previously, one of the broader benefits panelists saw in significantly increased communication between residents and families was a reduction in rumors about conditions in facilities.

A lot of the defense bar advocates took this opportunity with COVID to go to the courts and really paint this gloom-and-doom picture of a lot of our jails, trying to get their clients out of custody. So they weren't many coming in, but we had to fight that battle constantly in court . . . one of the positives that came out of this, it really helped us increase our communication with the courts, particularly with the judges to explain how many cases we had. A quick case in point, I got a call from one of the judges who's in charge of superior courts. . . . He said, "I heard you have 130 active cases in your jail today" And I said, "Your honor, we have two."

– Law enforcement management panelist

We've had a lot of inmates [who] submitted motions to the court for release and they all have a risk factor. They claim they can't be in jail, and we have to continually respond to the courts, tell them what we're doing to manage this and how many positives we have.

– Institutional corrections panelist

I can't control [rumors circulating in the public], but what I can control is putting out our own story, which I'm sure almost every system does. We have on our public webpage, a very detailed, informational package on everything we've done with COVID-19, why we've taken the steps we've done, including everyday numbers on our positivity rates and number of tests given, number of staff . . . we're up front with all of our information. And I think in addition to that, opening up the lines of communication with certain advocacy organizations to give them the truth of what you're doing, to honestly answer their questions. . . . Doing that, answering their questions, dispelling the rumors that are out there, that really helps.

– Institutional corrections panelist

We're doing nothing different than what the hospitals are doing. If somebody comes down with COVID and they're placed into observation, there's literally nobody that goes in that person's room except the nurse, and our inmates on observation have daily temperature checks, daily vital checks, nothing has changed there. It's nothing different than what hospitals are doing and, yeah, we get the inmates complaining and making phone calls and sending out messages on how cruel we are and how we're treating them. We have to explain what we're doing a lot to the courts and to family.

– Institutional corrections panelist

However, given damaged community trust and the perceived legitimacy of justice system agencies—and significant variation in that damage among jurisdictions across the nation—concerns about the credibility of information provided by facility leaders are perhaps not surprising. Reflecting some of these concerns, analysts argued for the development of "national standardization and accountability systems" to provide situational awareness of what is going on within correctional institutions, given variations in practice and disagreement between official information and reports by inmates of lack of supplies or care.[84]

Funding Pressures Will Shape What Agencies Can Do as They Continue Response

In our institutional corrections panel, there was less focus on funding pressures than for some of the other parts of the justice system. But the concern was present nonetheless. Even before the pandemic, there were concerns that corrections systems were not sufficiently resourced to successfully achieve all the ends society asks of them, particularly considering the increasing populations of inmates with serious mental health care needs, inmates with substance use treatment requirements, and aging populations who require care for both chronic and acute conditions. Given the economic effects of the pandemic, state and local budgets are under pressure, and corrections systems—even after bearing new costs associated with pandemic-management efforts—likely will not be immune from reductions. The significant reductions in population in response to the pandemic—if they are continued into the future—make the system look like a prime target for funding reduction. Although such funding reallocation over the longer term might be a necessary part of justice system realignment and reform efforts that reduce mass incarceration, in the short term, such pressures would result in systems losing the very space and flexibility that have been critical to enabling strategies to reduce the spread of COVID-19 in correctional facilities.

Funding reductions also would eliminate the opportunity to leverage the flexibility of smaller populations to focus available funding on programming and successful interventions (including education programs) in an effort to improve outcomes for incarcerated individuals. There has been long-standing concern about the ability of U.S. corrections strategies to successfully address individual criminogenic needs and effectively reduce recidivism among justice-involved populations. Cuts to corrections funding based only on short-term reductions in population would sacrifice the chance to make progress on outcomes, and—if progress can be made—to potentially realize more-substantial future efficiencies and cost savings resulting from less recidivism and lower levels of crime.

> Especially in our state, the economic impact has been devastating. We are very uncertain as to whether we're going to get any additional federal help. And so we're pressed to look at a lot of different things right now, and everything's on the table, unfortunately.
>
> – Institutional corrections panelist

---

[84] Watson et al., 2020, pp. 15, 18. In Watson and colleagues' more specific recommendations, they included public reporting of testing schedules and results for both incarcerated individuals and staff and public publication of prevention plans.

> I have a little bit of concern going forward that as the average daily populations (ADPs) are staying low for months, we're seeing some counties where the Board of Commissioners or Board of Supervisors say, "Well, since ADP is 40 percent, 50 percent, 60 percent less, then should your budgets be lowered by that amount?" And that gets to be a difficult conversation to tell them that you need the same amount of staff to be able to service this since we're already running at the slim margin. We didn't have extra staff, their housing units aren't being closed down, facilities aren't being shut down. So that ADP, even though it's low, the jail still is spread out and we need that staff.
>
> – Institutional corrections panelist

> Now that [in-custody populations] are declining . . . we've been able to create some space and space people out more and get back to facilities that had fewer people, which is obviously more COVID friendly. But the pressure is to save money and to consolidate— and to do exactly the opposite of what these lawsuits that have been brought against many of us have been about which is, "You can't socially distance in prison." So if you can't socially distance in prison, then why . . . move people back in together to close a prison to save money? So it's a push and pull and, as administrators, we're caught in the middle of it.
>
> – Institutional corrections panelist

Taking Stock and Moving Forward

In reflecting on the response to the pandemic, participants in our corrections panel were encouraged by the fact that staff and, in many cases, incarcerated individuals came together to respond to a common risk. But panelists also saw a challenge not to think in terms of the end of the pandemic and a return to "normalcy" because the risk of infectious disease in corrections facilities has come up in the past and likely will do so again in the future. Instead, the focus should be to plan to do better in such future events.

> It seems to be a little bit of a phenomenon that occurs when you have this kind of threat to the entire system that I think people—and, when I say people, I mean all staff, all incarcerated individuals—understand . . . the risk. That this virus is not going to differentiate a green uniform from blue uniform from a gray uniform, you're a human being, you're potentially at risk. So there's an acceptance that all of us are in this together. All of us have to be patient.
>
> – Institutional corrections panelist

> We shouldn't just think of "getting beyond COVID" and then, once we're beyond it, something like this is only going to happen once every a hundred years. The reality is we've always been talking about "what happens if we have a bad flu, a bird flu pandemic, SARS," and so on, and they didn't materialize the way COVID did. A future COVID could happen again. So I think we should inculcate into our own culture, all the structural things we have done well, and build upon those that could be expanded and/or improved.
>
> – Institutional corrections panelist

Promising Practices from the COVID-19 Pandemic Response

Because the COVID-19 pandemic represented such a challenge to carceral facilities, our panelists found a variety of substantial lessons learned to be valuable. One major lesson was the importance of corrections facilities not being hamstrung by the linked constraints of their infrastructure and the expectation to house as many inmates as possible in available space. Panelists whose agencies had reduced populations before the pandemic had flexibility that those that were operating near or above capacity did not. Although analysts examining the potential future for corrections facilities have identified a variety of ways that such systems as ventilation could reduce risk (which, according to a panelist with cross-cutting interactions with justice agencies, could have benefits for seasonal influenza and other diseases as well) and new ways to design waiting areas or housing to limit the chance of facilities becoming hotspots of disease spread,[85] the value of space to spread out and move populations around to protect them and isolate infected individuals will always be critical.

> The reduced population really helped us get creative. Now I have some space in the housing units, because a lot of my cells here, they're not strictly the two-man cells, they're four-man, eight-man, and then we have big dormitory-style units. We used to have 80 guys in there. The population has dropped. We've been able to create what we call a pretrial diversion unit. So we have social workers in there working with our staff to get these guys working with the courts and probation and the judges to get them out of here, back into the community for services there. And we also have one that I'm very proud of is a mental health unit, where we have a lot of folks with . . . really the tougher cases of mental illness, but who can survive in a more social setting instead of just a lone cell or a two-man cell, that's worked out very well. We can get them services on the floor, even in group sessions.
>
> – Law enforcement management panelist

Making changes in facilities—by upgrading their connectivity and bandwidth[86]—tie into another major lesson learned: that virtual and video visitation options, particularly those that put connectivity into the hands of individual residents, can have a variety of beneficial effects. More inmate communication to reduce rumors and increase the opportunity to provide programming while limiting resident movement was valuable from a facility management perspective, and was valuable to implement in a way that privileges those needs and benefits versus the business models of private providers of these services.

> I've heard from a number of facilities that, in response to shutting down visits, they have gone to video communication and that's been wildly popular. And it doesn't really cost that much. And, as opposed to paying outrageous prices for telephone contact, having video contacts with families allows people to maintain those connections and is really a critical thing to help with successful reentry. So I'm hoping that's going to flourish and continue.
>
> – Institutional corrections panelist

---

[85] "How COVID-19 Could Impact the Design of Detention and Correctional Facilities," HOK.com, April 30, 2020.

[86] "How COVID-19 Could Impact the Design of Detention and Correctional Facilities," 2020.

The benefits of virtualization for other management activities also were highlighted. When competing in a labor market where corrections careers often are not individuals' first choices, maintaining the benefit of telework could be a way to make these jobs more attractive in what is likely to be a demanding budget environment. The virtualization of court hearings to cut transport and security costs could contribute to saving money as well.

Working from home is not something as a department we ever embraced or even allowed. Our entire central office with the exception of probably about 50 people has been working from home throughout this pandemic. Some people have expressed that they've been even more productive than they would have been at work and it has improved their quality of life. And so, particularly in very tough budget times when cuts are being made and pay increases are difficult to come by, that's a perk that we can give to people that makes them feel valued and enhances their quality of life. I think, because we were forced to do it, now we're looking at it saying, "Okay, nothing bad happened, and our work still got done." So I think that is a silver lining because I probably would have never considered it and certainly not to the magnitude that we have.

– Institutional corrections panelist

To the credit of the courts, this has been a great impetus for change, for things that we've been pushing for decades: doing more video hearings, more telephone or video consultations with defense counsel rather than have all the security risks that come when you have to move prisoners around the county and bring people into the jail. This has accelerated that, it's probably taken 15 years off of the timetable that we were looking at before. The challenge will be to maintain what we gained going forward when this current emergency is over, because the tendency will be to go back to the way it was, where everyone was comfortable. So we can hold our ground and say, "No, we can't. We've discovered that there is a better way and that there is a more efficient way. So let's break through whatever barriers we have to with legislation or policy and make it happen."

– Law enforcement management panelist

A theme that recurred during multiple discussions was the value during the pandemic—and the importance going forward—of explicitly linking corrections to public health planning, given the impact that correctional health can have on public health.

My catchphrase is [that it is] public health *and* public safety [because of] how closely they're intertwined. And we've really gotten to know that over the years, as the comorbidity of various issues, folks who are in jail and prisons tend to be the sicker of the population, et cetera, et cetera. . . . So we've all gotten well versed kind of in that concept that the two cannot operate independently. What makes me very optimistic in this particular situation is [that] this is the first time in a crisis, in this huge nationwide crisis, that I remember jails [and] prisons getting any kind of focus whatsoever. Typically we've always been the forgotten population; out of sight, out of mind.

– Institutional corrections panelist

> Another key thing that [our county] did that I think . . . was really important is from day one, the jail system was on the county task force, so that as they were planning their public health response, the jails were at the table actively participating. I think that was extraordinarily important in terms of coordinating the response.
>
> – Institutional corrections panelist

At the macro scale, this was about corrections having a seat at the table during a crisis, but it also was about longer-term planning, with both public health entities and the hospitals and local medical systems that facilities depend on to care for their residents. Our participants put that in terms of a need for coordination. Other analysts put it more bluntly: "Community hospitals must be compelled to include nearby prisons and jails in their disaster planning process. . . . If necessary, state governors should compel area hospitals to accept patient transfers when needed."[87]

> It seems so obvious to me now that we should be having quarterly meetings with all these hospital administrators [of hospitals near corrections facilities], and they should be coming and visiting our facilities. . . . Had those relationships been stronger before COVID hit, it would have made dealing with the impact that they were feeling from our population [easier]. It would've made it a lot less stressful for everybody. So that's one thing that I definitely will be looking at going forward.
>
> – Institutional corrections panelist

Pandemic Pressure as a Driver of Broader Criminal Justice Innovation

In considering the future and how the pressures exerted on corrections systems might shape longer-term change in the justice system, panelists found impacts to be somewhat simpler than for some of the other parts of the justice system. Because of the serious risk posed by populations incarcerated in close proximity, the corrections system let a lot of people out at one time. Although populations in jails (e.g., for pretrial detention and violations of supervision conditions) made up a significant percentage of that reduction, there was real expedited release from prisons as well. Beyond the need for those reductions to manage the risk of infection within the system, such reductions responded to fundamental justice goals: Even if individuals were in the corrections system because they had broken the law, justice would not be served by not seeking to protect them from the pandemic.

---

[87] Williams et al., 2020.

I think that's one of the obvious takeaway points is that this crisis creates a really important opportunity—as crises often do—to educate policymakers and people who do have control [over justice system reform] to think in fresh ways about the overall costs of incarceration. Now, for those of us in the business, this is not a new discussion, but it rarely bubbles up in the way that it has around COVID . . . the pushback about reducing populations or reducing who we confine is predictable, and understandable, and actually well justified. We don't want to do anything that would threaten public safety. [But the pandemic has also showed that] confining large numbers of people in congregate facilities that [have high flows of people through them is risky too]. . . . If you were to design a system to rapidly disseminate COVID throughout your state—and throwing in [Federal Bureau of Prisons] and the immigration detention system, throughout the country—rapidly and effectively, you would design our detention and correctional system. . . . There is a threat to public safety associated with the way we do business now.

– Institutional corrections panelist

The broader outcomes of this strategy—beyond enabling more distancing and infection control within facilities—have not yet been fully assessed. However, like in other panels, there was a general view among our panelists, based on what they were seeing in their jurisdictions, that it did not seem to have had serious negative ramifications for public safety. If those conclusions hold up, dovetailing with the research needs discussed in the next section, the massive natural experiment in decarceration caused by the COVID-19 pandemic could reinforce broader arguments for reform and the reduction of mass incarceration in the United States.

As of late June, nearly 50,000 people have been released from jails and prisons as a direct response to the pandemic. And that's largely been successful, if we define success as people didn't come back into the system and were able to conclude their cases from the outside looking in.

– Community organizations panelist

We released thousands of people. A small number of them have had another encounter—they've been arrested, they've been returned to custody—but the numbers were single-digit percentages of people returning to custody over the weeks and months following. . . . We [corrections agencies] can participate in trying to manage the truth and limit the fear of what this means, so that this can be something sustainable in terms of [managing] the criminal justice population in jails and prisons more thoughtfully going forward.

– Institutional corrections panelist

We are all asking the same questions in every sector of the criminal justice system. Do we need to prosecute these people? Do we need to charge them with felonies at the same level? Do we need to seek felony dispositions [or incarcerate] technical parole violators? We have done a lot of intercessions in the name of public health, and we're seeing that, for the most part, it did not compromise public safety. So to me, that sets the table [for] . . . some of these initiatives [to continue] and make them structural within the criminal justice system.

– Institutional corrections panelist

Policy Development and Evaluation Needs to Better Inform Decisions in Both the Short and Longer Terms

Although the perception among the majority of our panelists was that the efforts to decarcerate had not had a negative public safety effect, there also was the view that their continuation should depend on evidence supporting that belief.[88] There are efforts underway to collect those data in some localities, but broad conclusions likely will require this remaining a national-level research priority. Variation in the ways that different areas have gone about this data-collection effort—which we discuss generally as a challenge or idiosyncrasy of the uneven U.S. response to COVID-19—will then become a research opportunity.

> A number of states are tracking recidivism rates specifically for those populations that qualified for early release under COVID. So [I] think it will be interesting. I know a lot of states are looking to see what the impact is [to] then see if we can move in the direction of some other kind of more institutionalized processes [to reduce incarcerated populations.]
>
> – Community organizations panelist
>
> I think it provides an opportunity for us to ask questions about the effectiveness of public safety, [where] public safety and public health are very closely associated, about whether we can do things differently. . . . Different jurisdictions did things different ways. Now's the time to go back and study. If you decrease the number of people who are being arrested for misdemeanor or charges being filed, all of those levers, if you targeted release, if you expanded compassionate release and then look at what were the impacts on public safety from the more traditional narrow perspective of crimes being committed, there's some lessons learned, there's some data we should be able to pull together to say that there were low-risk things we could do to reduce reliance on the mass incarceration tool and better focus our resources.
>
> – Institutional corrections panelist

Beyond these global questions leveraging the large-scale experiment of managing the COVID-19 pandemic, panelists also suggested the following researchable questions:

- Given concerns about the pandemic's effect on different racial and ethnic groups and disparities in incarceration, data need to be collected to better understand the burden of disease across demographic groups within facilities.[89]
- What can be learned from the significant differences in COVID-19 spread in separate correctional systems and even across facilities within the same system? Was the variation mostly attributable to the nature and time of introduction of the virus, or were there key

---

[88]   This was also a priority that was identified by the National Academies panel examining decarceration and COVID-19. The panel recommended "[assessing] changes in operations and targeted COVID-19 release mechanisms in correctional facilities to document the impact of such efforts on correctional health, public safety, public health, and racial equity" (Wang et al., 2020, p. 106).

[89]   This was also a priority that was identified by the National Academies panel examining decarceration and COVID-19 (Wang et al., 2020) and by the National Commission on COVID-19 and Criminal Justice (National Commission on COVID-19 and Criminal Justice, 2020b, p. 30).

differences in initial conditions (e.g., more- versus less-crowded conditions) or in the practices, policies, or infection-control actions taken that explain the different experiences?

- What have been the mental health effects of the pandemic on both incarcerated populations and correctional staff, and how long do such effects last?

- What disease-testing strategies are effective in minimizing infectious disease in correctional institutions, taking into account the limits of tests, their costs, and the information (and the uncertainty of that information) provided by a positive or negative result?

- Given concerns about individual isolation for disease prevention and controversy around the levels of transparency of correctional systems during the pandemic, can consensus models for such activities be developed that meet the needs of both corrections systems and advocates?

- Given the lessons learned from the pandemic and the significant infectious disease risks to both incarcerated populations and the public from high-density, mass incarceration, what should the capacity of existing correctional institutions be?

- What are the implications of the pandemic's lessons on the capacity of carceral facilities' medical care–delivery systems?

- How can corrections officers and staff be better protected from infection risks during large-scale outbreaks, including increasing their compliance with the use of available protective equipment?

- Are there architectural or other retrofitting options that would make correctional institutions more robust to future infectious disease threats?

- Can the effectiveness of virtual visitation and other virtual options be measured to support investments in their expansion?

- How can institutional corrections systems respond to budgetary pressures that could push toward a return to high-density facilities, therefore increasing vulnerability to infectious diseases?

Given the substantial remaining challenges with controlling the spread of COVID-19 and other infectious diseases within custodial facilities, answers to these research questions could make a significant contribution to improving future preparedness.

CHAPTER SIX

Community Corrections: Supervision and Service Provision

The community corrections system plays two roles within the justice system: as a *complement* to institutional corrections, where individuals serve sentences in custody for criminal behavior, and as an *alternative* to incarceration. In both cases, the goal of community corrections organizations is to facilitate justice-involved individuals' success in desisting from crime and reentering society. As a result, these organizations have dual roles: (1) the supervision and monitoring of those individuals' behavior and (2) the delivery of services, mentoring, and other assistance to facilitate supervisees' success (see Figure 6.1). These dual roles mean that this component of the justice system is complex, with critical roles for government corrections agencies—federal, state, and local probation, parole, and other types of community supervision agencies—and service providers both inside government (e.g., departments of public health or other social services agencies) and outside government (e.g., nonprofit service providers, medical and other treatment organizations, faith-based organizations).

Figure 6.1
Community Corrections Agencies

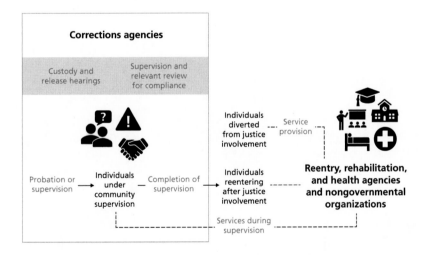

The activities of community corrections also bridge perspectives where the priority is the individual under supervision (e.g., how to help them get what they need to be successful) and broader public safety (e.g., the requirement to monitor effectively and, if the individual's behavior indicates that they are a danger to others, send them back into custody). Because of the variety of offenses that result in individuals being under correctional supervision, the types of activities that are involved in probation, parole, and other supervision can differ considerably across cases. The needs and challenges someone is likely to face when they are on juvenile probation for a nonviolent property crime are very different from those of a high-risk supervisee with repeated violent offenses. Supervision needs for individuals who are convicted of drug or property crimes are different from those of individuals convicted of sex offenses, and issues and challenges differ even among categories of sex offenses, some of which involve violence and some of which do not. Needs for treatment and other support services also can differ

Key Findings from Community Supervision and Service Provider Organizations' Response to the COVID-19 Pandemic

- Transitions to virtual models for both supervision and service delivery were made more difficult by major digital divides, with technical limitations for both supervisees and providing organizations. In some cases, technology had to be provided rapidly to staff and supervisees to allow activity to continue.

- Distanced and virtual supervision was viewed as beneficial by both staff and supervisees, increasing efficiency, allowing greater contact with supervisees, and reducing the burden of meeting justice obligations. It was viewed as a practice to continue, although outcome evaluation is needed.

- The pandemic resulted in a major reduction in the dosage of supervision for many people in the community corrections system, with reduced drug testing and less direct contact. So far, results appear positive, suggesting potential routes to further reform and improve the supervision system.

- Meeting the needs of individuals receiving treatment for substance use or mental health concerns was more difficult, requiring significant changes in models for treatment delivery.

- Community corrections organizations used virtual and work-from-home models that reduced infection risk and provided more flexibility to staff. However, balancing work and home life was a stressor for staff. Where in-person work was required, agencies used various cohorting models to reduce the exposure risk to large factions of their workforce.

- Efforts to decarcerate to reduce the risk of contracting COVID-19 in corrections institutions created a significant burden for supervision and service-provider organizations. For NGO service providers in particular, the demand for the services during this period was intense in some areas. Because of backlogs in other upstream parts of the justice system, community supervision participants expect another wave of cases in the future as those backlogs are resolved.

- There are major funding challenges facing both the government and NGO components of the community corrections system. These challenges will require more than considering how funding will affect individual entities in isolation. Instead, jurisdictions must address how the providers that serve their area are supported and how the different pressures on their individual funding streams will affect the viability of the system as a whole.

significantly from person to person. For example, the needs of someone coming out of prison and managing addiction issues will be very different from those of someone whose main needs are job training and placement assistance. These differences mean that there are both specializations within the community corrections sector, with individuals and programs focused on the needs of particular populations and customization of programming and supervision for different cases and circumstances.

Almost all of the activities of both supervision and service-providing agencies traditionally are delivered face to face. When putting the changes made in response to the pandemic into context, officers emphasized just how much supervision approaches rely on face-to-face contact: "About 70 percent of our work is in the community and there wasn't any kind of playbook, guidelines, or rules for how to respond to a situation like this."[1] Others cite even higher percentages of face-to-face work.[2] It is through contact and relationship-building that a community corrections officer forges a connection to the people they are supervising, and that relationship helps the officer most effectively help their supervisees. Even broader contacts and interactions within a supervisee's contacts and community might be necessary to effectively support reentry and desistance from recidivism. Treatment for mental health, addiction, and other concerns often is delivered in group settings, both to make it possible to help more people and because of the group dynamics and support that can be beneficial to recovery. As a result, the COVID-19 pandemic and the need to minimize contact to reduce the risk of transmission among staff and clients was a significant challenge to standard practices.

Because of the role they play in the justice system, community corrections agencies were a key enabler of the responses to the pandemic taken elsewhere. As we described in Chapter Five, release of as many people as possible who were being held in jails and prisons was a significant part of some response strategies to minimize COVID-19 spread within institutions. When they were released, those individuals came to community corrections agencies and service organizations, straining the capability of those agencies. In addition, because of the numbers of staff involved in delivering supervision and services, in some areas, agencies were called on to contribute in other ways to the pandemic response. Members of our panel noted such roles as managing protective equipment supplies, but other agencies described their officers being called on to assist other pandemic-response activities, including working in temporary shelters that were set up to allow greater social distancing or to provide alternative medical treatment sites.[3] Furthermore, community corrections officers were sometimes called on as backfill staff in correctional institutions when illness or quarantine sidelined prison or jail staff.[4]

---

[1] Comments of chief probation and pretrial officer Connie Smith of the Western District of Washington, in United States Courts, "Officers Innovate in the Field During COVID-19 Crisis," news release, June 11, 2020a.

[2] Holly Swan, Walter Campbell, and Nathan Lowe, *Pandemic Preparedness and Response Among Community Supervision Agencies: The Importance of Partnerships for Future Planning*, Rockville, Md.: Abt Associates, 2020.

[3] See discussion in American Probation and Parole Association (APPA), "Community Corrections Virtual Roundtable on the Coronavirus Pandemic," video, YouTube, April 8, 2020a.

[4] See discussion in APPA, "Community Corrections Virtual Roundtable: As the COVID-19 Dust Settles: Agency Efforts to Recover," video, YouTube, May 12, 2020b.

> It seems in times of crisis, people see [that our agency has] about 2,200 staff and 1,500 officers. They see a resource pool there. So suddenly, we were being directed to have our officers utilized distributing PPE, to help staff testing sites, if nothing else, being a presence. So [we] had to work around that because somebody had to still continue to make sure that supervision took place.
>
> – Community corrections panelist

Panelists from service-provider organizations also identified instances where they were called on to contribute in unusual ways, playing backfill and other roles where needed.

> One of the advantages of being a nonprofit is that as long as you want to do something and it's not illegal, and you can figure out how to do it, you are able to do it. So we were able to move really fast and we ended up doing some really strange things that we've never expected. Like when the correctional officers refused to screen visitors, for a couple of days, we were asked to screen visitors and do temperature checks or gift care packages to people who were unexpectedly released or work in the hotels where homeless people being released were being helped.
>
> – Community corrections panelist

Concern about how a pandemic or other disaster would affect community corrections was not new.[5] Like other parts of the justice system, the sector (through APPA) had developed pandemic planning resources some years before the COVID-19 pandemic, prompted by concerns about pandemic influenza and bioterrorism in the late 2000s. However, reflecting the decentralized nature and chronic research shortages in the U.S. community corrections system, uptake of these resources was not universal: According to information provided to APPA and Abt Associates by member agencies in response to a questionnaire early in the pandemic, although essentially two-thirds of agencies had crisis protocols in place, the remainder either did not have such protocols or the respondents were unsure whether they had them. Using these data, Swan, Campbell, and Lowe concluded that "it seems reasonable to conclude that APPA's pandemic influenza guidelines were not widely applied by community corrections agencies."[6]

---

[5]   In previous NIJ efforts to identify priorities for the sector, several high-priority needs focused on improving the sector's preparedness for different types of disasters (see Brian A. Jackson, Joe Russo, John S. Hollywood, Dulani Woods, Richard Silberglitt, George B. Drake, John S. Shaffer, Mikhail Zaydman, and Brian G. Chow, *Fostering Innovation in Community and Institutional Corrections: Identifying High-Priority Technology and Other Needs for the U.S. Corrections Sector*, Santa Monica, Calif.: RAND Corporation, RR-820-NIJ, 2015).

[6]   Swan, Campbell, and Lowe, 2020, p. 4.

> Back in, I believe it was 2008, 2009, APPA actually published some guidelines for preparing for emergency situations. And I think now everybody's going to be doing that. . . . I think now everybody's going to be really cognizant of the fact that they have to have some type of plan in place. We have to be strategic about everything we do.
>
> – Community corrections panelist

Like many of the members of other justice agencies who participated in our project, members of the community corrections panel noted that, at least initially, the assumption that the COVID-19 pandemic would be a short-term crisis versus a very long-term challenge affected how they planned and responded. For this sector, this difference was particularly important because, as the pandemic continued, efforts to reduce incarcerated populations (both through release and by using community-based alternatives to incarceration) continued as well. This meant that the flow of justice-involved individuals to supervision and services continued, even as the pandemic stressed agencies' capabilities to serve.

> We predicted several things at the onset of the pandemic. But one thing we didn't know was that it was going to go on for so long and our prison and our community corrections populations were going to drop so much with that.
>
> – Community corrections panelist
>
> I spoke to some staff yesterday, [and they said] "Chief, anytime we're going to be back in the office?" And I [said] "I don't think so. I think this is kind of normal and that's kind of another place where we have to figure out what is an operational posture that we can sustain indefinitely."
>
> – Community corrections panelist

However, local conditions and local responses to those conditions differed greatly. In a review of changes made in community corrections policies during the pandemic, Executives Transforming Probation and Parole (ExiT) identified states where major changes were made across multiple types of policies and practices and states where it appeared that no changes were made at all.[7]

> [Our courts] are decentralized, so . . . even though we do issue [overarching] policy. . . . It certainly can present challenges because particularly in an environment such as COVID, you have [areas] that are in different places for different reasons, as it relates to who's coming to work, who's holding court operations.
>
> – Community corrections panelist

The COVID-19 pandemic directly affected many community corrections organizations and service providers, with staff becoming ill and some dying. In their broad data call seeking

---

[7] EXiT: Executives Transforming Probation and Parole, "COVID-19 Response," webpage, undated.

to understand the effects of the virus on the sector (in which about 200 agencies from different parts of the country responded), Viglione and colleagues reported that approximately three in 20 agencies had at least one confirmed case of COVID-19 on their staff (and almost eight in 20 had at least one confirmed case among their clients).[8] Some of the agencies represented on our panel were significantly affected, with exposures leading to quarantines of large numbers of staff and many staff members ill with and lost to COVID-19. Community corrections officers and staff are included in some of the previously cited totals of practitioners who have lost their lives to COVID-19.[9]

> The first week, one of my offices had a staff meeting in a courthouse jury room with the entire office in there for four hours. And after the staff meeting, one of the people tested positive. So the entire county office was quarantined at home for 14 days. And we had to [immediately] figure out how to have other people supervise the thousand offenders that reported there. And then the next day, the governor told all state employees to go home. So I kind of threw our plan out the window pretty quickly there.
>
> – Community corrections panelist
>
> We had about 40 or more staff that have been sick. And we had several deaths that we also had to contend with. And then people's families also, our staff's families being sick. So it was a struggle.
>
> – Community corrections panelist

In considering the response of the community corrections system to the COVID-19 pandemic, it is useful to consider it as two complementary components: supervision and service delivery. The former role is largely the realm of government correctional agencies, although some private-sector firms are involved in contract supervision services as well. The latter is more complex and more associated with social services agencies, NGOs, and medical or treatment providers, but it is not a clear division of effort, and community corrections officers themselves play a bridging role in supervising and facilitating access to (and, sometimes, monitoring the supervisee's participation in) services and support. Some of the challenges are common across roles, and some are distinct to each; therefore, the discussion seeks to bring out both types of challenges.

Supervising and Delivering Services to Rapidly Increasing Numbers of Individuals Virtually and at a Distance

Reflecting the now relatively well-understood responses to the COVID-19 pandemic both inside and outside the justice system, efforts to reduce risk in the community corrections sector focused on distance and protective strategies for limiting disease transmission and, wherever possible, the use of virtual models for doing business to eliminate transmission risk. For both the supervision and service delivery components of community corrections, this shift involved

---

[8]   Jill Viglione, Lucas M. Alward, Ashley Lockwood, and Sara Bryson, "Adaptations to COVID-19 in Community Corrections Agencies Across the United States," *Victims & Offenders*, Vol. 15, No. 7–8, 2020.

[9]   American Correctional Association, undated.

some relatively significant changes from standard practices, and both types of components faced common challenges and concerns about the effectiveness of new ways of operating. However, those new models had advantages as well, some of which were responsive to concerns about the effect of justice involvement on individuals and communities.

> Certainly our mission hasn't changed, but how we've executed has changed pretty dramatically.
>
> – Community corrections panelist

Correctional Populations, Agencies, and Service Providers Face Significant Digital Divides
One common problem for both supervision and service delivery was a significant digital divide, which was a challenge across the justice system for virtual and other models of operation during the pandemic. As was the case elsewhere, the primary concern was the digital divide that exists for the justice-involved population,[10] but technology and connectivity shortfalls affected supervision and service-provider organizations as well. In the words of one provider, "About 75 percent of our staff and participants . . . actually had access to technology. They either had internet or they had a phone, a smartphone. That excluded about 25 percent of both staff and participants that couldn't receive the kind of services that we ended up doing remotely."[11]

> We smashed right into the digital divide for our clients. . . . Our [wraparound services] clients didn't have phones often. Or if they did, they didn't have internet access, or they didn't have a plan they paid for. So we ended up supplying a lot of phones and actually the city asked us to catch people coming out of jail and give them phones so that if they were being released to supervised release, it was possible to reach them. So that digital divide issue is a *huge* issue for our folks.
>
> – Community corrections panelist

This lack of access was a major barrier for supervision and service or treatment delivery, and, in some cases, both types of organizations provided technology and connectivity (e.g., a paid service plan) to their clients to make virtual models viable.[12] This avoided approaches where probation officers had to rely on clients' other family members' connectivity.[13] Representatives from organizations working with recently released individuals emphasized that people who were incarcerated for long periods might have even more-serious technologi-

---

[10] See discussion in APPA, "Community Corrections Virtual Roundtable: Probation Officers on the Front Lines Against COVID-19," video, YouTube, July 7, 2020c.

[11] See comments made by Eduardo Bocanegra, senior director, READI Chicago, in Council on Criminal Justice, "Facing COVID-19 in the Community," video, YouTube, May 12, 2020c.

[12] For some types of justice-involved individuals (e.g., some people convicted of sex offenses), restriction from access to the internet can be a condition of supervision, essentially resulting in an "enforced digital divide."

[13] Officer Connie Smith of the Western District of Washington in United States Courts, 2020a.

cal deficits than people who served shorter sentences.[14] Other challenges faced by reentering populations—notably housing instability—were mentioned as contributing to the digital divide: If someone did not know where they would be living from day to day, they would have similar uncertainty about their ability to connect to the internet for supervision or treatment.[15]

> Working with the local jail and doing some reentry work for the offenders, one of the significant issues we're having is getting the family or the group that's on the outside access to the communication devices to be able to do some of this remote work. So we struggled to get everybody with a camera on a phone, or to get a suitable internet speed or something of that nature. And this was particularly difficult with some of the populations that we serve, who just aren't as nimble at being able to acquire these things for many different reasons.
>
> – Community organization panelist

Digital divides affected organizations as well, in some cases limiting their ability to use alternative modes of service delivery. Organizations that had made previous investments in technology and connectivity had significant advantages in making the shift to virtual and distanced operations. But that advantage relied on the technology being familiar rather than bought but not yet leveraged.

> We were already operating virtual. The only offices we have are where day reporting centers are. We've moved away from brick and mortar to a paperless system, so we were already set up good with it. All of our officers were already working flex timed. So very little change in that regard.
>
> – Community corrections panelist
>
> We had Microsoft Surface tablets for all of the officers already. We were already set up with that. One of the things we did spend time doing, and we had the luxury to do, is bringing clients in, making sure clients had a way to be contacted using technology, training people on Zoom or Skype, whatever means we could set up communication.
>
> – Community corrections panelist
>
> I remember when I bought the iPhones for our staff, I [went] to offices and they [tried] to give them back to me. They [said,] "I'm never gonna use this phone. You might as well just take it [back]." And I'd say, "Well, just hold on to it. You might use it someday." And then the week after this started, I got all these emails that they never updated their software and now their phone doesn't work.
>
> – Community corrections panelist

Agencies that had not made these investments had more difficulty adapting; in some cases, agencies had to implement new technology as the pandemic intensified. And even agen-

---

[14]   Katelyn Newman, "For Prisoners Released Due to COVID-19, a Different World Awaits," *U.S. News and World Report*, April 15, 2020.

[15]   See discussion in APPA, 2020c.

cies that were well prepared could be affected by others who were suddenly reliant on finite bandwidth. Increases in use from many government agencies simultaneously swamped network capacity in some cases.[16]

> If you're paper-based, it's difficult to telework. If you have, you know, 135,000 files that haven't been scanned.
>
> – Community corrections panelist
>
> [Because of an initial infection in another office,] instead of phasing out, everybody was at home overnight. . . . We did have laptops and cell phones for our staff. Well, for our agents and supervisors, clericals did not. So that was a little bit of a challenge. And we ultimately just said, "Take your desktop off your desk and take that home. And we'll worry about getting you hooked up."
>
> – Community corrections panelist
>
> We tried as much as possible to give all the probation officers a smartphone, which was certainly an investment of money that we had to make, but that was fine and made sure that everybody had either agency-issued laptops or their home laptops that they could use to be able to access the remote [systems].
>
> – Community corrections panelist

Distanced or Virtual Supervision Involves Significant Change from Standard Practices

Although there was considerable variation across the country, many areas made quite substantial changes to community supervision practices in response to the pandemic.[17] According to an early assessment of the responses,

> The infiltration of COVID-19 into our criminal justice system has also affected our community corrections programming. With government buildings closed all over the nation, physical check-ins with probation and parole officers are suspended indefinitely to practice social distancing. States like Massachusetts have decreased the use of electronic monitoring as a supervisory tactic to avoid physical contact between the person fitting the device and the probationer or parolee. Probation and parole officers are using video and telephone calls to communicate with clients, rather than home or office visits.[18]

In broad guidance regarding reducing COVID-19 risk in community supervision contexts, most recommendations focused on reducing in-person contacts (including limiting drug testing), modifying in-person meetings to reduce risk (e.g., home visits by supervising officers, meeting outside), limiting conditions on release that could increase risk, expanding virtual options, and ending supervision terms early for low-risk individuals.[19] Others provided

---

[16] See discussion in APPA, 2020a.

[17] Researchers at the University of Central Florida developed a database of policy adaptations that is searchable by category (University of Central Florida, "Adapting Community Corrections in Response to COVID-19," database, undated).

[18] Marcum, 2020, p. 764.

[19] National Commission on COVID-19 and Criminal Justice, 2020a, pp. 32–33. See also Vera Institute of Justice and Community Oriented Correctional Health Services, *Guidance for Preventive and Responsive Measures to Coronavirus for Parole, Probation, and Clemency*, Brooklyn, N.Y., March 18, 2020.

guidance on how to "ration" supervision and time resources in the event that caseloads over-whelmed agency resources.[20] Other guidelines emphasized the potential importance of the probation or parole officer in providing information to reentering or supervised individuals on how to protect themselves from COVID-19 and reinforcing following guidance around isolation and quarantine, the use of face masks, and hand washing.[21]

> So as soon as we saw [lockdowns in other states,] that [gave us] time to prepare while we were in the offices before a potential lockdown, before community spread. So, what we initially did is we started looking at all of our key services from supervision, treatment, social services, court services, pretrial services. We actually learned from [a hurricane we experienced in our jurisdiction] to be prepared, to adapt on a dime when the entire system shut down and no one can go anywhere.
>
> – Community corrections panelist

Available data sources on the extent of changes in supervision policies reinforce the conclusion that there were substantial changes in some areas, but in practice, those changes—including the extent to which areas shifted to distanced and virtual models—were uneven. Beyond inventories of policies (such as the one developed by ExiT),[22] there were multiple efforts to collect data directly from agencies on how they were shifting their practices during the pandemic. As was the case for data collections for other portions of the justice system over the course of the pandemic, all of the following data collections were convenience samples with relatively low response rates, making it difficult to generalize results:

- Data collected by APPA and Abt Associates (between March and April 2020), identified large numbers of agencies that "suspended in-office reporting, in-person group activities, and home or field contacts."[23]
- Results of a similar data collection by the National Association of Pretrial Services Agencies (which was fielded between April and the end of May 2020) were comparable, with large percentages of respondents increasing telephone contacts and check-ins; temporarily suspending in-person contacts and check-ins in offices; and increasing the use of such technology as email, texting, video calls, and other methods.[24]
- A similar snowball sample data collection was done somewhat later in the pandemic (in June 2020) by Viglione and colleagues.[25] Their responses had heavier representation from smaller and rural agencies. In those agencies, changes in practice varied significantly, with nearly half reporting face-to-face contact with supervised individuals at about the same

---

[20]   National Council on Crime and Delinquency, *Community Supervision COVID-19 Guidance and Tips*, Washington, D.C., 2020.

[21]   American Society of Addiction Medicine, *Caring for Patients During the COVID-19 Pandemic: Managing Justice Involved People with Addiction During the COVID-19 Pandemic*, Chevy Chase, Md., September 18, 2020.

[22]   ExiT: Executives Transforming Probation and Parole, undated.

[23]   Swan, Campbell, and Lowe, 2020, p. 4. See also United States Courts, 2020a, for a discussion of virtual home visits using video streaming apps.

[24]   National Partnership for Pretrial Justice, undated. See also discussion in Hrdinova et al., 2020.

[25]   Viglione et al., 2020.

frequency as before the pandemic but between 10 and 20 percent reporting that they were holding no face-to-face meetings at all. However, the majority of their respondents also said that they were using such technology as phone check-ins, texting, email, and video.

The experiences of our panel members echo the broader picture from the data collections.

Our officers, for the very first time, are text messaging their clients, they're doing some things that they weren't doing before. And I really am looking forward to seeing what those outcomes are of all of these changes.

– Community corrections panelist

In March, April, while we're trying to get our bearings, I was fine with waiving some residential contacts and all of that. But [now] we're not seeing people in the office, unless there's an absolute safety, tactical reason why you need that. Other than that, it's work from home, but maintain your field contact standards, [and] use technology to substitute those in-person contacts that may have been in an office setting. And that's been really helpful.

– Community corrections panelist

We basically substituted, if you were in a medium risk category of supervision and you were seen every two weeks, that would happen virtually. And if you were in another subset of . . . [cases]—what we call RAW cases, robberies, assaults, and weapons cases—then you also got an in-person visit at home, socially distant with PPE. And then, [for] responding obviously to other emergencies as they came up, we still had teams of people in an office that we were able to deploy. That actually has worked very well. In fact, I would say people have *more* contact than the baseline contact they're supposed to have.

– Community corrections panelist

We did allow our staff to do contact visits to what we consider our low-risk offenders via either telephone or virtually, which has never been done in the parole system. We did telephonic contacts [before], but it didn't replace your normal face-to-face contact. So we eliminated the requirement for face-to-face contacts for low-risk offenders on our regular caseloads. We also allowed the officers to do different types of what we call home visits. Instead of actually going into the client's home, we made exceptions to those rules so we could maintain the six feet or more social distancing when we saw the clients in the field. That made a huge difference. I mean, if you go in a parole office today, when you would normally have 20 to 30 people in the office, you're probably going to see about one-third of the staff there. Everyone else is in the field.

– Community corrections panelist

What we did was we actually developed a . . . virtual supervision template with alternative procedures that apply to every program from electronic monitoring to drug testing, to personal contacts and supervision.

– Community corrections panelist

According to one of our panelists, in addition to existing technological alternatives for contacting clients, some systems used dedicated smartphone apps focused on supervision, combining elements of electronic monitoring that might be provided by GPS or an ankle monitor with communications capability. By the time of our workshops, some community corrections systems were starting to open up again and resume more face-to-face interactions. Other publicly reported examples included agencies in Wisconsin and Mississippi, which began to resume some in-person supervision in midsummer.[26]

When making these changes, there was a need to make sure that clients understood the situation and what their obligations were under the altered supervision approach. Our panelists emphasized the need for strong and varied communication options because not everyone would pay attention to the same channels during the disruptive circumstances of the pandemic. From the data collected in data calls by others, this focus on communication was reportedly not universal. According to data in Swan, Campbell, and Lowe, "less than half of [probation or parole] agencies had made any sort of announcement to their clients about the changes [to supervision practices] or the pandemic."[27]

> [One lesson from past disasters was] it was really important to be able to communicate in multiple media platforms, not just texting and emailing with clients. We started a Facebook page. . . . We started a Twitter account. We didn't have [either or those] before. We made a lot of adjustments to our website in terms of [providing information on], "If you've lost contact with your officer, here's where you need to call. Here's what you do." We continued to put out quite a bit of information all over the place in terms of what to do, which really helped when the lockdown came.
>
> – Community corrections panelist

The pandemic also stressed technological elements of standard supervision models, including ankle monitors and other devices. Deploying those devices involves direct contact between staff and supervisees. But because these devices have practical challenges, such as technical glitches and batteries dying—and because they usually must be inspected to ensure that they are still being worn by the individual, have not been tampered with, and are functioning as expected—contact might be required to keep a device running even after it is in use. As a result, some states made significant reductions in the number of individuals assigned to electronic monitoring in an effort to reduce contact. One state representative was quoted in the press as saying that their state is "only putting ankle bracelets on people for whom the state 'couldn't figure out a way not to do it.'"[28] This was certainly not universal, however. Some other jurisdictions indicated that they had increased the use of electronic monitoring as a path to keep people out of correctional institutions.

---

[26] Comments of Sarah Krahn and Jay Laufenberg in National Association of Counties, "Community Supervision During COVID-19: Implications for Change," webinar, August 5, 2020; "Limited Visits to Begin at Probation, Parole Offices in July," WTOK, June 30, 2020.

[27] Swan, Campbell, and Lowe, 2020, p. 4.

[28] Beth Schwartzapfel, "Probation and Parole Officers Are Rethinking Their Rules as Coronavirus Spreads," The Marshall Project, April 3, 2020a.

> [In our county, our electronic monitoring] program went up by at least a thousand people. Initially we were having some issues, just basic supply issues, but also staffing for the monitoring. As we're getting ready for our next fiscal year to start, we actually started shifting some of our staff around to transition over to the electronic monitoring side of the things, because it just grew so quickly and we didn't have the resources in place. So, of course, the stakeholders feel better cause they can say, "Oh, they're not in the jail" . . . but no one's doing anything to actually try to support the program the way it needs to be supported to make sure that we're still running a secure program.
>
> – Institutional corrections panelist
>
> We started thinking about inspecting equipment. Electronic monitoring, I think is one of the best examples. We actually changed our procedures to allow for a virtual inspection of that equipment. . . . Now, if they don't have a phone, there's where your creativity, your innovation, comes in. Take a time-stamped picture of it with a weather channel and the time behind you, things like that.
>
> – Community corrections panelist

Drug testing is frequently part of supervision. The process, including observation during sample collection, generally requires close contact between staff and supervisees. Particularly early in the pandemic, some areas suspended testing in an effort to reduce the chance of COVID-19 transmission. In a data call to community corrections professionals, Viglione and colleagues found that the majority of their respondents had decreased the use of drug testing, and the National Partnership for Pretrial Justice data call found similar results.[29] In some cases, respondents made infrastructure changes (e.g., adding a window to restrooms) so that collections could be observed while maintaining social distance.[30] Reduction—although not elimination—of testing was echoed by our participants and by practitioners in other contexts.[31]

> We didn't do any urinalysis in the field. We went from random and targeted urinalysis just to random. So that knocked down about 50 percent of our urinalysis that we were currently doing monthly. So now we do those in the office and we schedule those so we can have limited clients in the office at the same time.
>
> – Community corrections panelist

Other alternative approaches to testing were explored, including transdermal patches to detect the use of drugs by supervised individuals,[32] remote devices that combined GPS moni-

---

[29] Viglione et al., 2020.

[30] National Partnership for Pretrial Justice, undated.

[31] Comments of Ellen Donnarumma, vice president for justice services, Community Resources for Justice, in Council on Criminal Justice, 2020c; Schwartzapfel, 2020a.

[32] Courtney Tate, "Amarillo Probation Officers Making Adjustments to Supervise Offenders Through COVID-19 Pandemic," *KFDA News*, April 29, 2020.

toring with a breathalyzer operated by the individual under supervision themselves,[33] and the use of oral fluid swab testing.

> For drug testing, we were a urine-based state. And so we had to buy [oral fluid collection] swabs and get those out distributed across the state. So people could start drug testing [supervisees'] homes with swabs.
>
> – Community corrections panelist
>
> In criminal justice, the integrity of testing of observed collections is such an important part of accountability [for behaviors like drug and alcohol desistance]. So, we kind of invented this new term *quasi-observed*, what can we do to make staff and the participant comfortable? Could we do different procedures to give adequate space? . . . Let's look at alternatives [like] the transdermal drug patch versus urine testing, which gives a different kind of detection, a different kind of functional wearability of it as opposed to urine testing . . . alternative testing methods that were very important to us [for managing safety, but] that still kept accountability and integrity in the testing process.
>
> – Community corrections panelist

The other major change in practice, which reflected the desire to limit the number of people in custody and therefore at risk of spreading COVID-19 in the corrections system, was limiting the use of technical violations of probation and parole conditions.[34] In some states, individuals who were jailed because of technical violations were an early class of prisoners who were released to reduce incarcerated populations.[35] In both the APPA/Abt Associates and National Partnership for Pretrial Justice data, on the order of half of respondents indicated that their agencies had suspended or reduced revocations of supervision for most violations.[36] Some case studies of local areas cite greater use of "alternative sanctions" for technical violations.[37] Examples of such sanctions from the literature include completion of additional online courses, house restrictions, use of summons (rather than issuing warrants), and more-frequent virtual check-ins.[38] In some states, people were not reincarcerated even if they relapsed in substance use during supervision, and instead were provided with additional support and treatment.[39] In a Council on Criminal Justice discussion about the changes in practices, panelists argued that, at least at that point, in May 2020, the cuts in revocations for technical violations had "no

---

[33] Tommy Simmons, "'A Little More Creative': How the Coronavirus Has Changed Probation, Parole in Idaho," KTVB7, May 3, 2020.

[34] National Conference of State Legislatures, 2020. This is also consistent with the recommendations of Wang et al., 2020.

[35] Schwartzapfel, 2020a.

[36] Swan, Campbell, and Lowe, 2020; National Partnership for Pretrial Justice, undated.

[37] See, for example, Buncombe County Justice Services Department, undated.

[38] Peter Wagner and Emily Widra, "Five Ways the Criminal Justice System Could Slow the Pandemic," *Prison Policy Initiative* blog, March 27, 2020; Simmons, 2020.

[39] Simmons, 2020.

obvious effect on crime rates,"[40] suggesting that the changed policies might be worthwhile to maintain after the pandemic to save money and reduce justice involvement.

> You're pretty much locked out of jails, which we used a lot for violations. And so now you have to come up with a new way of imposing sanctions and handling violations and all of this stuff. It's all laid out in policy and procedure, and so getting those changes put in place as quickly as possible [was a challenge].
>
> – Community corrections panelist

Delivering Distanced or Virtual Counseling, Treatment, and Reentry Services Is Challenging

Echoing concerns that were raised by some of our law enforcement panelists, participants in the community corrections panel noted that the early part of the COVID-19 pandemic was extremely challenge for counseling, treatment, and reentry services providers, and many shut down completely while they worked through how to operate under the new conditions. Those shutdowns—and the financial challenges that followed rapidly on their heels—limited the ability of many individuals to get services and strained community corrections models that rely heavily on social services agencies and nongovernmental service providers.[41] In a data collection from reentry service providers in April 2020, the Council of State Governments found that three-quarters of the 126 programs that responded to their call for information had either "stopped providing some services or closed operation entirely."[42] The majority of the respondents to the data call were concerned that access to services would be significantly reduced in spite of the majority indicating that they were making greater use of technology in delivering services.

However, there was a short-term effort to shift to virtual and distanced models to continue to deliver services, as there was across the rest of the sector.[43] That shift included developing plans for distancing, cleaning protocols, facility upgrades for ventilation, and alternative outdoor delivery models, even for sensitive areas, such as drug treatment. According to a community corrections panelist, "We have set up open-air or van dosing [for the delivery of medication-assisted treatment] outside our facilities for those who are symptomatic and often do onsite testing in collaboration with the Department of Public Health." Some other treatment providers went to a similar drive-by model where counselors met with individuals at their homes outside.[44]

---

[40] Comments of Ellen Donnarumma, vice president for justice services, Community Resources for Justice, in Council on Criminal Justice, 2020c.

[41] See discussion in APPA, 2020a.

[42] The Council of State Governments Justice Center, "Survey Shows Reentry Services Halting Across U.S.," April 22, 2020.

[43] For another review that discusses how service delivery needed to shift to address supervisees' needs during the pandemic, see Alisha Desai, Kelley Durham, Stephanie C. Burke, Amanda NeMoyer, and Kirk Heilbrun, "Releasing Individuals from Incarceration During COVID-19: Pandemic-Related Challenges and Recommendations for Promoting Successful Reentry," *Psychology, Public Policy, and Law*, 2020.

[44] See discussion in APPA, 2020c.

> And we [wraparound service provider organizations] got hit like a ton of bricks with no prep time, no chance to know this was coming. And we adapted and we readapted and we kept readapting as information kept changing, everything changed all the time.
>
> – Community corrections panelist
>
> We lost initially our program services that we had. We have some key components of our programming [provided through contracts and] I think everybody was like, "What is this? What's happening?" And then our programs [provided by NGOs], they pivoted right away. And then they were able to go virtual and we lost maybe a half step as we sort of regrouped mentally here. But they really stepped up, especially the mentoring-type programs.
>
> – Community corrections panelist

Others made a shift to virtual learning models for delivery of educational programs, mirroring changes occurring elsewhere:

> Given the impact of COVID-19 on the economy and certain occupational sectors, vocational service providers have also had to adapt services. For example, distance learning was being used to provide some vocational training as a replacement for transitional jobs.[45]

Online treatment programs for violence prevention—for example, programs focused on individuals who have been domestic abusers—adopted virtual models for functions, including "remote . . . counseling, group or individual sessions, intake processing for new abusers, and monitoring completion of assignments as part of their rehabilitation program."[46] Practitioners emphasized that the alternative models were important but did not work for everyone: Technological barriers and the digital divide were concerns for some accessing treatment and services, and—even if those barriers were surmountable—there were concerns that some clients used technological frustration as an excuse to drop out of treatment.[47]

Given the economic fallout of the COVID-19 pandemic and increasing numbers of people released to community supervision and reentry in response to infection risk inside facilities, panelists emphasized that they were seeing increasing levels of need,[48] including for basic needs, such as food and shelter.[49] According to Anne Precythe, director of the Missouri Department of Corrections,

> The most basic things that people leaving prison need are jobs and treatment. Both of those have shifted significantly in many places. The jobs don't exist [and] the employers who were

---

[45] Stephanie Holliday, Sarah B. Hunter, Alex R. Dopp, Margaret Chamberlin, and Martin Y. Iguchi, *Exploring the Impact of COVID-19 on Social Services for Vulnerable Populations in Los Angeles: Lessons Learned from Community Providers*, Santa Monica, Calif.: RAND Corporation, RR-A431-1, 2020, p. 5.

[46] Emezue, 2020.

[47] See discussion in APPA, 2020c.

[48] This is consistent with the recommendations for reentry support laid out in Wang et al., 2020.

[49] See, for example, discussion in Vera Institute of Justice, 2020a; Alison O. Jordan and Melvin H. Wilson, *Addressing COVID-19 and Correctional Facilities: A Social Work Imperative*, Washington, D.C.: National Association of Social Workers, Social Justice Brief, June 2020; Newman, 2020.

totally able and willing to hire [justice-involved individuals] they're not hiring right now so that's a challenge. Treatment modalities have shifted totally to technology for the most part and not everybody is comfortable using that. But the other one that comes to mind is housing, and in some places, shelters and housing have become more challenging.[50]

And that rising need was happening at the same time that disease-control measures and other pressures were reducing the capacity of programs to deliver as much to as many people.

> The social distancing, the reduction in activity, has reduced the services, and that's been very significant in terms of counseling, in terms of reentry, in terms of all kinds of things.
>
> – Community organization panelist
>
> What we're seeing is rising need. We're seeing rising need around substance abuse treatment, around mental health treatment. We're seeing the population we serve dealing with greatly increased trauma, increased homelessness, real risk of hunger and [a] hard time finding jobs. All of that. We're also seeing a rise in violent crime. We're seeing a rise in domestic violence. We're seeing a rise in overdoses.
>
> – Community corrections panelist

Just as participants in our law enforcement panel emphasized how much the remainder of the justice system depended on people getting the treatment that they needed, community corrections panelists focused on how agencies had tried to make sure that happened.

> We don't want somebody that needs substance abuse [counseling] not to get treatment. Somebody that needs mental health services, we want them to get the services that they need. So coordinating that and working with our contracted providers, working with our local mental health authority providers [was critical for] determining the best way to continue to provide the services with everyone's safety in mind. So we went to a virtual visits when we could. If there was enough room in the contractor's current location where they could social distance and do small groups of less than ten that was done. Telemedicine was already being done [and] that increased as well. So those types of things, obviously we don't know the outcomes yet, but we've had very positive feedback from not only the clients, but from the providers and the parole officers. We are definitely thinking that's something we're going to continue.
>
> – Community corrections panelist

Mental Health

For reentry in particular, access to mental health services is a key element for supporting justice-supervised individuals. The strain and stress associated with the pandemic was an added threat to their success, particularly given economic impacts and job losses, which fell heavily on industries and job categories that employed reentering people.[51] To limit contact,

---

[50] Council on Criminal Justice, 2020b.

[51] See discussion in APPA, 2020a.

virtual counseling and telehealth models were used to increase the ability to maintain continuity of care. In their data, which were collected from a sample of staff connected to community corrections, Viglione and colleagues found that the majority of their respondents were using telehealth services for mental health treatment.[52] Others went to distanced in-person models to limit infection risk while maintaining care delivery that is more in line with usual procedures. In an effort to reduce the chances of breaks in continuity, in some cases, institutional corrections agencies sent individuals home with a longer supply of needed medications and with a prescription to allow for more time to connect with care as part of reentry supervision.[53]

> One of the things we quickly moved to [in outpatient therapeutic programs], which was a significant investment in staffing time was, instead of taking groups of 25, we broke into groups of five. It helped us look at social distancing, maintain boundaries, but we added a lot of additional time and resources from a staffing perspective just to maintain the continuity of services with what we felt were the most fragile populations.
>
> – Community corrections panelist
>
> The feedback we've had from our clients has been very interesting. Some people have told us, they do feel more comfortable talking [in a virtual setting]. It just seems safer. They're not as stressed out. I'm looking at attendance rates and people are saying "I'm able to make my meetings." Our counselors are able to do more individual sessions.
>
> – Community corrections panelist

Our panelists also expressed concerns about the inability to meet the needs of individuals with mental health conditions during reentry becoming a roadblock to releasing them as part of COVID-19 prevention efforts.[54] One participant described that, particularly for individuals with serious mental illness, they were "getting stuck" in custody because of the perception that they were more difficult to decarcerate safely.[55]

---

[52]   Viglione et al., 2020.

[53]   For example, in Virginia, the Department of Corrections "is now releasing offenders with three months' worth of medication rather than the usual one month. This will ensure that returning citizens have adequate time to establish care in the community and comply with socially distancing requirements" ("Legislature Approves Authority for Virginia DOC to Release Some Offenders Early," *Independent Messenger*, April 28, 2020). See also the comments of Sarah Krahn in National Association of Counties, 2020.

[54]   See, for example, discussion in APA, 2020.

[55]   Others have argued that this was, in part, because persons with mental illness have less resources to post bail in the pretrial context (APA, 2020).

> Some of them came back to us and said that even as we've dropped the jail population overall by 25 or 30 percent, the problem that we're seeing is that the portion of people with serious mental illnesses is starting to creep up, because for that group of people in our jail, we're having much more difficulty figuring out how to connect them with some of the other supports, the supports like housing that they may not have had when they were in the community.
>
> – Community corrections panelist
>
> For people with serious mental illnesses, re-entry needs and the perception that people could not be easily and safely transitioned back into the community was, for many jails, a barrier to letting people with serious mental illnesses go, even if they met the local jurisdiction's assessment of charge and risk that would have allowed them to be released.
>
> – Community corrections panelist

Substance Use Disorders

Substance use disorder treatment is extremely sensitive to maintaining continuity of care, particularly when medications are involved that support desistance from use. Just as the added stress of the pandemic could prove difficult for individuals who are dealing with mental health issues, that stress can make maintaining sobriety more difficult.[56] Furthermore, the effects of the pandemic have raised concerns about the availability of support to these individuals: "The pandemic has also suspended some of the social supports that are both lifeline and requirement for many on probation and parole, including Alcoholics Anonymous and Narcotics Anonymous meetings, appointments with counselors and therapy groups."[57]

> I've also heard about a heightened vulnerability among those people who have substance abuse disorders. So that's becoming a problem also. And I know that there are a couple of departments that I've spoken to recently, some of the smaller departments in rural areas, particularly those that you're accustomed to hearing about all of the meth addiction and things like that is it's just completely gone berserk. So those are the types of things that I think departments are going to have to really look at.
>
> – Community corrections panelist

Speaking directly to this challenge, the American Society of Addiction Medicine developed a set of guidelines for maintaining treatment. These guidelines included providing released individuals with a naloxone rescue kit in case of overdose; providing a path to uninterrupted access to medication-assisted treatment (for example, "the probation or parole officer could be assigned the responsibility of ensuring the individual is able to access their community treatment providers to assure uninterrupted treatment"); providing take-home medications and prewritten prescriptions to limit gaps in treatment; making connections with

---

[56] Ernie Fletcher, Dave Johnson, Robin Thompson, and Grace Lamb, *A Holistic Approach to Corrections Early Release COVID-19 Strategies*, London, Ky.: Fletcher Group, May 14, 2020.

[57] Schwartzapfel, 2020a.

community organizations; and addressing the housing needs of reentering individuals.[58] The guidelines also emphasized the need to understand individuals' health status and vulnerability to COVID-19 in shaping a flexible approach to treatment.[59]

> We know that if people are at increased risk for coming home and having overdoses or using the emergency departments, this would be problematic for our health care system at large.
>
> – Community corrections panelist

As was the case for mental health treatment, Viglione and colleagues found in their data collection from community corrections staff that the majority of respondents were using telehealth services for substance use treatment.[60] In addition, mirroring the effort to not reincarcerate people because of technical violations of their supervision, in some areas, there were efforts that sought to limit reincarceration of individuals as a result of substance use violations of probation and parole conditions.[61]

> Some of the ways that telehealth and the use of technology has helped to decouple medicine from a physical location is particularly important for people on community supervision and people who are at reentry. We've seen that in the jurisdictions that are rural and really didn't have access to specialized health care and specialized substance use care. The loosening of the regulations around telehealth and the ability to pay for it differently has made a big difference in being able to get people care and that's particularly important. Because we are seeing significantly more overdoses, that people who are formally incarcerated are at really high risk. So I think those two things are the things that are, have been standing out for me. And certainly telehealth doesn't replace the in-person connection, but it's certainly better than not having [treatment available].
>
> – Community corrections panelist

Multiple analyses have reported that treatment providers have shifted to harm-reduction approaches, providing medications and other supports to help maintain desistance from more-serious substances during pandemic-imposed stay-at-home periods that make treatment more difficult. According to Holliday and colleagues, "substance use treatment providers have been increasing their use of harm reduction approaches . . . to help reduce overdoses from more-serious substances, reduce withdrawal problems, and help clients to shelter in place."[62] Panelists cited challenges with providing take-home medications for treatment of opioid use disorders, which is critical because the country is simultaneously dealing with mortality from the opioid

---

[58] American Society of Addiction Medicine, 2020, p. 3.

[59] See also Vera Institute of Justice and Community Oriented Correctional Health Services, 2020.

[60] Viglione et al., 2020.

[61] Mick Stinelli, "Report Recommends Reducing Incarceration for Substance Use Violations," *Pittsburgh Post-Gazette*, October 18, 2020.

[62] Holliday et al., 2020, pp. 5–6.

use epidemic and the COVID-19 pandemic. Early on, regulations made such models difficult to implement, although as the pandemic progressed, there were changes made to facilitate treatment.

> One of the bigger barriers from the community-based provider perspective is the speed and agility at which governmental systems and regulatory bodies move to respond to conditions on the ground. And many times, we're seeking guidance—sometimes permission—and support to carry out our work or even sometimes broaden our scope of work. And it can be really difficult to get that response and to get that support.
>
> – Community corrections panelist

Others wonder whether these changes presage models that will survive the pandemic to make treatment more accessible in the long term:

> In just a matter of weeks, swift modifications in our opioid treatment regulations that the Substance Abuse and Mental Health Administration announced in March 2020 have revealed an alternative reality by which patients with opioid use disorder in the U.S. can now access treatment. Longer take-homes for methadone—which previously were only allowed after a patient completed years of daily visits to clinics—are now considered standard. Buprenorphine treatment initiation—previously requiring a lengthy evaluation process by a waivered physician followed by frequent monitoring—can now be done over a simple phone call. Mandates for supervised urine drug screens and in-person behavioral counseling sessions have been largely relinquished or adapted to be remote. At the same time, the drive to prevent the spread of COVID-19 in detention centers has led to the unprecedented dismissal of thousands of low-level drug charges, which would have otherwise led to the incarceration of many drug users with minimal or no access to effective treatment.[63]

RAND Corporation work echoed the conclusion that changes had the potential to significantly expand access to drug treatment.[64]

Employment Services

As noted earlier, some providers substituted distance learning for their traditional model of transitional jobs building work experience because those jobs are not available in the current economic environment. However, in spite of such efforts, the success of individuals in reentry and supervision is inevitably going to be harder in a tougher economy because a key contributor to such success is stable employment. This issue was echoed in a Council on Criminal Justice panel in May 2020: "Individuals returning home from jails and prisons will be in competition with an even larger pool of people for even fewer jobs, making it even more difficult than usual. And having a criminal conviction makes it much more difficult."[65]

---

[63] Noa Krawczyk, Michael I. Fingerhood, and Deborah Agus, "Lessons from COVID 19: Are We Finally Ready to Make Opioid Treatment Accessible?" *Journal of Substance Abuse Treatment*, Vol. 117, 2020.

[64] Holliday et al., 2020, p. 8.

[65] Comments made by Bobby Scott, U.S. Representative, in Council on Criminal Justice, 2020c.

> Our clients have been the most marginalized in the employment sector as it is. And their skill sets may not be aligned with the new economy as it ramps up, and they're going to be the last ones hired anyway. So what is that going to do? Our officers are scrambling a little bit about, where do I focus now? . . . But really equipping people to be more employable, that was part of probation work, but I'm very afraid for our clients, for their economic sustainability and financial health. And so, so that's one area that I think is going to be a huge challenge.
>
> – Community corrections panelist

Housing and Other Support

Because many individuals who are held in jail or have been otherwise incarcerated are at very high risk for homelessness,[66] the final area of reentry need supporting correctional population reduction was housing.[67] Indeed, some of our participants noted the need to provide housing as a barrier to managing risk inside facilities because of policies that prevented the release of someone who would end up on the street; during the pandemic, this meant that that person was potentially at risk of both infection with and spread of COVID-19.

> We had people that state and city corrections *could* release, but if they were homeless, they *would not*. And so they were staying there [in custody] and they were terribly at risk. Prior to the pandemic, half the folks being released from state prison to [the city] were being dumped in the city shelter because they were homeless, [so this likely affected a lot of people].
>
> – Community corrections panelist

Clients being homeless posed challenges for the delivery of other services; they might not have reliable connectivity for virtual programming and might not be able to find private locations to participate in sometimes very sensitive treatment programs.

> Where do they go to have a confidential conversation? If you try to do a counseling session, where can they be, where they don't have other people hearing deeply personal things?
>
> – Community corrections panelist

One approach to meeting this need was standard transitional housing models, but congregate living arrangements were at risk for the spread of COVID-19, and there were examples

---

[66] In some areas, this was a driver for limiting release: "Counties are shut down right now. The resources in the community are very limited. So as concerned as I am that someone would test positive for COVID inside the prison and die from that disease, I'm equally as concerned that we would engage in early release, and release someone into the community into the homeless population and [then they] test positive and die in the community" (Colette Peters, director, Oregon Department of Corrections, in Council on Criminal Justice, 2020b).

[67] For example, efforts to minimize spread in facilities "led to an increased need to provide housing because more individuals who are experiencing or at risk for homelessness have been diverted from the county jail system" (Holliday et al., 2020, p. 5).

of shelters that had to be shut down because of infection.[68] And if people in transitional housing do not have places to which to transition, managing that model becomes difficult:

> One thing I've been struck by is that within this environment of trying to safely move as many [incarcerated] folks home as possible, we're left with a lot of people, particularly in our residential reentry centers, who don't have anywhere to go. They are with us in the community now, finishing their sentences, but they can't go home because they have nowhere to go. That poses a whole different series of complications both for the operation of the centers and individuals.[69]

> One [area] that's been impacted by the pandemic is our community-based congregate living situation. So residential reentry centers, halfway houses, homeless shelters, all of those have been impacted in different ways and many of them are a part of the community correctional system more broadly. A lot of the residential providers have worked hard to move folks to home confinement situations. But again, if there's not an address to return to that then creates congestion in a residential facility, which creates a possibility for community spread.
>
> – Community corrections panelist

Different areas and organizations used different models to try to meet shelter needs under pandemic conditions (with some similarities in approach to models pursued by victim services providers, which we discuss in Chapter Seven). For example, the city and county of San Francisco probation department partnered with NGOs to lease hotel rooms to provide housing for justice-involved individuals who would otherwise be homeless.[70] Some organizations in New York were reported to be providing hotel rooms and vacation rental company Airbnb apartments to recently released individuals who otherwise would have had nowhere to go.[71] The city itself was sheltering thousands of people in hotels.[72] Montana responded to housing needs by increasing discretion in the use of housing vouchers to support reentry.[73] Other areas delivered food and other necessities to individuals under supervision to support social distancing.[74]

---

[68] See discussion in APPA, 2020c.

[69] Comments of Ellen Donnarumma, vice president for justice services, Community Resources for Justice, in Council on Criminal Justice, 2020c.

[70] Office of the Mayor, "Mayor London Breed and Adult Probation Department Announce Supportive Housing Program for People in the Criminal Justice System During COVID-19," San Francisco, Calif., news release, May 7, 2020.

[71] The willingness of hotels and motels to participate in these efforts reportedly varied across the country. See, for example, discussion in Vera Institute of Justice, 2020a.

[72] Abigail Kramer, "Out of Jail and Homeless: City Struggles to Stop Covid-19's Spread," The New School, Center for New York City Affairs, May 5, 2020.

[73] Steve Bullock, Governor, State of Montana, "Directive Implementing Executive Orders 2-2020 and 3-2020 Related to State Correctional and State-Contracted Correctional Facilities," memorandum to Montanans and all officers and agencies of the State of Montana, April 1, 2020.

[74] Examples were reviewed by ExiT: Executives Transforming Probation and Parole, undated.

> We've seen a lot of jurisdictions across the country buying up old motels or old hotels. And they've emptied out the congregate homeless shelters. So what happens at the conclusion of this pandemic . . . to [all of these] single-occupancy or double-occupancy units that are much more humanizing and safe than big, large, homeless shelters? What's going to happen to those assets? And how will that impact the provision of homeless services going forward?
>
> – Community corrections panelist
>
> We did have to get involved with our city health department for those people who were in isolation [when they were scheduled to be released], who said that they had nowhere to go. I'm trying to find beds in the community. And everybody really tried to get on board.
>
> – Institutional corrections panelist

Benefits of Virtual Community Corrections and Services

Although virtual models were forced on traditionally in-person efforts by necessity, participants in our panels saw significant benefits from the perspective of both the community corrections practitioners and the supervisees.[75] With the flexibility provided by virtual connections, officers found that they were spending more total time interacting with supervisees than when all of their contact had been in scheduled in-person meetings. Officers were connecting with their supervisees in off hours and could provide support more flexibly. Participants reported that many officers felt that they had stronger relationships as a result of more-frequent contact, potentially making it more likely that probation and parole processes will achieve their goals. That potential for increased success is reflected in evidence-based correctional practices in addressing supervisees' criminogenic needs.[76] Some practitioners have argued that the increased use of technology has made it easier for probation officers to connect with younger supervisees because they are communicating in a way that is more "in tune" with younger audiences.[77] In cases in which those juveniles were still living at home, virtual models meant that when contact with the family was needed, they could easily be brought into the conversation. Furthermore, the virtual window into the home provided in a FaceTime or Skype call gave a much more informative picture of family dynamics than a formal in-office interview.

> On average, prior to this, we were only spending six minutes of time per offender [in] face-to-face field contacts. Virtually, on average, we were spending 23 minutes of time with these individuals. So obviously, core correctional practices, the more time you spend with them, the greater the likelihood of having an impact, and you don't have all these distractions of the house, the safety issues. So it really was very direct.
>
> – Community corrections panelist

---

[75] Also see the comments of Anne Precythe, director, Missouri Department of Corrections, in Council on Criminal Justice, 2020b.

[76] Faye S. Taxman and Steven Belenko, *Implementing Evidence-Based Practices in Community Corrections and Addiction Treatment*, New York: Springer, 2012.

[77] See discussion in APPA, 2020a.

We're doing a lot virtually, we've learned some tricks and silver linings, that we're going to keep forever. I love the idea that on Friday nights and Saturday nights, when our clients are most at risk, when our office normally would be closed, we can be reaching them.

– Community corrections panelist

I talk to parole and probation officers across the state, they say they feel better connected now to their offenders than they did before. Before, I think a lot of people would wait until that report day in the office to have their communications. And you got ten people in the lobby waiting to see you, and you're churning through them. Now, they can FaceTime them. They can Google Duo them, they can text them, they can call them. So they're having more frequent communications with the people that they're supervising. And the feedback that I'm getting is that they feel like they're more connected to them. And so I think that's a really positive thing that's come out of this.

– Community corrections panelist

In our juvenile work, we ask the family to come [into the office] also. Our officer's report that they can see family dynamics much better when it's virtual, because there are people walking around the house with their phone. You're watching who's hugging who, and who's kind of arguing with whom. . . . That is just a much more fluid way of interacting. It made us realize how much of a mask and a guard people have when they come into our offices to meet with their officer. In people's regular course of life, it's a much richer experience. It can be, again, not for everybody, but I think that's something that we can take with us.

– Community corrections panelist

As was the case in other parts of the justice system, virtual models erased some constraints that distance imposed on traditional approaches. In terms of getting supervisees into medical or counseling programs, newly reentering individuals might have had to wait for a slot to open in a program that was near enough to them to make attending practical. With telehealth models, community corrections leaders could place clients virtually in programs anywhere in their state, which could make it possible to get treatment started much more rapidly.[78]

Virtual models also had convenience and other benefits for supervisees. Just as having to come into court can be a significant burden on supervisees and could put their employment at risk, supervisees having to take time off to go to in-office supervision meetings also can be tough, particularly if they do not have their own transportation. According to a participant in an August 2020 National Association of Counties webinar, "Transportation is an issue in our county, we have no public transportation, so people who don't drive have to find rides into the office. . . . We took away that as a barrier for them."[79] Participants in our workshop who had surveyed their clients said that the ability to easily meet with probation officers without taking (often unpaid) time off work was a major improvement for them. Not having supervisees congregating in facility waiting rooms could be a net positive for outcomes by limiting a situation

---

[78] Comments of Sarah Krahn in National Association of Counties, 2020.

[79] Comments of Susan Rice, chief probation officer, Miami County, in National Association of Counties, 2020.

in which individuals with varied criminal histories (e.g., a low-risk, first-time convicted individual versus a high-risk, violent career criminal) could come into contact with one another.

> I got a question from an officer yesterday: "Hey, after this is over, if that's ever going to happen, do you see us using our office like we used to?" Yes and no. The idea of having an office, that came from the eighties when we couldn't be reached by cell phone or pagers. So it's probably time to move off of that. And, for somebody who's doing well to be able to step away from their job and use FaceTime or some kind of videoconferencing app to talk briefly with their officer and then get back to work instead of taking half a day off, which is probably without pay, just makes complete sense. At the same time . . . that doesn't work well for everybody. And if it doesn't meet the needs of that individual, don't use it.
>
> – Community corrections panelist

However, beyond the convenience of not having to travel to appointments, participants and others have pointed out that the greater comfort level of clients who are calling from their homes is a substantial benefit:

> For some people, coming into the office to meet with us can be very overwhelming for them, especially if they have a lot of trauma in their past. So being able to meet with them virtually really helped with that, because I think they felt more comfortable being able to talk to somebody through a phone app from their home, and we were at home, and it seemed to really strengthen some of the relationships that we had with our clients.[80]

That comfort and the willingness to open up has the potential to make supervision more effective and improve the benefits clients get from the process.

> On the client side . . . we saw [some] people that opened up. That no matter what we tried to do [in person] to create a safe environment, they just were hesitant. They're hesitant to trust. Their experiences taught them [that] you can't trust somebody with a badge or authority, but when it's by videoconference, it's like, "Well, at least I know you're not arresting me right now." And they opened up more.
>
> – Community corrections panelist

Concerns About the Effectiveness of Virtual Community Corrections and Services

Although our participants discussed major benefits from virtual and distanced models, they had concerns about whether they were effective as well. They also were aware that assessing effectiveness was going to be a necessary part of decisions about what changes to maintain after the pandemic recedes. A significant concern was that, as a result of digital divides and the fact that virtual models do not work for everyone, these approaches simply cannot reach everyone who needs counseling and other services.

---

[80]   Comments of Susan Rice, in National Association of Counties, 2020. Also see discussion in APPA, 2020c.

> [Although there were benefits to reaching some people virtually,] *I think we lost the most vulnerable people.* The people who were relapsing, the people who had nowhere to live, the people who were sleeping on the subways. And so we decided as soon as we possibly could, we were going to open up again and we did that. . . . What we lost [with virtual models] was the community that was about self-help and about change.
>
> – Community corrections panelist

Multiple members of our panel were skeptical that virtual connections were adequate substitutes for in-person relationship-building—for counseling, treatment, and many supervision needs. There was particular tension with recent initiatives that sought to increase contact to improve supervision outcomes. According to one panelist who has experience with multiple corrections agencies, for some specific supervision needs (including monitoring and treatment for some high-risk individuals convicted of sex offenses), in-person meetings are critical.

> Part of what mattered was that we were the safe place where they could be and where they could get a meal and where they could be around people who weren't drugging and where they had role models of people who'd made it through what they were struggling with. And now were seasoned professionals who were role models. So a lot is lost. *You cannot look at somebody's postage stamp–sized face and know they're wringing their hands or that they smell because they haven't been able to shower. There are huge things we cannot do.* And our dose of contact has diminished dramatically. So there are things we've learned. There are things we're not going to do again, if we can possibly get out of them.
>
> – Community corrections panelist

> The challenge with [certain sex offense] cases and we're going to see a significant spike in them soon [given backlogs in the court system] is the assessment. And the assessment, we think *requires* personal contact with the offender . . . and that's a significant challenge because there is somewhat of a—I don't want to say mystery—but there's a lot of unknown factors in the [sex offender] world. You know, it's not as simple as "hands-on" sex offenses where you can pretty much conclude that they have the propensity for violence . . . so [for many sex offenses,] that's an assessment that we still believe the in-person assessment is going to be necessary to jump in.
>
> – Community corrections panelist

> We touch about 55,000 individuals a month across our universe of services. Many of those we see multiple times each month. So our first reaction was how do we maintain continuity of services without touch? . . . What we do in treatment and education services became a major concern when we thought about intensive outpatient, supportive outpatient aftercare education courses. Fortunately, we were a bit ahead of the curve in being able to move to a virtual environment. We had done programs in virtual settings of trying to touch rural communities, but many of these had not done in that virtual medium. So that was a challenge of how quickly we can adapt to maintain continuity.
>
> – Community corrections panelist

> In the past three years, our policies have been driven by requirements to see offenders spontaneously after hours, things like that. And we really started to see a positive effect. Now that we're not doing that and, and our drug testing was reduced by 65 percent, what type of outcome will that have? We're not sure. We're going to look at it because maybe we were testing too often in the first place.
>
> – Community corrections panelist

Managing Community Corrections Agencies During a Pandemic

Navigating the pandemic required agencies to make significant changes to how they managed themselves internally—not just how they delivered services to their clients. Some of these management changes dovetailed with shifts in delivery, including work-from-home models, while others responded to other staff and agency needs.

Virtualizing Agency Management and Operations

In many of the areas represented by our panelists, the pressure of the pandemic led to decentralized and distributed agency operations with much greater numbers of staff working from the field or from home than had been the case previously. Although it was not uniform across all areas, the requirement to minimize risk by distributing the workforce reduced resistance to flexible working models in some agencies.

> People have been pressing us [to be] able to work from home, especially in investigations and that kind of stuff. And the city was not necessarily allowing us to do it.
>
> – Community corrections panelist
>
> One of the benefits to the working remotely is before that, if somebody came up positive or had contact with somebody who had COVID well, now we have to figure out well, who was at the office when you were, and now we've lost all of those folks for two weeks. . . . It's helped us be in a position where "I'm sorry, you're not feeling well, and we hope you feel better," but it's not impacting a group of 30 more people that don't need to be in [the office], so that's been helpful.
>
> – Community corrections panelist
>
> One thing that I think has been a great takeaway for me is that I'm hearing that there's a lot more trust in probation and parole officers, that there has to be a lot more discretion given to them to do their jobs . . . we see that people can still be productive and effective without being in an office from nine to five every day.
>
> – Community corrections panelist

Having officers work from home was a challenge from the perspective of maintaining a boundary between domestic and professional life, which could be even more challenging for officers involved in some types of supervision. For example, participants cited supervision of individuals convicted of sex offenses, which can involve the review of materials to which officers would not want their family members exposed.

> Keeping the boundaries [between] work and personal certainly matters and implicates timekeeping and all that stuff. So that gets a little trickier, but I think it's not insurmountable.
>
> – Community corrections panelist
>
> One of the challenges in our sex offender management program specifically is that part of their job is viewing graphic material on a daily basis. They're now doing that *in their homes* with children in their surroundings. So it presents lots of challenges.
>
> – Community corrections panelist

Virtual technologies also had advantages for agency leadership, where the transition made it easier to communicate with large numbers of staff at the same time.

> [For communicating with staff, with virtual platforms] I can speak to a couple of hundred of them at a time and take questions. And that only makes good sense going forward and expands our reach, particularly with a large agency that's very spread out. There's just a huge upside to that. Same thing with management . . . it's great to be able to reach the entire management team of probably 140 people all at one time. One message. Everybody hears the same thing at the same time. It just makes really good sense.
>
> – Community corrections panelist

Because of the connections among components of the justice system, virtualization in the courts also affected community corrections. Panelists made similarly positive points about the convenience and savings associated with virtual hearings from the community corrections point of view, but there also were questions raised, as there had been for virtual trial processes.[81]

> Initially some states . . . and counties have returned to actually doing parole revocation hearings in facilities. We switched from that model to a video system, which we already had in place with most facilities.
>
> – Community corrections panelist
>
> And parole, particularly, we find that when you're trying to make decision on discretionary release, eye contact is important. Body language, the mood in the room, and all that is lost with technology, it really is. . . . It's difficult to conduct hearings whether you're trying to either not talk over anyone or anticipate what somebody might say on a monitor, and it hasn't worked as well as we would've liked.
>
> – Community corrections panelist

Keeping Staff Safe and Minimizing Department-Level Risk Using Modified In-Person Staffing Models

As the concerns about the effectiveness of virtual models suggested, some things have to be done in person. Beyond client interactions that must be conducted in person, such tasks as

---

[81] Comments of Sarah Krahn in National Association of Counties, 2020.

firearms training cannot be done over Zoom. And not all community corrections officers transitioned to virtual models uniformly. As a result, agencies had to identify approaches to minimize risk during in-person activities—and when the virus did not cooperate, things got complicated.

> It seemed like everything became complicated, even training somebody in maintaining their firearms certification. That's about the only training we're doing. Even something like that, I think our first time back on the range, even limiting students, spreading them out, it's outdoors, all that kind of stuff . . . [and] somebody ends up positive. And so now everybody that was on the range that week, now you're all out two weeks. It just seemed like, not that our work is simple in normal times, but nothing is simple in the midst of all of this.
>
> – Community corrections panelist

Like other justice system organizations, probation and parole agencies used staff rotations and shift adjustments to minimize the risk of staff exposures or to break employees into cadres so that, if exposure occurred, the entire agency would not have to shut down.[82] Agencies used PPE, although in data calls done early in the pandemic (e.g., the APPA/Abt Associates survey), staff reported concerns about the availability of PPE for use during in-person interactions.[83] Similar points were made during our panels.

> We took into consideration appropriate PPE, like everyone else has done, [but] kind of slowly went that way. I remember back in March where like nobody [was wearing] a mask, we tried to follow the CDC guidelines. And then it made us sound like we didn't know what we were talking about, but now everyone is following the CDC guidelines. And we tried to adapt as they adapted, and [as they] make changes, we do the same thing.
>
> – Community corrections panelist
>
> Everyone wanted N95 masks, everyone wanted to stay at home. You got a lot of emails about "Why do I [have] to supervise offenders? You're putting my life at risk." And so, as information came out, we tried to communicate as best we could, but then it's managing shifting from our 105 offices to doing everything in the field.
>
> – Community corrections panelist

However, when outbreaks or exposures occurred—like in the training context described earlier—participants discussed the importance of connections with public health departments to be able to assess the effect on the agency and minimize both individual risk and operational impacts.[84]

---

[82] Swan, Campbell, and Lowe, 2020, p. 4. See also discussion in APPA, 2020c.

[83] Swan, Campbell, and Lowe, 2020, p. 3.

[84] The National Commission on COVID-19 and Criminal Justice recommended institutionalizing such connections to sources of medical knowledge, including public health agencies (National Commission on COVID-19 and Criminal Justice, December 2020b, p. 33).

> We've learned that there was one stakeholder that we didn't have a lot of communication with, and it's proven to be pretty beneficial. And that's communication with the local health department. Whenever we've had outbreaks in certain areas, we've invited the health department or asked them to come to our probation offices and do testing on all of our staff. And that's been beneficial because there's been a lot of staff that have tested positive that were asymptomatic. And if they would have walked into our probation offices with staff in there and possibly have vendors in there, the spread of the virus would have really run rampant throughout that office.
>
> – Community corrections panelist

Managing Staff Mental Health and Stress

As staff concerns about the availability of PPE suggest, the pandemic was a major stressor for community corrections and service provider staff. Like others across the economy who are dealing with children going to school remotely, concerns about disease risk among family members, and the potential loss of friends and relatives to COVID-19, corrections and reentry practitioners had competing needs. Flexible work schedules were noted as an important part of trying to manage staff stress and helping individuals balance family and work obligations.[85] Although virtual models of working had benefits, these models also increased work stresses because supervisees calling at odd hours made it more difficult for practitioners to maintain a separation of work and home life.

> We joked, "Hey, telecommuting is fun when it's your choice, but nobody's liking it right now," especially with kids present and all that stuff. I think we do have to be sensitive to that. There are certain parts of our workforce that are not performing well in that environment. We can either move on from them or adapt that environment. And I think that's something we need to really listen for the answer.
>
> – Community corrections panelist
>
> The younger people were definitely on board with talking to their probation officers (POs) virtually. [But] the POs then [had] their work hours kind of expanded, because people were calling at all hours of the day and night.
>
> – Community corrections panelist
>
> Everything that we're disrupting in their work, is on top of, "Now you're a stay-at-home school teacher, and now you're a chef." And now four of you were in a house trying to work from home and that's like best case, that's for folks that their spouse didn't lose a job, or don't have a spouse, or they don't have help. . . . So keeping the psychological state of our employees supported and in mind has been critical.
>
> – Community corrections panelist

Depending on staff members' family situations, the pressures on them could be even higher. For example,

---

85 See discussion in APPA, 2020a.

We did a very small analysis of some of the staff who are doing [this] work. We learned just in one site . . . about 30 percent of our staff there were single parents. . . . I can only imagine how much of struggle [it] is for a lot of our frontline staff who often had to have a second job or a part-time job or in many cases what we're also learning is, [for married staff], that their spouses, their partners have also lost their job.[86]

These pressures increased the importance of leaders and managers staying engaged with staff and maintaining a connection with them—not just about work but also about the individuals' personal circumstances. According to a participant in an April 2020 APPA meeting,

We also had staff who are losing relatives to the virus, and they're mourning and they have to deal with stuff, so it's a relentless assault on the psyche as well as the actual physical manifestations of this. So I don't think I will ever be able to do enough to ensure their wellness, but we're certainly trying.[87]

Decisionmaking Elsewhere in the Justice System Affected Community Corrections Entities

As the receiver of justice-involved individuals who have completed their path through the court system (to probation) or institutional corrections (to supervised release), the community corrections system is in the position to be affected by changes made in multiple branches of the justice system. Immediate actions taken to reduce infection risk (e.g., by increasing releases form jails and prisons) meant that an initial wave of supervisees came to the community corrections system. However, in the longer term, the backlogs building in other parts of the justice system represent pulses of demand for supervision and services that will reach providers as the situation progresses.

Decarceration to Reduce COVID-19 Risk Hit Supervision and Service Providers Hard

The push to move people out of institutions meant that community corrections and reentry services providers had many new cases to serve. These cases included early releases for individuals who had served their sentences and pretrial release and supervision, which was specifically called out by our participants as a concern. This push toward decarceration hitting already cash-strapped community corrections agencies and service providers was also a focus in a Council on Criminal Justice panel discussion: "Participants said that while warranted, the expedited jail and prison releases caused by fears of COVID-19's rapid spread have not been met with a commensurate increase in community support services."[88] Others noted the issue of the sheer numbers involved:

I think we need to have better communication and better coordination around the overall picture for people coming home and then the actual support network of groups that are doing that work . . . but we're talking huge numbers here, huge cuts and then huge numbers of people coming home . . . [and] we've got to understand how we're going to support

---

[86] Eduardo Bocanegra, senior director, READI Chicago, in Council on Criminal Justice, 2020c.

[87] APPA, 2020a.

[88] Eduardo Bocanegra, senior director, READI Chicago, in Council on Criminal Justice, 2020c.

the people, the providers on the ground to actually do the work—in an environment where even more people are going to be released and going to have needs for more critical access to reentry support.[89]

> We're often a forgotten end of the criminal justice system. But we work as a system and our courts have been doing everything just about virtually. They're not having jury trials right now. *For a while it was just pleaing people to get them out of jail. The number of people on bond supervision increased. It tripled. We were ill prepared for that.*
>
> – Community corrections panelist
>
> The pretrial system is very weak. . . . We talk a lot about reentry, but when people are getting out on bond and they don't have a place to stay and they don't have support and because the dockets are backed up, they're out even longer with really no help. Some of those issues just have to be addressed. That was one of the things that we dealt with when there was a push to get people out of jail. I don't want to push people out at midnight that don't have a place to go. I mean, it's almost cruel. Not everyone has family to pick them up. Not everybody has transportation. Some of the shelters were shut down. Some of the nonprofits really did take a long time to be able to shift. You know, I think there are things that we're going to have to look at very hard.
>
> – Community corrections panelist

In some cases, requirements that reentry services must be available to assist people transitioning out of custody were a barrier to implementing decarceration in response to the pandemic. And in one case cited by one of our participants, reentry providers opposed changes that would lead to significant short-term releases because they felt that they did not have the capacity to address the needs.

> A [challenge a] number of states faced with trying to do early releases was the need to have reentry planning and without the ability to connect with those community organizations that actually presented even a statutory barrier in some cases.
>
> – Community organization panelist
>
> There's legislation that was just passed by the New Jersey state legislature, which . . . would lead to the quick release of up to 4,000 people who are soon to be released anyway. It's a response, not just to COVID, but to future emergencies, future health crises. . . . There was opposition to that legislation from reentry service providers . . . people who typically are allied in this movement and this work, but who basically said that because of [their] budget crisis, [they] cannot support the release and reentry of this many people on an expedited timeline.
>
> – Community organization panelist

---

[89] Samra Haider, executive director of programs and chief strategy officer, Center for Employment Opportunities, in Council on Criminal Justice, 2020c.

Expecting a Future Wave of Cases to Manage

Our participants were at least as concerned about the long term as they were about the short-term increase in cases. They were acutely aware of case backlogs building in other parts of the justice system, which, at the minimum, were pending flows of cases that would come to them when operations resumed. Their concern was magnified by the fact that—rather than sending all of those pending cases to institutions—a greater reliance on diversion to supervision (which echoes some of the discussion in our courts panel) could be viewed as a faster path to release the pressure of backlogs elsewhere in the system. That strategy would further magnify the potential future load for community corrections and service providers to shoulder.

> One of the things we have a concern with is [the] judicial emergencies. This time last year we would have already had about 40,000 startups [of new cases under supervision] and we've only had about 15,000. The concern is now what's going to happen when the courts open back up and we have to be prepared to absorb those high volume of cases? I think we've been around long enough that there'll be a lot of blue-light specials going on just to move them onto our caseloads. And we certainly have to be prepared for that.
>
> – Community corrections panelist
>
> We may get more people on probation . . . I think it's important for our field to also recognize that . . . when people need to move cases, they're going one [way] or the other. They're going [to] prison, or they're going to go on some kind of supervision. I mean, the dismissals are already happening, those have not slowed down. With the financial crunch that probation is in . . . that's a crushing blow. I mean we may not even have enough staff to manage anything, if we can't work through it.
>
> – Community corrections panelist

Different Funding Challenges for Government and Nongovernment Organizations

Money and severe funding shortfalls in this part of the justice system were explicit concerns expressed by participants from both supervision and service organizations about the capacity of the system to serve current and future caseloads. For government agencies and government-funded providers, budget cuts to respond to reductions in tax revenue have hit hard:

> For instance in a place like [our city,] you're seeing a 25 percent increase in people released from the jail into the community. Yet the city . . . understandably has to make some serious budget cuts and so even [our program] had to have our capacity cut by 50 percent because of those budget cuts. I think what we need to do and what we need to kind of figure out a way that we can push is to make sure that some of the response around the needs to release more people and have more people in the community is met with the same investment in reentry support.[90]

---

[90]   Samra Haider, executive director of programs and chief strategy officer, Center for Employment Opportunities, in Council on Criminal Justice, 2020c.

Participants in our panel had faced direct budget cuts and had to find ways to reduce expenditures even during a period of increased demand for their services.

> [We were] notified in April that by July 1st we needed to cut 2 percent, that's around $2.3 million. Thankfully we're able to do that without [layoffs.] But it was tight.
>
> – Community corrections panelist

Others have termed this likely penny-wise and pound-foolish because cuts in programming that are intended to keep people out of the justice system might mean that more money will have to be spent later if their reentry fails and they are arrested and incarcerated again—not to mention the additional victimization that would result. For example,

> [d]iscretionary community-based programming is frequently the first to be cut, but evidence-based community programming often has a large return on investment and is inexpensive in comparison to traditional crime responses. In addition, community-based approaches promote holistic, comprehensive approaches to public safety and may improve the perceived legitimacy of anti-crime efforts.[91]

Such cuts also have hindered some agencies' ability to shift to technology approaches that would make it easier for them to continue operating effectively through the pandemic. As a result, the cuts might result in both short-term and long-term consequences in terms of community corrections effectiveness and staff and community risk exposure.

> I think now six months into it, I think people have adjusted to this, and I think we will be better in the end. We're looking at a lot of technology. The complicated part of that is . . . budget issues. Technology costs money and you need to use it right now. And your budgets are being slashed, we had to go through layoffs and our staffs have had furlough days. And *so it's tough with the budget situation as well as trying to purchase some technology that can be used.*
>
> – Community corrections panelist

One particular monetary challenge is that, reflecting the fee-for-justice model used in many areas, agencies and service providers often are dependent on money paid by individuals under supervision or treatment.

> The other thing that I think [is important] is the economic hit from the shutdowns. So not only were people struggling with trying to protect their families and deal with the virus, [but also] losing their job, losing employment, just was a huge thing. For our departments, a good portion of our basic operating funds are those from clients. Obviously that's not the funding methodology we wanted, but we've taken big hits from that. And, you know, we had to do hiring freezes and adjust to that.
>
> – Community corrections panelist

---

[91]   National Commission on COVID-19 and Criminal Justice, 2020a, p. 34.

> A majority of what we do are offender funded, participant pay programs, and we quickly realized the stress involved there. We're a for-profit [service provider] organization and we've always been involved in collecting money from the individuals for their services because that's a necessary part of serving the system. But, you know, we quickly reacted by saying, you know, we've got to show tolerance and patience and work with individuals.
>
> – Community corrections panelist

The suspension of collection of supervision fees, in addition to reflecting the challenges to supervised individuals in the pandemic economy, also helped "encourage people in financially precarious situations to observe social distancing."[92] The suspension of restitution payments to victims, however, would have that effect at the expense of crime victims. In their data collection in June 2020, Viglione and colleagues found that the suspension of fee collection was relatively rare, although a larger number of agencies were not issuing violations for late fee payment.[93]

Our participants emphasized that the consequences of these resource shortfalls could be dire, particularly for nonprofit service providers. They also noted that if that part of the system fails, there will be no one with the capacity to deliver the reentry and treatment services on which the success of community corrections programs depends.

> We are in unconscionable uncertainty about funding. We are looking at potential cuts. We're looking at potential retroactive cuts. The state of nonprofits before the COVID pandemic was fragile. [A] study in 2016 found that one in eight social service providers were technically insolvent. And for housing nonprofits, one in three were technically insolvent. We get funded at 80 percent of what it costs to do the job. We get paid late. Right now, we are dealing with unexecuted contracts and we don't know what's going to happen. The choice is closing the programs down or gambling that a promise that's not supported by an existing contract will be kept. . . . But most importantly, some of the nonprofit providers that you rely on are going to cut services dramatically and even more important, many of them won't be there next year or in two years. So I think there's a crisis because probation relies on the community providers. And they're going to go under.
>
> – Community corrections panelist

Available multiorganization data support our panelists' concerns:

In April, two-thirds of reentry service providers reported that they either had or were considering reducing services because they faced significant financial stress. Safety net health care providers are also under extreme stress. This raises serious concerns that people who

---

[92] Vera Institute of Justice and Community Oriented Correctional Health Services, 2020, p. 2.

[93] Viglione et al., 2020.

are leaving prison or jail are not able to access the services they need to successfully transition back to their communities, including services needed to mitigate COVID-19.[94]

In addition, respondents to a Council of State Governments data call to reentry providers found that, by April 2020, some already had to lay off staff.[95] These challenges demand that the community corrections sector do more than consider how funding and support will affect individual entities in isolation. Instead, it must address how the network of providers that serve an area are supported and how the different pressures on their individual funding streams will affect the viability of the system as a whole.

> There is grave concern about the survival of the nonprofits that you rely on for services because the needs are going up and the services are deeply jeopardized right now. So I think having a broader swath of concern than your individual agency is really important right now, protecting the services that you rely on is really important.
>
> – Community corrections panelist

Taking Stock and Moving Forward

The effects of the pandemic on community corrections providers were significant. Although in some other sectors, the effects of the pandemic or infection-reduction efforts helped in the short term to manage pressures—for example, the reduction in calls for service experienced by law enforcement—many of those efforts added workloads to community supervision and service provider organizations that were under stress and faced funding constraints before the COVID-19 pandemic. Financial pressures on these organizations—both within government and in the NGO sector—and their threat to the medium- to long-term functionality of this component of the justice system was one of the strongest messages from our participants. According to our panelists, unless ways of funding both supervision and services for these populations are found, when the wave of demand implied in the backlogs elsewhere in the system makes it to community corrections, the sector might not be robust enough to weather it.[96]

At the same time, the economics of the pandemic hit not just agencies and organizations but also the individuals they were serving, making it tougher for the individuals under supervision and treatment to succeed.

---

[94] Wachino, 2020, p. 2.

[95] The Council of State Governments Justice Center, 2020.

[96] This is consistent with one of the final recommendations of the National Commission on COVID-19 and Criminal Justice (which was published as this report was in the final stages of writing) for a need to "build community-based capacity to provide services to justice-involved populations during public health emergencies." The Commission also recognized the need for stable funding support for these efforts (National Commission on COVID-19 and Criminal Justice, 2020b, p. 15).

> So we are having the devil of a time doing what we normally do very well, which is linking people to jobs. And to the extent that we can, we're using transitional work as a way of helping people get into the mode of working and hoping to support their families. But these are limited ten-week slots that we have. And I don't think most of the restaurants are going to open again. We work with the bodegas, with the small stores. A lot of them are not going to survive.
>
> – Community corrections panelist

In spite of the major pressures that the pandemic has put on this part of the justice system, it also has driven adaptation and creativity, with agencies responding to the risk caused by the spread of COVID-19 in communities and the need of the sector, according to a panelist, to "change the way that they operate, but . . . pretty much continue [their] work unabated."

> The best thing about this, it's made us realize that you have to adapt to situations. Not that you hope for a pandemic, but . . . this has given us an opportunity to do things which maybe should have [been] considered long ago, but [agencies] haven't had the opportunity, the financial necessity or even—I won't say creative *ability*, but it makes you think outside the box, which I think is . . . very, very healthy.
>
> – Community corrections panelist

Promising Practices from the COVID-19 Pandemic Response

Among the changes made during the pandemic that panelists argued should be preserved were the shifts to teleworking models that provided more flexibility to both staff and leaders, helped conserve resources, and had potential benefits for recruiting and retention.[97]

> With telework, we made more progress in the first 30 to 60 days of the pandemic toward teleworking than we did in the previous six or seven years.
>
> – Community corrections panelist
>
> We went to Microsoft Office 365 and Teams. And honestly, from now on, there is not going to be any meeting that is citywide that I'm going to have in person. Maybe once a year, every six months to see people? Because you miss people? But the Teams thing has worked really well to keep up with certain things. Before, it was a struggle to schedule those people, and they had to come from all different places. So we were able to move pretty smoothly into our operational work virtually.
>
> – Community corrections panelist

---

[97]   See discussion in APPA, 2020a.

> I think as employers we have to continue to look for ways to be competitive. Certainly, there's an economic downturn, but prior to that, there wasn't, and it was getting harder and harder. So how do we take some of the flexibility that we've used here and bring that and normalize it, certainly not in a way that would impact service delivery at a high-quality level, but I think we're going to continue to compete with employers that have found it not just *possible* to work in this environment but *profitable*. So we're going to have to adapt in government in ways . . . that maybe we haven't in the past.
>
> – Community corrections panelist

Virtual access to the courts was viewed as beneficial to members of the public, and virtual supervision models and telehealth or teletreatment as part of community corrections practice was as well. Virtual models made it less burdensome for people to check in during supervision and could allow them to begin to receive services even if programs in their local area were full. The extent of the use of virtual models likely will depend on evaluations of their outcomes, given concerns about the importance of personal relationships during supervision and counseling, but hybrid models could be an approach to preserve the advantages of virtual models while minimizing potential concerns about efficacy.

> To be able to have the conversations and the connections virtually you have to have had a relationship first. I think it's much harder to build that first relationship phase virtually. So the first six weeks is that intense phase of getting to know the client, the kind of stuff that is going to probably stay in person. But I think nobody's now wedded to the office being the in-person location. That in-person [location] can be in their neighborhood. It can be in any number of places. And then if that person actually prefers video or whatever, we're much more nimble and can do that.
>
> – Community corrections panelist

The other major advantage of virtual models is the ability to adapt supervision to the needs of individuals—a "one-size-fits-one" approach, in the words of one of our panelists—and therefore better meet their needs. Being able to more flexibly adjust the dose of supervision given to each person reflects the understanding that too much supervision can be bad for outcomes for some individuals,[98] but—potentially more importantly—it allows resources and attention to be conserved for the supervisees who will benefit most.

---

[98] Schwartzapfel, 2020a; see discussion in APPA, 2020c.

> We have many, many, many individuals under our supervision who do not need our services. That's just a fact. Just as they don't need to be in prison, they don't need to be under our supervision. They truly do not need our services. And I think it's come to a time where we've got to quit talking about not having the necessary resources and talk about how are we managing our resources to create the time that's needed with those high-risk, high-need individuals. The one-size-fits-one [model]. . . . I think that we've kind of shied away from just admitting that we, we can no longer be everything to everybody. And I think sometimes as a profession, we want to take that on. We think because they come to us, we're supposed to do something with them instead of pushing back and say[ing], maybe they should've never come to us to start with.
>
> – Community corrections panelist

Pandemic Pressure as a Driver of Broader Criminal Justice Innovation

When considering the potential for broader change in this portion of the justice system as a result of the pandemic, participants noted specific policy changes, such as putting the legislative and technology infrastructure in place to be able to do better in similar future circumstances,[99] but they also discussed more-fundamental shifts.

> I don't think instinctively that as a system we're inclined to be introspective. . . . I think if there is a silver lining, [it's that] we are being *forced* to be introspective. Ironically, some of the things that we were considering well before the pandemic where "old-school resistance prevailed," now we're really considering it. And it could be that it's the best approach.
>
> – Community corrections panelist

In looking toward the future, participants viewed the cost pressures created by the pandemic as a likely impetus for broader innovation and change and a point on which actors across the political spectrum might find common ground. Coupled with the potential for those pressures to push toward less incarceration for cost purposes, the strain on supervision and services was viewed as likely to cause a reexamination of who really needed to be supervised.

> We are the best return on investment for dealing with felons or people that have committed crimes in our communities. When we look at probation and we say we're $5 a day to supervise [someone], opposed to $50-plus to be incarcerated, I think with the budget constraints that we're going to have within our states, legislators are going to catch on to that.
>
> – Community corrections panelist

---

[99] For example, our participants noted the need for areas to have legislation on the books for compassionate and medical release of incarcerated individuals in the event of future infectious disease emergencies to provide the ability to respond more effectively. The example cited was the New Jersey legislation that was enacted and allowed the release of a significant number of individuals to reduce incarcerated populations (Lauren del Valle and Leah Asmelash, "New Jersey Releases More Than 2,200 Eligible Inmates Under Nation's First Public Health Crisis Sentencing Law," CNN, November 4, 2020).

> [Releasing into supervision] is a fiscally responsible thing to do. And it doesn't keep people in prison any longer than they need to be. So I look at this as a unique opportunity . . . you have conservatives saying, we have too many people in prison, it's too expensive. We need to get people out. And you have progressives saying that this country should be ashamed of itself for having so many people behind bars. So this is a great opportunity for us to use this pandemic to actually do something about that. And a lot of prison populations have been drastically reduced because COVID gave us the fiscal responsibility, the impetus, but also the courage. And I'm going to use that word, the courage to do this, and we need to do more of it because you know what we did before clearly wasn't working.
>
> – Community corrections panelist
>
> I think that seeing those revocation rates go down fairly sharply, and particularly for technical violations, is something that we're looking at as a real potential positive. It's something to move forward. . . . It's built on reform that was pre-COVID, but COVID really escalated it to a level that we hadn't expected.
>
> – Community organization panelist

Virtual models also can reinforce existing experiments around showing that supervision did not have to be done in a community corrections office or other facility—and that what probation officers and service providers did was about the people being served and not the place where that service was being delivered. To the extent that cost reductions must continue, agencies "de-infrastructuring" could be a way to do so.

> I think it's going to be more important now than ever for those of you who are at the helms of your organizations to really look at the cost of brick and mortar.
>
> – Community corrections panelist
>
> The thought was, we've got to continue our day-to-day operation, and we've got to continue to drive that in the midst of the pandemic instead of having the pandemic drive our business. A few other things, we realized that it reaffirmed that *it's about the people under supervision and not the places of supervision*. That was big. We had just undergone a time-based study and we had moved our system from a contact-based to a time-based system. And so we, we were getting our toes in the water and kind of, it forced us to jump on in. That's a big paradigm shift where we're now, it's, it's all about the time that you're devoting to a case instead of how many times you're seeing an individual.
>
> – Community corrections panelist

However, several of our panelists argued that the experience in the pandemic—where supervision dosage has been drastically reduced for some people and where services are being delivered in very different ways—should drive people to support more-fundamental justice reform. According to a participant in a National Association of Counties webinar, if there are not significant increases in negative outcomes, the writing will be on the wall for pre-pandemic supervision approaches:

[Given what we have observed when programming has been limited during the pandemic,] what does that mean for us? Does that mean we were over-supervising before? And I think the answer to that question is probably yes. I think we found that we can still do a lot of the things that we used to do, but do them in a little different way and still be able to help people and get them through their term of supervision.[100]

The significant experiment in both decarceration and more-focused supervision provides support for the idea that less invasion into the lives of justice-involved individuals might produce similar or better outcomes and might make it possible for community supervision and its associated services to be a more effective *substitute* for incarceration.

> Some of the shifts in community supervision . . . I think COVID has really laid bare opportunities for criminal justice reform more broadly.
>
> – Community organization panelist
>
> The mission of probation and parole is really as an alternative to incarceration and it hadn't really been working that way in a . . . lot of places in the United States. And so the big picture for me is post-pandemic we're not going to try to go back to exactly what we were before. . . . And we've learned that there are these populations that were in jail and prison that didn't need to be there. And everyone agreed on that within a matter of days or weeks.
>
> – Community corrections panelist

This potential—which was highlighted by both members of our panel and others from the sector—is particularly important given the focus on equity and racial justice that was emphasized in the protests that occurred in summer 2020. Less-intensive supervision, and more-supportive rather than punitive supervision, have been components of broader calls for the reform of community corrections practices.[101] Practitioners have even argued that the suite of approaches and capabilities of supervision agencies and their networks of partners are the model that is being called for to respond to community concerns:

[How do we] actually explain to the community what we actually do? . . . Because everybody knows the social climate of . . . defund[ing] programs and police and law enforcement and, if you listen closely, our communities are asking for things that parole and probation departments across the nation already have. . . . We have people that are so diverse in our departments—that have mental health background[s], psychology degrees, counseling, case management, all that stuff the community asked for [during the recent protests], we *already* have it.[102]

As a result, beyond opportunities for innovation and reform within community corrections, change in this area could provide a template for broader system change.

---

[100] Comments of Susan Rice in National Association of Counties, 2020.

[101] See, for example, the discussion of the proposals of the REFORM Alliance (which predated the 2020 protests) described in Van Jones, "Atlanta Police Shooting Is About Probation, Not Just Police," CNN, June 18, 2020.

[102] Alex Jones, probation and parole officer, Multnomah County Justice Reinvestment Program, in APPA, 2020c.

If we put our mind to it, we can figure out a way to have a civilized society without incarcerating so many people. I think the implications for community corrections is that there's going to be a shift toward getting people out and getting them into community corrections. I think that's just smart and it probably bodes that business is about to start booming even more for people in community corrections. And I think we have to think about how we should be doing this efficiently and effectively.

– Community corrections panelist

There seems to be a lot more compassion from even some of the officers that have considered themselves more law enforcement types. Speaking to a lot of them, they say, "I need to make sure that the softer side of me is shown when I'm working with people," because they're really understanding that not only is it hard for just everybody, but it's particularly hard for people who have criminal records, for people who have already difficult economic situations in their lives. And I think that's really starting to resonate for a lot of people. And a couple of people have mentioned the whole Black Lives Matter piece, the whole racial justice piece. I think that also has opened up their eyes in terms of how they deal with, the type of rapport they have, with the people in their caseload. . . . You wish [the pandemic] hadn't happened, but I see that as a silver lining—that we've learned to be a little bit more compassionate and understanding of people's plight.

– Community corrections panelist

Policy Development and Evaluation Needs to Better Inform Decisions in Both the Short and Longer Terms

As practitioners from other sectors did, members of our panel emphasized the importance of evaluation to substantiate positive impressions of supervision and delivery models necessitated by the pandemic.[103] Some have such evaluation efforts underway within their own agencies.

We formed a subcommittee that is actually measuring outcomes on the effects of our alternative monitoring procedures. Like what are the outcomes associated with that? I think the best example of that is drug testing and treatment. So, we have a lot of districts that went toward telemedicine and there are pros and cons of telemedicine. The pros obviously are those who didn't have transportation are able to engage. We are now experiencing some I'll call it accountability issues as to did they really participate for that long, and are they engaged and how appropriate is group treatment through Zoom, particularly for sex offenders.

– Community corrections panelist

---

[103] Other organizations have identified key questions that should be examined to assess the changes made in response to the COVID-19 pandemic. For example, in the APPA and Abt Associates report, priorities included why some agencies were better prepared and able to adapt than others, how responses differed between urban and rural areas, and which of the changes made in response to the pandemic were in progress before the pandemic. Echoing our panel, the authors noted the need for an evaluation of virtual versus in-person contact; the factors shaping the effectiveness of alternative supervision models; the effect of reductions in supervision intensity, arrests, and revocation on success; and the effectiveness of virtual treatment programs (Swan, Campbell, and Lowe, 2020).

> It's critical to get the data and do the research and figure out who's benefiting, and have it really focused on the outcomes. There are people that have opioid use disorder, if they're not on the medicines, you're going to have bad outcomes. So if you can keep the focus on that, they may not need your [community corrections] services. Likewise, somebody who's got a mental illness but is not getting the help they need for their mental illness [are] not going to do well [no] matter what you do if you don't have that treated.
>
> – Community corrections panelist

The following key research and evaluation questions came out of our discussion:

- Given the importance of employment as a component of reentry and a driver of success, can the effect of the pandemic's economic dislocation on justice-involved individuals be directly measured to better understand supervision success rates going forward?
- Are virtual models as effective as in-person supervision, counseling, and treatment? What factors determine any differences in effectiveness? How have key outcomes—both from the individual and societal perspective—been affected by the shift?
- How have digital divides across different parts of the community corrections system—including government agencies, NGO service providers, and entities serving urban and rural communities—affected the ability to continue operations through the pandemic?
- How has reduction of the use of such techniques as drug testing or electronic supervision affected outcomes? Do the changes made provide a template for reducing costs and intrusion into supervisees' lives going forward?
- How have the major changes to the use of revocations—and, therefore, a significant reduction in a flow of individuals back into institutional corrections—affected outcomes?
- How can both supervision agencies and the service providers on which they depend be sustainably funded, given what we have learned during the pandemic?
- What are the full net savings for corrections agencies from virtual models? Estimates should include variable costs (e.g., staffing, transportation time) and potential savings from infrastructure costs. What are the net savings to the individuals under supervision?
- How can the effects of the changes made as a result of the pandemic be distinguished from the effects of other initiatives (e.g., bail reform) that were already underway in some areas?[104]
- What data need to be collected now—because they are otherwise likely to be lost—and what questions can be taken on when the immediate disruption of the pandemic has

---

[104] Members of both our community and community corrections panels emphasized the need to distinguish the effects of the pandemic from those of other initiatives for fear of positive reform efforts being scuttled unfairly. According to one participant,

> One thing that's interesting for New York is that COVID occurred after bail reform was passed in New York. So there was already movement in New York State to give low-level offenders appearance tickets, as opposed to having them sit in the county jail. . . . I worry about misuse of data. In New York State [we] have seen major bail reform. And what we've seen is misuse of data, blaming rise in violence on bail reform. When the numbers just don't bear it out, but it works as a story and it works in the media and to see us regress, I think would be a tragedy.

passed? For example, understanding which individuals received different doses of virtual supervision or services might be difficult to reconstruct after their programs are complete.

Understanding how changes in supervision—particularly the significant reduction in revocations and the backflow of individuals into institutions—pair with the use of virtual technologies that make it easier for many people to successfully participate in the supervision process could contribute significantly to changes that improve the efficiency of the justice system and also advance reform goals.

CHAPTER SEVEN

Victim Services Providers

Victim service providers (VSPs) play a core role in ensuring that the needs of victims are met, both helping survivors recover from the effects of criminal behavior and ensuring that the criminal justice system meets their needs and facilitates their involvement in investigation, court, and corrections processes (see Figure 7.1). The roles played by VSPs vary and include legal assistance; justice-related advocacy and support (for example, supporting a crime victim as they testify during the trial of the accused perpetrator); and other support services, such as providing counseling, shelter, and mental health treatment. Some support providers are specialists who focus on specific types of crime (e.g., domestic violence survivor support organizations), specific populations (e.g., the needs of a particular cultural or non-English-speaking community), or specific types of services. Others are generalists, providing a broad slate of services across crime types or populations. There are a wide variety of different organizational models for service delivery, including service provision that is connected to law enforcement agencies, court systems, prosecutors' offices, hospitals, campuses, and independent NGOs. Different groups can operate individually or in collaboration with each other.

Figure 7.1
Victim Services Providers

Given the risks created by the COVID-19 pandemic, the activities of VSPs were stressed in different ways. Many of the services provided to victims of crime are generally done in person—for example, sheltering in a domestic violence shelter, in-person counseling with a mental health practitioner, direct provision of food assistance—which was risky for both the individuals needing support and the paid staff or volunteers involved in delivering that support. The requirement to continue to meet victims' needs under these conditions challenged organizations in many ways and required as much or greater adaptation and innovation than in other justice agencies.

> Service providers have been so creative and, and trying to help survivors and working with the resilience that survivors have and that these programs have as good problem solvers, but they are struggling.
>
> – Victim services panelist
>
> We're seeing a lot of faith-based outreach work, wraparound services, the ministries that many congregations provide in their communities, struggling to be able to figure out how to pivot during this time of COVID-19 to continue those sort of outreach and ministry initiatives that they have in place.
>
> – Community organization panelist

However, because the endeavor of effectively serving victims is inherently tied to the actions taken by the justice system with respect to the alleged perpetrators of those crimes, VSPs also were challenged by the changes made in the system to manage COVID-19 risk. Victims and their needs represent one of the three key perspectives that must be reflected in considering justice system changes, and the nature of the crisis meant that many of the changes made cut against the needs of victims. Responding to the risk of COVID-19 in courts and corrections agencies required broad and global actions, reducing prosecution or speeding the release of whole classes of justice-involved individuals. These actions made it impossible to consider the particulars of individual cases, leaving some victims' concerns unexamined and likely unaddressed. VSPs therefore had to adapt to the effects of those changes on their practices to continue to pursue their missions under the pandemic-imposed conditions.

> At least on the misdemeanor level, a lot of the cases with the exception of domestic violence and other crimes that involve a victim, they're pretty much not being prosecuted. People are not being arrested. There's no court. . . . The same is for lower-level felonies as well. . . . Even with domestic misdemeanor, domestic violence cases, everyone is out of custody and, while we're filing them, there's literally nothing happening. . . . So we're just really focused on victim safety and not so much conviction in those cases.
>
> – Victim services panelist

The conditions imposed by the pandemic and the public health responses to manage them—including such interventions as stay-at-home orders and quarantine—also changed the nature of victimization and the needs of clients who were contacting VSPs. As we discussed in Chapter Two, the pandemic shifted and increased many victim needs. Such actions as stay-at-home orders appear to have pressurized domestic violence or family abuse situations; they also made it more difficult to identify cases of abuse and for victims to reach out for help. Such crimes as identity theft and fraud shifted, with particular concern about the elderly being targeted. Furthermore, concerns arose that the pandemic environment made it less likely for all victims to seek help because of fear of COVID-19 infection, assumptions that the pandemic would have shut down programs, or the belief that others might need assistance more than they do. Financial constraints and the realities of safely providing help also constrained delivery capacity in some programs. Like in other parts of the justice system, such trends have the potential for creating a backlog of need that will be realized as conditions improve.

Some agencies have reported that hotline calls are shorter and, when callers do get in touch with hotlines, those calls tend to be more frantic or more panicked, which may indicate that victims of abuse are only reaching out to hotlines during the pandemic when violence is especially severe or life-threatening.

— Community organization panelist

If you're trapped in your house with your abuser all day, it's really difficult to get to a private room to call the police or call a domestic violence agency to, um, indicate that you need some assistance, right, because there's additional harm or risk of harm associated with making those calls.

— Community organization panelist

We had a big concern about children being sheltered in place with abuse and no way to know what to do.

— Victim services panelist

Survivors are struggling to access the services that they need. They're reporting that they need services for longer periods of time. They need more-intensive services. And [providers are] seeing an increase in survivors coming back, folks that they had worked with who had moved beyond the immediate needs and . . . living independently and not using services, are coming back.

— Victim services panelist

The different intensities of the pandemic and the disparate responses to it across states and localities mean that service providers have been operating in very different conditions. An area that did not lock down to reduce viral transmission would not have experienced the same changes as one that did. As a result, changes in crime and, therefore, changes in crime victim need are geographically dependent, reflecting the localized variation in the pandemic and its impacts.

[Looking across VSPs in many areas,] there are very clear regional differences in demand. A lot of that depends on regional approaches to sheltering, to COVID policies, to COVID practices that are established by local governments. And that in turn influences how people interact with law enforcement agencies within those regions in general.

— Victim services panelist

The actions of the remainder of the justice system are shaped by existing inequalities and structural issues in the country, and so are the efforts of VSPs. Because the effects of crime fall very heavily on economically disadvantaged and marginalized communities, they are compounded by those structural realities, and the responses to them by VSPs must take both into account. Language issues meant that culturally specific VSPs became involved in providing information about COVID-19 and prevention in addition to their usual roles. The economic effects of the pandemic and job losses cut into individual and community resources to weather both the pandemic and victimization during this period. And although the pressures for justice system reform are not *focused* on service providers, the willingness of people affected by crime to reach out for assistance is affected by trust and legitimacy concerns, meaning that the effectiveness of VSPs is *shaped* by the current environment.

> Programs were overwhelmed with the amount of work they were doing providing basic information about the disease, what the stay-at-home orders meant, mask requirements, etc. That information was not and is still not available in the languages that folks speak. Up to 40 percent of our community don't feel comfortable speaking in English.
>
> —Victim services panelist

> The CDC send a lot of materials to domestic violence and sexual assault organizations. But they were translated into Spanish, but not into other African and Asian dialects. That translation is expensive and takes a lot of time.
>
> —Victim services panelist

> Crime can happen to anyone, regardless of your status of wealth or your ability, but it impacts people on the margins differently. People who are already poor, who are homeless, who are people of color who have experienced trauma in their lives are more severely impacted by any type of crime.
>
> – Victim services panelist

> Many [survivors] don't have access to health care and live in parts of the city that are underserved (e.g., food deserts). Half of the city doesn't even have a hospital. To get to a hospital, you had to use public transportation and that's dangerous. These barriers are baked into the system. Survivors are isolated with their abusers, but also unable to access resources. We heard this from survivors in gentrified areas and areas that were cut off. These are complications for everyone in the community.
>
> – Victim services panelist

> Something that we're [seeing and] hearing from other [city] agencies is [that] calls or those seeking help in the immigrant communities [have dropped]. We know that they have been historically the hardest hit often with needs [but] because of their fear to come forward and seek services [they are not] get getting the assistance. It's just another barrier for them.
>
> – Victim services panelist

The challenges created by the pandemic for providers of victim services required significant innovation and adaptation.[1] Such groups and agencies, which often depend on less-stable funding streams than other justice agencies, are relied on by people who—even if COVID-19 was not the dominating factor in their environment—are experiencing some of the worst periods of their life and are in great need of support and assistance. Changes made by these agencies in delivery models, staffing approaches, and services made it possible to continue their efforts, but the levels of need—and the expectation that those needs will only increase over the longer term—suggest that maintaining support for crime victims will get tougher over time.

Key Findings from VSPs' Response to the COVID-19 Pandemic

- VSPs went to virtual and remote working models to continue to operate and reach crime victims during the pandemic, but providers had reservations about cybersecurity, the ability to deliver services securely, and the effectiveness of some counseling and intervention delivered by phone or videoconferencing. New approaches to delivering some services appear promising to continue after the pandemic recedes.

- Some critical services, including shelter and food, require in-person interaction, and delivering them in a safe way was more difficult and costly for providers.

- Bandwidth limitations and the digital divide can hamper serving all those who need assistance.

- Pandemic conditions, including stay-at-home orders and visitor restrictions at such sites as hospitals, made it more difficult to reach victims. New approaches had to be developed to do so that might be valuable to maintain after the pandemic.

- Providers faced significant challenges protecting their staff because of being at a lower priority for access to protective equipment. Providers working from home faced the additional challenges of stress and managing the collision of their work and home lives.

- VSPs had difficulty with staffing levels, and recruiting during the pandemic was a challenge.

- Changes made by police and the courts in how they responded to some crimes—including nonarrest or rapid release of some individuals—made it tougher to meet the needs of crime victims.

- Many provider organizations face acute funding shortages from changes made by government, reduced revenues from fines paid by justice-involved individuals, reduced philanthropy, and financially strapped businesses that are unable to provide pro bono services or in-kind contributions. The pandemic has put the continued viability of many service providers at significant risk.

---

[1] For a discussion of responses by providers in one state, see Jaclyn Houston-Kolnik, Hannah Feeney, and Rebecca Pfeffer, *Impact of COVID-19 on North Carolina's Victim Service Providers*, Washington, D.C.: RTI International, 2020.

> I think it's creating unprecedented times for us to adapt our programming and the way we approach some of these issues, especially the burden that is placed on community-based organizations to respond, not just for a short period of time, but for an extended period of time. This compassion fatigue and worker fatigue is a real serious issue that I think is going to be felt for years to come.
>
> – Community organization panelist

Using Virtual Victim Services Models Helped, but Shelter and Food Cannot Be Delivered Virtually

Like in other parts of the justice system, there was a major effort across the victim services sector to transition to virtual modes of operation, both to continue serving populations through the pandemic and to protect staff (which we discuss in greater detail in the following sections). This included staff working from home and greater use of telephone and video options for service delivery.[2] According to a RAND report,

> Many services and operations switched to virtual modes, including video- and telephone-based communication methods. This included service delivery with clients (e.g., therapy and case-management sessions, document signing), staff meetings, and supervision. Many staff were working from home. Certain community-based outreach services and office-based services have continued when essential, but have been scaled back as much as possible.[3]

Groups supporting the sector also provided guidance and tools to help organizations select technology for virtual service provision and remote work.[4] Participants in our panels and available resources emphasized the need to train staff to go virtual because of the major shift from traditional service delivery.

> Right in the beginning of COVID when our state shut down and people were told to stay home, probably about 75 percent of our agency went remote. The shelters stayed in person. We have a street work project that works with runaway homeless youth that stayed in person and our [child advocacy center] stayed in person. But every other program went remote.
>
> – Victim services panelist

---

[2]   Alyssa Elman, Risa Breckman, Sunday Clark, Elaine Gottesman, Lisa Rachmuth, Margaret Reiff, Jena Callahan, Laura A. Russell, Maureen Curtis, Joy Solomon, Deirdre Lok, Jo Anne Sirey, Mark S. Lachs, Sara Czaja, Karl Pillemer, and Tony Rosen, "Effects of the COVID-19 Outbreak on Elder Mistreatment and Response in New York City: Initial Lessons," *Journal of Applied Gerontology*, Vol. 39, No. 7, July 1, 2020.

[3]   Holliday et al., 2020, p. 5.

[4]   For example, National Network to End Domestic Violence, Technology Safety, "Response to the COVID-19 Pandemic," webpage, undated.

> [In pivoting to remote services,] the level of services these organizations were able to provide depended on their ability to get support from their localities or states. [Where we are located], the response was robust—the [local government] quickly got resources to service providers to help them transition to remote service provision. Also, the response on the part of service providers was quick. Both providers and service recipients have experienced technology issues. Providers needed to provide laptops and iPads to survivors so that they could participate in listening sessions. That's the experience across the board.
>
> – Victim services panelist
>
> This underscores the needs to invest in mobile advocacy. Organizations that at one time were like "How does that work?" . . . had to figure it out. We expect increased investment in mobile advocacy services. The ability to stay in contact with the community and provide services is good.
>
> – Victim services panelist
>
> You need to build in time to train personnel on functionality and use of new platforms, new communication methods. Just rolling out the software isn't enough. You need to teach people how to use it, teach them how to navigate through the system, really educate them on privacy settings or transfer of information and how to communicate that to the people that they serve in plain language.
>
> – Victim services panelist

Like in other parts of the justice system, the transition to virtual operations was much easier for organizations that had made previous technology investments and were not starting from limited capability when the pandemic hit. The smoothest transition required an organization to already have the technology and have experience using it.

> Back in October a year ago, I transitioned everybody to laptops, which they fought and screamed . . . [about, but] now they're all thanking me because they can all work from home or wherever. So we have a lot of people working remote, but their computers that are linked as if they were sitting in the office. So they're making calls to victims, they're checking in with them.
>
> – Victim services panelist
>
> I think one thing I wish we had done differently was been ready for virtual. We had Zoom all that time and I don't know why we just didn't use it. I do know with what we do at [our service providing organization], a lot of our stuff is relation-based and people getting in person and hearing each other's stories.
>
> – Community organization panelist

Because of the sensitivity of providing intervention services to individuals who might be in dangerous circumstances or counseling on sensitive issues of victimization, there has been a considerable focus on providing safe ways to reach out for support. Adding the ability for text contact for services has been a priority because texting does not require access to a private area where a phone conversation could be held without being overhead.[5] However, even ubiquitous methods, such as texting, have cybersecurity vulnerabilities; abusers could use various types of spyware or tracking software "to covertly and overtly monitor the online presence of the person they are abusing to maintain coercive and even deadly control."[6] Other platforms for videoconferencing are not immune to concerns about cybersecurity and questions from providers about whether their access controls are sufficient for use in sharing sensitive personal health information.

> Domestic violence programs started adding text capacity to their hotlines and helplines. The domestic violence hotline certainly got a lot of chats and texts because, when you're stuck in the same apartment or house or your room with the perpetrator, you needed a silent way to reach out. So we saw many people adding those services. Also, everybody [is] trying to figure out what are secure platforms . . . to meet with survivors. I love Zoom, but it's not actually a secure platform. It doesn't comply with the Violence Against Women Act's requirements for confidentiality. So a lot of people [are] really trying to figure that out.
>
> – Victim services panelist
>
> I think that there are . . . some sites, some agencies that have made a choice [to use a particular technology platform that may be easier to adopt but] that we know . . . isn't as secure as we'd want it, but we'd rather do it in a less secure fashion than not offer services.
>
> – Victim services panelist
>
> [Regarding] the challenges of setting up remote work and the confidentiality and the cybersecurity and all of those things. They can be done. We're doing it. We've just been doing it for six years, so we didn't have to stand it up quickly, but there are, there are ways to do it.
>
> – Victim services panelist

Participants in our panel cited benefits from virtual access with respect to victims being able to get protective orders during the pandemic, although others pointed out that protective orders have to be served to go into effect, and some areas are resisting doing in-person process service, reducing the impact of issuing the orders. Panelists also cited the unexpected positive benefits of increasing engagement in the justice process because of the ease of joining proceedings virtually. They noted greater utilization of counseling services; fewer people missed appointments than was the case when all counseling was done in person.

---

[5]   Peter D. Kramer, "Domestic-Abuse Victims Can Now Text, Chat to Be Heard by Counselors, Not Their Abusers," lohud.com, August 13, 2020; Emezue, 2020.

[6]   Emezue, 2020, p. 5.

> Anecdotally, we're also hearing a lot of law enforcement agencies talk to us about the flip to virtual services, virtual platforms, *increasing* victim engagement, *increasing* access to services, giving victims more control over how they participate, who they have with them when they participate, when they talk to people [and] for how long, [and] that's been an incredibly positive thing that's come out of it.
>
> – Victim services panelist
>
> What we're getting from the psychiatrist counselors that we're talking to [is that they] are seeing a higher rate of people showing up for their appointments, less no-shows, which is really, really good, especially when you're trying to expand access to health, especially mental health.
>
> – Community organization panelist

However, participants cited challenges with virtual models of service delivery, including from breakdowns in the way that virtual models are being used in some parts of the justice system. For example, although some states have sought to address breakdowns in courts and others accepting electronic signatures on legal documents to limit stress on victims and reduce the need for them to come into offices or courts,[7] participants noted multiple examples of places in the system that have not made that transition effectively.

> Immigrants with pending immigration relief based on their victimization have been put into even further limbo. [Since] Social Security offices were closed down, even folks who did get [their status] approved that should have led to the creation of a Social Security card, they're generally required to go in person to pick [it] up. Because the offices are closed, they cannot get a Social Security card. The only option that the offices have provided is to send in their original immigration documents in the mail, which is of course unsafe to do. So, [the options] we've given immigrant survivors is either having no access to benefits and services that require a Social Security number or to lose proof of their immigration status at a time when that's of the utmost danger.
>
> – Victim services panelist
>
> [One challenge is] trying to find ways to provide wraparound services to victims. It's hard to schedule appointments for victims. It's hard to even connect with victims to get them to sign necessary paperwork. And so basically what we've been trying to do is find safe places where the street outreach team feels comfortable meeting with the victims while also protecting themselves.
>
> – Community organization panelist

Although virtual service provision allowed some programs to keep operating when they might have otherwise halted providing assistance, they were not always able to serve the same number of people as they could using traditional methods, which is a concern when overall needs are increasing. Limits in capacity have led some to focus on those with the greatest needs,

---

[7]   Office of Victim Advocate, undated.

although not serving others is creating a backlog of unserved individuals whose needs might compound over time.

> Most of the providers that we work with have tried to move to remote services, but had to restrict intakes. . . . I think they're focusing their responses on folks who are coming back into contact, and those cases that they have with expanded needs and increased needs. And so I think that's causing a backlog, and making it harder for survivors who are just coming out of their situation or being identified for the first time to get access to the services that they need.
>
> – Victim services panelist

Finally, some people are getting sick of video meetings, which suggests a difficulty in sustaining service delivery through these mechanisms in the long term.

> We're getting feedback [from the people we serve] that they are tired of Zoom. They don't want to do any more Zoom meetings. They don't want to do any more webinars. . . . So that is a little bit concerning to me on how we're going to make sure that we reach those people.
>
> – Community organization panelist

Digital Divides Limit Virtual Service Delivery

As was the case for the transition to virtual court processes, the digital divides across the country and among different socioeconomic classes affected the virtualization of victim services. Since the beginning of the pandemic, examinations of the adaptation of victim services to this environment described the importance of digital connectivity and the challenges its absence caused:

> Novel digital modalities are not without their shortcomings. For example, survivors (and even abusers in treatment) may face inherent structural and practical barriers to accessing digitalized services while sheltered in-place. Specific challenges may include internet connectivity issues (in low- or dead-zone internet coverage areas) and in no-tech and low-tech situations, leading to high-data burden and accessibility issues.[8]

> Essentially, a victim must have full access to the internet or unfettered, private access to an active phone line in order to report a crime against [an abuser] during this pandemic. Even these seemingly simple requirements can quickly exclude vast numbers of domestic violence victims from accessing help in an emergency or reaching the appropriate resources.[9]

Concerns about digital divide issues came up frequently in both our victim services and community organization panels. Participants noted it repeatedly as a particular concern for

---

[8]   Emezue, 2020, p. 4.

[9]   Hansen and Lory, 2020, p. 735.

rural areas, where fast internet and cellular system coverage might be limited or even non-existent. The digital divide issues can have a greater impact on individuals from vulnerable populations or communities, creating equity concerns in access to assistance and services. In some cases, creative approaches are needed to make access possible for populations in particularly difficult circumstances: "For example, one agency described distributing solar chargers so that individuals without stable housing still had access to their mobile devices and could stay in touch with outreach teams and caseworkers."[10] Such efforts are needed because if the populations that services are intended to reach do not have access to virtual platforms, success in developing virtual options will not matter.

> We can have the best [virtual] services possible, but if people don't have a laptop or broadband, it equates to no services.
>
> – Victim services panelist
>
> Some of these smaller programs [we work with], serving more vulnerable survivors have said, "People only have phones, they don't have laptops. We don't have laptops. We can't afford laptops. Survivors can't afford laptops. You have to make this relevant to me." Because, I'm over here [saying], "We've got all these great resources on how to do virtual services." And, then we hear from folks like, "Hey, make that relevant to me."
>
> – Victim services panelist

Although there have been some efforts to reduce these digital divide issues over the course of the pandemic—for access to services and also in the context of access to education for online schooling—concerns persist.

> We work in some rural areas that still have poor access to internet. We have seen some good initiatives of getting the connected devices out there, but there is still a technological divide that is very present.
>
> – Community organization panelist
>
> Bandwidth, cloud services, cell phone access, internet access hotspots, a lot of people prior to COVID were even depending upon libraries and public spaces, but those all got shut down. We're having a couple of communities talk about trying to get hotspots that they can place in community accessible areas and then kind of rotate them based on how much they're being used.
>
> – Victim services panelist

---

[10] Holliday et al., 2020, p. 6.

> With these new online text hotlines and online services, we have to remember that those sort of services aren't accessible to everyone. That some women may be more able to access a strong Wi-Fi signal than women in low-income communities, for instance. So the importance of . . . providing in-person services in addition to additional layers of [virtual] services in the future will be important.
>
> – Community organization panelist

Even individuals who have technology access might not have the expertise to use it effectively for high-pressure events, such as testifying at a virtual hearing, and efforts to assist them remotely are challenging. Lack of technology can hurt individuals' ability to apply for such public benefits as unemployment as well, which might be difficult to manage on a device with a small screen, such as a mobile phone.

> If victims were going to . . . testify, they couldn't come into a courtroom. Everything is done remotely. So the technology gap has been really spotlighted on the fact that many people do not have access to the internet. They don't have computers at home. They don't know how to navigate through setting up a Blue Jeans call or [other videoconferencing software] to be able to provide their testimony remotely. And that's put a lot of pressure and a lot of stress on victims of crime who are trying to figure out how to get a restraining order; it has to be done remotely. Going to family court, it's done remotely. And the, the issue is that the victim advocates, if there are any, they're also remote.
>
> – Victim services panelist

Members of disadvantaged populations might not have access to bank accounts, making easier modes of delivering financial assistance (e.g., checks) impractical for them and increasing the logistical challenges of delivering aid. As a result, panel members emphasized that alternative plans were needed that addressed the constraints of COVID-19 infection prevention but did not fully depend on digital access or assumptions about victims' access to banking and other services.

Some Services Are Tougher to Deliver at a Distance

Although there are important services that are impossible to deliver virtually, even some that technically can be provided over the phone or video are difficult to provide well. Our participants argued that there were basic limits in what can be done in an activity that requires making personal and emotional connections with the individuals being helped: "We're trauma-informed, and it's been hard to take that approach on the phone." Those limitations are leading to a desire to move service provision back in person as quickly as possible, pending the ability to manage COVID-19 risk. The experiences of some programs that have started to do so have provided support for that assessment.

> But the truth is we are not as effective in our jobs of helping people heal or helping people get beyond their trauma or their experience, or not as effective without having some kind of contact or interaction.
>
> – Victim services panelist
>
> When we were shut down, we learned to do everything remotely or to the extent we could. But now that we're starting to open up again . . . we're really seeing that it makes a difference when we're in the room, even if we're six or ten feet away from the person, it makes a difference when we have that personal contact. And I can say that for victims, talking about family law, talking about getting [a] restraining order, or even [talking] about being a victim of crime over [the] computer just is not effective. It doesn't have the holistic humanity that we bring to this whole issue.
>
> – Victim services panelist
>
> While the lawyers in my office would say, "Well, this is really efficient. I can do all my work from home," and yes they can, but the victim advocates are saying it doesn't work for us. We need to have personal contact with people. We need to be able to let them know that we really care about them.
>
> – Victim services panelist

There appear to be conflicting pressures between virtual models and coming back in person in providing services to children, including family-focused service provision and supervision. Both in discussions and in literature analyses, some suggest that virtual models are working well, and are potentially better than in-person attendance for high-stress events, such as court hearings.[11] Others have explored the use of virtual visitation between caseworkers and children being served and for family visits.[12] According to one analysis,

> While face-to-face visitation and training is preferable, teleconferencing can be used to reinforce familial bonds in the interim while face-to-face visitation is not possible. Application of this software is expansive with state agency case workers, Court Appointed Special Advocates, and Guardians Ad Litem being able to arrange frequent virtual visits with children in foster care to ensure they are healthy and well cared for during shelter-in-place. Moreover, supervised visitation with both parents and siblings can be arranged and monitored by the person in charge of supervision so that the visit can be controlled and recorded if required (this is particularly easy with software such as Zoom). Conferencing can also be used for the purpose of distance education, with one example being direct parental training and coaching as a complement to other online training that may be available.[13]

Participants in our panels viewed this as a valuable option; they criticized some court systems for not making it well known and available broadly to all populations.

---

[11] Reed and Alder, 2020.

[12] Karen Oehme, Kelly O'Rourke, and Lyndi Bradley, "Online Virtual Supervised Visitation During the COVID-19 Pandemic: One State's Experience," *Family Court Review*, Vol. 59, 2021.

[13] Chad Posick, April A. Schueths, Cary Christian, Jonathan A. Grubb, and Suzanne E. Christian, "Child Victim Services in the Time of COVID-19: New Challenges and Innovative Solutions," *American Journal of Criminal Justice*, Vol. 45, 2020, p. 686.

> People don't have laptops or access to computers. If they had done that for people to be able to see their attorneys, that would have been helpful. The court [here] hides things. It's hard for us to learn about options. Our clients don't know their options. For custody cases, there are problems with supervised visitation. There are problems with clients not seeing their children for large periods of time.
>
> – Victim services panelist

However, the view that in-person visits are better for children has led some to begin to develop guidelines to resume them: Some sources note the "potential for permanent psychological harm if children are unable to see their parents and siblings, especially during a time of crisis, and call for continued in-person visits in lower risk cases, based on guidance from public health officials."[14]

Pandemic-Induced Isolation Requires New Strategies to Reach Victims

Similar to the challenges faced by community-based violence prevention interventions discussed in Chapter Three, VSPs struggled to reach the people they are trying to serve because of infection-prevention decisions made by hospitals in particular. The inability to contact victims where their need is greatest and most salient reduces the chances of building a relationship to help them recover from crime. In some cases, programs became more proactive in their outreach, calling victims directly in an effort to forge the connections needed.

> What happened was all of our hospitals stopped allowing the rape crisis advocates into the hospital for forensic exams, which was a huge issue. And so victims were really having to navigate the medical system by themselves. A lot of people were afraid to go to the hospital because there was so much fear that going into a hospital would expose them to COVID and that was probably close to correct. What we also saw was that law enforcement, when victims would call, law enforcement was less likely to actually go into a house where a victim was living. And we saw a big drop in domestic violence and sexual assault and child abuse reports.
>
> – Victim services panelist
>
> What we did was through our family justice center [was] they were calling victims. And in the first go round of our calls from the justice center to survivors of domestic violence, 147 told us they needed to be out of their house because they were being sheltered with the abuser.
>
> – Victim services panelist

Some service providers supplemented these efforts with other communication modes in an attempt to address the effect of the digital divide on these populations (which could mean that an isolated victim had no way to determine that services were still available) or the issue

---

14   Rachel Blustain, "COVID-19 Creates Deep Uncertainty in NYC's Child-Welfare System," *City Limits*, March 30, 2020.

that children who are not going to school have less contact with mandated reporters who note and trigger responses to abuse situations.

> Some of our clients don't have laptops. Some of them don't even have a cell phone. Many of them don't have Wi-Fi. So what does that mean? And it's not even just for us to be able to connect with them or for them to connect with us, but early on, it was "How do we let them know that there is help out there, that [even though] the buildings are closed, there's still help available?"
>
> – Victim services panelist
>
> We spent a lot of time—and not just our agency, but other agencies [and the city government]—reaching those in the community to let them know that the police were still responding, that shelters were still open, the hotline was still available 24/7, that you could still, even though the courts shut down, you could still petition for an order of protection.
>
> – Victim services panelist
>
> So we did, we also did [public service announcements], and we ran them on kid-based TV programs and worked with the school district to be able to outreach to the children. Because again, we saw a big drop in the number of kids or child abuse cases.
>
> – Victim services panelist

In other cases, new approaches were developed in collaboration with law enforcement to try to identify victims in need of assistance, particularly given the observation that many people were not calling the police or service agencies for help until their situation reached a higher threshold of threat and violence than usual. Those higher stakes increased the importance of recognizing when individuals need help during any contact with them.

> I think it will be important for police departments to work with agencies to assess how best to connect victims with services. So instead of just responding to the call and arresting or not arresting, but connecting victims with services in the community that can provide follow-up, given there might be less ability for victims to protect themselves successfully during this time.
>
> – Community organization panelist
>
> We knew before COVID happened that coordinated community response in terms of domestic violence was a useful strategy to reduce risk and harm. And I think even more so now a coordinated community response is important for domestic violence. So . . . when police are responding, [particularly] if victims aren't calling the police until things get especially severe or are unable to call the law enforcement as often as they usually would, when they are responding, are [the officers] doing effective risk assessment in the field? Are they assessing the risks victims face within these new circumstances? And are they coordinated with community domestic violence agencies to help victims connect with those resources?
>
> – Community organization panelist

Other agencies explored different approaches in an effort to make it possible for victims to request help, including adding contact information to boxes provided by food banks, posting flyers at grocery stores, and making other public service announcements.[15] It also was reported that law enforcement in some areas established code words that individuals who were previously victimized could use to covertly call for help.[16] According to one of our panelists, in another area, behavioral health staff joined medical providers in staffing a county COVID-19 testing site to ask abuse-screening questions of people who were coming to be tested, providing an alternative opportunity to reach victims who might be sheltering with their abusers.

> Some places worked really hard to let people know that "shelters were still open, that they would put you up in a hotel if they would need it. [That they] have great hygiene and social-distance measures in place, please come." So some states really did a lot of outreach and people came and they [report now that they] are packed, [that] demand is high. In other places, they didn't do a lot of outreach and people thought, "Of course there'll be no one to help me." And so they saw calls go down because people didn't know that they had that option.
>
> – Victim services panelist

Safely Serving Victims During Pandemic Conditions Is More Difficult

For services that had to be provided in person, where emergency sheltering of individuals at risk is the central example, providers had two main options: (1) Seek ways to make usual methods of delivery of those services safer by taking risk-reducing measures, or (2) find other approaches to deliver them. Providers did both.

Health Protocols Were Implemented for Shelters but Reduced Capacity to Serve

Shelters that continued their operation did so by implementing health protocols to reduce the chance of COVID-19 spread. Provider coalition organizations have developed resources to help organizations implement safety protocols that work in their contexts.[17] These measures included health screening, which has become commonplace in many contexts. Like for all organizations that operate in facilities that were not built with disease-transmission prevention as a primary design concern, infrastructure constraints meant that safer operations necessitated lower-capacity sheltering operations. In some cases, sheltering organizations added quarantine requirements in which individuals needed to stay at hotels (which we discuss in more depth in the following section) before entering a group shelter, which made it harder to rapidly respond to victim needs.

---

[15]   IACP, "Supporting Victims of Domestic Violence During the COVID-19 Pandemic," webpage, May 18, 2020d.

[16]   Elman et al., 2020.

[17]   For example, see National Network to End Domestic Violence, "Resources on the Response to the Coronavirus (COVID-19)," webpage, March 12, 2020, updated November 20, 2020.

> But some of the things we heard right away [from frontline providers] were providers doing phone screens prior to serving someone in person and to ask some of those health-related questions, maybe different or even lower capacity in shelter settings, where they were trying to put into place social distancing or other sorts of methods.
>
> – Victim services panelist
>
> We are a low-barrier shelter. So we try to say yes to individuals who might hear no from other organizations or programs. . . . COVID has made it more complicated to be low barrier because we do have to require either a negative COVID test coming in or a quarantine period.
>
> – Victim services panelist

These measures were not always enough to make abuse survivors comfortable in shelter situations, and a panelist described individuals leaving shelters because they did not think they were safe there from COVID-19—even if that meant returning to live with their abuser. In addition, some of the safety measures that can contribute to reducing the risk of infection might be difficult for some individuals given their victimization history. For example, wearing masks was described as traumatizing for some types of violence victims because of feelings of being restrained or claustrophobic behind the mask. Mask-wearing also was cited as a cause of serious stress for some people of color because of concerns about interacting with police and others with their faces covered and about how it would be perceived.

Constraints around reducing the chance of transmission have made some service programs less viable (e.g., group counseling or youth-focused programming), in some cases because of the willingness of individuals to come in to participate. Staffing shortages (which we discuss later) also have led to constraints on the ability of programs to serve the same numbers of people or to operate at all.

> We have eliminated some of our programs, but they are programs that are really our preventative program . . . we've eliminated them for the primary reason because it's difficult to bring groups into the building.
>
> – Victim services panelist

Greater Use of Hotel-Based Sheltering Was Valuable but Costly

In spite of efforts to keep COVID-19 out of shelters, incidents of exposures in shelters did occur and resulted in some having to close down and substitute more-expensive hotel-based sheltering strategies for more–resource-efficient group living models.

> The other problem that we had was that one or two women in a shelter tested positive and they had to move everyone out of the shelters. So for quite some time, the shelters were without people living there around the issues of COVID and exposure to other people or quarantining people. So we've used a lot of hotel rooms and other ways to try to keep people, particularly domestic violence victims and their children, safe during this time.
>
> – Victim services panelist

Hotel-based sheltering was a strategy cited by multiple members of our panel. The use of hotels was attractive; there was low occupancy because of greatly reduced tourism and business travel from the pandemic. However, as areas shifted focus to try to restart tourism, hotel accommodations became less available and forced providers to adopt alternative strategies, from putting people up in tents to suggesting that they live in their cars.

> We have in-kind donations from two hotel brands and, with a service provider on the ground, we're able to coordinate and provide hotel stays for people kind of as a stop-gap between accessing some sort of more stable housing situation. Pre-pandemic, a lot of what we saw was a request for like one or two nights, maximum three, often to get through the weekend if it's Friday at 4:00 p.m. and [the program] had shelter for the person, but the program starts on Monday. . . . What we've seen through the pandemic is this increased need for longer periods of time. Whether because someone needs to quarantine before entering a new housing situation or a shelter setting, or just because the resources are more scarce or there's less availability, and so it's a lot harder to figure out a stopgap solution.
>
> – Victim services panelist

> It's been tough for communities. In many, they were putting survivors up in hotels and then all the hotels had to be used for firefighters or as tourism came back, all the hotels were getting used to build back up in tourism. So in South Dakota, for example, as the Sturgis motorcycle rally was coming in, the local [domestic violence] programs literally were buying tents to put domestic violence survivors in because there was nowhere else. Folks were talking about survivors living in their cars. That became a part of safety planning. . . . It's been desperate and heartbreaking.
>
> – Victim services panelist

Where accommodations were not being provided pro bono by hotel companies, the costs of providing rooms as alternative shelters added up quickly. Some panelists described getting specific grants to help cover the costs, while others had to cover the increases by eliminating other expenditures from their budgets.

> We've had to shift budget line items from some things that were also needed, but shift all of that to hotel funds. And so we've been doing some grant writing, trying to figure out how to increase some of our funds for things like hotels, but that piece isn't going to end even after we reopen if we're requiring a two-week quarantine in order to enter the facility.
>
> – Victim services panelist
>
> So we were able to get a grant to be able to move domestic violence victims and their children out of the location [where they were being forced to shelter in place with their abuser] to be able to pay for up to six months. But that's only six months. We saw a lot of women coming to us who were living in their car, had moved into their cars to get away from the abusers.
>
> – Victim services panelist

Maintaining Staff Capacity and the Safety and Health of a Diverse Provider Workforce Is a Challenge

The ability of service provider organizations to continue operating depends on their staff, and if their staff members get sick, they cannot help the people they serve. In some cases, operations might depend on relatively small numbers of people, and if they get sick, activities might have to stop completely.

> We also have a lot of sites where there's not a lot of redundancy in victim service programs, so there's only maybe two victims service providers for an entire agency. And we've had some where those two people have been exposed. We've had active diagnoses of COVID and it may be two people, [but] it shuts down the entire program. And so there's no one to step in and provide those services in their stead while they are either recovering or not recovering.
>
> – Victim services panelist
>
> We know that if we don't take care of ourselves and take care of our staff, we're not going to be able to take care of our clients.
>
> – Victim services panelist
>
> We're an example of your worst-case scenario of when your program has to shut down because of COVID staffing issues. We wound up moving residents into hotels, which changed our caseload, and the way case management worked. Our social worker's done a great job adapting to that, but what we're finding is putting people in hotels creates so many more complications and requires a lot more [work] related to case management.
>
> – Victim services panelist

To Serve Clients, Providers Had to Protect Their Staff

The transition to virtual operations was part of organizations' strategy for protecting their staff from COVID-19. However, as we discussed with respect to other criminal justice organizations, service-providing organizations had to maintain in-person activities to perform key parts of their roles. Across the social services sector, that required developing safety protocols to limit the chance of COVID-19 spread. For example, a RAND review of safety measures implemented across multiple types of service providers included the following common components:

> Organizations noted that when staff are in the office or in the field, they are taking extra precautions, such as using PPE, including masks, screens, and seat covers; engaging in physical distancing; implementing screening protocols for COVID-19; and staggering shifts. Some organizations were not requiring staff to participate in field-based activities, instead relying on staff who volunteer that they feel comfortable doing so. There has also been an increased frequency of cleaning protocols for high-risk areas (e.g., common spaces, vehicles).[18]

Like other justice agencies, some service providers (particularly those in congregate settings, such as shelters), reportedly used cohort models, where "staff and clients [are assigned] to specified groups to minimize the risk of infection spread."[19]

Developing and implementing those policies could be a heavy lift for some organizations: For the same reason that smaller, lower-resource NGOs would be at risk from a significant percentage of their staff becoming ill, they also would not have the time and resources to develop safety plans. One panelist said that it would be "untenable" for them to go back to in-person options. Given the demands on their time in attempting to serve their backlog of clients, there is simply not time available to develop the policies and procedures needed to return to working in their traditional offices.

> I've got an entire new policy around workplace health, workplace safety. That has changed things pretty dramatically. Everybody's with a mask, even in the office. If there are two people in the hallway, one has to face the wall while the other walks by. We take this health questionnaire. We have some offices where two people share an office. Now they can't be in the office at the same time, so they have to stagger their times. So we've really [made] a big sea change in how we're actually physically structured.
>
> – Victim services panelist
>
> The policy, these procedures and plans that need to be put in place, even for us to go back into the office . . . [spending the time doing that now,] that's untenable for us. Our demand is such that we can't spend our time trying to do that, particularly when we're more productive at home.
>
> – Victim services panelist

Some panelists also cited challenges in implementing protective plans because of difficulty getting PPE and other supplies. Particularly early in the pandemic, VSPs were not prioritized as essential and therefore could not get protective equipment.

[18] Holliday et al., 2020, p. 5.

[19] Holliday et al., 2020, p. 6.

> One of the things that came up for us as a challenge early on, because we had to stay open and provide services, is we were really low on the totem pole for any kind of PPE. You couldn't find it. And so we learned a valuable lesson about keeping it in stock.
>
> – Victim services panelist

Managing staff safety in the context of initiatives involving multiple providers or justice system agencies—e.g., a multidisciplinary team model for case management and service delivery—involves additional layers of challenges. Different agencies might have different policies, even if they are seeking to work together and be transparent about what they are doing to manage COVID-19 risk. Defaulting to virtual meetings for such programs was one approach to reducing that complexity.[20]

> Managing multiple agencies and their health issues [in centers where there is multi-agency collaboration, even when] they're being open and addressing it with us, is sometimes a bit of a challenge.
>
> – Victim services panelist

Mental health concerns regarding provider staff also were prominent on the panel. Like others who work in the justice system and are exposed to second-order trauma from responding to crimes and assisting victims, service providers' jobs are stressful under the best of circumstances. Under pandemic conditions, provider staff have all of the added stressors of family, health, and other challenges, and, as panelists emphasized, because of the relatively low pay of frontline providers, they might not have the financial resources to cushion the pandemic's impact. Working from home increases the difficulty in separating work life from home life, potentially magnifying stress. Because many provider staff members also are members of minority groups, the national protests focused on social justice and equity concerns in the justice system might affect them in very personal ways. All of these combine to create major pressures on a workforce that crime victims depend on to help them deal with their victimization.

> I can't say enough about the need [to] provide support for staff. This is hard work, it has always been hard work, [but] it's become even harder . . . with the confluence of COVID and the racial unrest [and] police violence. . . . We constantly are looking at how we can do a better job so that all of our staff feel supported and feel supported in a real meaningful way.
>
> – Victim services panelist

---

[20] Elman et al., 2020.

> One of the things that we've also seen that I think indirectly has an impact on the clients we serve is the significant impact that this has had on our staff. We know that often the client-facing staff . . . are the lowest-paid or from communities [in which] many of our staff have been impacted directly by COVID where a family member has died, or they themselves have gotten sick with COVID. They are taking care of ill family members. . . . What does that mean for me if I have a underlying health condition, or I have children at home, and even for those who are working remotely, we're hearing from our staff [about] more enhanced vicarious trauma.
>
> – Victim services panelist

Protecting staff from COVID-19 infection and the stresses of worrying about their and their families' health—particularly when working in emergency shelter settings—also might create tensions between policies around meeting staff and client needs. Such tensions have to be navigated; the needs of both groups must be met for service delivery to be effective.

> It's going to mean things like taking temperature twice a day, it's going to mean a lot more questions about where you [are] going [and] who [you are] going to be around. Things that don't feel good to residents, but that become necessary to make staff feel safe coming to work.
>
> – Victim services panelist
>
> So during the initial lockdown . . . for women in our shelter who were used to being in situations where they couldn't come and go on their own, and who felt controlled, that triggered a lot of them. And so we actually had some clients who wound up leaving just because they felt such anxiety with being stuck in, um, in a house. . . . [But] some staff . . . were terrified at the idea of residents being able to kind of come and go on their own and potentially bring the virus back in. So we're still trying to figure out when we reopen . . . what that means now that the [state-imposed] restrictions are a little bit looser.
>
> – Victim services panelist

Staffing Shortages and Challenges Recruiting

Providers cannot serve victims if they do not have the staff available to do so. Participants on our panel described situations in which they had to shut down some operations because staff were scared to work under pandemic conditions. Responses to that fear of infection also increased staff burden and workload. For example, a panelist cited an example of staff members working alone and for extended periods to try to limit their exposure to others, but with substantial risk of burnout and mental health consequences.

> We partner with two different agencies who also provide trauma treatment and trauma therapy. They've lost all of their staff. And so that's a big gap. We [even] have the grant to pay, but they don't have the staff. And it's very difficult to hire right now for victim advocates or for therapists and people that provide that kind of service.
>
> – Victim services panelist

> We had to temporarily close our shelter because we didn't have enough staff. So we lost a couple of staff members over the summer, who were just scared to come to work. We can't do residential care remotely, so people had to come. We're a 24-hour shelter, so if we don't have enough people to fill all of those shifts, then we had to close temporarily.
>
> – Victim services panelist

> Part of the challenge in a residential setting is that because people are nervous about exposure, in many cases one person is doing the work of many others and working extended hours to avoid coming into contact with others. You're seeing organizations that need to hire staff to provide relief to those who have been working constantly.
>
> – Victim services panelist

Although panelists described efforts to be more flexible in scheduling and work models to help staff deal with stressors around child care or other factors, they also cited examples of agencies that would not allow such flexibility and were losing staff members as a result.

> I would say in a lot of jurisdictions, there's also decisions being made for victim service personnel who are also facing care of children, care of loved ones while working from home and agencies not being flexible to allow that to happen. [In some cases,] where if the agency sets expectations and they can't meet those expectations, they have to voluntarily relinquish their positions.
>
> – Victim services panelist

Replacing or supplementing staff was described as very difficult or even impossible under the combination of pandemic conditions and resource constraints. However, one panelist mentioned being able to hire skilled staff who were laid off by financially struggling hospitals. Finding staff who are already trained is valuable; panelists cited similar challenges to other justice agencies in onboarding and hiring new employees. In this case, the challenge is compounded by trying to train staff to provide compassionate care to victims in a virtual environment where supervision and mentoring by experienced providers is much more difficult.

> We don't pay very well. Frontline staff don't make a lot of money. And so, we're trying to find people who care about this issue and victim services and can approach things from a trauma-informed care perspective. And so we're not just hiring for a position, we're trying to hire the right temperament and all of that. . . . Trying to find staff who can actually meet the needs of clients for what [the organization] budgeted has been difficult.
>
> – Victim services panelist

> We could probably reopen using a temp agency that focuses on social services staff. But they add 50 percent just off the bat on top of the hourly rate.
>
> – Victim services panelist

> The challenge of hiring new staff and doing it remotely [is considerable]. But on top of that, then you've got the challenges of onboarding and training that new staff remotely and how to build and ensure that staff are providing victim-centered services. If you're not sitting in the room with them, if you can't have a senior case manager or clinical director overseeing, sitting in with someone while they're providing direct services, [it is much more difficult] ensuring that the services are being provided appropriately and understanding when and how to intervene to provide better support to staff.
>
> – Victim services panelist

Panel members cited circumstances where, in decisions made about managing workforce COVID-19 risk, the needs of victim service provision fell through the cracks: Decisions were made that affected activities in ways that might not have been fully understood a priori. This was noted in particular for volunteer-based victim services activities that were connected to other entities. In some cases, the decisions were based on risk—those entities wanted to limit overall COVID-19 risk by categorically designating volunteers as nonessential. This was very similar to circumstances observed in correctional institutions, where key program providers were kept out of facilities to limit risk. In other cases, the decisions were simply practical—e.g., volunteer personnel had not been issued agency laptops or phones, so they could not work from home. For some programs, this meant that services to entire classes of victims had to be halted.

> We have a few sites that have interns and volunteers that support victim service programs and efforts. Many of the agencies made a hard stop on volunteer participation during COVID, [with] most of them citing a risk level that they weren't willing to take on for nonemployed personnel. . . . And that of course affects service [delivery].
>
> – Victim services panelist

> There are some programs that eliminated services to an entire victimization category. What we often recommend with a program starting up services, is to have interns and volunteers providing services to expanded victimization categories. So nonviolent crimes, identity theft, burglaries, robberies, those types of things. And when those personnel, when the volunteers and interns went away, so did the services to those victims. Then programs had to regroup and figure out how to spread their three existing paid personnel even further, or make a decision to stop services to particular categories.
>
> – Victim services panelist

Changes in Other Parts of the Justice System Affect Providers and Victims

The ability of organizations to provide victim services—even if they are not *directly* connected to justice system agencies—can be significantly affected by the decisions and actions taken by criminal justice agencies and actors. For example, VSPs that were connected to law enforcement agencies were affected by the decisions made by those agencies in terms of what crimes merited response and how staff were deployed. One panelist put it very bluntly: "[In some agencies, leaders] determined that victim service personnel were nonessential employees and so immediate access and on-call response diminished." In other instances, the effects on service provision might have been inadvertent, as a result of decisions not to pursue certain crimes, such as prostitution (therefore eliminating chances to identify and respond to human trafficking), or because of the reassignment of staff who traditionally were accompanied by service providers to other duties.

> The police didn't really want to do anything related to prostitution, that they saw that as low-level and they didn't want to put people at risk and in the jail system in terms of putting people into that situation.
>
> – Victim services panelist
>
> At least in the beginning, the officers who were assigned to human trafficking [in the metro police department near us] were reassigned, so instead of doing what they normally do, they were assigned to do things like go to shops and restaurants and make sure that they were closed down or make sure that people were wearing masks.
>
> – Victim services panelist
>
> [Particularly early in the pandemic,] there were decisions made around police response to crimes that—depending on how the victim service personnel were structured or placed in the organizational chart—also impacted demand for services or [delivery of] services. So, for example, if we have [a department] where the victim service personnel are partnered or paired with an investigative unit versus a patrol response unit, many of the investigators were [reassigned to] frontline positions. They were taken off investigative details. . . . And [the victim service personnel] weren't reassigned along with the investigator or sworn personnel that they normally work with.
>
> – Victim services panelist

Within the court system, practical changes to reduce COVID-19 risk had direct effects on service provision. Hospitals did not allow victim advocates entry as part of their infection-control strategies, and similarly, a participant cited an example of a court system initially refusing to allow victim support persons to attend court hearings, even though the right to such support is protected by law. Some victims needed considerable help navigating the new virtual court processes, which were available in large part to ensure that access to protective orders and other justice services was preserved during the pandemic. And just as there were concerns about virtual processes being sufficiently formal to be impactful for the accused, similar questions were raised for victims. In the words of one participant, "I appreciate . . . what courts are doing and [they are] really still trying to engage victims, but just recognizing how hard that is for victims, who want [their] day in court and . . . [it ends up being] a Zoom meeting."

> We have a helpline for folks who are going through the legal system [and are representing themselves]—it's called women's law. And we saw a COVID-related increase [in calls of] 350 percent. Unsurprisingly, a huge number [were] people [asking], "What do I do to access courts digitally?" So we had to put together all kinds of resources about in each state, [including] how might you get a restraining order right now.
>
> – Victim services panelist

> Some courts are just starting to open up, but we do a lot of preliminary hearings where we have to put witnesses on. So all of that's being done remotely. Being able to support victims while they're in family court, or in the restraining order court, or criminal court, everything, all the advocacy is done remotely . . . so that's, that's really impacted the staff. And I'm not just talking about the victim witness people, but also our attorneys and the investigators and the police. It's really shifted to more remote.
>
> – Victim services panelist

However, the court-centered changes that potentially have the greatest effect on victims of crime are the decisions made about what crimes to prosecute and how accused individuals are managed after arrest (if they are arrested at all under pandemic conditions). As we discussed in the chapters focusing on law enforcement and the courts, there was a major initiative in some jurisdictions to arrest fewer people to reduce populations within the justice system. Although many of the crimes that were deprioritized were "less serious," that did not mean that they did not have victims and, as a result, the decision to take broad categorical action to limit case flow by offense type missed key individual differences that might exist among cases. As one panelist emphasized, repeated "less serious" offenses perpetrated by the same person against the same person can have at least as great if not a greater impact than a single "more serious" event. And although not all victims of crime necessarily *want* prosecution as part of the path to a just outcome, some do, and the decision not to prosecute any such crimes denies them that path to justice.

> In addition to the courts being closed . . . [they] issued a mandate that suspended any requirement of cash bail for misdemeanor-level or low-level felonies. And unfortunately in [our state], human trafficking is still not considered a serious and violent felony under the law. So we saw cases where victims were calling the police, somebody was getting arrested and then they were being released immediately. And so what happened after that was after a couple of weeks of the police driving someone to a jail and then them getting out immediately, they stopped bringing them to jail. So we had a big issue of trying to keep people safe, victims of crime safe from a perpetrator.
>
> – Victim services panelist
>
> There's a big move in [our state] to . . . take away authority of the [district attorney] to proceed with filing certain charges [even over the objection of victims], but secondly, a big effort to reduce the footprint in the criminal justice system. And that . . . directly impacts victims of crime in so many ways.
>
> – Victim services panelist
>
> I think in terms of serving victims, a lot of times when there are resource depletion or staffing issues, or just time-management issues, I think everybody tends to default to the more serious crimes as the one who get the response from the people in the system. I think that for some victims, what we see is this perpetual misdemeanor, low-level involvement has a much more significant impact on their daily life. And so, it's not always the best choice and it's not always in line with victim healing or with what they need from the system to kind of wash away low-level crime.
>
> – Victim services panelist

Not having an accused person held for a time in jail—particularly in cases of interpersonal violence, such as domestic or child abuse—takes away a window of time that service providers used to act to protect victims. Those actions included making connections to different services, arranging for shelter, and taking steps to remove them from the situation in which the harm occurred.

> In terms of accountability, healing, even in terms of safety sometimes, having the criminal justice system respond to [low-level offenses] provides them enough breathing room to allow for other organizations, other service providers to do effective safety planning . . . when those kinds of accountability measures go away, they aren't getting connected in the same way with the other service providers who can supplement those services and supplement healing for the victim in ways that the criminal justice system can't.
>
> – Victim services panelist
>
> Safety planning and services provision often takes quite a bit of time and planning. So agencies may need to adapt specific [guidelines] to how to effectively provide safety services to victims in these different and tighter circumstances.
>
> – Community organization panelist

It also has created a requirement for some services—sometimes services that are required by law—to become much more agile to be effective. The example cited by multiple panelists was victim notification, or making the victim aware that the accused, who might have been arrested only hours before, was already being released as a result of pandemic limitations on jail custody. In addition to citing examples where this did not happen, panelists described how it created new demands on them as service providers to be able to more quickly get word to clients about their circumstances and risk.

> We also heard about instances where survivors would have no idea that their abuser has been released until they run into them on the street.
>
> – Victim services panelist
>
> We've had to create a 24-hour line where if somebody is arrested for the crime of interpersonal violence, or if there's a victim of the crime and the [perpetrator is] going to be released within 12 hours, we have to notify the victims. And so we've set up a completely new system where the police notify us that somebody has been taken to jail. Either they're going to be released [or, as] the policies work now, they'll have a risk assessment with the idea of releasing [them] back into the community. So 24/7, we're getting information in and calling victims to give them a heads up.
>
> – Victim services panelist

Acute Funding Concerns Threaten Victim Service Delivery

The budget cuts that have affected many justice agencies have hit victim services efforts that are funded out of municipal revenues. As one participant summarized, "The city budget for victim services have been cut. Less people are getting served because there's less money. Cases are not being picked up as fast as they were." Like in other parts of the justice system, the funding of these services through court filing fees or fines—although a predictable and protected source in normal times—has proven vulnerable in the pandemic as those revenue streams have collapsed as a result of policy decisions (such as closing the courts or reducing traffic enforcement) or the effects on the broader economy.

> Sadly with the economy, we're anticipating—it hasn't happened yet, knock on wood—that we're going to see hits to our budget. It's going to impact staffing and also [funds available for client assistance]. . . . So as the need goes up, sadly, the funding will potentially go down.
>
> – Victim services panelist
>
> In some states, some of the court fees that would normally have been paid actually go to fund some of those community services. And so without the court operating as normal, they're seeing reductions in funding for some of those services.
>
> – Community organization panelist
>
> Crime victim compensation, which . . . funds medical expenses and time off from work, funeral expenses, mental health counseling, and things like that [for victims]. A lot of state comp programs are dependent on . . . you guessed it: things like traffic tickets and fines and fees. And so comp programs are seeing a major source of their funding at the state level completely drying up. And that is something that's going to have a profound and awful impact on the capacity to be able to remunerate victims for their financial losses that result from crime.
>
> – Victim services panelist

The diversity in organizations that operate in the victim services space means, however, that not all such efforts are tied to tax revenues and compete for funds with other city or state priorities. Some are funded by federal grants or from grants from other sources. According to a panelist, although grant money is sometimes viewed as less desirable than line items in a municipal budget, with the pandemic hammering budgets, the "soft money" of grants has the advantage of not being fungible and, therefore, is not as readily reallocated to other priorities.[21] Some run community fundraisers, bringing in operating funds from annual banquets or galas. Some are funded through donations, in kind or financially, from private-sector organizations. However, all of these alternative sources also have been hit hard by the economic damage of the pandemic.

> We get limited grants. We're funded quite a bit by corporate America. We get industry sponsorships and those have all been frozen. None of them want to spend money right now.
>
> – Victim services panelist

---

[21] Another observation made by a participant was that even agencies that are supported by grant funds might have encountered difficulties producing their specific deliverables—if restrictions related to COVID-19 make in-person service provision or training impossible. That would require the renegotiation of deliverables.

They had to cancel all their April Sexual Assault Awareness Month fundraising. And now they've canceled October Domestic Violence Awareness Month fundraising. And many typical funders have lost a lot of money, so in-kind service donations are really down. As an example, a lot of shelters said, "We need to install free-standing sinks so that people can wash their hands and not have to go into the bathroom" . . . or "We need to get rid of carpeting and put down like laminate flooring to be able to just kinda hose it down with Lysol." Normally you would work with a local plumbing company, a local flooring company who would donate those services in kind, [but] those small local businesses are closed and may be closed forever. And so that whole local community that you depend on as a service provider is strained and it all starts to fall apart.

– Victim services panelist

Grant funds are drying up. Several people have talked about foundations and corporations. They are affected financially by the pandemic. And so those funds are drying up. The effect of that is really, really devastating, especially to community-based organizations.

– Victim services panelist

The breakdowns in fundraising hurt the ability of organizations to get federal funds; some require local matching funds to be eligible for funding.

A lot of the trafficking services grants have a . . . match requirement for the federal grants. And so service providers who can't have volunteer groups come in, aren't able to have interns in the office. [Organizations that] aren't able to get those in-kind donations or hold those fundraisers are struggling to figure out how to meet those match requirements on those grants.

– Victim services panelist

Although there were some relief funds that could be used by providers, all organizations—and particularly smaller ones—do not have experience pursuing and managing federal grants. That lack of experience was a barrier to their taking advantage of such funding streams as the Paycheck Protection Program or CARES Act funding.

Culturally specific organizations haven't been able to access payroll protection loans that would help them keep staff and access funds for resources. Organizations have to have existing relationships with banks to use those mechanisms. There is also a threshold fund requirement. Culturally specific victim services organizations are left out of those opportunities.

– Victim services panelist

[The first issue was] navigating the CARES Act and other relief packages. Most people just did not know what this meant for their community members, but also for the community-based organizations that were also in need of these funds. So they were trying to seek out information on how to actually continue to provide services, and as well as navigate these policies that were not always clear to most people.

– Community organization panelist

Some [service providers] have been able to access some of the emergency funding that came through the federal government, but federal funding is challenging. Some of the money came through the Department of Housing and Urban Development. If you are a program that hadn't worked with [Housing and Urban Development] funding before, it's hard.

– Victim services panelist

Sites have been reporting to us that a lot of people doing the work aren't necessarily specialized in understanding grant processes, procurement processes, [request for proposal] processes, financial processes. [How] to navigate all of those inner layers of systems. And some of the times we're working with agencies that have ten personnel. And so, you know, having the depth of knowledge to try and navigate all of those systems to meet the needs based on people's skills and experience is incredibly challenging at times.

– Victim services panelist

Taking Stock and Moving Forward

As a result of many factors—for example, victim services and the access needed to deliver them not being viewed as essential in some cases, clients not being willing to seek help, shifts in crime and needs, and the effects of pandemic control measures—participants in our panels saw a significant backlog in unmet need among victim populations. In some cases, that need is already starting to be realized; for example, when steps were taken to better link VSPs to investigation and response activities by law enforcement so that service provision could be resumed.

I think, in general, within the last two to three months, we're seeing a much higher integration of . . . victim services personnel [back into response by the police]. We're now seeing people who are getting more comfortable with technology involving victim services personnel again, and now that demand has [increased], *it's almost crippling in some of the organizations.* Because now there's just a huge influx of victims that were not seeking services before, or that had experienced a delay in response due to sheltering restrictions [or because they] didn't feel comfortable reporting certain circumstances. [So] now there's almost an explosion of victimization being reported to law enforcement that was not prior reported. So [there is a] drastic difference in the first three months [of the pandemic] to the past three months in terms of how law enforcement–based victim service personnel are being utilized, being included, being incorporated, and the demands placed on their services.

– Victim services panelist

That need—which our panelists expected to continue to be present for a long time given the economic and other dislocations that have occurred as a result of the pandemic—is hitting just as funding streams are drying up as a result of the economic fallout. And, in spite of the tendency of service providers to continue to meet all needs even as resources decline, our panelists cautioned that the scope of needs are such that that is likely not going to be possible.

> I think it's also helpful just to think about it's going to be years before real recovery happens. I mean . . . you've got a really high rate of unemployment just across the board. And so when you talk about helping a population who doesn't have credit, who doesn't have job experience, who doesn't have a resume, trying to provide some of those supports just for employment, which is essential for any sort of long-term independence and self-sufficiency.
>
> – Victim services panelist
>
> Sometimes we have to say, no, we just can't do the same level that we were doing before, or no, we can't do that program anymore if we really can't fund it without hurting the whole entity. So it's just something that we're really bad at in our sector.
>
> – Victim services panelist

Promising Practices from the COVID-19 Pandemic Response

Our VSP panel participants identified fewer potentially promising lessons from the pandemic that appeared valuable to carry forward than members of our other panels. However, the panelists did note the importance of partnerships and collaborations in accessing resources and facilitating service delivery in ways that would not be possible for individual organizations. This included community networks for getting support, although cautionary statements about the effect of the pandemic on the availability of donations demonstrated that—in an event as broadly disruptive as the COVID-19 pandemic—there were limits to the capacity of those networks.[22]

> One of the biggest lessons learned for us . . . is just how critical partnerships and collaborations are, particularly those that have been created before a pandemic. We could not have done everything that we were able to do if it wasn't for our collaborations in the systems, child welfare, criminal justice, housing, with local community-based organizations, culturally-based organizations. I can't say enough about how critical government agencies were that we had these relationships that we could just build on that enabled.
>
> – Victim services panelist
>
> One of the things that I've seen a lot of is more informal community support networks getting coordinated in my own community and other communities where people are supporting people in their own communities with donations and support services. And hopefully I think that will continue.
>
> – Victim services panelist

---

[22] This is consistent with one of the final recommendations of the National Commission on COVID-19 and Criminal Justice (which was published as this report was in the final stages of writing) for a need to "build community-based capacity to provide services to justice-involved populations during public health emergencies." The Commission also recognized

Some of the alternative methods that law enforcement and others were forced to develop to reach victims seemed promising to continue. Some panelists believed that the alternative approaches were identifying victims of crime who might not otherwise have been identified, and therefore would not have been served previously. One of our panelists pointed out that the only crime—and, therefore, the only victims—the criminal justice system is aware of are the ones that get reported. So if the goal is to serve all victims, efforts have to look beyond what police or court systems are doing. New approaches for reaching victims might be a starting point to find people in need of help who would not have been identified before.

> Most victims of crime will never interact with the criminal justice system. There are no charges filed, there is no prosecution. So if we're talking about victim services and access to the support they need and justice, as they define it, if we're only talking about the criminal justice system, we're missing most of crime victims.
>
> – Victim services panelist

There was enthusiasm for some of the technological options that were pursued by agencies during the pandemic, although less enthusiasm than was expressed by other panels about similar applications. There was most interest in the use of telehealth and telecounseling options because both appeared to be strategies for increasing access. However, as we discuss in the section on research needs, there were questions about whether clients could be served as effectively and whether they would be as satisfied with virtual service delivery—of all types of services, not just telehealth—which suggests a desire for more evidence before arguing for their retention.

> [One thing from the pandemic that] we hope will remain is the implementation of telehealth. . . . I know across the nation, we have a shortage of the psychologists and psychiatrists . . . [so alternative telehealth options are] giving people more access to the care that they need.
>
> – Community organization panelist
>
> [Reaching out to colleagues who are delivering mental health services virtually,] nobody has seen a decrease in caseload, all of them have reported increases. . . . I don't know what is driving that, but it's been heartening to hear that victims are continuing and even increasing their access to mental health services, both in the immediate, short, and long term after the trauma of victimization.
>
> – Victim services panelist

Members of the panel saw opportunities in further technology adoption in the sector to address other challenges for victims. Primary among these opportunities was the potential for virtual platforms to include on-demand impartial translation services so that non-English speakers would have more-ready access to translators who could facilitate their engagement with and involvement in the justice process.

---

the need for stable funding support for these efforts (National Commission on COVID-19 and Criminal Justice, 2020b, p. 15).

Pandemic Pressure as a Driver of Broader Criminal Justice Innovation

In some of the other parts of the justice system, the pressures of the COVID-19 pandemic were seen by panelists as pushing changes that have been considered in the broader context of criminal justice reform. This was less the case for victim services, which is not surprising given the fact that this part of the system is not the focus of as much pressure to reform as police, courts, or corrections. However, there were lessons from the pandemic and the responses to it that are relevant for thinking about change in the longer term, although more from the perspective of change in the broader system than change in victim services specifically.

The first longer-term lesson that came out of the panel discussions across our victim service and community organization panels was how the needs of people linked to the criminal justice system—in this case, crime victims—are intimately linked to other policy interventions. That specific intervention was the eviction moratorium that provided housing stability, which, unsurprisingly shaped need for emergency shelter requirements for victims. However, that moratorium was viewed as only delaying need, not unlike actions taken elsewhere in the system that delayed rather than eliminated flows of people going into the justice process, and therefore contributed to the development of a backlog of need in the system.

> Housing stability is one of the biggest predictors of post disaster recovery. And if [when eviction moratoria expire,] these community members don't have a place to stay or know how long they can stay in their home, that has rippling consequences.
>
> – Community organization panelist
>
> We've actually received some referrals from law enforcement who are working with women who have said, "Right now I'm actually in a situation that is okay because there's a rent moratorium, but as soon as that goes away, I'm going to be kicked out of where I am and then I'll give you a call."
>
> – Victim services panelist

Beyond the connection of victims' needs with broader policies, the most important lessons from the victim services panel for broader reform efforts are cautionary ones. Many of the responses taken by other parts of the justice system in response to the pandemic were discussed in our panels as prototyping implementation of systematic reforms. Reducing the incarceration of low-level, perceived low-risk individuals as a group, for example, has been framed as a path to reform, and was a key strategy for reducing the population in jails, courts, and prisons during the pandemic. However, feedback from our panelists pointed out that those categorial interventions neglected the fact that perpetrators within those groups might have had significantly different effects on victims, and their nonarrest or early release could make protecting victims of past abuse much more difficult. As a result, it would appear that—of the three perspectives on change in the justice system: justice agencies, justice-involved individuals and their communities, and victims of crime—the needs of the latter might have been the least considered or reflected in the strategies for responding to the COVID-19 pandemic.

Policy Development and Evaluation to Better Inform Decisions in Both the Short and Longer Terms

In considering research and evaluation to support victim services delivery during this and potential future infectious disease environments and the lessons from the COVID-19 pandemic response to date, a variety of questions came out of the discussions. Those questions varied, from fundamental concern about both the efficacy of and victim satisfaction with alternative service delivery modes to how such models as sheltering in hotels, which were forced on providers by the pandemic, compare with more-common ways of providing shelter. Given the differences in viewpoints about virtual models for service delivery—even between organizations that are focused on victims and community corrections agencies that also have service-provision requirements—are there unique barriers to virtual models here or strategies through which virtual technologies could be adapted to better serve this sector?

A lot of these flexible practices need to stay intact after this is over. But I'd also love to see just some, you know, then some thought around not only satisfaction with transitioning services, but actual impact on case outcomes from a criminal justice perspective. Victim engagement is cited a lot for whether cases progress through the system. And so if we're able to increase engagement, are we keeping track of what that's doing to case outcomes?

– Victim services panelist

We are really excited to see research on the need for housing and alternative kinds of housing supports. Do we have any information about how hotels and motels differed from a traditional domestic violence shelter? How has flexible funding been used, and what are the impacts on reported rates of domestic violence and sexual assault, and how do they differ?

– Victim services panelist

Beyond questions of efficacy and satisfaction, the following questions appear to be relevant to informing post-pandemic practices:

- Given differences in data on needs reflected in calls to helplines versus calls to police, how can the totality of the changes in victim service demand caused by the pandemic be better characterized?
- Changes in reporting behavior by victims during the pandemic risks future analyses of crime and justice responses reaching distorted conclusions. For example, if many victims delay reporting because of fear of COVID-19 or other reasons, crime at different stages of the pandemic may appear lower than it actually was. How can this be addressed in research and evaluation studies?
- Given concerns about the digital divide significantly affecting the ability of victims from locations with low broadband or little communications infrastructure accessing services and participating in the justice process, can levels of true access be better mapped to inform assessment of the impact of virtual models? Such assessments could build on or support other analyses that are relevant to access for virtual education and remote work.
- Given resource constraints and victims in need of sheltering, can better strategies be identified to reduce infection risk in group shelters while keeping barriers to utilization low for clients?
- How can organizations that might not have as strong a technology infrastructure as government criminal justice agencies more effectively address the information security and other concerns with delivering services remotely? Similar to questions raised in the past

regarding law enforcement,[23] are there challenges (e.g., with legal discoverability) with providers using personally owned devices in performing their roles?

- Given the importance of services to victims of crime and the importance of supporting their involvement in the justice process, how can sustainable support for organizations delivering those services be put in place, given the vulnerability revealed by the pandemic and its economic consequences?

Research to address these needs could contribute to a better understanding of the effect of shifts in crime during the pandemic on the population and better prepare and sustain service-providing organizations to meet the population's needs in future incidents of infectious disease.

---

[23] See, for example, the discussion in John S. Hollywood, Dulani Woods, Andrew Lauland, Sean E. Goodison, Thomas J. Wilson, and Brian A. Jackson, *Using Future Broadband Communications Technologies to Strengthen Law Enforcement*, Santa Monica, Calif.: RAND Corporation, RR-1462-NIJ, 2016.

CHAPTER EIGHT

Conclusions: Considering the System-Wide Effects of the COVID-19 Pandemic on Public Safety, Health, and Justice

Across our panel discussions, one theme that recurred was how the shock of the pandemic had forced a speed of change that was unprecedented for a system that—for good reason—is often quite risk averse. In describing normal operations before the pandemic, panelists cited examples of the potential for change, but concern about the consequences or deference to precedent and established practices held that change back.

> Law enforcement and the justice system as a whole are by definition—and by necessity in many ways—risk averse. The idea is that you as an individual actor, as a police officer, as a corrections officer, whatever it may be, you cannot fail. Someone who's in your care or custody cannot go out and do a bad thing because that reflects poorly on you, on your department, on the system as a whole, [and so] it's a very, very risk-averse system.
>
> – Community organization panelist
>
> Our parole board, they were slapping GPS on every single person they parole . . . [because they] were fearful of what might happen. In our field that drives a lot of the decision-making, unfortunately.
>
> – Community corrections panelist
>
> [There were many opportunities to bring in more technology], even prior to the pandemic, but that the defense bar or the bench was reluctant or unwilling to engage in.
>
> – Institutional corrections panelist

The pressure of the COVID-19 pandemic *forced* change on the system, and multiple risks—for example, of altering usual practices, of releasing many people from custody or supervision, or of moving away from arrest as central to law enforcement action—had to be accepted to respond to the greater risk posed by the virus. And the changes made in response were significant and the speed of that change was near unbelievable for some of our panelists.

> Really, it's the pace of change. [It's] unprecedented in my experience in over 32 years of court administration.
>
> – Court system panelist

> I think this pandemic has pushed people forward necessarily in a really positive direction . . . there's all sorts of operational benefits to the agency . . . it's something that we've been pushed into, we being the system collectively, and we're going to grab hold of it and try and push it further as a policy change.
>
> – Institutional corrections panelist

Common Challenges and Resulting Innovations Across the Justice System

The pressures placed on the justice system by the pandemic affected parts of the justice system in different ways, but, in many cases, the responses to those challenges had common causes and demanded similar responses. As a result, in our panels' deep dives into each component, the following common themes and corresponding needs emerged for research and evaluation to assess the value of maintaining changes made after the pandemic recedes:

- **Shifts in crime and need that occurred during the pandemic had implications throughout the entire system.** The pandemic resulted in reductions in some types of reported crimes but increases in others; these shifts were shaped by the effects on behavior and the responses taken to control infection. Increases in such offenses as domestic and family violence simultaneously created needs (e.g., the requirement for courts to maintain access to protective orders, the need for law enforcement to change how they responded to some calls), made some strategies for responding more difficult (e.g., the decision in some areas to generally not arrest individuals accused of misdemeanors), and magnified demands on service providers to meet victims' needs. Some of those changes might enable better response to such concerns as domestic violence going forward. The nature of the pandemic created needs within the justice system, causing stress among incarcerated individuals and practitioners across justice organizations that built on similar concerns that preceded the pandemic.

- **Physical infrastructure can put unforgiving constraints on responses to infectious disease.** Responding to the pandemic required space to physically distance, and the high density of many facilities in the criminal justice system made that exceedingly difficult—and required such strategies as decarceration to create the needed space. Across our panels, participants described difficulties in using distance to manage the disease—in small police stations, in court buildings where the design goal had been to fit as many courtrooms in as possible, in overcrowded jails and prisons, and in congregate shelters for reentry and to serve victims of crime.

  From one perspective, those challenges raise questions about what the true capacity of the current justice system infrastructure should be and whether it should be much lower than the pre-pandemic approaches of high-density facilities (unless investments are made to make that infrastructure less vulnerable to future pandemics). However, the experience led some of the panelists to argue for the value of "de-infrastructuring" future justice activities—i.e., with more people working in the field, working from home, and using other distributed approaches to reduce the need for physical buildings and offices.

- **A massive shift to virtual access to justice and services could be valuable to both justice agencies and society, but it could leave areas and individuals behind.** For some time, analysts and practitioners have argued that there could be substantial benefit from adding telepresence and other virtual technologies to the justice system. Those benefits were dramatically realized during the pandemic. However, the pandemic led agencies to apply virtual models for tasks and functions that had not been the focus before. The expansion of online police services saved officers time. Virtual connections between courts and correctional facilities were valuable to both systems, allowing some tasks to be done with less transportation cost and security risk than physically moving people from place to place. The ability for members of the public to connect virtually—to go to court, to speak with incarcerated family members, to report during community supervision, and to receive services—saved them money and time, and made their participation in justice processes much less burdensome.

However, our panelists raised questions about efficacy as well: While some panels were nearly unanimous on the value of virtual modes, others cautioned that—particularly for counseling and service delivery—the effectiveness of virtual modes might not be sufficient. And although there are clearly some types of virtual interactions and processes that are entirely unproblematic (e.g., providing individuals virtual ways to file paperwork or perform other transactions), important questions remain about the effect of virtual modes on the outcomes of trials and other hearings. Therefore, additional evaluation is needed to assess whether justice truly is deliverable virtually.

Furthermore, although the potential value of virtual connections was clear to many, the issue of the digital divide came up across essentially all of our panels. Not every justice agency or supporting organization has invested in technology that will allow it to rapidly "go virtual."[1] Not everyone in every area of the country has ready access to technology and connectivity. To the extent that the justice system maintains virtual models, the needs of those populations without access to technology must be addressed so that the increase in access to justice for some is not offset by a decrease in access for others. However, potentially limited access to virtual justice is only one result of the shortfalls in digital infrastructure that exist in many areas of the country. Both before and during the pandemic, shortcomings in the availability, speed, and capacity of internet infrastructure in poorer or more-rural areas has affected economic activity, the education system, and other societal functions. Efforts to address the digital divide to facilitate virtual justice system models would pay dividends in many other areas as well.

- **A justice *system* can respond more effectively in a crisis than a group of justice organizations acting independently.** In our panels, several participants flagged the importance of organizations collaborating to effectively respond to crises of this magnitude. The importance of collaborating with public health agencies came up multiple times, and the information and guidance health experts could provide to justice agencies was noted as important.[2] Other collaborations were highlighted as well, such as sharing protective equipment, bringing together information, coordinating different elements of response, and cooperating to try to meet the needs of both justice-involved individuals and crime victims' needs. Our panels provided a multitude of examples where the decisions in one

---

[1] The National Commission on COVID-19 and Criminal Justice also recommended upgrading the digital infrastructure of the criminal justice system—i.e., focusing on the *internal* system shortfalls in capability and digital divides (National Commission on COVID-19 and Criminal Justice, 2020b, p. 16).

[2] The National Commission recommended institutionalizing such connections to sources of medical knowledge, including public health agencies (National Commission on COVID-19 and Criminal Justice, 2020b, p. 33).

part of the system affected others and, although those choices might have been unavoidable in the face of the crisis, more coordination and information-sharing might have cushioned the effects of those choices throughout the system.[3]

- **Serious challenges remain for successfully protecting the health and safety of emergency responders and critical personnel during large-scale disasters.** Large-scale events, whether natural or manmade, have created serious challenges with regard to protecting the health and safety of emergency responders and critical personnel. Echoing the experiences of 9/11, panelists questioned whether today's responders would have long-term consequences from COVID-19. The potential for long-term physical effects is still uncertain, although it appears to be a significant concern for some. It is certain, however, that mental health consequences from the stresses of the pandemic already are occurring, with some justice agencies taking significant action in response. As was the case for 9/11, there likely will be a need to remain attentive to how the consequences of this disaster evolve and how both the availability and use of protective options by practitioners and key personnel shape those consequences.

Although these areas represented common themes across most or even all of our panels, they are also areas in which research and evaluation are needed going forward. For some of the common innovations that were viewed as beneficial, evaluation is needed to support the relatively broad optimism among our participants about the value of preserving them. For the common challenges, research is needed to both evaluate the concerns and prepare to address them going forward.

Across these themes, there is also the critical challenge to assess what data need to be collected now, as the pandemic continues, for fear of losing the chance to assess what we have learned and how the changes made have performed. For example, in some agencies, there have been significant differences in the doses of justice intervention received by different people, and solid information about how those doses varied might become very difficult to reconstruct after their involvement in their programs is complete. In Table 8.1, we bring together the variety of research and evaluation needs suggested by panelists in the panel discussions and discussed throughout this report.[4]

What the system did—and the value of it continuing to do some of those things—is part of the story, and the collection of data to support research and evaluation efforts going forward can help support the case for maintaining some of those practices. But some of the most important lessons from the pandemic come from what the system *did not* do, including the choice to not arrest many people and not require many individuals to complete their original sentences or periods of detention for some crimes and violations. Lessons can be learned from

---

[3]   One of the final recommendations of the National Commission on COVID-19 and Criminal Justice (which was published as this report was in the final stages of writing) was maintaining "standing coordinating panels for public health emergency preparedness" of criminal justice agencies (National Commission on COVID-19 and Criminal Justice, 2020b, p. 13).

[4]   The National Commission argued for the development of minimum standards across a wide variety of these topic and practice areas to strengthen preparedness for the next pandemic. It also called for a "national research agenda concerning COVID-19 and criminal justice" for which the questions in this report could provide a jumping-off point; furthermore, the results of such questions could support standards development (National Commission on COVID-19 and Criminal Justice, 2020b, p. 31).

what that inaction means for potential changes that could be made to the justice system of the future.

> I think one thing that jumps out for us is that there should have been, or there needs to be, more discussion about measuring the actual processes that our partners are engaged in when they're responding in response to COVID. You know, a lot of people are talking about outcomes and how we can be responsive to communities, but no one's measuring what they're doing very well. That's both the community partners and the law enforcement partners. . . . My concern about that is . . . six months from now, let's say this thing passes, and a lot of municipalities [will be able to] talk about what they *think* they did, but they won't be any actual process-related data that we can use to connect to the outcomes that we're all interested in.
>
> – Community organization panelist

Decarceration and Reductions in Arrests Opened a Window to Ask More-Fundamental Questions About the Criminal Justice System

Although a slate of common problems and novel innovations from the pandemic is valuable for the justice system, the value of those lessons learned likely pales in comparison with what we can learn from the massive experiment represented by the changes made in arrest, incarceration, and supervision in response to the pandemic. Although a major increase in the use of virtual technology might be valuable, the broader policy changes made could help set the stage for a very different future for the justice system overall.

Because reducing the density of people in the justice system was a key part of responding to infectious disease risk, the responses—less arrest, less detention, more releases, and less supervision—by definition lightened the touch of the justice system on society for an extended period. As more than one of our panelists observed, those changes were in line with reforms that some organizations and communities have argued should be made for some time. Their implementation in response to the COVID-19 pandemic benefited from past efforts piloting and evaluating similar interventions to varying degrees. As a result, the more fundamental question coming out of the pandemic is not "Does the justice system keep using video conferencing?" Instead, it is "Does the justice system sustain wide-reaching changes in how it does business to reduce the level of incarceration in the country going forward?"[5]

The views of our panelists differed in terms of what the future likely will hold. Some felt that there would be an almost gravitational pull to move back to usual practice once the disruption of the pandemic lets up and the risk of COVID-19 no longer dominates decisionmaking—and, if the system does not prepare to resist that pull and maintain beneficial changes, the opportunity to learn from this crisis could be lost. Others thought that the lessons learned were so compelling that there would be no way to go back after having seen the potential for a much cheaper, less intrusive, and—possibly—comparably effective approach to criminal justice. Members from both perspectives agreed on the need for research

---

[5]   The final report of the National Commission on COVID-19 and Criminal Justice also argued for the expansion of diversion and alternative interventions to reduce the flow of such individuals into the justice system (National Commission on COVID-19 and Criminal Justice, 2020b, pp. 21–24).

Table 8.1
Key Research and Evaluation Questions Identified from Panel Discussions

Category	Law Enforcement	Court System	Institutional Corrections	Community Supervision	Victim Services
Understanding COVID-19's effects on criminal justice	• What explains the differences from place to place in how crime and victimization changed during the pandemic? • What is the extent of the long-term physical and mental health consequences of COVID-19 for law enforcement officers? How has the pandemic affected officer suicide, which was a significant concern before the pandemic?	• Can the effects of the pandemic on plea bargaining behavior and outcomes be identified and measured? Can concerns about the potential coerciveness of COVID-19 in correctional facilities (i.e., increasing bargaining power of prosecution) be distinguished from ways that the push to reduce jail and prison populations might lead to a greater desire to reach agreement rapidly?	• Given concerns about the pandemic's effect on different racial and ethnic groups and disparities in incarceration, data need to be collected to better understand the burden of disease across demographic groups within facilities. • What have been the mental health effects of the pandemic on both incarcerated populations and correctional staff, and how long do such effects last?	• Given the importance of employment as a component of reentry and a driver of success, can the effect of the pandemic's economic dislocation on justice-involved individuals be directly measured to better understand supervision success rates going forward?	• Changes in reporting behavior by victims during the pandemic risks future analyses of crime and justice responses reaching distorted conclusions. For example, if many victims delay reporting because of fear of COVID-19 or other reasons, crime at different stages of the pandemic may appear lower than it actually was. How can this be addressed in research and evaluation studies? • Given differences in data on needs reflected in calls to helplines versus calls to police, how can the totality of the changes in victim service demand caused by the pandemic be better characterized?

Table 8.1—Continued

Category	Law Enforcement	Court System	Institutional Corrections	Community Supervision	Victim Services
Improved disease management	• How has the level of community trust and the public perception of the legitimacy of police departments affected their ability to contribute to managing COVID-19? Have more-trusted departments been more effective or been provided with access to sensitive data or other resources to enable pandemic response? Are there other roles that law enforcement could productively play in public health response? • How can areas better plan for future pandemics to limit the conflicts and imprecision in public health orders (e.g., what businesses were classified as essential, what level of enforcement by police is appropriate or useful) that made law enforcement participation in managing the crisis more difficult and controversial? Can a consensus be reached around definitions and categories to make it possible to respond more quickly, collaboratively, and effectively to future outbreaks?	• Can resources be developed to educate court system stakeholders about Health Insurance Portability and Accountability Act (HIPAA) requirements regarding the sharing of COVID-19 case information to enable protection of both staff and the community?	• What can be learned from the significant differences in COVID-19 spread in separate correctional systems and even across facilities within the same system? Was the variation mostly attributable to the nature and time of introduction of the virus, or were there key differences in initial conditions (e.g., more- versus less-crowded conditions) or in the practices, policies, or infection-control actions taken that explain the different experiences? • What disease-testing strategies are effective in minimizing infectious disease in correctional institutions, taking into account the limits of tests, their costs, and the information (and the uncertainty of that information) provided by a positive or negative result?		• Given resource constraints and victims in need of sheltering, can better strategies be identified to reduce infection risk in group shelters while keeping barriers to utilization low for clients?

Table 8.1—Continued

Category	Law Enforcement	Court System	Institutional Corrections	Community Supervision	Victim Services
Improved disease management (continued)	• Are there more-effective ways to address the increase in mental health calls that has been observed during the pandemic, and how might alternative models inform consideration of police reform efforts? • How can law enforcement officers be better protected from infection risks during large-scale outbreaks, including increasing their compliance with the use of available protective equipment?		• Given concerns about individual isolation for disease prevention and controversy around the levels of transparency of correctional systems during the pandemic, can consensus models for such activities be developed that meet the needs of both corrections systems and advocates? • How can corrections officers and staff be better protected from infection risks during large-scale outbreaks, including increasing their compliance with the use of available protective equipment? • Given the lessons learned from the pandemic and the significant infectious disease risks to both incarcerated populations and the public from high-density, mass incarceration, what should the capacity of existing correctional institutions be?		

Table 8.1—Continued

Category	Law Enforcement	Court System	Institutional Corrections	Community Supervision	Victim Services
Improved disease management (continued)			• Are there architectural or other retrofitting options that would make correctional institutions more robust to future infectious disease threats? • What are the implications of the pandemic's lessons on the capacity of carceral facilities' medical care–delivery systems?		
Assessing the outcomes of reductions in arrest, incarceration, and supervision	• What have been the effects of nonarrest policies and actions taken in response to lower-level crimes during the pandemic? Do initially positive perceptions hold up over the longer term?	• Has the significant reduction in pretrial detention and money bail had an effect on appearance rates?	• How has the reduction in detention, reduction in jail use, and expedited release from prison incarceration affected crime and recidivism rates? • How can the effects of the changes made as a result of the pandemic be distinguished from the effects of other initiatives (e.g., bail reform) that were already underway in some areas?	• How has the substitution of supervision for incarceration, and the reduction in the amount of supervision for many individuals, affected crime and recidivism rates? • How have the major changes to the use of revocations—and, therefore, a significant reduction in a flow of individuals back into institutional corrections—affected outcomes? • How has the reduction of the use of such techniques as drug testing or electronic supervision affected outcomes? Do the changes made provide a template for reducing costs and intrusion into supervisees' lives going forward?	

Table 8.1—Continued

Category	Law Enforcement	Court System	Institutional Corrections	Community Supervision	Victim Services
Assessing the outcomes of reductions in arrest, incarceration, and supervision (continued)				• How can the effects of the changes made as a result of the pandemic be distinguished from the effects of other initiatives (e.g., bail reform) that were already underway in some areas?	• What are the differences in outcomes for individuals served in alternative housing supports or hotel or motel models versus standard sheltering?
Assessing distanced criminal justice models	• What have been the effects of alternative work schedules and models on staff and law enforcement agencies, and how should those effects shape the decision to continue them over the longer term? • What should be measured to better assess the effects of pandemic restrictions on alternative approaches, such as violence-reduction interventions, and assess the effectiveness of efforts to create virtual options for generally relationship-intensive face-to-face interventions?	• Is there a measurable effect on case outcomes of trial participants being socially distanced or wearing face coverings? • How can courts proactively identify alternative facilities where jury trials could be held in the community? • Can tools be developed to solicit community input on case prioritization to ensure that community views are reflected in which cases are allocated scarce court resources and acted on for backlog reduction?	• Can the effectiveness of virtual visitation and other virtual options be measured to support investments in their expansion?		

Table 8.1—Continued

Category	Law Enforcement	Court System	Institutional Corrections	Community Supervision	Victim Services
Assessing virtual delivery of justice services	• How satisfied has the public been with the provision of virtual police services during the pandemic, and how much have those alternative models saved departmental resources? • How effective have efforts to train staff and new officers virtually been? Over time, how do the skills and capabilities of officers who went to the Academy in cyberspace differ from those of officers who were trained in person? • What technologies are needed to support more law enforcement practitioners in flexible work models (e.g., systems to better enable dispatchers to work remotely)? • Did digital divides among different groups in the public affect the effectiveness of communication and other strategies? Were alternatives used by departments that encountered such problems effective?	• Have remote-appearance options reduced failure-to-appear rates? • Do victims of crime have a different perception of whether justice is served in remote hearings and proceedings? • How do jurors perceive the experience of serving on a virtual jury? • In virtual proceedings, do outcomes differ from those of in-person court processes on measurable factors, such as bail, sentences, or other outcomes? • Could online dispute-resolution processes be applied in the criminal area to help reduce the backlog while maintaining procedural justice? • Does the potential for integrating virtual technology into future court operations suggest a need to revisit court design and security standards? • If virtual juries are used, are there issues maintaining the representativeness of the jury pool?		• Are virtual models as effective as in-person supervision, counseling, and treatment? How have key outcomes—both from the individual and societal perspective—been affected by the shift? • What are the net savings from virtual models, including staffing and transportation time and cost, and also infrastructure and other costs? What are the net savings to the individuals under supervision? • How have digital divides across different parts of the community corrections system—including government agencies, NGO service providers, and entities serving urban and rural communities—affected the ability to continue operations through the pandemic?	• How effective are virtual models for delivering services to victims, and how satisfied are those victims with the outcomes (including virtual court participation)? • How can organizations that might not have as strong a technology infrastructure as government criminal justice agencies more effectively address the information security and other concerns with delivering services remotely? Similar to questions raised in the past regarding law enforcement, are there challenges (e.g., with legal discoverability) with providers using personally owned devices in performing their roles? • Given concerns about the digital divide significantly affecting the ability of victims from locations with low broadband or little communications infrastructure to access services and participate in the justice process, can levels of true access be better mapped to inform assessment of the impact of virtual models?

Table 8.1—Continued

Category	Law Enforcement	Court System	Institutional Corrections	Community Supervision	Victim Services
Assessing virtual delivery of justice services (continued)		• How has the shift to virtual proceedings affected self-represented litigants? • Can the positive effects of virtual proceedings on litigants—in easier access, lower costs, and other factors—be quantified? If costs are lower, is access to justice increased? • Can the effects of streaming or broadcasting court proceedings online be measured to allow for the weighing of broader access versus greater exposure for victims, defendants, and other parties?			• Given the importance of services to victims of crime and the importance of supporting their involvement in the justice process, how can sustainable support for organizations delivering those services be put in place given the vulnerability revealed by the pandemic and its economic consequences?
Improving justice funding models	• Given likely funding constraints on departments going forward, what are the implications of the types of programs and initiatives that will be cut? How do such cuts interact with reform efforts arguing for the reallocation of resources from police budgets?	• How have the mechanisms through which court systems are funded affected their ability to respond to and operate through the pandemic?	• How can institutional corrections systems respond to budgetary pressures that could push toward a return to high-density facilities, therefore increasing vulnerability to infectious diseases?	• How can both supervision agencies and the service providers on which they depend be sustainably funded given, what we have learned during the pandemic?	

and evaluation on this question most of all, to either support the argument to maintain these approaches or make reasoned decisions about which of them should be modified or discarded going forward.

> I think there's a real crossroads question about whether we're going to start regressing to mass incarceration again, or whether we're going to invest in protection of the community by prevention.
>
> – Community corrections panelist
>
> We're never going back to the way things were. We're going to have to change the way we're going, and it's going to be a different world that we're in.
>
> – Court system panelist
>
> I think there's a real opportunity to fundamentally shift the reach of the criminal justice system in the lives of the poorest people in the community. But there's also tremendous resistance. . . . I think it's going to be up to researchers to be able to really evaluate the impact of COVID and bail reform and these arguments around police legitimacy and the link between that and crime to really help us better understand the impact of all of those and what it means for supervision in the community.
>
> – Community organization panelist

Even though we are looking through the lens of the pandemic, the questions about maintaining more-substantial changes in practice going forward are fundamentally a continuation of the debate about the kind of justice system the United States wants. Both within and outside criminal justice agencies, many have lamented the number of missions and tasks that have been left for the justice system to perform—responding to crime, managing mental health crises, substance use intervention, and addressing routine neighborhood problems and frictions. Indeed, in our discussions, one panelist pointed to what police departments were asked to do during the pandemic as the most recent example of society asking the justice system to do something that others should have been responsible for—and funded to do.

> The criminal legal system has become the largest bucket into which we dump *all* of our problems . . . [as the legal system] . . . you are responsible for victims, families, for reentry, for law enforcement relationships, for case integrity, for judicial norms, all of that just falls into this big bucket. . . .
>
> So if there's a way to look to jurisdictions that have really thought meaningfully about what it means to really shrink the number of questions and responsibilities that the system addresses—and not just in terms of where we deploy police or who gets arrested—I mean, the number of questions the system is willing to answer and is unwilling to answer . . . that for me would be the primary example of what we should be thinking about post-pandemic.
>
> And then, the next time a crisis hits, maybe with fewer questions to answer, the legal system can be a little more adept in terms of how it responds to people's needs and how it works to save lives.
>
> – Community organization panelist

> In many of these communities, the best-funded institution to take on the burden of COVID response and public health work was . . . the criminal justice system. And so what I hope for the future is a reinvestment in the independent public health institutions that can operate totally independently and have the resources to do so without relying on the criminal justice system, which I think inevitably the more you get police departments into the work of public health workers, the more it erodes trust in the process.
>
> – Community organization panelist

However, as the quote from our community organizations panelist in the introduction to this report noted, there are at least the following three fundamental perspectives from which such changes need to be examined:

- the justice system itself and how changes affect its functioning and effectiveness
- justice-involved individuals and their communities, which are significantly affected by decisions about policing, incarceration, and approaches to justice
- members of the public who are affected by crime; how the system is designed also must meet their needs and achieve just outcomes from their perspective.

This need to consider multiple perspectives came up repeatedly across our panels in different ways. When we looked across the different parts of the justice system, there were some changes made by agencies that were beneficial from all of these perspectives. For example, although not all of our panelists agreed that transparency across the justice system had increased, increasing the amount of information agencies were sharing about what they were doing was useful for other justice agencies, for communities and justice-involved individuals (e.g., residents within correctional facilities), and for victims of crime who were involved in the justice process and for awareness of what was happening.

> Jurisdictions . . . collecting and making that information public, that's particularly important, but also not just quantitative data. It's really important to hear from the people who are both in the system, as people who are impacted by it, *and* the people [who] operate the system on why they think this is important and to have those voices out there. So I think that innovation or rethinking is particularly important and we are already seeing sort of the uptick in going back to the way we were before.
>
> – Community corrections panelist

In contrast, many of the changes made in response to the pandemic by justice agencies focused on the first two of these perspectives: changes made to maintain the functioning of the system and to protect both criminal justice practitioners and justice-involved individuals from the risk of viral spread. Some of those changes had real effects on victims of crime and on the ability of justice agencies and service providers to meet their needs. Conversely, there was at least one example of a change that cut the other way: the decision to livestream many court proceedings to preserve public access while the courthouse was physically closed. That decision most-directly served the need of the system for proceedings to be transparent and the needs of crime victims and the broader public for access, but it imposed potentially serious new costs on justice-involved individuals, whose day in court became exponentially more public than a traditional, in-person proceeding. As a result, in considering the path forward, how major changes affect different populations served by the justice system will be important.

However, even with the difficulty in finding changes that meet the needs of all three of these groups simultaneously, the pandemic and the natural experiment created by the justice system's response to it have created an opportunity to do so. Returning to the argument of our community organization panelist,

> in this pandemic . . . all three of those groups have had to respond or have been impacted by the decisions that are being made, and *all* of them are being affected by the crisis. . . . [Before the pandemic], if you look at those three things as three points on a triangle, you can only ever work within two of them and the third is left to feel the consequences of the changes. But we have a moment here where everyone is in this together in a way that they never have been before.

In the discussions across multiple panels, there was a view that learning from this experience and moving toward a more cost-efficient and lighter-touch justice system could be an instance where consensus could be built across the political spectrum. Essentially, consensus among actors and groups that might disagree on many other things could be built around arguments for less intervention in society, for saving justice resources for the cases and criminal threats in which they are really required, for the justice system playing fewer roles, and for saving money that will be needed for other priorities. But finding that path forward will require consideration and research that can speak to the outcomes of the changes—and how they affected all three of these central groups.

I think there is a lot of support in the general public for the concept of scaling back on mass incarceration. And I think that is one of the very few things that consistently—in the last five or ten years—has been a bipartisan issue that pretty much everybody can agree that we want to cut back incarceration.

– Institutional corrections panelist

Some of the change that I didn't think was possible included reducing our jail population by a third and keeping it there.

– Court system panelist

I think one of the hugest impacts, and will be a lesson learned later on, is *who should actually be in jail*? We had a response to a pandemic, and these collaborations with our stakeholders, our district attorneys, our public defenders, our law enforcement, those doing the arresting. We've made these agreements and now a lot of people who would have been in jail are now being supervised in the community. Well, if that is not having an effect on public safety, do those folks really need to be in jail in the first place, or can they be supervised in another capacity?

– Institutional corrections panelist

> This is an opportunity to the extent that it allows us to thin [the] prison population, have people put onto supervision, and then also give supervision a chance to thin those people that they cannot manage because of the numbers that are being released and saving community supervision for those that really need it. And I think that's really the key here. I mean, there can be something positive out of this.
>
> – Community corrections panelist

The Crisis in the Justice System Caused by the Pandemic Will Not Disappear the Moment the Virus Is Defeated

Just as individuals who have been infected with COVID-19 can suffer long-term health consequences even after they have recovered, the justice system will suffer from long-term effects in functioning and performance after the pandemic is under control, according to our panelists. A key transition described in nearly all of our panels was the point that agencies stopped viewing the pandemic as something that would pass rapidly, and instead as a prolonged crisis—a marathon, not a sprint. Because of how agencies responded to the immediate pressure of the pandemic, enduring pressures—backlogs of cases, demands, and needs—were created that might take years to work through, even after pre-pandemic capacity is restored. In Figure 8.1, we identify points in the system from beginning to end where the flow of people and cases had been stopped because of concerns about capacity.

Figure 8.1
Pressures Building at Different Points in the Justice System from Backlogs and Capacity Constraints

We work as a system and our courts have been doing everything just about virtually . . . but a real downside, and we're looking at this statewide, is the dockets aren't moving . . . and the backlog is huge. You know, I've seen it, the court shut down, obviously [after the hurricane we experienced]. I saw the impact of that. But the courts are going to have to be able to function and at over a hundred percent to be able to actually even make a dent into the docket. So, I don't know if that's going on in other places or not, but there's a backlog and it's a big deal.

– Community corrections panelist

Even when reductions in concern about COVID-19 allow the resumption of more-normal operations, each roadblock represents either a building pressure of demand or a narrowing of the throughput of the system that will mean that the justice system's recovery will be a long-term process. That recovery will be complicated by the scars that the pandemic almost certainly will leave on municipal budgets, on the philanthropic funding streams on which many service providers rely, and on the economy as a whole. The fiscal and economic fallout means not only are justice agencies likely going to have fewer resources to address the backlogs but also that that need in particular will continue to expand as some stresses experienced by individuals and families during the pandemic persist.

We've seen, across the board, a huge economic impact on survivors, and the stark racial disparities that we see in COVID infections and deaths, we've also seen with impact on economics for survivors, [including] survivors reporting that they can't access the food that they need . . . these are going to be ongoing needs, right? *What we have seen across many other disasters, natural disasters, manmade disasters, is the demand tends to go up and be sustained after the crisis recedes.* So the more COVID starts to recede, we think we'll see more people coming forward and saying, "All right, I stuck it out when I was afraid to leave during COVID and I need help now." So we expect we will see increased calls, increased demands for shelter, particularly an increased demand for housing assistance in the coming months to two years, right as the economy struggles to rebuild and survivors are putting their lives back together. That's going to be an ongoing investment that's needed.

– Victim services panelist

Building Toward a Safer and More Just Future While Weathering the Long-Term Consequences of the Pandemic

Many of the ways in which the COVID-19 pandemic put pressure on individual justice agencies and stressed the seams in the justice system—as the country dealt with the spread of the virus both unevenly and divergently—were not a surprise. Long before the COVID-19 pandemic, there was concern about the consequences of the number of people channeled into the justice system in the United States. Over the years, the focus of calls for reform regarding mass incarceration have focused on the consequences for justice-involved individuals and their communities, and how the intermingling of responses to mental health issues, substance use, and crime has created major concern about the system's overall effectiveness. Beyond such concerns, the pandemic made undeniable that the public safety goals of criminal justice and public health are inexorably intertwined, and that past efforts to prepare the system for pandemic threats had only limited success. That connection means that improving preparedness for future disease threats has become an additional reason to revisit the country's approach to criminal justice in the hope that any future infectious disease outbreak will find a system that is better positioned to weather the storm.

> So I would argue, when disaster strikes, who survives? Well, it's those who plan ahead, it's those who prepare for what we thought was unthinkable.
>
> – Law enforcement management panelist

Many of the responses by justice agencies to the COVID-19 pandemic came out of policy experiments and innovations that existed well before, although the pressure of responding pushed their adoption to a breakneck pace. Across our panels, participants repeatedly expressed how much change had happened very quickly and how flexible and creative staff in their agencies and organizations had been to keep pushing their missions forward. That innovation—which proved that organizations that had long been viewed as difficult to change can adapt very quickly—was a key source of hope that changes could continue to be made going forward. One of the explanations for the slow pace of change in the justice system, in spite of years of concerns regarding its effectiveness, efficiency, and fairness, was that it was a system that *could not* and potentially *should not* make rapid change. The pandemic proved that argument to be incorrect. Many parts of the system made big changes and did so rapidly. By showing what was possible, that demonstration opens up new possibilities for the future and weakens past explanations for sluggish innovation and reform.

> The pandemic was not the disruption that we wanted in the court system, but maybe the disruption we needed to really make change happen. . . . [W]e're a big old-fashioned institution that doesn't change very easily. And this pandemic has really pushed the pace of change.
>
> – Court system panelist
>
> I think that the biggest thing that I would say about staff since the beginning of COVID is that I think that their creativity and their willingness to be creative has gone up significantly. Even though in the back of their head, they're still saying, well, we've never done it that way, it's much more apparent that the way we did it isn't going to work right this minute. And if we're going to do anything, we've got to be more flexible.
>
> – Law enforcement management panelist

Because of COVID-19, which has claimed the lives of numerous members of criminal justice and service organizations, of medical professionals—including those treating justice-involved individuals who became infected—and of people across the country overall, seeking to realize the potential for improvement and change in the justice system seems to be a critical goal. From what has been learned in responding to this crisis, our panelists saw a chance for innovation that could make the criminal justice system both more effective in managing public safety *and* fairer to those who become justice-involved. In our discussions, panelists talked about the inherent tensions that exist within the system between the desire to craft justice interventions that are effective at the individual level and responding uniformly across large categories of people, offenses, or problems. Responses to the pandemic to reduce the population of justice-involved individuals, allowing the system to focus on fewer people at a time, make customizing intervention for greater effectiveness easier. Technologies that the pandemic forced on a usually risk-averse justice system, most notably virtual modes of interaction and supervision, further enable the development of one-size-fits-one models that can conserve resources, improve fairness, reduce the intrusiveness of the justice system in the lives of individuals and their communities, and be more effective. Although the likely enduring fiscal pressure on the justice system might make this sort of innovation practically important, learning from the pandemic to build a stronger justice legacy could be, in the words of one of our panelists, a way to find a "thin silver lining" in a very dark time for the country.

Project Participants

In selecting our panelists, we sought participants from across the country who represented criminal justice, service provision, and community organizations with expertise and experiences relevant to understanding the response of the justice system to the COVID-19 pandemic. Panelists' geographic locations are shown in Figure A.1, and the full listing of panelists is provided in Table A.1.

Figure A.1
Locations of Origin for Panelists

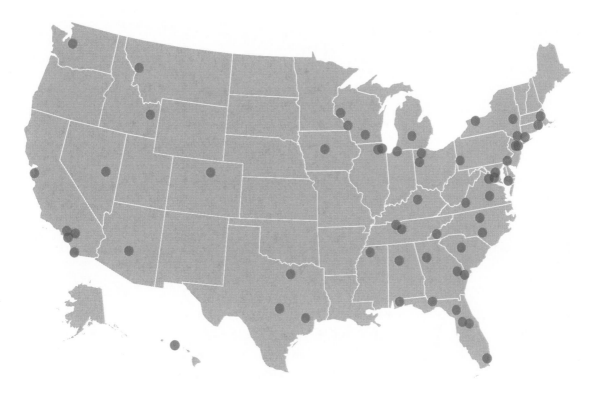

Table A.1
Panel Participants and Organizational Affiliations

Name	Affiliation
Armando Aguilar	Miami Police Department (Florida)
Scott Allen	University of California, Riverside, School of Medicine
Irshad Altheimer	Rochester Institute of Technology
Jeffrey Alvarez	NaphCare, Inc.
Ed Alverez	Bay Area Rapid Transit Police Department
Anthony Annucci	New York State Department of Corrections and Community Supervision
Jamie Aten	Humanitarian Disaster Institute
Eric Atkinson	Menomonie Police (Wisconsin)
Wesley Attwood	National Institute for Occupational Safety and Health
Rich Austin	Milton Police Department (Georgia)
Julie Marie Baldwin	American University
Veronica Ballard Cunningham	American Probation and Parole Association
Nicole Banister	National Governors Association
Mike Barnett	San Diego County Sheriff's Department (California)
Ana Bermudez	New York City Department of Probation
David Blumberg	Maryland Parole Commission and International Association of Paroling Authorities
John Boman	Bowling Green State University
Erika Brooke	University of Florida
Alana Brown	The Safe Sisters Circle
Jean Bruggeman	Freedom Network USA
Patrick G. Brummond	Wisconsin's 7th Judicial Administrative District
Nelson Bunn	National District Attorneys' Association
Jimmy Chapman	Roanoke County Police Department (Virginia)
Michael Cimino	Maricopa County Adult Probation (Arizona)
Darryl Coleman	Harris County Sheriff's Office (Texas)
Brenda Cooke	New York City Department of Correction
Kevin Coppinger	Essex County Sheriff's Office (Massachusetts)
Trent Cornish	Probation and Pretrial Services Office, Administrative Office of the U.S. Courts
Karma Cottman	District of Columbia Coalition Against Domestic Violence; Ujima (The National Center on Violence Against Women in the Black Community)
Maureen Curtis	Safe Horizon
Megan Cutter	National Human Trafficking Hotline
Ayesha Delany-Brumsey	Council of State Governments
Adrian Diaz	Seattle Police Department (Washington)
Barbara Duncan	Salisbury Police Department (Maryland)
Amy Durall	International Association of Chiefs of Police
Terry Fain	Recovery Monitoring Solutions
Erin Forry	American Society of Crime Laboratory Directors
Matthew Guariglia	Electronic Frontier Foundation
Jane Gubser	Cook County Department of Corrections (Illinois)
Howard Hall	Roanoke County Police Department (Virginia)

Table A.1—Continued

Name	Affiliation
J. Andrew Hansen	Western Carolina University
Shannon B. Harper	Iowa State University
Cherie Harris	Kirkland Police Department (Washington)
Dylan Hayre	American Civil Liberties Union
Christopher Hines	Loudon County Sheriff's Office (Virginia)
Rene Hinojosa	Texas Department of Criminal Justice
Grace Huang	Asian Pacific Institute on Gender-Based Violence
Linda Jackson	Virginia Department of Forensic Science
Scott Jackson	Montana State Crime Laboratory
Wesley Jennings	University of Mississippi
Kim Jones	National Alliance on Mental Illness–Georgia
Katie Kaukinen	University of Central Florida
Kevin Kempf	Correctional Leaders Associations
Karl Kim	National Disaster Preparedness Training Center
A. J. Kramer	Office of the Federal Public Defender for the District of Columbia
James Krause	Fairfax County Police Department (Virginia)
Lance Leslie	Maricopa County Sheriff's Office (Arizona)
Beth Luthye	Salvation Army of Central Maryland
Thomas Lyons	Cook County Adult Probation (Illinois)
Russ Marlan	Michigan Department of Corrections
Teresa May	Harris County Community Supervision and Corrections Department (Texas)
Yeny McIntyre-Nalbone	Putnam County Child Advocacy Center (New York)
Stephanie McKenny	Los Angeles Police Department (California)
Catherine Meyers	Center for Children, Inc.
Roy Minter	Savannah Police Department (Georgia)
John Mueller	Yonkers Police Department (New York)
Michael Nail	Georgia Department of Community Supervision
John Nevin	Michigan Supreme Court
John Nicoletti	Nicoletti-Flater Associates
James Nolette	Fayetteville Police Department (North Carolina)
Nancy O'Malley	Alameda County District Attorney's Office and California District Attorney Association
JoAnne Page	Fortune Society
Chad Posick	Georgia Southern University
Gerry Prieto	Long Beach Police Department (California)
Thomas Prol	Sills Cummis & Gross
Allison Randall	National Network to End Domestic Violence
Marcus W. Reinkensmeyer	Administrative Office of the Courts, Supreme Court of Arizona
Jody Rich	Brown University
Charles Richardson	Loudon County Sheriff's Office (Virginia)
Edwin Roessler	Fairfax County Police Department (Virginia)
Dan Satterberg	King County Prosecuting Attorney's Office (Washington)
Anne Seymour	Medical University of South Carolina, National Crime Victims Research and Treatment Center

Table A.1—Continued

Name	Affiliation
Keri Kei Shibata	University of Notre Dame Police
April Singleton Clarke	South Carolina Department of Corrections
David Slayton	Texas Office of Court Administration
Susan Sorenson	Ortner Center on Violence and Abuse, University of Pennsylvania
Ben Stickle	Middle Tennessee State University
Megan Stoltz	International Association of Chiefs of Police
Jonathan Sury	National Center for Disaster Preparedness
Samuel Anderson Thumma	Arizona Court of Appeals, Division One
Marsha Travis	Davidson County Sheriff's Office (Tennessee) and American Jail Association
Eva Velasquez	Identity Theft Resource Center
David Voth	Ohio Crime Victim Services
Emily Wang	Yale University
Jeff Washington	American Correctional Association
Heidi Washington	Michigan Department of Corrections
Michael White	Arizona State University
Joe Winkler	Florida Department of Corrections
Garrett L. Wong	Superior Court of California, County of San Francisco
Steve Woolworth	Evergreen Treatment Services and International Community Corrections Association

References

Adelstein, Janna, "Courts Continue to Adapt to COVID-19," Brennan Center for Justice, September 10, 2020. As of December 8, 2020:
https://www.brennancenter.org/our-work/analysis-opinion/courts-continue-adapt-covid-19

Adolph, Christopher, Kenya Amano, Bree Bang-Jensen, Nancy Fullman, Beatrice Magistro, Grace Reinke, and John Wilkerson, "Governor Partisanship Explains the Adoption of Statewide Mandates to Wear Face Coverings," *medRxiv*, September 2, 2020. As of January 18, 2021:
https://www.medrxiv.org/content/10.1101/2020.08.31.20185371v1

Alfonso, Fernando, III, "The Pandemic Is Causing an Exponential Rise in the Online Exploitation of Children, Experts Say," CNN, May 25, 2020.

Altheimer, Irshad, Janelle Duda-Banwar, and Christopher J. Schreck, "The Impact of Covid-19 on Community-Based Violence Interventions," *American Journal of Criminal Justice*, Vol. 45, 2020, pp. 810–819.

American Bar Association Task Force on Legal Needs Arising out of the 2020 Pandemic, *Summary Report: Survey Regarding Legal Needs Arising from the COVID-19 Pandemic*, Chicago, Il., May 2020. As of December 8, 2020:
https://www.americanbar.org/advocacy/the-aba-task-force-on-legal-needs-arising-out-of-the-2020-pandem/

American Correctional Association, "The Wall of Honor," webpage, undated. As of December 7, 2020:
http://www.aca.org/ACA_Prod_IMIS/ACA_Member/Wall_of_Honor.aspx

American Probation and Parole Association, "Community Corrections Virtual Roundtable on the Coronavirus Pandemic," video, YouTube, April 8, 2020a. As of December 9, 2020:
https://www.youtube.com/watch?v=fAAgaZ7JNXg&app=desktop

American Probation and Parole Association, "Community Corrections Virtual Roundtable: As the COVID-19 Dust Settles: Agency Efforts to Recover," video, YouTube, May 13, 2020b. As of December 9, 2020:
https://www.youtube.com/watch?v=aJeHLjmKlao&feature=youtu.be&t=1

American Probation and Parole Association, "Community Corrections Virtual Roundtable: Probation Officers on the Front Lines Against COVID-19," video, YouTube, July 7, 2020c. As of December 9, 2020:
https://www.youtube.com/watch?v=oBTDJE2K8ak&feature=youtu.be

American Psychiatric Association, *The Impact of COVID-19 on Incarcerated Persons with Mental Illness*, Washington, D.C., 2020.

American Society of Addiction Medicine, *Caring for Patients During the COVID-19 Pandemic: Managing Justice Involved People with Addiction During the COVID-19 Pandemic*, Chevy Chase, Md., September 18, 2020.

Anti-Defamation League, "Reports of Anti-Asian Assaults, Harassment and Hate Crimes Rise as Coronavirus Spreads," *ADL Blog*, June 18, 2020. As of December 7, 2020:
https://www.adl.org/blog/reports-of-anti-asian-assaults-harassment-and-hate-crimes-rise-as-coronavirus-spreads

APA—*See* American Psychiatric Association.

APPA—*See* American Probation and Parole Association.

Ashby, Matthew P. J., "Initial Evidence on the Relationship Between the Coronavirus Pandemic and Crime in the United States," *Crime Science*, Vol. 9, No. 6, 2020.

Asher, Jeff, "Murders Are Rising. Blaming a Party Doesn't Add Up." *New York Times*, September 28, 2020.

Association of State and Territorial Health Officials, "Public Health and Information Sharing Toolkit: Authorities and Limitations in Sharing Information Between Public Health Agencies and Law Enforcement," webpage, undated. As of December 8, 2020:
https://www.astho.org/Programs/Preparedness/Public-Health-Emergency-Law/Public-Health-and-Information-Sharing-Toolkit/Authorities-and-Limitations-in-Sharing-Information-Issue-Brief/

Baldwin, Julie Marie, John M. Eassey, and Erika J. Brooke, "Court Operations During the COVID-19 Pandemic," *American Journal of Criminal Justice*, Vol. 45, 2020, pp. 743–758.

Barnes, Stephen R., Louis-Philippe Beland, Jason Huh, and Dongwoo Kim, *The Effect of COVID-19 Lockdown on Mobility and Traffic Accidents: Evidence from Louisiana*, Essen, Germany: Global Labor Organization, GLO Discussion Paper Series 616, 2020.

Bella, Timothy, "A GOP Sheriff Vowed Not to Enforce Arizona's Coronavirus Restrictions. Now He's Tested Positive," *Washington Post*, June 18, 2020.

Bender, Adam, "COVID-19 Could Change Views Toward Remote 911 Operators," *Communications Daily*, June 15, 2020. As of December 8, 2020:
https://communicationsdaily.com/article/2020/06/15/
covid19-could-change-views-toward-remote-911-operators-2006120038

Blustain, Rachel, "COVID-19 Creates Deep Uncertainty in NYC's Child-Welfare System," *City Limits*, March 30, 2020. As of January 18, 2021:
https://citylimits.org/2020/03/30/covid-19-creates-deep-uncertainty-in-nycs-child-welfare-system/

Boman, John H., IV, and Owen Gallupe, "Has COVID-19 Changed Crime? Crime Rates in the United States During the Pandemic," *American Journal of Criminal Justice*, Vol. 45, 2020, pp. 537–545.

Bowles, Laken, "Tennessee Will Stop Providing COVID-19 Patient Data to Law Enforcement, First Responders," *News Channel 5 Nashville*, May 27, 2020. As of December 8, 2020:
https://www.newschannel5.com/news/tennessee-will-stop-providing-covid-19-patient-data-to-law-enforcement-first-responders

Boyd, Thomas P., State Court Administrator, Michigan Supreme Court, "Virtual Jury Trials," memorandum to all judges, Lansing, Mich., July 20, 2020.

Bradbury, Shelly, "Colorado Courts Catapulted Online Amid Coronavirus Pandemic," *Denver Post*, August 16, 2020.

Bragg, Ko, and Kate Sosin, "Inside the COVID Unit at the World's Largest Women's Prison," *PBS News Hour*, October 19, 2020. As of December 9, 2020:
https://www.pbs.org/newshour/health/inside-the-covid-unit-at-the-worlds-largest-womens-prison

Brennan Center for Justice, *Prosecutors Responses to COVID-19*, Washington, D.C., March 27, 2020, updated July 15, 2020.

Brooks, Rosa, and Christy Lopez, *Policing in a Time of Pandemic: Recommendations for Law Enforcement*, Washington, D.C.: Georgetown Law Innovative Policing Program and Edmond J. Safra Center for Ethics, April 10, 2020.

Buchanan, Molly, Erin D. Castro, Mackenzie Kushner, and Marvin D. Krohn, "It's F**ing Chaos: COVID-19's Impact on Juvenile Delinquency and Juvenile Justice," *American Journal of Criminal Justice*, Vol. 45, No. 4, 2020, pp. 578–600.

Bullock, Steve, Governor, State of Montana, "Directive Implementing Executive Orders 2-2020 and 3-2020 Related to State Correctional and State-Contracted Correctional Facilities," memorandum to Montanans and all officers and agencies of the State of Montana, April 1, 2020.

Buncombe County Justice Services Department, *Buncombe County Fact Sheet: On Addressing COVID-19 in Our Local Justice System*, undated. As of December 8, 2020:
https://www.buncombecounty.org/common/jrac/safety-justice-challenge/covid-19-factsheet.pdf

Bureau of Justice Assistance, Public Safety Officers' Benefits Program, "About PSOB," webpage, undated. As of December 8, 2020:
https://psob.bja.ojp.gov/about/

Candler, Blake, "Court Adaptations During COVID-19 in the World's Two Largest Democracies," *SSRN*, May 24, 2020.

Carter, TaLisa J., "COVID-19 in the Common Area: The Pandemic Is Reinforcing the Interconnected Nature of Corrections," *Urban Wire* blog, June 16, 2020. As of January 18, 2021:
https://www.urban.org/urban-wire/
covid-19-common-area-pandemic-reinforcing-interconnected-nature-corrections

Centers for Disease Control and Prevention, "COVID Data Tracker: United States COVID-19 Cases and Deaths by State," webpage, undated. As of December 7, 2020:
https://covid.cdc.gov/covid-data-tracker/#cases_deathsper100k

Centers for Disease Control and Prevention, National Center for Health Statistics, "Excess Deaths Associated with COVID-19," webpage, updated December 2, 2020. As of December 7, 2020:
https://www.cdc.gov/nchs/nvss/vsrr/covid19/excess_deaths.htm

Chammah, Maurice, "The Rise of the Anti-Lockdown Sheriffs," The Marshall Project, May 18, 2020. As of December 7, 2020:
https://www.themarshallproject.org/2020/05/18/the-rise-of-the-anti-lockdown-sheriffs

Chappell, Bill, and Paige Pfleger, "73% of Inmates at an Ohio Prison Test Positive for Coronavirus," NPR, April 20, 2020. As of December 9, 2020:
https://www.npr.org/sections/coronavirus-live-updates/2020/04/20/838943211/
73-of-inmates-at-an-ohio-prison-test-positive-for-coronavirus

Chari, Karishma A., Alan E. Simon, Carol J. DeFrances, and Laura Maruschak, *National Survey of Prison Health Care: Selected Findings*, Washington, D.C.: U.S. Department of Health and Human Services, National Health Statistics Reports, No. 96, July 28, 2016.

Chavez, Nashelly, and Lori A. Carter, "Santa Rosa Police Department Fined $32,000 Over Workplace Coronavirus Outbreak, Detective's Death," *The Press Democrat*, September 22, 2020.

Collins, Dave, "Jury Duty? No Thanks, Say Many, Forcing Trials to Be Delayed," Associated Press, November 22, 2020.

"Coronavirus in the U.S.: Latest Map and Case Count," *New York Times*, undated.

Council on Criminal Justice, "Facing COVID-19 in the Courts," video, YouTube, April 16, 2020a. As of December 8, 2020:
https://www.youtube.com/watch?v=4ux55R23jIs

Council on Criminal Justice, "Corrections and COVID-19: Challenges and Strategies," video, YouTube, April 30, 2020b. As of December 9, 2020:
https://www.youtube.com/watch?v=FKbCr3LrzCo

Council on Criminal Justice, "Facing COVID-19 in the Community," video, YouTube, May 12, 2020c. As of January 18, 2021:
https://www.youtube.com/watch?v=qJzuBr49OCA

The Council of State Governments Justice Center, "Survey Shows Reentry Services Halting Across U.S.," April 22, 2020. As of December 9, 2020:
https://csgjusticecenter.org/survey-shows-reentry-services-halting-across-u-s/

The COVID Tracking Project, "The Data," data set, updated October 2, 2020. As of October 2, 2020:
https://covidtracking.com/data

Cramer, Amelia, "How Interagency Trust Can Foster an Optimal Jail Response to COVID-19," MacArthur Foundation Safety and Justice Challenge blog, April 8, 2020. As of December 8, 2020:
https://www.safetyandjusticechallenge.org/2020/04/how-interagency-trust-can-foster-an-optimal-jail-response-to-covid-19/

Criminal complaint, *United States v. Fox, Croft, Garbin, Franks, Harris, and Caserta*, case 1:20-MJ-416-SJB, W.D. Mich., October 6, 2020. As of December 8, 2020:
https://www.justice.gov/usao-wdmi/press-release/file/1326161/download

Czeisler, Mark É., Rashon I. Lane, Emiko Petrosky, Joshua F. Wiley, Aleta Christensen, Rashid Njai, Matthew D. Weaver, Rebecca Robbins, Elise R. Facer-Childs, Laura K. Barger, Charles A. Czeisler, Mark E. Howard, and Shantha M. W. Rajaratnam, "Mental Health, Substance Use, and Suicidal Ideation During the COVID-19 Pandemic—United States, June 24–30, 2020," *Morbidity and Mortality Weekly Report*, Vol. 69, No. 32, August 14, 2020, pp. 1049–1057.

Damien, Christopher, "Man Tests Positive for COVID-19 During Trial; Attorneys Say Court Isn't Protecting Public," *Desert Sun*, August 14, 2020.

del Valle, Lauren, and Leah Asmelash, "New Jersey Releases More Than 2,200 Eligible Inmates Under Nation's First Public Health Crisis Sentencing Law," CNN, November 4, 2020.

Derr, Brendon, Rebecca Griesbach, and Danya Issawi, "States Are Shutting Down Prisons as Guards Are Crippled by Covid-19," *New York Times*, January 1, 2021.

Desai, Alisha, Kelley Durham, Stephanie C. Burke, Amanda NeMoyer, and Kirk Heilbrun, "Releasing Individuals from Incarceration During COVID-19: Pandemic-Related Challenges and Recommendations for Promoting Successful Reentry," *Psychology, Public Policy, and Law*, 2020.

Diamond, Shari Seidman, Locke E. Bowman, Manyee Wong, and Matthew M. Patton, "Efficiency and Cost: The Impact of Videoconferenced Hearings on Bail Decisions," *Journal of Criminal Law and Criminology*, Vol. 100, No. 3, 2010, pp. 869–902.

Draper, Brandon Marc, "And Justice for None: How COVID-19 Is Crippling the Criminal Jury Right," *Boston College Law Review*, Vol. 62, No. 9, E. Supp. I.-1, 2020, pp. I.-1–I.-10.

Dugdale, Emily Elena, "They Got the Memos, But LA Cops Still Aren't Wearing Masks," *Laist*, July 6, 2020. As of January 18, 2021:
https://laist.com/2020/07/06/they_got_the_memos_but_l-a_cops_still_arent_wearing_masks.php

Duncan, Alexandra, Noah Sanders, Maria Schiff, and Tyler N. A. Winkelman, "Adaptations to Jail-Based Buprenorphine Treatment During the COVID-19 Pandemic," *Journal of Substance Abuse Treatment*, Vol. 121, February 2021.

Elman, Alyssa, Risa Breckman, Sunday Clark, Elaine Gottesman, Lisa Rachmuth, Margaret Reiff, Jena Callahan, Laura A. Russell, Maureen Curtis, Joy Solomon, Deirdre Lok, Jo Anne Sirey, Mark S. Lachs, Sara Czaja, Karl Pillemer, and Tony Rosen, "Effects of the COVID-19 Outbreak on Elder Mistreatment and Response in New York City: Initial Lessons," *Journal of Applied Gerontology*, Vol. 39, No. 7, July 1, 2020, pp. 690–699.

Emezue, Chuka, "Digital or Digitally Delivered Responses to Domestic and Intimate Partner Violence During COVID-19," *JMIR Public Health Surveillance*, Vol. 6, No. 3, July–September 2020.

Ervin, Storm, and Sara Batomski, "We Need to Do More to Support Victims of Domestic Violence During the Pandemic," *Urban Wire* blog, April 21, 2020. As of December 8, 2020:
https://www.urban.org/urban-wire/we-need-do-more-support-victims-domestic-violence-during-pandemic

ExiT: Executives Transforming Probation and Parole, "COVID-19 Response," webpage, undated. As of December 9, 2020:
https://www.exitprobationparole.org/covid-19-response

Fair, Matt, "Witnesses Not Safe with Livestreamed Trials, Philly DA Says," Law360, September 14, 2020. As of December 9, 2020:
https://www.law360.com/articles/1310031

Farr, Stephanie, "N.J. Has Charged More Than 1,700 for Violating Stay-at-Home Orders but Just a Handful of Citations Have Been Issued in Pa.," *Philadelphia Inquirer*, April 21, 2020.

"FBI Investigating COVID-19 Data Breach in South Dakota," Associated Press, August 21, 2020. As of December 8, 2020:
https://apnews.com/article/cfdfc0b77303664b165faf4866887612

Federal Trade Commission, "FTC COVID-19 and Stimulus Reports: Age and Fraud," Tableau Public, data set, June 11, 2020, updated December 4, 2020a. As of December 7, 2020:
https://public.tableau.com/profile/federal.trade.commission#!/vizhome/COVID-19andStimulusReports/AgeFraud

Federal Trade Commission, "FTC COVID-19 and Stimulus Reports: Map," Tableau Public, data set, June 11, 2020, updated December 4, 2020b. As of December 7, 2020:
https://public.tableau.com/profile/federal.trade.commission#!/vizhome/COVID-19andStimulusReports/Map

Fletcher, Ernie, Dave Johnson, Robin Thompson, and Grace Lamb, *A Holistic Approach to Corrections Early Release COVID-19 Strategies*, London, Ky.: Fletcher Group, May 14, 2020.

Fraternal Order of Police, "COVID-19 Line-of-Duty Deaths," webpage, updated December 7, 2020. As of December 7, 2020:
https://fopcovid19.org/news/covid-19-line-of-duty-deaths/

Frazier, Stephanie, "Sheriff's Office Providing Backup After Entire East Texas Police Department Tests Positive for Virus," *KLTV News*, July 29, 2020. As of December 8, 2020:
https://www.kltv.com/2020/07/29/sheriffs-office-providing-backup-after-entire-east-texas-police-department-tests-positive-virus/

Freudenthal, Bethany, "Most Staff at Sunland Park Police Department in Quarantine, County and State Officials Helping," *Las Cruces Sun News*, June 19, 2020.

Friese, Greg, "Face Masks: Here's What Cops, Firefighters, Medics and COs Have to Say About Use, Policy and Effectiveness," *Police1*, July 31, 2020. As of December 8, 2020:
https://www.police1.com/police-products/wmd-equipment/ppe/articles/face-masks-heres-what-cops-firefighters-medics-and-cos-have-to-say-about-use-policy-and-effectiveness-oy4meLGHK1wzg57H/

FTC—*See* Federal Trade Commission.

Gonzalez, Jennifer M. Reingle, Rebecca Molsberry, Jonathan Maskaly, and Katelyn K. Jetelina, "Trends in Family Violence Are Not Causally Associated with COVID-19 Stay-at-Home Orders: A Commentary on Piquero et al.," *American Journal of Criminal Justice*, October 7, 2020.

Goodison, Sean E., Jeremy D. Barnum, Michael J. D. Vermeer, Dulani Woods, Siara I. Sitar, and Brian A. Jackson, *The Law Enforcement Response to Homelessness: Identifying High-Priority Needs to Improve Law Enforcement Strategies for Addressing Homelessness*, Santa Monica, Calif.: RAND Corporation, RR-A108-6, 2020. As of December 9, 2020:
https://www.rand.org/pubs/research_reports/RRA108-6.html

Goodman, Gail S., Ann E. Tobey, Jennifer M. Batterman-Faunce, Holly K. Orcutt, Sherry Thomas, Cheryl M. Shapiro, and Toby Sachsenmaier, "Face-to-Face Confrontation: Effects of Closed-Circuit Technology on Children's Eyewitness Testimony and Jurors' Decisions," *Law and Human Behavior*, Vol. 22, 1998, pp. 165–203.

Gould, Jens, "State to Scrutinize Local COVID Enforcement as Part of Aid Decisions," *Santa Fe New Mexican*, July 28, 2020.

Gourdet, Camille, Amanda R. Witwer, Lynn Langton, Duren Banks, Michael G. Planty, Dulani Woods, and Brian A. Jackson, *Court Appearances in Criminal Proceedings Through Telepresence: Identifying Research and Practice Needs to Preserve Fairness While Leveraging New Technology*, Santa Monica, Calif.: RAND Corporation, RR-3222-NIJ, 2020. As of January 18, 2021:
https://www.rand.org/pubs/research_reports/RR3222.html

Gover, Angela R., Shannon B. Harper, and Lynn Langton, "Anti-Asian Hate Crime During the COVID-19 Pandemic: Exploring the Reproduction of Inequality," *American Journal of Criminal Justice*, Vol. 45, 2020, pp. 647–667.

Grant, James, and Kierra Sam, "Police, Advocates Say COVID-19 Pandemic Is Fueling Spike in Domestic Violence Cases," 12News, October 23, 2020.

Haffajee, Rebecca L., and Michelle M. Mello, "Thinking Globally, Acting Locally—The U.S. Response to COVID-19," *New England Journal of Medicine*, Vol. 382, No. 22, May 28, 2020.

Hager, Eli, "Your Zoom Interrogation Is About to Start," The Marshall Project, July 20, 2020. As of
December 8, 2020:
https://www.themarshallproject.org/2020/07/20/your-zoom-interrogation-is-about-to-start

Hale, Thomas, Anna Petherick, Toby Phillips, Sam Webster, Beatriz Kira, Noam Angrist, and Lucy Dixon,
"Coronavirus Government Response Tracker," University of Oxford, Blavatnik School of Government
webpage, undated. As of December 7, 2020:
https://www.bsg.ox.ac.uk/research/research-projects/coronavirus-government-response-tracker

Hansen, J. Andrew, and Gabrielle L. Lory, "Rural Victimization and Policing During the COVID-19
Pandemic," *American Journal of Criminal Justice*, Vol. 45, July 17, 2020, pp. 731–742.

Hart, Dionne, "Health Risks of Practicing Correctional Medicine," *AMA Journal of Ethics*, Vol. 21, No. 6,
June 2019, pp. 540–545.

Harvey, Anna, Orion Taylor, and Andrea Wang, *COVID-19, Jails, and Public Safety*, Washington, D.C.:
Council on Criminal Justice, National Commission on COVID-19 and Criminal Justice, updated December
2020.

Heiss, Jasmine, Oliver Hinds, Eital Schattner-Elmaleh, and James Wallace-Lee, *The Scale of the COVID-19–
Related Jail Population Decline*, Brooklyn, N.Y.: Vera Institute of Justice, August 2020.

Holliday, Stephanie Brooks, Sarah B. Hunter, Alex R. Dopp, Margaret Chamberlin, and Martin Y. Iguchi,
*Exploring the Impact of COVID-19 on Social Services for Vulnerable Populations in Los Angeles: Lessons Learned
from Community Providers*, Santa Monica, Calif.: RAND Corporation, RR-A431-1, 2020. As of December 9,
2020:
https://www.rand.org/pubs/research_reports/RRA431-1.html

Hollywood, John S., Dulani Woods, Andrew Lauland, Sean E. Goodison, Thomas J. Wilson, and Brian A.
Jackson, *Using Future Broadband Communications Technologies to Strengthen Law Enforcement*, Santa Monica,
Calif.: RAND Corporation, RR-1462-NIJ, 2016. As of December 9, 2020:
https://www.rand.org/pubs/research_reports/RR1462.html

Houston-Kolnik, Jaclyn, Hannah Feeney, and Rebecca Pfeffer, *Impact of COVID-19 on North Carolina's
Victim Service Providers*, Washington, D.C.: RTI International, 2020.

"How COVID-19 Could Impact the Design of Detention and Correctional Facilities," HOK.com, April 30,
2020. As of December 9, 2020:
https://www.hok.com/news/2020-04/
how-covid-19-could-impact-the-design-of-detention-and-correctional-facilities/

Hrdinova, Jana, Douglas A. Berman, Mark E. Pauley, and Dexter Ridgway, *Documenting the Challenges (and
Documents) as Ohio Courts Respond to COVID-19*, Columbus, Ohio: Ohio State University, Moritz College of
Law, Drug Enforcement and Policy Center, 2020.

IACP—*See* International Association of Chiefs of Police.

Ingraham, Christopher, "COVID-19 Has Killed More Police Officers This Year Than All Other Causes
Combined, Data Shows," *Washington Post*, September 2, 2020.

International Association of Chiefs of Police, "Organizational Readiness: Ensuring Your Agency Is Prepared
for COVID-19," webpage, March 26, 2020a. As of December 8, 2020:
https://www.theiacp.org/resources/document/
organizational-readiness-ensuring-your-agency-is-prepared-for-covid-19

International Association of Chiefs of Police, "COVID-19 Public Health Protections," webpage, April 1,
2020b. As of December 8, 2020:
https://www.theiacp.org/resources/document/covid-19-public-health-protections

International Association of Chiefs of Police, "Law Enforcement Officer Exposure to COVID-19," webpage,
April 15, 2020c. As of December 8, 2020:
https://www.theiacp.org/resources/document/law-enforcement-officer-exposure-to-covid-19

International Association of Chiefs of Police, "Supporting Victims of Domestic Violence During the COVID-19 Pandemic," webpage, May 18, 2020d. As of December 9, 2020:
https://www.theiacp.org/resources/document/
supporting-victims-of-domestic-violence-during-the-covid-19-pandemic

Jackson, Angie, "COVID-19 Cases Among Marquette Prison Staff Double in One Day," *Detroit Free Press*, October 15, 2020.

Jackson, Brian A., D. J. Peterson, James T. Bartis, Tom LaTourrette, Irene T. Brahmakulam, Ari Houser, and Jerry M. Sollinger, *Protecting Emergency Responders: Lessons Learned from Terrorist Attacks*, Santa Monica, Calif.: RAND Corporation, CF-176-OSTP, 2002. As of December 8, 2020:
https://www.rand.org/pubs/conf_proceedings/CF176.html

Jackson, Brian A., Ashley L. Rhoades, Jordan R. Reimer, Natasha Lander, Katherine Costello, and Sina Beaghley, *Practical Terrorism Prevention: Reexamining U.S. National Approaches to Addressing the Threat of Ideologically Motivated Violence*, Homeland Security Operational Analysis Center operated by the RAND Corporation, RR-2647-DHS, 2019. As of December 8, 2020:
https://www.rand.org/pubs/research_reports/RR2647.html

Jackson, Brian A., Joe Russo, John S. Hollywood, Dulani Woods, Richard Silberglitt, George B. Drake, John S. Shaffer, Mikhail Zaydman, and Brian G. Chow, *Fostering Innovation in Community and Institutional Corrections: Identifying High-Priority Technology and Other Needs for the U.S. Corrections Sector*, Santa Monica, Calif.: RAND Corporation, RR-820-NIJ, 2015. As of December 9, 2020:
https://www.rand.org/pubs/research_reports/RR820.html

Jackson, Brian A., Michael J. D. Vermeer, Kristin J. Leuschner, Dulani Woods, John S. Hollywood, Duren Banks, Sean E. Goodison, Joe Russo, and Shoshana R. Shelton, *Fostering Innovation Across the U.S. Criminal Justice System: Identifying Opportunities to Improve Effectiveness, Efficiency, and Fairness*, Santa Monica, Calif.: RAND Corporation, RR-4242-NIJ, 2020. As of December 9, 2020:
https://www.rand.org/pubs/research_reports/RR4242.html

Jackson, Donny, "COVID-19 Could Have Lasting Impacts on 911 Practices, Speakers Say," IWCE's Urgent Communications, April 6, 2020. As of December 8, 2020:
https://urgentcomm.com/2020/04/06/covid-19-could-have-lasting-impacts-on-911-practices-speakers-say/

Jennings, Wesley G., and Nicholas M. Perez, "The Immediate Impact of COVID-19 on Law Enforcement in the United States," *American Journal of Criminal Justice*, Vol. 45, 2020, pp. 690–701.

Johns Hopkins University School of Medicine, "COVID-19 United States Cases by County," data set, updated December 6, 2020. As of December 7, 2020:
https://coronavirus.jhu.edu/us-map

Johnson, Jeremiah P., "Police Response to COVID-19: Innovation and Diffusion by a Policy Community of Practitioner-Scholars," *Police Forum*, Vol. 29, No. 1, April 2020, pp. 48–53.

Jones, Van, "Atlanta Police Shooting Is About Probation, not Just Police," CNN, June 18, 2020.

Jordan, Alison O., and Melvin H. Wilson, *Addressing COVID-19 and Correctional Facilities: A Social Work Imperative*, Washington, D.C.: National Association of Social Workers, Social Justice Brief, June 2020.

Jouvenal, Justin, and Michael Brice-Saddler, "Social Distancing Enforcement Is Ramping Up. So Is Concern That Black and Latino Residents May Face Harsher Treatment," *Washington Post*, May 10, 2020.

Katz, Josh, Abby Goodnough, and Margot Sanger-Katz, "In Shadow of Pandemic, U.S. Drug Overdose Deaths Resurge to Record," *New York Times*, July 15, 2020.

Keeshan, Charles, "Court: Police Have No Right to COVID-19 Patients' Names, Addresses," *Daily Herald*, June 28, 2020.

Kindy, Kimberly, "Inside the Deadliest Federal Prison, the Seeping Coronavirus Creates Fear and Danger," *Washington Post*, April 10, 2020.

Konda, Srinivas, Hope Tiesman, Audrey Reichard, and Dan Hartley, "U.S. Correctional Officers Killed or Injured on the Job," *Corrections Today*, Vol. 75, No. 5, November/December 2013, pp. 122–123.

Krafka, Carol L., and Molly Johnson, *Electronic Media Coverage of Federal Civil Proceedings: An Evaluation of the Pilot Program in Six District Courts and Two Courts of Appeals*, Washington, D.C.: Federal Judicial Center, 1994

Kramer, Abigail, "Out of Jail and Homeless: City Struggles to Stop Covid-19's Spread," The New School, Center for New York City Affairs, May 5, 2020. As of December 9, 2020:
http://www.centernyc.org/reports-briefs/2020/5/5/
out-of-jail-and-homeless-city-struggles-to-stop-covid-19s-spread

Kramer, Peter D., "Domestic-Abuse Victims Can Now Text, Chat to Be Heard by Counselors, Not Their Abusers," lohud.com, August 13, 2020. As of December 9, 2020:
https://www.lohud.com/story/news/local/rockland/new-city/2020/08/13/
center-for-safety-change-coronavirus/3353100001/

Krawczyk, Noa, Michael I. Fingerhood, and Deborah Agus, "Lessons from COVID 19: Are We Finally Ready to Make Opioid Treatment Accessible?" *Journal of Substance Abuse Treatment*, Vol. 117, 2020.

Kruesi, Kimberlee, "COVID-19 Data Sharing with Law Enforcement Sparks Concern," Associated Press, May 19, 2020.

Kust, James, "These Wisconsin Sheriffs Say They Won't Enforce Gov. Tony Evers' Statewide Mask Order," *TMJ 4 News*, July 31, 2020. As of December 8, 2020:
https://www.tmj4.com/news/coronavirus/these-wisconsin-sheriffs-say-they-wont-enforce-gov-ton
y-evers-statewide-mask-order

Kuznitz, Alison, "Mask Ambassadors Will Soon Help Charlotte Area Residents Follow COVID-19 Rules," WBTV, August 6, 2020. As of December 8, 2020:
https://www.wbtv.com/2020/08/06/mask-ambassadors-will-soon-help-charlotte-area-residents-fol
low-covid-rules/

Lageson, Sarah Esther, "The Perils of 'Zoom Justice,'" *The Crime Report*, September 1, 2020.

Lantz, Brendan, and Marin R. Wenger, *Bias and Hate Crime Victimization During the COVID-19 Pandemic*, Tallahassee, Fla.: Florida State University Center for Criminology and Public Policy Research, May 2020.

Lattimore, Pamela K., James Trudeau, K. Jack Riley, Jordan Leiter, and Steven Edwards, *Homicide in Eight U.S. Cities: Trends, Context, and Policy Implications—An Intramural Research Project*, Washington, D.C.: National Institute of Justice, December 1997.

"Law Enforcement Agencies Refuse to Enforce Mask Orders," *Herald-Star*, July 27, 2020. As of December 8, 2020:
https://www.heraldstaronline.com/news/local-news/2020/07/
law-enforcement-agencies-refuse-to-enforce-mask-orders/

"Law Enforcement Officer Tests Positive for COVID-19, Exposes 41 APD Employees," *KOB 4 News*, April 19, 2020. As of December 8, 2020:
https://www.kob.com/albuquerque-news/
apd-officer-tests-positive-for-covid-19-exposes-41-other-employees-/5704033/

Lee, David, "Texas Judge Holds First Virtual Jury Trial in Criminal Case," Courthouse News Service, August 11, 2020. As of December 8, 2020:
https://www.courthousenews.com/texas-judge-holds-first-virtual-jury-trial-in-criminal-case/

"Legislature Approves Authority for Virginia DOC to Release Some Offenders Early," *Independent Messenger*, April 28, 2020. As of December 9, 2020:
https://www.emporiaindependentmessenger.com/news/article_90e181f6-88b4-11ea-b1d9-6bddf2e14cb0.html

Lehmann, Christine, "COVID Biggest Cause of Police Deaths This Year," WebMD, October 12, 2020. As of December 8, 2020:
https://www.webmd.com/lung/news/20201012/police-at-high-risk-for-covid-19-race-to-adapt

LeMaster, C. J., "As COVID-19 Forces Closure of Edwards Police Dept., 3OYS Explores Other Agencies' Pandemic Policies," *WLBT News*, June 19, 2020. As of December 8, 2020:
https://www.wlbt.com/2020/06/19/
covid-forces-closure-edwards-police-dept-oys-explores-other-agencies-pandemic-policies/

Leslie, Emily, and Riley Wilson, "Sheltering in Place and Domestic Violence: Evidence from Calls for Service During COVID-19," *Journal of Public Economics*, Vol. 189, September 2020.

"Limited Visits to Begin at Probation, Parole Offices in July," WTOK, June 30, 2020. As of December 9, 2020:
https://www.wtok.com/2020/06/30/limited-visits-to-begin-at-probation-parole-offices-in-july/

Lum, Cynthia, Carl Maupin, and Megan Stoltz, *The Impact of COVID-19 on Law Enforcement Agencies (Wave 1)*, Washington, D.C.: International Association of Chiefs of Police and the Center for Evidence-Based Crime Policy at George Mason University, April 13, 2020a.

Lum, Cynthia, Carl Maupin, and Megan Stoltz, *The Impact of COVID-19 on Law Enforcement Agencies (Wave 2)*, Washington, D.C.: International Association of Chiefs of Police and the Center for Evidence-Based Crime Policy at George Mason University, June 25, 2020b.

Marcum, Catherine D., "American Corrections System Response to COVID-19: An Examination of the Procedures and Policies Used in Spring 2020," *American Journal of Criminal Justice*, Vol. 45, 2020, pp. 759–768.

The Marshall Project, "How Prisons in Each State Are Restricting Visits Due to Coronavirus," webpage, March 17, 2020, updated November 25, 2020a. As of December 9, 2020:
https://www.themarshallproject.org/2020/03/17/tracking-prisons-response-to-coronavirus

The Marshall Project, "A State-by-State Look at Coronavirus in Prisons," webpage, updated December 2020b. As of December 7, 2020:
https://www.themarshallproject.org/2020/05/01/a-state-by-state-look-at-coronavirus-in-prisons

Mascia, Jennifer, "Pushed Out of Hospitals by COVID, Anti-Violence Programs Try to Adapt," The Trace, October 5, 2020. As of December 8, 2020:
https://www.thetrace.org/2020/10/coronavirus-pandemic-gun-violence-shootings-up-louisville/

McGuinness, Dylan, "Houston to Spend $6.2M in COVID-19 Funds to Expand HPD Domestic Abuse Teams," *Houston Chronicle*, November 9, 2020.

McNamara, Maura, "Correctional System Recommendations for Responding to COVID-19: A Toolkit," New York: New York City Department of Corrections, 2020.

Meagher, Tom, and Damini Sharma, "COVID Tracking in Prisons," GitHub webpage, undated. As of November 1, 2020:
https://github.com/themarshallproject/COVID_prison_data

Mellis, Alexandra M., Marc N. Potenza, and Jessica N. Hulsey, "COVID-19-Related Treatment Service Disruptions Among People with Single- and Polysubstance Use Concerns," *Journal of Substance Abuse Treatment*, Vol. 121, February 2021.

Mello, Michelle M., Jeremy A. Greene, and Joshua M. Sharfstein, "Attacks on Public Health Officials During COVID-19," *JAMA*, Vol. 324, No. 8, 2020, pp. 741–742.

Michigan Justice for All Task Force, "Chief Justice Tells Congress of Michigan's Virtual Court Successes," No. 3, September 2020.

Mohler, George, Andrea L. Bertozzi, Jeremy Carter, Martin B. Short, Daniel Sledge, George E. Tita, Craig D. Uchida, and P. Jeffrey Brantingham, "Impact of Social Distancing During COVID-19 Pandemic on Crime in Los Angeles and Indianapolis," *Journal of Criminal Justice*, Vol. 68, May–June 2020.

Mohs, Marielle, "Coronavirus in MN: Gov. Walz Signs Executive Order Giving COVID Case Data to 911 Dispatch Centers," *WCCO CBS Minnesota*, April 11, 2020. As of January 18, 2021:
https://minnesota.cbslocal.com/2020/04/11/
coronavirus-in-mn-gov-walz-signs-executive-order-giving-covid-case-data-to-911-dispatch-centers/

Mojica, Adrian, "Police: Man Who Tested Positive for COVID-19 Charged with Escape for Leaving Quarantine," *WZTV Nashville*, May 10, 2020. As of December 8, 2020:
https://abc3340.com/news/nation-world/
police-man-who-tested-positive-for-covid-19-charged-with-escape-for-leaving-quarantine

Monares, Freddy, "Bozeman Attorneys Quarantining After Defendant Tests Positive," *Bozeman Daily Chronicle*, July 10, 2020. As of December 8, 2020:
https://www.bozemandailychronicle.com/coronavirus/
bozeman-attorneys-quarantining-after-defendant-tests-positive/
article_13f77855-50f1-5d84-95f2-1844097fb96c.html

Montgomery, David, "COVID-19 Curbs Community Policing at a Time of Diminishing Trust," *PEW Stateline* blog, October 1, 2020. As of December 8, 2020:
https://www.pewtrusts.org/en/research-and-analysis/blogs/stateline/2020/10/01/
covid-19-curbs-community-policing-at-a-time-of-diminishing-trust

Montoya-Barthelemy, Andre G., Charles D. Lee, Dave R. Cundiff, and Eric B. Smith, "COVID-19 and the Correctional Environment: The American Prison as a Focal Point for Public Health," *American Journal of Preventive Medicine*, Vol. 58, No. 6, June 2020, pp. 888–891.

National Association of Counties, "Community Supervision During COVID-19: Implications for Change," webinar, August 5, 2020. As of December 9, 2020:
https://www.naco.org/events/community-supervision-during-covid-19-implications-change

National Center for State Courts, "Coronavirus and the Courts," webpage, undated a. As of December 8, 2020:
https://www.ncsc.org/newsroom/public-health-emergency

National Center for State Courts, "The Evolving Nature of 'Essential Services' and 'Urgent Matters,'" webpage, undated b. As of December 8, 2020:
https://www.ncsc.org/newsroom/public-health-emergency/newsletters/essential-services

National Center for State Courts, "New Data Shed Light on Pandemic-Related Backlogs," webpage, undated c. As of January 18, 2021:
https://www.ncsc.org/newsroom/at-the-center/2020/new-data-shed-light-on-pandemic-related-backlogs

National Center for State Courts, *Preparing for a Pandemic: An Emergency Response Benchbook and Operational Guidebook for State Court Judges and Administrators*, Williamsburg, Va., 2016.

National Commission on Correctional Health Care, "COVID-19 Weekly Roundtable for Law Enforcement and Correctional Health Care Webinar," blog post, March 20, 2020, updated May 15, 2020. As of December 9, 2020:
https://www.ncchc.org/blog/
covid-19-weekly-roundtable-for-law-enforcement-correctional-health-care-webinar

National Commission on COVID-19 and Criminal Justice, *Recommendations for Response and Future Readiness: Interim Commission Report*, Washington, D.C.: Council on Criminal Justice, October 2020a.

National Commission on COVID-19 and Criminal Justice, *Experience to Action: Reshaping Criminal Justice After COVID-19*, Washington, D.C.: Council on Criminal Justice, December 2020b.

National Conference of State Legislatures, "Criminal Justice System Responses to COVID-19," webpage, November 16, 2020. As of December 8, 2020:
https://www.ncsl.org/research/civil-and-criminal-justice/criminal-justice-and-covid-19.aspx

National Council on Crime and Delinquency, *Community Supervision COVID-19 Guidance and Tips*, Washington, D.C., 2020.

National Emergency Number Association, *How 9-1-1 Is Changing in a COVID-19 World: 9-1-1 and COVID-19 Report Series*, Alexandria, Va., May 8, 2020.

National Law Enforcement Officers Memorial Fund, "COVID-19 Related Law Enforcement Fatalities," webpage, undated. As of December 7, 2020:
https://nleomf.org/covid-19-related-law-enforcement-fatalities

National Law Enforcement Officers Memorial Fund, "Officer Deaths by Year: Year-by-Year Breakdown of Law Enforcement Deaths Throughout U.S. History," webpage, September 29, 2020. As of December 7, 2020:
https://nleomf.org/facts-figures/officer-deaths-by-year

National Network to End Domestic Violence, "Resources on the Response to the Coronavirus (COVID-19)," webpage, March 12, 2020, updated November 20, 2020. As of December 9, 2020:
https://nnedv.org/latest_update/resources-response-coronavirus-covid-19/

National Network to End Domestic Violence, Technology Safety, "Response to the COVID-19 Pandemic," webpage, undated. As of December 9, 2020:
https://www.techsafety.org/covid19

National Partnership for Pretrial Justice, "COVID-19 Sparks 'Unprecedented' Pretrial Reforms, Survey Shows," webpage, undated. As of December 8, 2020:
http://www.pretrialpartnership.org/news/covid-19-sparks-unprecedented-pretrial-reforms-survey-shows/

The National Police Foundation, "Coronavirus (COVID-19): Resources for Law Enforcement—COVID-19 Law Enforcement Impact Dashboard (Data from Impact Survey 2 & 3)," webpage, undated. As of December 8, 2020:
https://www.policefoundation.org/covid-19

Needles, Zack, "Law.com Trendspotter: Virtual Civil Jury Trials Are Definitely Divisive—and Likely Inevitable," *Law.com*, September 13, 2020. As of December 8, 2020:
https://www.law.com/2020/09/13/law-com-trendspotter-virtual-jury-trials-remain-divisi
ve-but-are-they-inevitable/

Neff, Joseph, and Beth Schwartzapfel, "Infected, Incarcerated—and Coming to an ICU Near You?" The Marshall Project, April 16, 2020. As of December 9, 2020:
https://www.themarshallproject.org/2020/04/16/infected-incarcerated-and-coming-to-an-icu-near-you

Nelson, Blake, "More Law Enforcement Officers Calling Helplines as Protests and Coronavirus Pandemic Add Stress to Stressful Job," Officer.com, September 10, 2020.

Nelson, Bryn, and David B. Kaminsky, "A COVID-19 Crisis in U.S. Jails and Prisons," *Cancer Cytopathology*, Vol. 128, No. 8, August 2020, pp. 513–514.

Neuman, Scott, "Florida Sheriff Orders Deputies and Staff Not to Wear Face Masks," NPR, August 12, 2020. As of December 7, 2020:
https://www.npr.org/sections/coronavirus-live-updates/2020/08/12/901756223/
florida-sheriff-orders-deputies-and-staff-not-to-wear-face-masks

Nevin, John, "Michigan's Justice System Reaches 1 Million Hours of Zoom Hearings," Lansing, Mich.: Michigan Courts News Release, September 17, 2020.

New Jersey State Bar Association, *Report of the Committee on the Resumption of Jury Trials of the New Jersey State Bar Association Pandemic Task Force: Part Two*, New Brunswick, N.J., September 2, 2020a.

New Jersey State Bar Association, *Notice to the Bar and Public: COVID-19—Update on Court Operations During "Phase 2.5" of the Supreme Court's Post-Pandemic Plan*, New Brunswick, N.J., September 22, 2020b.

New Yorkers for Responsible Lending, "Implementation of Virtual Court Appearances in Nonessential Matters," letter to Judge Lawrence K. Marks, New York, April 15, 2020.

Newman, Katelyn, "For Prisoners Released Due to COVID-19, a Different World Awaits," *U.S. News and World Report*, April 15, 2020. As of December 9, 2020:
https://www.usnews.com/news/healthiest-communities/articles/2020-04-15/
prisoners-released-due-to-coronavirus-enter-a-different-world

Novisky, Meghan A., Chelsey S. Narvey, and Daniel C. Semenza, "Institutional Responses to the COVID-19 Pandemic in American Prisons," *Victims and Offenders*, Vol. 15, Nos. 7–8, 2020, pp. 1244–1261.

O'Donnell, Brenna, "COVID-19 and Missing & Exploited Children," *National Center for Missing and Exploited Children* blog, July 16, 2020, updated October 20, 2020. As of December 7, 2020:
https://www.missingkids.org/blog/2020/covid-19-and-missing-and-exploited-children

Oehme, Karen, Kelly O'Rourke, and Lyndi Bradley, "Online Virtual Supervised Visitation During the COVID-19 Pandemic: One State's Experience," *Family Court Review*, Vol. 59, 2021.

Oesterle, Tyler S., Bhanuprakash Kolla, Cameron J. Risma, Scott A. Breitinger, Daniela B. Rakocevic, Larissa L. Loukianova, Daniel K. Hall-Flavin, Melanie T. Gentry, Teresa A. Rummans, Mohit Chauhan, and Mark S. Gold, "Substance Use Disorders and Telehealth in the COVID-19 Pandemic Era: A New Outlook," *Mayo Clinic Proceedings*, Vol. 95, No. 12, December 2020, pp. 2709–2718.

Office of the Mayor, "Mayor London Breed and Adult Probation Department Announce Supportive Housing Program for People in the Criminal Justice System During COVID-19," San Francisco, Calif., news release, May 7, 2020. As of December 9, 2020:
https://sfmayor.org/article/
mayor-london-breed-and-adult-probation-department-announce-supportive-housing-program-people

Office of Victim Advocate, "COVID-19 Guidance," webpage, undated. As of December 8, 2020:
https://www.ova.pa.gov/Resources/COVID-19%20Guidance/Pages/default.aspx

Officer Down Memorial Page, "Line of Duty Deaths by State," webpage, undated. As of December 1, 2020:
https://www.odmp.org/search/browse

Park, Catherine, "1 in 4 Young Asian Americans Experienced Anti-Asian Hate Amid COVID-19," *FOX 5 News*, October 5, 2020. As of December 7, 2020:
https://www.fox5dc.com/news/1-in-4-young-asian-americans-experienced-anti-asian-hate-amid-covid-19

Payne, Brian K., "Criminals Work from Home During Pandemics Too: A Public Health Approach to Respond to Fraud and Crimes Against Those 50 and Above," *American Journal of Criminal Justice*, Vol. 45, 2020, pp. 563–577.

PERF—*See* Police Executive Research Forum.

Phillips, Kristine, "Police Agencies Are Using Drones to Enforce Stay-at-Home Orders, Raising Concerns Among Civil Rights Groups," *USA Today*, May 3, 2020.

Police Executive Research Forum, "Changes in Domestic Violence Calls, and the Police Response, in the COVID Environment," *PERF Daily COVID-19 Report*, April 3, 2020a. As of December 7, 2020:
https://perf.memberclicks.net/covidapril3

Police Executive Research Forum, "How Has the COVID-19 Pandemic Impacted Crime Rates?" *PERF Daily COVID-19 Report*, May 12, 2020b. As of December 7, 2020:
https://perf.memberclicks.net/covidmay12

Police Executive Research Forum, *PERF Daily COVID-19 Report*, May 21, 2020c. As of December 8, 2020:
https://perf.memberclicks.net/covidmay21

Police Executive Research Forum, *PERF Daily COVID-19 Report*, August 3, 2020d. As of December 8, 2020:
https://www.policeforum.org/covidaugust3

Police Executive Research Forum, *PERF Daily COVID-19 Report*, September 16, 2020e. As of December 7, 2020:
https://perf.memberclicks.net/covidsep16

Police Executive Research Forum, "PERF Analysis Reveals a Spike in Some Violent Crimes This Year," *PERF Critical Issues*, webpage, November 18, 2020f. As of December 7, 2020:
https://perf.memberclicks.net/criticalissuesnov18

Pollard, Michael S., Joan S. Tucker, and Harold D. Green, Jr., "Changes in Adult Alcohol Use and Consequences During the COVID-19 Pandemic in the U.S.," *JAMA Network Open*, Vol. 3, No. 9, 2020.

Posick, Chad, April A. Schueths, Cary Christian, Jonathan A. Grubb, and Suzanne E. Christian, "Child Victim Services in the Time of COVID-19: New Challenges and Innovative Solutions," *American Journal of Criminal Justice*, Vol. 45, 2020, pp. 680–689.

Prison Policy Initiative, "Responses to the COVID-19 Pandemic," webpage, June 2020. As of December 8, 2020:
https://www.prisonpolicy.org/virus/virusresponse.html

Prost, Stephanie Grace, Meghan A. Novisky, Leah Rorvig, Nick Zaller, and Brie Williams, "Prisons and COVID-19: A Desperate Call for Gerontological Expertise in Correctional Health Care," *Gerontologist*, Vol. 61, No. 1, February 2021, pp. 3–7.

Puglisi, Lisa B., Giovanni S. P. Malloy, Tyler D. Harvey, Margaret L. Brandeau, and Emily A. Wang, "Estimation of COVID-19 Basic Reproduction Ratio in a Large Urban Jail in the United States," *Annals of Epidemiology*, Vol. 53, January 2021, pp. 103–105.

Rainey, Rebecca, and Maya King, "Defund the Police? It's Already Happening Thanks to the COVID-19 Budget Crunch," *Politico*, August 15, 2020. As of December 8, 2020:
https://www.politico.com/news/2020/08/15/defund-the-police-coronavirus-budget-395665

Reed, Allie, and Madison Alder, "Virtual Hearings Put Children, Abuse Victims at Ease in Court," *Bloomberg Law*, July 23, 2020. As of December 8, 2020:
https://news.bloomberglaw.com/us-law-week/virtual-hearings-put-children-abuse-victims-at-ease-in-court

Reverby, Susan M., "Can There Be Acceptable Prison Health Care? Looking Back on the 1970s," *Public Health Reports*, Vol. 134, No. 1, 2019, pp. 89–93.

Richards, Edward P., "A Historical Review of the State Police Powers and Their Relevance to the COVID-19 Pandemic of 2020," *Journal of National Security Law & Policy*, Vol. 11, No. 1, October 19, 2020, pp. 83–105.

Richards, Edward P., Katherine C. Rathbun, Corina Solé Brito, and Andrea Luna, *The Role of Law Enforcement in Public Health Emergencies: Special Considerations for an All-Hazards Approach*, Washington, D.C.: U.S. Department of Justice, Bureau of Justice Assistance and Police Executive Research Forum, September 2006.

Rihl, Juliette, "'It Almost Broke Me': How the Pandemic Strains Mental Health at Pittsburgh's Jail," *The Crime Report*, September 16, 2020.

Romine, Taylor, "NYPD Creates Asian Hate Crime Task Force After Spike in Anti-Asian Attacks During COVID-19 Pandemic," CNN, August 18, 2020.

Rosenfeld, Richard, and Ernesto Lopez, *Pandemic, Social Unrest, and Crime in U.S. Cities*, Washington, D.C.: Council on Criminal Justice, National Commission on COVID-19 and Criminal Justice, July 2020.

Rovner, Josh, "COVID-19 in Juvenile Facilities," The Sentencing Project, webpage, December 4, 2020. As of December 9, 2020:
https://www.sentencingproject.org/publications/covid-19-in-juvenile-facilities/

Rubin, Rita, "The Challenge of Preventing COVID-19 Spread in Correctional Facilities," *JAMA*, Vol. 323, No. 18, 2020, pp. 1760–1761.

Russo, Joe, Michael J. D. Vermeer, Dulani Woods, and Brian A. Jackson, *Data-Informed Jails: Challenges and Opportunities*, Santa Monica, Calif.: RAND Corporation, RR-A108-1, 2020a. As of December 9, 2020:
https://www.rand.org/pubs/research_reports/RRA108-1.html

Russo, Joe, Michael J. D. Vermeer, Dulani Woods, and Brian A. Jackson, *Risk and Needs Assessments in Prisons: Identifying High-Priority Needs for Using Evidence-Based Practices*, Santa Monica, Calif.: RAND Corporation, RR-A108-5, 2020b. As of December 9, 2020:
https://www.rand.org/pubs/research_reports/RRA108-5.html

Russo, Joe, Dulani Woods, George B. Drake, and Brian A. Jackson, *Building a High-Quality Correctional Workforce: Identifying Challenges and Needs*, Santa Monica, Calif.: RAND Corporation, RR-2386-NIJ, 2018. As of December 10, 2020:
https://www.rand.org/pubs/research_reports/RR2386.html

Russo, Joe, Dulani Woods, George B. Drake, and Brian A. Jackson, *Leveraging Technology to Enhance Community Supervision: Identifying Needs to Address Current and Emerging Concerns*, Santa Monica, Calif.: RAND Corporation, RR-3213-NIJ, 2019. As of December 9, 2020:
https://www.rand.org/pubs/research_reports/RR3213.html

Russo, Joe, Dulani Woods, John S. Shaffer, and Brian A. Jackson, *Caring for Those in Custody: Identifying High-Priority Needs to Reduce Mortality in Correctional Facilities*, Santa Monica, Calif.: RAND Corporation, RR-1967-NIJ, 2017. As of December 9, 2020:
https://www.rand.org/pubs/research_reports/RR1967.html

Saloner, Brendan, Kalind Parish, Julie A. Ward, Grace DiLaura, and Sharon Dolovich, "COVID-19 Cases and Deaths in Federal and State Prisons," *JAMA*, Vol. 324, No. 6, 2020, pp. 602–603.

Scannell, Kara, "Nowhere to Go: Some Inmates Freed Because of Coronavirus Are 'Scared to Leave,'" CNN, April 4, 2020.

Schmidt, Samantha, "The Centers Helping Child Abuse Victims Have Seen 40,000 Fewer Kids Amid the Pandemic," *Washington Post*, August 19, 2020.

Schnepel, Kevin T., *COVID-19 in U.S. State and Federal Prisons*, Washington, D.C.: Council on Criminal Justice, National Commission on COVID-19 and Criminal Justice, September 2020.

Schuchat, Anne, "Public Health Response to the Initiation and Spread of Pandemic COVID-19 in the United States, February 24–April 21, 2020," *Morbidity and Mortality Weekly Report*, Vol. 69, No. 18, May 8, 2020, pp. 551–556.

Schwartzapfel, Beth, "Probation and Parole Officers Are Rethinking Their Rules as Coronavirus Spreads," The Marshall Project, April 3, 2020a. As of December 9, 2020:
https://www.themarshallproject.org/2020/04/03/
probation-and-parole-officers-are-rethinking-their-rules-as-coronavirus-spreads

Schwartzapfel, Beth, "COVID-19 Has Trapped Thousands of Parolees in Prison," *Slate*, May 7, 2020b. As of December 9, 2020:
https://slate.com/news-and-politics/2020/05/covid-19-probation-parole-limbo.html

Servick, Kelly, "Pandemic Inspires New Push to Shrink Jails and Prisons," *Science*, September 17, 2020. As of December 9, 2020:
https://www.sciencemag.org/news/2020/09/pandemic-inspires-new-push-shrink-jails-and-prisons

Shapiro, Joseph, "As COVID-19 Spreads in Prisons, Lockdowns Spark Fear of More Solitary Confinement," NPR, June 15, 2020. As of January 8, 2021:
https://www.npr.org/2020/06/15/877457603/as-covid-spreads-in-u-s-prisons-lockdowns-spark-fear-of-more
-solitary-confinemen

Shjarback, John, and Obed Magny, *Policing During the Pandemic: California Officers' Experiences*, Sacramento, Calif., June 2020.

Simmons, Tommy, "'A Little More Creative': How the Coronavirus Has Changed Probation, Parole in Idaho," KTVB7, May 3, 2020. As of December 9, 2020:
https://www.ktvb.com/article/news/crime/
a-little-more-creative-how-covid-19-has-changed-probation-parole-in-idaho/
277-ad46e588-d77a-4da9-aba2-1ee3b86a06fa

Slayton, David, *Jury Trials During the COVID-19 Pandemic: Observations and Recommendations*, Austin, Tex.: Office of Court Administration, August 28, 2020.

Smith, Allan, "Police Departments Face One-Two Punch: Defund Protests and Coronavirus," *NBC News*, June 28, 2020. As of December 8, 2020:
https://www.nbcnews.com/politics/politics-news/
police-departments-face-one-two-punch-defund-protests-coronavirus-n1232182

Smith, Carl, "All Rise: Virtual Court Is Now in Session," *Governing.com*, September 16, 2020. As of December 8, 2020:
https://www.governing.com/now/All-Rise-Virtual-Court-Is-Now-in-Session.html

Sorenson, Susan B., Laura Sinko, and Richard A. Berk, "The Endemic Amid the Pandemic: Seeking Help for Violence Against Women in the Initial Phases of COVID-19," fact sheet, Philadelphia, Pa.: Ortner Center on Violence & Abuse, University of Pennsylvania, undated. As of December 7, 2020:
https://upenn.app.box.com/s/pjz63g3ud4zrgnwekz5xavi8pdte3q1u?mc_cid=eec71cafaa&mc_eid=997adef761

Sourdin, Tania, Bin Li, and Donna Marie McNamara, "Court Innovations and Access to Justice in Times of Crisis," *Health Policy and Technology*, Vol. 9, No. 4, December 2020, pp. 447–453.

Stinelli, Mick, "Report Recommends Reducing Incarceration for Substance Use Violations," *Pittsburgh Post-Gazette*, October 18, 2020.

Stobbe, Mike, and Adrian Sainz, "Pandemic Could Be Contributing to Spike in U.S. Overdose Deaths," *Washington Post*, November 10, 2020.

Storm, Jennifer, Joyce Lukima, Julie Bancroft, Meg Garvin, Diane Menio, Natasha McGlynn, Angelis Padilla, Karen C. Buck, Laura Vega, Karen Hinkle, and Carline Menapace, "Victim Advocates Request Changes to Procedures in Philadelphia Courts," Philadelphia, Pa.: Office of Victim Advocate, September 15, 2020.

Strom, Kevin J., Andre Richards, and Renée J. Mitchell, *Defund the Police? How to Chart a Path Forward with Evidence and Data*, Washington, D.C.: RTI International, July 22, 2020.

Supreme Court of Arizona Plan B Workgroup, "Minimizing the Digital Divide During Jury Selection," memorandum, July 30, 2020a.

Supreme Court of Arizona Plan B Workgroup, "Guidelines for Arizona Courts: Court Emergency Needs Checklist to Work Remotely," memorandum, September 1, 2020b.

Supreme Court of the State of Arizona, *COVID-19 Continuity of Court Operations During a Public Health Emergency Workgroup Best Practice Recommendations*, Phoenix, Ariz., May 1, 2020.

Swan, Holly, Walter Campbell, and Nathan Lowe, *Pandemic Preparedness and Response Among Community Supervision Agencies: The Importance of Partnerships for Future Planning*, Rockville, Md.: Abt Associates, 2020.

Tate, Courtney, "Amarillo Probation Officers Making Adjustments to Supervise Offenders Through COVID-19 Pandemic," *KFDA News*, April 29, 2020. As of December 9, 2020:
https://www.newschannel10.com/2020/04/29/amarillo-probation-officers-making-adjustments-supervise-offenders-through-covid-pandemic/

Taxman, Faye S., and Steven Belenko, *Implementing Evidence-Based Practices in Community Corrections and Addiction Treatment*, New York: Springer, 2012.

Tessler, Hannah, Meera Choi, and Grace Kao, "The Anxiety of Being Asian American: Hate Crimes and Negative Biases During the COVID-19 Pandemic," *American Journal of Criminal Justice*, Vol. 45, 2020, pp. 636–646.

UCLA—*See* University of California, Los Angeles.

United States Commission on Civil Rights, "The U.S. Commission on Civil Rights Calls for Adequate Healthcare in Prisons and Detention Centers During the COVID-19 Outbreak," press release, Washington, D.C., March 20, 2020.

United States Courts, "Officers Innovate in the Field During COVID-19 Crisis," news release, June 11, 2020a. As of December 9, 2020:
https://www.uscourts.gov/news/2020/06/11/officers-innovate-field-during-covid-19-crisis

United States Courts, "As Courts Restore Operations, COVID-19 Creates a New Normal," news release, August 20, 2020b. As of December 9, 2020:
https://www.uscourts.gov/news/2020/08/20/courts-restore-operations-covid-19-creates-new-normal

University of California, Los Angeles, "UCLA Law: COVID-19 Behind Bars Data Project," webpage, undated. As of December 9, 2020:
https://law.ucla.edu/academics/centers/criminal-justice-program/ucla-covid-19-behind-bars-data-project

University of Central Florida, "Adapting Community Corrections in Response to COVID-19," database, undated. As of December 9, 2020:
https://ccie.ucf.edu/adapt-cc/database/

U.S. Bureau of Labor Statistics, "Injuries, Illnesses, and Fatalities: Census of Fatal Occupational Injuries (CFOI)—Current," webpage, updated December 17, 2019. As of December 7, 2020:
https://www.bls.gov/iif/oshcfoi1.htm#2018

U.S. Department of Health and Human Services, Office for Civil Rights, *COVID-19 and HIPAA: Disclosures to Law Enforcement, Paramedics, Other First Responders and Public Health Authorities*, Washington, D.C., undated.

"U.S. Hate Crime Highest in More Than a Decade—FBI," *BBC News*, November 17, 2020. As of December 7, 2020:
https://www.bbc.com/news/world-us-canada-54968498

Vargas, Ramon Antonio, "After High-Ranking NOPD Officer Contracts Coronavirus, Union Calls on Department to Test All Cops," *NOLA.com*, June 25, 2020. As of December 8, 2020:
https://www.nola.com/news/coronavirus/article_397822ae-b734-11ea-a01c-53e0f1f3b919.html

"Vehicle Theft in L.A. Up 17% During COVID-19 Pandemic," *KTLA 5 News*, May 25, 2020. As of December 7, 2020:
https://ktla.com/news/local-news/vehicle-theft-in-l-a-up-17-during-covid-19-pandemic/

Vera Institute of Justice, "COVID-19 and Jail Releases Webinar," video, YouTube, April 17, 2020a. As of December 9, 2020:
https://www.youtube.com/watch?v=Bmt7fjmeOKU

Vera Institute of Justice, "COVID-19 and Policing Webinar," video, YouTube, April 17, 2020b. As of December 7, 2020:
https://www.youtube.com/watch?v=le5H7U9tbWw

Vera Institute of Justice and Community Oriented Correctional Health Services, *Guidance for Preventive and Responsive Measures to Coronavirus for Parole, Probation, and Clemency*, Brooklyn, New York, March 18, 2020.

Vermeer, Michael J. D., Dulani Woods, and Brian A. Jackson, *Would Law Enforcement Leaders Support Defunding the Police? Probably—If Communities Ask Police to Solve Fewer Problems*, Santa Monica, Calif.: RAND Corporation, PE-A108-1, 2020. As of December 8, 2020:
https://www.rand.org/pubs/perspectives/PEA108-1.html

Viglione, Jill, Lucas M. Alward, Ashley Lockwood, and Sara Bryson, "Adaptations to COVID-19 in Community Corrections Agencies Across the United States," *Victims & Offenders*, Vol. 15, No. 7–8, 2020, pp. 1277–1297.

Vogt, R. J., " Racial Disparity Spurs Challenge to NYPD COVID Policing," Law360, May 31, 2020. As of December 8, 2020:
https://www.law360.com/articles/1278161/racial-disparity-spurs-challenge-to-nypd-covid-policing

Wachino, Vikki, "Testimony of Vikki Wachino, CEO, Community Oriented Correctional Health Services to the National Commission on COVID-19 and Criminal Justice," testimony before the National Commission on COVID-19 and Criminal Justice, Washington, D.C., September 3, 2020.

Wadhwani, Anita, "State Health Department Gives Names, Addresses of Tennesseans with COVID-19 to Law Enforcement," *Chattanooga Times Free Press*, May 8, 2020.

Wagner, Peter, and Emily Widra, "Five Ways the Criminal Justice System Could Slow the Pandemic," *Prison Policy Initiative* blog, March 27, 2020. As of December 9, 2020:
https://www.prisonpolicy.org/blog/2020/03/27/slowpandemic/

"Wake County Closes Courtroom After Defendant Shows Up with COVID-19," *WRAL.com*, June 16, 2020, updated June 17, 2020. As of December 9, 2020:
https://www.wral.com/coronavirus/
wake-county-closes-courtroom-after-defendant-shows-up-with-covid-19/19147386/

Wallace, Megan, Liesl Hagan, Kathryn G. Curran, Samantha P. Williams, Senad Handanagic, Adam Bjork, Sherri L. Davidson, Robert T. Lawrence, Joseph McLaughlin, Marilee Butterfield, et al., "COVID-19 in Correctional and Detention Facilities—United States, February–April 2020," *Morbidity and Mortality Weekly Report*, Vol. 69, No. 19, May 6, 2020, updated May 15, 2020, pp. 587–590.

Wang, Emily A., Bruce Western, Emily P. Backes, and Julie Schuck, eds., *Decarcerating Correctional Facilities During COVID-19: Advancing Health, Equity, and Safety*, Washington, D.C.: The National Academies Press, 2020.

Watson, Crystal, Kelsey Lane Warmbrod, Rachel A. Vahey, Anita Cicero, Thomas V. Inglesby, Chris Beyrer, Leonard Rubenstein, Gabriel Eber, Carolyn Sufrin, Henri Garrison-Desany, Lauren Dayton, and Rachel Strodel, *COVID-19 and the U.S. Criminal Justice System: Evidence for Public Health Measures to Reduce Risk*, Baltimore, Md.: Johns Hopkins Center for Health Security, 2020.

Weichselbaum, Simone, "Have COVID-19? Cops May Have Your Neighborhood on a 'Heat Map,'" The Marshall Project, June 9, 2020. As of December 8, 2020:
https://www.themarshallproject.org/2020/06/09/
have-covid-19-cops-may-have-your-neighborhood-on-a-heat-map

Welsh-Huggins, Andrew, "In Cities Across U.S., Voters Support More Police Oversight," Associated Press, November 21, 2020.

White, Michael D., and Henry F. Fradella, "Policing a Pandemic: Stay-at-Home Orders and What They Mean for the Police," *American Journal of Criminal Justice*, Vol. 45, 2020, pp. 702–717.

Widra, Emily, and Dylan Hayre, *Failing Grades: States' Responses to COVID-19 in Jails & Prisons*, Northampton, Mass.: Prison Policy Initiative, June 25, 2020.

Widra, Emily, and Tiana Herring, "Half of States Fail to Require Mask Use by Correctional Staff," *Prison Policy Initiative* blog, August 14, 2020. As of December 9, 2020:
https://www.prisonpolicy.org/blog/2020/08/14/masks-in-prisons/

Williams, Brie A., Cyrus Ahalt, David Cloud, Dallas Augustine, Leah Rorvig, and David Sears, "Correctional Facilities in the Shadow of COVID-19: Unique Challenges and Proposed Solutions," *Health Affairs Blog*, March 26, 2020.

Winberg, Michaela, "Some Philly Police Aren't Wearing Masks, and the City Won't Enforce the Rule," Billy Penn newsletter, June 30, 2020. As of December 8, 2020:
https://billypenn.com/2020/06/30/
some-philly-police-arent-wearing-masks-and-the-city-wont-enforce-the-rule/

Winton, Richard, Matt Hamilton, and Benjamin Oreskes, "LAPD Has Quarantine Site for Officers: Biltmore Hotel in Downtown L.A.," *Los Angeles Times*, April 15, 2020.

Wisconsin Courts COVID-19 Task Force, *Chief Justice's Wisconsin Courts COVID-19 Task Force: Final Report*, Madison, Wisc., May 2020.

Witwer, Amanda R., Lynn Langton, Duren Banks, Dulani Woods, Michael J. D. Vermeer, and Brian A. Jackson, *Online Dispute Resolution: Perspectives to Support Successful Implementation and Outcomes in Court Proceedings*, Santa Monica, Calif.: RAND Corporation, RR-A108-9, forthcoming.

Yadavalli, Anita, Christiana K. McFarland, and Spencer Wagner, *What COVID-19 Means for City Finances*, Washington, D.C.: National League of Cities, May 2020.

Yoon-Hendricks, Alexandra, and Michael McGough, "Sacramento Sheriff, Other Capital Agencies Won't Enforce Newsom's Mask Order. Here's Why," *Sacramento Bee*, June 19, 2020, updated June 20, 2020.